THE SHAPE OF REASON

◆ THE SHAPE OF REASON ◆
Argumentative Writing in College

S E C O N D E D I T I O N

John T. Gage
University of Oregon

Macmillan Publishing Company
New York

Collier Macmillan Canada
Toronto

Editor: Eben W. Ludlow
Production Supervisor: Charlotte Hyland
Production Manager: Valerie Sawyer
Text and Cover Designer: Jane Edelstein
This book was set in Berkeley Old Style by Carlisle Communications, Ltd., and was printed and bound by Book Press.
The cover was printed by The Lehigh Press, Inc.

Macmillan Publishing Company
866 Third Avenue, New York, New York 10022

Collier Macmillan Canada, Inc.
1200 Eglinton Avenue East
Suite 200
Don Mills, Ontario M3C 3N1

Library of Congress Cataloging-in-Publication Data

Gage, John T.
    The shape of reason : argumentative writing in college / John T. Gage.— 2nd ed.
        p.   cm.
    Includes index.
    ISBN 0–02–340041–2
    1. English language—Rhetoric.   2. Reasoning.   I. Title.
PE1431.G34   1991
808'.042—dc20   90–45549
                              CIP

Printing: 1 2 3 4 5 6 7   Year: 1 2 3 4 5 6 7

Acknowledgments appear on page 286, which constitutes a continuation of the copyright page.

*This book is dedicated
to the memory of
Sally Gage*

♦ A NOTE TO STUDENTS ♦

Argumentative writing is writing that reasons its way to a conclusion. It addresses ideas that the writer takes seriously enough to want to explore and support with good reasons. This book is about this process: writing as reasoned inquiry.

You are invited to engage in this process by responding critically to the ideas of others and by writing about your own ideas in such a way that you try to earn the understanding and assent of your audience. In this way, you are invited to use writing to enter an intellectual dialogue that should be a central part of your experience of college. This approach has some consequences in the way I have written this book.

First, I have tried to challenge you to think about ideas and about writing. I want you to make up your own minds about everything in this book.

Second, this book treats the writing process as moving from a sense of the whole argument to the discovery of specific parts, rather than building separate "skills" in isolation from complete writing intentions. This means that you will not be asked to produce writing merely for the sake of practicing some part of a whole composition (such as sentences or paragraphs), although you will be asked to write thesis statements and "enthymemes" (see Chapter 4 for a definition of this term) that represent the whole intention of an essay and the line of reasoning that it will develop.

Third, this book treats the form of an essay as something that is *generated* by the writer rather than as something *imposed* on the writer. I want you to generate the structures that give your essays their own unique shape based on your ideas, rather than try to fill up "empty forms" imposed from outside. Form follows function. Ideas come first.

Fourth, I have placed the process of reasoning through an argument and generating the structure of an essay within the context of critical reading and research. Critical reading and research underlie the process of inquiry, which requires some kind of response to others' ideas and some basis of knowledge from which to respond. So, I have treated argumentation here as a matter of finding and presenting the best possible reasons you can for your reader's understanding and assent, and not as a matter of trying to "win" your case by overpowering the "opposition." I have tried to underplay persuasion, as your aim, in favor of inquiry. Critical reading is a kind of prerequisite to inquiry, because it challenges us with ideas we may not have thought about. Research involves finding out anything we need to know to be sure we are responding and inquiring responsibly.

Finally, I have tried to be honest with you about why I think argumentative writing matters. Thinking and writing are not processes that you can ever expect to "master." By doing them you learn the rewards of intellectual accomplishment as well as experience the limits of human understanding. Thinking is an adventure that requires risks. It always balances certainties with uncertainties. By facing both, we learn to live with our own uncertainties and to be more tolerant of the beliefs of others.

So, I urge you to treat this book and the writing that it invites you to do as an adventure in thinking. We are all in this together. The possibilities are endless.

♦ A NOTE TO
INSTRUCTORS ♦

In *The Shape of Reason*, I have presented argumentative writing as a large enough category to contain the kinds of intellectual and compositional skills that students should be practicing in college. Argumentative writing, for me, does not focus on one mode of developing ideas to the exclusion of another. The process of coming to conclusions may engage the writer in every possible kind of compositional pattern, depending on the nature of the issue and the writer's situation. I have presented argumentation as a process of inquiry into questions at issue that is best pursued if guided by principles but not governed by rules. Consequently, I have adapted the classical rhetorical concept of the enthymeme as the central basis for the invention and structuring of arguments, an approach that blends classical insights about rhetorical reasoning with contemporary understandings of the composing process. This helps to remove logic from the sometimes scary realm of rules and formulas by treating reasoning as a natural and informal process.

I have included other features in the book that I hope will make the approach more effective. Extended discussions of important terms, such as *structure, thesis, enthymeme,* and *style,* show how these concepts are flexible and shaped by the purposes to which we, as writers, put them. Each chapter ends with "Questions for Thought, Discussion, and Writing" that call for independent evaluation of the ideas in the chapter. I have written some narrative examples of a student thinking about ideas, coming up with a thesis and reasons, and structuring an essay, not as a model to be copied, but as an illustration of the process. I have tried to connect all the issues to the research process rather than to isolate that process from writing.

Instructors familiar with the first edition might be interested in the most significant changes that I have made in this second edition.

1. I have added reading selections after each chapter, to be read and analyzed according to the concepts being discussed in that chapter. The selections are also meant to generate discussion of ideas for students to write about.

Three provocative and challenging readings, on themes found in the chapter readings, form a new appendix. With this change, the book may now be used with or without a supplementary reader.

2. I have shortened individual chapters in response to many helpful comments from students and teachers.

3. In Chapter 3, on the thesis, I have made explicit use of "stasis" theory, grouping stasis questions according to the nature of the question at issue and showing how they affect reasoning.

4. Chapter 4 on reasoning has been changed considerably, primarily to bring the idea of the enthymeme forward to frame the entire discussion so that the enthymeme is not presented merely as a kind of syllogism. Informal reasoning is discussed in advance of formal logic, which is presented as one way to think about the enthymeme. Stephen Toulmin's terminology is introduced as a complementary way to describe informal reasoning.

5. Chapter 5 on structure now begins with the concept of using a structural enthymeme as a guide to thinking about form as a consequence of reasoning. Several examples of structural enthymemes are illustrated, each with different potential structures as possibilities for development.

6. In place of a separate chapter on research, new "Implications for Research" sections have been added to appropriate chapters, so that the issue of research is linked more directly to the reasoning and writing processes.

The approach to writing taken in *The Shape of Reason* will work best if students discuss ideas freely and write essays that respond honestly to the issues and arguments that develop during such a discussion. It invites and enables you to respond to students' ideas and writing as a critical thinker and writing consultant. It is in this way that I hope the book serves to enliven teaching as well as learning. This process is one from which both instructors and students never cease to learn.

I urge you to discuss your discoveries and questions about this approach with your colleagues, and thereby to form a discourse community of your own about your mutual insights and concerns. I have written the *Instructor's Manual* for the book in such a way that it can provide a basis for such discussions as well as specific advice about teaching the book. In the second edition of the *Instructor's Manual*, I have benefitted greatly from Kathleen O'Fallon's co-authorship. She provides a different perspective from mine, having taught this approach in different settings and with the interests of different colleagues to negotiate, and our collaboration has led to a more useful guide to teaching argumentative writing than I could have produced on my own.

In the first edition of this book, I acknowledged my debt to my own teachers and friends and to sources for ideas from Aristotle to Wayne Booth. Since then, many teachers and many students have told me about their experience with that edition, and I am grateful to all of them. I am especially indebted to the following people for specific suggestions or other forms of help with this edition: Frederick J. Antczak, Paul Armstrong, Douglas Babington,

Margaret Bayless, Walter H. Beale, Linda Bensel-Meyers, Grant Boswell, Nancy Bradbury, Michael Bybee, Keith Comer, Mary Coté, Jim Crosswhite, Elizabeth Deis, Ann Dobyns, Carol Faulkner, Rick Filloy, Lowell Frye, Richard Fulkerson, John Garvin, Carolyn Hill, Martin Jacobi, Monica C. Johnstone, Ann Kemmy, Don Kraemer, Cindy La Com, Anne Laskaya, Nancy M. Lowe, Michael G. Moran, Kathleen O'Fallon, William Petty, Bart Queary, Arthur Quinn, Marilyn Reid, Diana Rhoads, Patricia Roberts, Jeannie Thomas, Victor J. Vitanza, and Jeffrey Walker.

Once again, as ever, Robin and Molly Gage are those without whom nothing.

J. T. G.

◆ CONTENTS ◆

3   ASKING QUESTIONS, GENERATING IDEAS   53

4   GIVING REASONS   96

WRITING AND THE COLLEGE COMMUNITY

DISCOURSE COMMUNITIES

All of us are individuals, but we coexist with other individuals in communities. We belong to, or interact with, a variety of communities, each of which makes different demands on us, and which we, in turn, affect in different ways. As a member of your generation you are part of one kind of community, as a college student you are part of another, as a family member you belong to another sort of community, and as a person who holds certain political beliefs you are part of another sort of community. Such a list of examples could go on practically indefinitely: different communities for different aspects of our lives. Each of us belongs to a large number of overlapping communities.

Although we share some characteristics with the other members of each community we belong to, as individuals we are also unlike those members in other ways. A community is defined by some characteristic that unites its members, but diversity among people is present in every community. Diversity may be set aside to one degree or another for the good of the community, or it may become an obstacle to cooperation. Communities are dynamic things in which the members are always seeking cooperation but not at the expense of loss of individuality.

Some communities may be called **discourse communities**. A discourse community is any kind of community in which the members attempt to achieve cooperation and assert their individuality through the use of language. We are all members of a variety of discourse communities, each of which uses language in different ways. Family communities have their own ways of using language, some of which you use only when you are among family members (and some of which you may try to avoid). Political communities have their own ways of using language. Communities of natural scientists use language in some ways unique to them, as do communities of artists, athletes, businesspeople, farmers, and others. Language, since it is adaptable to any purpose, takes on characteristics that help the community to achieve its ends. Communities define themselves to a greater or lesser degree by the way in which they use language.

The uses of language in any discourse community go beyond specialized vocabularies. Yes, certain communities may have words that only members of those communities know or use. Such words are called jargon—words that you know by virtue of being part of some discourse community, words that nonmembers of that community do not know. But, more importantly, each community differs (more or less) in other ways in its use of language: Different forms of language (such as oral or written, spoken or sung, formal or informal, letters or essays, and so on) may predominate in the discourse of a group; language may be valued differently (language has a different value in the discourse of visual artists, say, than it does in the discourse of newspaper journalists); the purposes of language may vary (such as selling merchandise, persuading voters, praying, reporting information, telling jokes, telling stories, or telling lies). Such differences also overlap from community to community.

As a college student, you are a part of several discourse communities, each of which values language differently and uses it for different purposes. The language used in your biology and math classes will differ from the language used in your history and English classes. It will differ in vocabulary as well as in style. Short answers, lab reports, and factual questions may be more appropriate to some kinds of disciplines, whereas whole essays, speculative questions, and discussions may be favored in others.

Despite such differences, these discourse communities are also part of a larger discourse community: the college community itself. Like any other community, the scholarly community of the college or university has goals that in part determine how it uses language.

The purpose of the scholarly community is to inquire and to share with others the products of inquiry—understanding and knowledge. This is the central purpose that unites its members and that motivates them to cooperate with each other, despite differences among individuals. **Inquiry**, seen as the active search for answers to questions, suggests certain values and uses that language has in such a community. If language is used in such a community to inquire and to share knowledge, it will be used in certain ways, not ways that are necessarily better or worse than other ways but that are more suited to these goals. Language is valued in such a community for its ability to aid inquiry and to share understanding and knowledge honestly and precisely.

Diversity of point of view is not only respected in a college community, then, but it is actively sought. A community in which all members think alike on the most important questions is unlikely to inquire into those questions, since there will be no alternative points of view. Diversity of opinion is a prerequisite to inquiry and should be valued as such. This is why a scholarly community is one that seeks to open issues of any kind to further questioning by seeking other points of view, rather than to close off questioning by failing to listen to the challenging ideas of others who differ.

As college students, you are invited to join a community of inquiring minds. As learners, you are expected to do more than receive information passively. Like all other members of this discourse community, you are expected to participate actively in the open questioning of that information, listen to all sides, make judgments, and present those judgments to others coherently. The activities you are asked to go through in college—reading, discussion, writing, research, experiments, and so on—have a purpose beyond the acquisition of information in each class. They are meant to help you become better able to cope with the intellectual demands of a complex world, a world in which you will frequently be called upon to make independent decisions among competing ideas in the interest of one or another community to which you belong. Such decisions have to be made on the basis of reasoned thought, not by flipping a coin or following the crowd or a charismatic leader. An education prepares you to exercise judgment.

JUDGMENT AND WRITING

Judgment applies to all those occasions when we must decide what to do with information in its raw form. Do we accept it or deny it? How do we measure its significance or value? How should we use it? How does it relate to other bits of information? If people did not exercise judgment, their knowledge would be a useless hodgepodge of unrelated and equally significant bits of information. No educated person can do without the quality of judgment that enables her or him to make sense of all those bits. Yet there are no rules or procedures that can be followed to learn to exercise it. Judgment is learned only by practicing it. It is the act of judiciously appraising, discriminating, sorting, adapting, transforming, and applying ideas. Inasmuch as all of these actions require choice, judgment is learned best when one is faced with alternative answers.

Writing argumentative essays in college—a community of inquiring minds—is an opportunity to practice and improve this kind of judgment. If you choose ideas for your essays that are worth writing about, in response to problems that require careful reasoning to solve, you will be challenging yourself on many levels to exercise your best judgment. Writing is not simply an act of finding the right words; it involves looking at issues from different points of view, examining different positions and potential reasons for holding them, and thinking about potential structures and ways of presenting ideas to a reader. In performing such mental acts, you will be enhancing your understanding of the ideas you write about and your ability to reason while you improve as a writer.

It is important to remember that no writing class by itself can teach you to write at your best. All writers, even if they seem to write effortlessly, learn to write better each time they take on and complete a new writing challenge. Each new writing task is a challenge of its own, and the best a writing class can do is to create situations that will allow you, or invite you, to meet the challenge. You will become a better writer, but the rate will be imperceptible, just as the rate at which you learn to think better is imperceptible. Both changes happen slowly, in small increments, as a result of the challenges you face in more than one class and outside of class as well.

If you are thinking about these challenges, you may not always feel your writing is improving when in fact it is. As you improve as a writer, you will naturally take on slightly more challenging writing tasks and find yourself writing about somewhat more difficult issues. As you respond to new writing situations, you may feel inadequate, simply because they will require you to go beyond what you already know how to do. A feeling of inadequacy (which you share with all writers, whether they will admit it or not) is therefore nothing to worry about. It is the way you should feel if you are learning.

Writing, as this book stresses, is a process of finding and structuring reasons. When we face a writing task, and when that task emerges from our attempts to find cooperation in a community of diverse opinions, writing becomes more than an attempt to put the right words in the right order. It becomes a search for reasons. It is in this way that the serious attempt to compose your thoughts in writing will often lead you to the very important discovery of what you think and why you think it.

Thus, writing is at the very center of what you do as you participate actively in a discourse community of inquirers. Any college student in any class can read, listen, take notes, pass objective tests, and even think deliberately about what it all means. But writing about the information with which you are presented in college has an effect that none of these other activities alone can produce. Writing causes you to clarify the information and the problems that come with it, to work out positions for yourself and to explore reasons for holding those positions. Writing, because it is undertaken to communicate, must be clear, and thus forces clarity upon us. But if writing is also undertaken to influence the discourse community's thinking, that is, to be understood and believed, then it forces more than clarity upon us. It also forces us to find the best reasons we can. Any act of writing that does not stop with the mere assertion of unrelated bits of information will force the writer to search for good reasons, and in that process the writer's judgment is being exercised as well as the writer's composing skills. Judgment and skills grow together.

THIS BOOK AND YOU

The assumptions I have made about the importance of writing in college have led me to approach reason and structure as the central elements of good writing. This book is intended to guide you through a process of thinking and composing that will result in thoughtful, well-structured essays about ideas that matter to you.

The chapters are organized to focus on aspects of this process, but you will find as you compose essays that these aspects are not as separate as the parts of the book suggest. Books about writing must inevitably make distinctions among principles and stages of composing that are arbitrary and artificial in order to spread them out into a sequence of chapters. Ideas and choices that may occur to a writer in any order or all at once must be taken apart and given the appearance of a necessary order. In this book, the order will be as follows.

Chapter 1 will go on from the previous discussion of writing in a college community to look at how the specific purpose of a piece of writing gives it structure. Chapter 2 will explore the process of reading and responding critically, and Chapter 3 will give you some advice for finding something to say in your writing that represents a meaningful idea in relation to a question at issue. Chapter 4 will discuss the process of finding adequate support in the form of reasons, and Chapter 5 will discuss the process of using that support as the basis for structuring your writing. Chapter 6 will help you revise your writing and make decisions about style. As you can already see, these matters are not separate from each other; the book will address significant issues repeatedly, but not, I hope, redundantly. I have tried to take you, as my reader, through a process of thinking at several levels of sophistication. By the time I get around to putting a technical term of any kind to a concept, for instance, you will have become familiar with that concept in a nontechnical way. The closing sections in Chapters 2, 3, 4, and 5 will discuss the implications of the ideas in those chapters for the research writer.

Although abstract, this arrangement is meant to represent a process that is intuitively followed by every writer: being confronted with the conflicting ideas of others, responding with ideas of one's own, and developing one's reasons into a form and into language that will enable them to be understood and believed by others. As you give each stage your conscious attention, you can experience a process of thinking from which to draw as you compose, even though your actual acts of composing will never be completely self-conscious or divided into stages.

Each chapter ends with examples of argumentative writing that you are invited to read and discuss from the point of view of the concepts in the chapter. Further readings are found at the end of the book in the Appendix. These readings are not meant to serve as models for you to imitate as you compose essays. There are no ideal models for a well-reasoned, well-structured essay, because no two pieces of writing arise from the same situations or need to satisfy the same conditions. In fact, if you read them carefully, you will probably find certain things about each of the essays that you would not want to imitate. They are meant instead to have two other functions. The first is to help you to investigate and assess how other writers have faced the challenge of inquiry, reasoning, and writing that the chapters discuss. As you analyze them, you can see more deeply into the process of thinking and writing that you will follow, in your own way, as you compose essays that respond to the unique circumstances of your own thinking. The second function of these readings is to confront you with the ideas of others, ideas that may challenge you to argue for your own. The authors of these readings, in this way, will become part of the larger discourse community in which you participate as you use writing to explore your own thinking on similar issues. These readings can become the beginning of an intellectual inquiry that takes you into further exploration of your own and others' arguments.

Ideally, as you use this textbook, you are engaged in active, open, reasonable discussion with others about the ideas in this book and in any other reading you may be doing for your writing class. Ideally, the members of the class will form a discourse community of inquiring minds, people who engage in an exchange of ideas and who will attempt to offer each other reasonable grounds for changing each others' minds. Ideally, the members of this community, who share your concern about the issues you discuss but who may not share your responses to those issues, will become the audience to whom you write. And you, in turn, will become part of the audience they need to address. In such a class, the activities of thinking, discussing, writing, and judging will not be separate. They will merge and reinforce each other.

My purpose in this book is to invite you to struggle with and find your way among real ideas, ideas that matter. The positions you forge for yourself will be your own positions, reasoned about and structured in such a way that you will feel a sense of achievement in each essay that you write. If you enter the process of reasoning and writing discussed in this book in a willing and thoughtful way, you will be writing essays that represent your best thinking on issues that are important to you. Writing classes should be just as concerned with the important issues of a complex world as any other college class. Students who are asked to write about the teacher's favorite idea just to practice writing or who churn out empty-headed compositions on prefabricated topics, like "My Favorite Movie" or "How to Change a Tire," are doomed to write boring stuff for an already bored teacher. And they are cheated of the opportunity to use writing to learn what they really think and why. So, let's get real. I want you to learn to write, but I also want you to write to learn. It's my intention to enable you to use writing to learn where you stand in the ongoing discussion of ideas that demand serious attention from thinking people. Serious does not mean solemn, though. I also hope you will find the process interesting and fun.

PURPOSE AND DESIGN

As an active participant in the discourse communities of your college and your classroom, you will have two main purposes: to find your own way among the ideas of others as you read and listen to them, and to present the result of your inquiry in writing. Finding out what you think is what enables you to know what purpose will guide the composition of your writing. In saying this, however, I do not mean that writing comes only after thinking. The search for ideas, the process of inquiry itself, can and should go on in writing and is helped by the attempt to find the right words and sentences for what you mean. Writing itself can generate ideas, and is often the way we find our meanings. Consequently, this book will ask you to write at every stage of your thinking, and to rewrite at every stage as well. But before we get to that, we should talk about the idea of purpose and how it is a guide to writing, even though in the process of writing new purposes may be discovered. Finally, when a piece of writing is made into a whole composition intended for an audience, it will represent the purposes you have chosen and discovered in the process of writing it.

The shape that any piece of writing takes on results from the writer's overall sense of purpose. If we think of that shape as the progress from part to part in a composition, it may become easier to see that some sense of a destination, a goal to be reached, is what gives the writer—and the reader—a sense that the parts are held together in meaningful ways. We feel, as we read, that each new part is somehow justified by what went before it and that together they are progressing toward some conclusion. You have probably encountered writing that lacked this quality, and your response was to wonder, at some point as you slogged through it, "How did I get here?" You had this experience because the writer had somehow failed to make a transition from one part to the next, failed, that is, to connect the parts in a way that suggested forward progress. Thus, both the reader's sense of progress in prose and the writer's control of this quality come from the same source: a clear sense of an intention that accounts for the necessity of each of the parts and their relations.

That thought reminds me of an episode in *Alice's Adventures in Wonderland,* when Alice encounters the Cheshire Cat sitting goodnaturedly in a tree. She asks the Cat:

> ". . . Would you tell me, please, which way I ought to go from here?"
> "That depends a good deal on where you want to get to," said the Cat.
> "I don't much care where—" said Alice.
> "Then it doesn't much matter which way you go," said the Cat.
> "—so long as I get *somewhere,*" Alice added as an explanation.
> "Oh, you're sure to do that," said the Cat, "if you only walk long enough."

Lewis Carroll is having fun here with an idea that is central to an understanding of human actions of all kinds, including writing. That idea may seem self-evident, but it sometimes escapes us: Intention determines choice. When we face a choice of one or another way of acting, it is our intention that guides us. Sometimes, of course, we are not certain whether one or another way will, in fact, serve our intention, but the kind of deliberation that we enter into in that case still concerns the relationship of means to ends. What Carroll illustrates is that if we have no intended *end,* then the *means* that we choose hardly matters. In reference to the way in which we shape writing, we might say that if we have no destination to guide our selection of parts and their relations, it hardly matters what parts or what relations we choose. If we have no end in mind to use as a reference point for decisions along the way, any shape will do as well as another.

Whole compositions have unique shapes, or structures, then, because they have unique intentions. Generating the unique structure for your own composition must start with some degree of clarity about your own intentions. The self-evident relation between means and ends in composing gives you three principles to help ensure that the writing you create will present the reader with functionally related parts:

1. Try to be as clear as possible about what purpose you want your writing to achieve.
2. Use your intended purpose as the test for deciding whether any given part is necessary and whether any additional parts are needed.
3. Make your own sense of your purpose clear to the readers too, so that they can follow the parts and the transitions between them as they progress through the writing.

The purpose of a composition is its *whole* purpose, the sum of its parts. Its *structure* is the way in which those parts are held together to achieve that purpose. The purpose of a whole piece of writing is best described as an idea. Of course, compositions contain more than one idea, but they must all somehow relate to each other because they serve an overall idea of some kind.

EARNED CONCLUSIONS

The overall or central idea that holds the parts of a composition together is sometimes called a **thesis**. Later, I will discuss thesis statements more fully and their role in helping you to generate structure. Now it is enough to say that the purpose of any piece of nonfiction prose writing is to provide the audience with sufficient ideas within its structure to enable them to understand and to accept its main idea.

We can speak of many different kinds of actions that ideas perform within a composition, such as *to show, to explain, to illustrate, to develop,* or *to support.* But one kind of action takes in all such particular actions and makes them necessary; that action is *to earn.* Whatever else the ideas in a composition do, they are there in order that the writer can earn the reader's attention or assent. It is one thing to assert an idea. It is another to earn it.

I have chosen this word *earn* to characterize the act of relating ideas to a thesis because it suggests a kind of ethical edge that other words do not.

Ethical suggests fairness and respect toward the reader. But even more, when a writer has an idea that she or he wishes to put forth for others to understand and accept, the word *earn* brings with it a sense of responsibility to make the writing do justice to that idea. A thesis is not just any idea, picked out of thin air for no other reason than to have something to write about. A thesis is a special kind of idea, one that you choose because you believe it and want it to be believed by others. It is an idea you choose to write about because you feel a sense of investment in it and want others to feel that same sense. It is such a sense of investment that makes composing seem worth the effort. If you were to compose without regard to your commitment to the central idea, you would be in Alice's predicament of not knowing which way you ought to turn because you don't much care where it is you go. When you care about an idea, you have a reason to enter the process of searching for other ideas to use to earn that idea.

At one time or another, all writers have the experience of writing like Alice, lost in a confusing wonderland of words, thinking, "If only I write long enough I'm bound to get *somewhere*." In fact, you may have found that writing can lead you into unexpected and interesting discoveries when you let yourself explore ideas freely. I hope you, like many students, have experimented with free writing in which you "just wrote" without knowing, or without caring, where you would go in the end. In the process, you may have stumbled onto a new thought that seemed very interesting or a purpose that you didn't know you had. There are many ways of coming upon ideas and purposes, and free writing can certainly be one of them. If you have had the experience of discovering what you wanted to say *as* you were engaged in writing, you were open to new ideas. But the experience didn't end there. You probably also realized that once you made the discovery you became responsible for doing something with all your free writing to tie it somehow to that new idea, that new conclusion. Once the new idea was there, new responsibilities came along. Unless you were writing in the form of free association, as in a journal, you realized that the writing you did to stimulate this new idea could not necessarily stand as a composition *about* that idea. This awareness came from a feeling of being responsible, a feeling that once you knew just what you wanted to say you somehow accepted the job of making sure that everything else you wrote was relevant to that thought. Your journal entry, for instance, may have generated the thought, but then the thought had to generate the composition.

Either way, writing is an act of inquiry. Once you know what it is you want to write about—and this decision will involve much more than free writing, but include reading and discussion, too—inquiry becomes a process of looking into the implications of your idea and potential means of supporting it. It is in this way that having one idea leads to the discovery and testing of other ideas. If you take responsibility for earning your main idea, you begin to see that there are many, too many, possible things to say *about* it, and you have to begin testing some of those things to see whether they are worth putting into your writing or leaving there. Writing is a process of accepting and rejecting many possible ideas, in light of the overall idea they are meant to support. As you decide which ideas to include, you are judging the quality of your own thoughts. You are doing more than "just writing." You are inquiring, which is another name for thinking about what you think.

QUESTIONS FOR THOUGHT, DISCUSSION, AND WRITING

1. Think about your own attitudes toward your education and honestly ask yourself whether you generally seek challenges on your own or whether you mostly look for an easy way out of an assignment. Perhaps you can describe situations of each kind. What made the difference?
2. Think about an experience you have had in which you felt that what you already knew was adequate to solve a significant problem. Think about another experience in which your knowledge was not adequate to solve such a problem. Then compare what you learned from these two experiences.
3. Describe an experience in which you came to a clarification of your own thinking through writing.
4. Before reading any further in this book, describe the approach to writing you expect it to take. What *responsibilities* will you be asked to take as a writer? What do you feel about taking them?
5. Have you ever discovered your own intention in a piece of writing after you had begun to write? What did you do with the writing you had already done as a result of this discovery?
6. What does it mean to you to hear that you should be conducting genuine *inquiry* into your ideas as you write? What does *earning* your ideas mean to you?
7. In each of the three essays that follow, identify the main idea, or thesis, and then identify other ideas that the writer uses to *earn* that thesis. In each case, try to ask yourself how the ideas are structured to make a whole: What makes each part of the essay necessary? Why are they arranged in this order? Having identified what you think are the supporting ideas, try to assess whether they provide you with sufficient grounds for accepting the conclusion. By what means do you judge whether they do or not?

♦ **READINGS** ♦

WE CAN KILL EXIT POLLING BY LYING OUR HEADS OFF

Linda Ellerbee

In 1967, the good citizens of Kentucky entered their voting booths to elect a lieutenant governor, which would not exactly be your basic cosmic moment in American politics except for one thing.

When they exited their voting booths, some of the good citizens of Kentucky were stopped by strangers with earnest faces and clipboards.

"Pardon me, sir, I'm with CBS News, and I wonder if you'd mind telling us who you just voted for?"

"What? Oh, well . . . sure, I guess. I mean, why not? What could it hurt?"

That's when The Exit Poll was born.

In 1980, we found out what it could hurt.

That's when The Exit Poll turned into The Thing That Ate California.

Eighty-six million Americans voted for president that year. Thirty-six thousand of them were "exit polled."

Who won the race?

NBC won, that's who.

At 8:15 p.m., Eastern Standard Time, NBC News, based on information gathered from its own exit polls, declared Ronald Reagan the next president.

Next ABC News declared Reagan the winner.

Then Carter went on television and conceded.

And all this happened while the real polls were still open in about one third of the country.

In Hawaii, people were still out to lunch.

Not surprisingly, there were geographically unfortunate citizens who, having already heard the final score, figured the game was over and, so instead of voting, stayed home to watch TV.

While it's doubtful this had any significant effect on the Carter-Reagan race, it almost certainly altered the outcome in some other, less grand but equally important political contests.

We who committed television for a living defended exit polls as a matter of Journalistic Principle. We said we conducted exit polls and broadcast the results because we believed in the The Public's Right to Know. That's what the First Amendment was all about, we said.

We lied.

We conducted exit polls because we could conduct exit polls.

Once again, technology had brought television to a place common sense was still trying to locate on the map.

In 1984, the networks were asked, nicely, to give up exit polling or at least to keep the results to themselves until after everybody had a chance to vote.

Even children who cannot stay out of closets on Christmas Eve can sometimes be made to wait until Christmas morning before they tell everybody else in the house what Santa Claus brought them.

Besides, there is no journalistic principle compelling us to tell the public everything we know the minute we know it.

We are allowed to think. Why, we might even be supposed to think.

It's happened before. It happened in 1979 when all three television networks knew there were Americans hiding in the Canadian Embassy in Iran—knew it but did not report it, not until those Americans were safely out of Iran.

And the First Amendment survived.

However, when it comes to election night, our scoop addiction is too tough to cure without help.

That's why there's talk of going so far as to have all the polls in all the states close at the same time.

Call it Eastern Television Time.

That would slow down the projections, anyway.

Sure, it would be inconvenient for the states and for the voters but, hey, that's journalism, folks.

Or maybe we could take it one step further and get rid of those pesky voting booths altogether. That would simplify everything. Remember the man who ran for the Senate in 1986 and, when he lost, demanded a recount on the basis that he'd won in the exit polls?

Huh?

Time now to screw our courage to the sticking place and do what's right.

Exit polling must die.

All we need is a plan, something sneaky, dishonorable and immoral enough to do the job. Something grossly unfair.

I thought you'd never ask.

They may put me in television jail for this, but if you do exactly what I'm about to tell you to do, we can make Tuesday The Day The Exit Poll Died.

Election day. We enter the booth, vote, exit the booth, smile earnestly back at the people with their clipboards and say we'll be happy to tell them how we voted. Yes, in every race.

Then we take a deep breath, look 'em straight in the eye—and lie. We lie our heads off.

From one end of the ballot to the other.

From sea to shining sea.

WHO KILLED BENNY PARET?

Norman Cousins

Sometime about 1935 or 1936 I had an interview with Mike Jacobs, the prizefight promoter. I was a fledgling reporter at that time; my beat was education but during the vacation season I found myself on varied assignments, all the way from ship news to sports reporting. In this way I found myself sitting opposite the most powerful figure in the boxing world.

There was nothing spectacular in Mr. Jacobs' manner or appearance; but when he spoke about prize fights, he was no longer a bland little man but a colossus who sounded the way Napoleon must have sounded when he reviewed a battle. You knew you were listening to Number One. His saying something made it true.

We discussed what to him was the only important element in successful promoting—how to please the crowd. So far as he was concerned, there was no mystery to it. You put killers in the ring and the people filled your arena. You hire boxing artists—men who are adroit at feinting, parrying, weaving, jabbing, and dancing, but who don't pack dynamite in their fists—and you wind up counting your empty seats. So you searched for the killers and sluggers and maulers—fellows who could hit with the force of a baseball bat.

I asked Mr. Jacobs if he was speaking literally when he said people came out to see the killer.

"They don't come out to see a tea party," he said evenly. "They come out to see the knockout. They come out to see a man hurt. If they think anything else, they're kidding themselves."

Recently, a young man by the name of Benny Paret was killed in the ring. The killing was seen by millions; it was on television. In the twelfth round, he was hit hard in the head several times, went down, was counted out, and never came out of the coma.

The Paret fight produced a flurry of investigations. Governor Rockefeller was shocked by what happened and appointed a committee to assess the responsibility. The New York State Boxing Commission decided to find out what was wrong. The District Attorney's office expressed its concern. One question that was solemnly studied in all three probes concerned the action of the referee. Did he act in time to stop the fight? Another question had to do with the role of the examining doctors who certified the physical fitness of the fighters before the bout. Still another question involved Mr. Paret's manager; did he rush his boy into the fight without adequate time to recuperate from the previous one?

In short, the investigators looked into every possible cause except the real one. Benny Paret was killed because the human fist delivers enough impact, when directed against the head, to produce a massive hemorrhage in the brain. The human brain is the most delicate and complex mechanism in all creation. It has a lacework of millions of highly fragile nerve connections. Nature attempts to protect this exquisitely intricate machinery by encasing it in a hard shell. Fortunately, the shell is thick enough to withstand a great deal of pounding. Nature, however, can protect man against everything except man himself. Not every blow to the head will kill a man—but there is always the risk of concussion and damage to the brain. A prize fighter may be able to survive even repeated brain concussions and go on fighting, but the damage to his brain may be permanent.

In any event, it is futile to investigate the referee's role and seek to determine whether he should have intervened to stop the fight earlier. That is not where the primary responsibility lies. The primary responsibility lies with the people who pay to see a man hurt. The referee who stops a fight too soon from the crowd's viewpoint can expect to be booed. The crowd wants the knockout; it wants to see a man stretched out on the canvas. This is the supreme moment in boxing. It is nonsense to talk about prize fighting as a test of boxing skills. No crowd was ever brought to its feet screaming and cheering at the sight of two men beautifully dodging and weaving out of each other's jabs. The time the crowd comes alive is when a man is hit hard over the heart or the head, when his mouthpiece flies out, when the blood squirts out of his nose or eyes, when he wobbles under the attack and his pursuer continues to smash at him with poleaxe impact.

Don't blame it on the referee. Don't even blame it on the fight managers. Put the blame where it belongs—on the prevailing mores that regard prize fighting as a perfectly proper enterprise and vehicle of entertainment. No one doubts that many people enjoy prize fighting and will miss it if it should be thrown out. And that is precisely the point.

GETTING A BIG BANG OUT OF CREATION THEORIES

Noel Riley, S.M.

As one who wears two hats (or should I say a hat and a veil?), I am both angered and embarrassed when the origins of our universe are posed as a conflict between Genesis and evolution.

My hat? I have a master's degree in chemistry from St. Louis University, and have taught science and religion for more than 25 years. My veil? I am a Roman Catholic nun, a member of the Sisters of Mercy community. I firmly believe both in God and in evolution. My embarrassment? That "believers" should espouse a discredited fundamentalist view of creation, one that merits the scorn and ridicule of the scientific community. My anger? That there are some well-meaning people who confront the young with a false choice: *either* the biblical story of creation *or* evolutionary theory. My thesis? There is no intrinsic conflict between faith and science, between God the creator and evolutionary theory.

The book of Genesis was probably written between the 10th and 6th centuries B.C., much later than the oral traditions from which it sprang. What scientific knowledge did the inspired authors have? Only the knowledge of their time, which is the case with our generation, too. Was the science faulty? Certainly, unless you think the earth is flat, supported by a large turtle, with waters above and below, and kept in check by an enclosed firmament. Did the authors of Genesis intend to teach science? Certainly not. As Roman Catholic theologian Robert Bellarmine wrote some four centuries ago, "The Bible was written to show us how to go to heaven, not how the heavens go!" And, as St. Augustine observed in the 4th Century, "The gospels do not tell us that our Lord said, 'I will send you the Holy Ghost to teach you the course of the sun and moon'; we should endeavor to become Christians and not astronomers."

What Genesis does is relate—in simple, figurative language that could be understood by primitive people—the fundamental principles of salvation and the description then popular of the origins of the human race. Let us consider a few examples of this figurative language and the underlying message.

In Genesis, God is shown as a master craftsman fashioning the world in six days and resting on the seventh. Jews were required to keep the Sabbath as a day of rest, which is the most reasonable explanation for depicting God as resting on the Sabbath, too.

The creation story uses a liturgical or mnemonic device, "God saw that it was good," to mark each great event of creation. Once it was considered necessary to think of "the days" as periods of time representing some thousands of years each. But the days can be understood simply as normal 24-hour periods, forming the literary framework of what was probably a prehistoric hymn. The use of this literary device had a practical purpose; it made memorization and recitation easier, for we are speaking of people who were largely illiterate.

The primitive cosmology of Genesis was used to teach that God created all things and to emphasize his transcendent power, and his love and concern for us. This view contrasted with the pagan epics, then widespread, in which creation was depicted as a struggle between the gods and the forces of chaos. The Hebrew people lived among idolaters and were surrounded by those who worshiped animals. The point of Genesis is that God is to be worshiped because it was He who created all these things.

And why is Eve described in Genesis as being formed from the side of Adam? To demonstrate that she is of the same nature as man, unlike animals, and does not deserve the subordinate position assigned women in pagan society.

The biblical story of creation has a religious purpose. It contains, but does not teach, errors. The evolutionary theory of creation, in contrast, has a scientific purpose, and the search for truth is the province of astronomers, geologists, biologists and the like. These two purposes are distinct, and both offer truth to the human mind and heart. The mistake scientists make is drawing philosophical and religious inferences and deductions unwarranted by the scientific data; the mistake of religious leaders is using the Bible as a science textbook.

At the time of the controversy over Galileo's theory of the universe, Bellarmine warned: "I say that if a real proof be found that the sun is fixed and does not revolve around the earth, but the earth around the sun, then it will be necessary, very carefully, to proceed to the explanation of the passages of Scripture which appear to be contrary, and we should rather say that we have misunderstood these than pronounce that to be false which is demonstrated."

Far from taking God out of the universe, the theory of evolution gives us a more sublime conception of God's creative act. He operates through the laws of nature that He has established. I am indebted to contemporary philosopher John O'Brien for an analogy: Just as it shows more skill for a billiards player to get all eight balls in the pockets in one stroke, rather than eight (or nine!), so it is a loftier conception of God to imagine a single creative act, with secondary causes operative thereafter.

Today scientists trying to explain the origins of the universe favor the "big bang" theory. Does this contradict Genesis? Not at all. In fact, if I were tempted to embrace a discredited concordism, I would see in the first "big bang" the creative hand of God, and His lofty words: "Let there be light!"

Indeed, let there be more light in our discussions, for the believer need fear not truth, but ignorance.

♦ 2 ♦

CRITICAL READING

HOW WE READ

In this chapter, I want to go into the question of what it means to believe what we read. Why is it that we sometimes think ideas are obvious while at other times we do not want to believe them? We understand ideas in relation to all of the ideas that surround them in any given piece of writing that we read, and we somehow adjust our beliefs to fit what we already know. The act of believing is the result of a decision, and we can decide how *much* belief to give to any idea based on how well it connects to other ideas and to what we know independently. The process of giving and withholding belief can be carried out in a rational or an irrational way. We are rational when we decide to make up our minds or not based on reasons. Each time we see a reason, we have to figure out whether it is a good one. So, reading is a process of making our way between the extremes of too much unreasonable belief (when the reasons to believe aren't good enough) and too much unreasonable doubt (when the reasons to *dis*believe are not good enough). Keeping this delicate balance is much easier said than done.

At least two kinds of beliefs are asked of us when we read. We are asked to believe the *information* presented by the writer, and we are asked to believe the *ideas* that are asserted about that information. In both cases, we read with some awareness that we do not *have* to believe something just because a writer says it. The question is: What kind of mental process do we go through to help us decide whether to believe the information and ideas we read?

Whether we are habitual readers, casual readers, or infrequent readers, we are all readers, and a lot of what we know and think has been the result of *how* we have read whatever we happen to have read. *Somebody* must be reading all those ads for toothpaste with guileless innocence, even if *we* all know not to believe them. And somebody, similarly, must be reading our favorite self-help book (the one we keep nodding "yes" to without questioning) as if it were nothing but propaganda. We change our reading habits to fit the nature of the reading matter and our reasons for reading it. It would be silly to adopt the same guarded stance when reading the comic page that we might adopt when reading the advertisements. But might the comics ever be trying to sell us anything? Are they not sometimes asking for our belief in certain ideas? You bet they are. We might change our reading habits to fit the occasion, and we should, but we might not want to give up our ability to think critically about what we read.

Whether rightly or wrongly, we often rely on reading when we want a source for some piece of information. We may not believe everything that we read, but we nevertheless know that if we are to have reliable information, we probably ought to seek it in a reliable written source. Part of becoming educated is learning about the usefulness of such sources. We don't usually study a subject with the idea that we will commit everything we learn about it to memory. We know there are some things about it that we can look up if we have to. We study that subject with the idea that we can go on reading about it with a better sense of understanding.

I've said that we know these things. Perhaps I should say we assume them. To what extent should we rely on reading as a source of information? What does it mean to have found a reliable source? By what means do we decide that a given piece of information is true?

A CASE IN POINT

Let's consider an example, although you should be warned at the beginning that the example is loaded. Let's keep things simple for the moment and not try to deal with controversial matters of belief; let's stick to "facts." Suppose, for whatever reason, you decide to read up on the history of the bathtub, a subject on which you ought to be able to find reliable information. You look up *Bathtub* in an encyclopedia and discover an article that contains this information:

> The Victorian tub was frequently a hooded affair, usually made of wood, copper, or iron. Bathroom fixtures were often disguised out of a desire for modesty. The tub, for example, might have a cover resembling a sofa or chaise lounge. Home bathroom facilities gradually became common in western Europe, Canada, and the United States. The White House in Washington, D.C., did not have a bathtub until 1851, and a generation later a bathroom in the house was still a mark of the wealthy class.*

---

* *The Encyclopedia Americana* (1982), 3, 351.

You may have noticed that some of this information is vague. The words *frequently* and *usually* in the first sentence tell us that the author cannot be categorical about *all* bathtubs during the Victorian age. The author does the same with *often* in the next sentence and *might* in the next. He or she is hedging. You might be beginning to ask, "What *does* this writer know for sure?" But then you find something straightforward and precise: "The White House . . . did not have a bathtub until 1851." Now, there's what you're looking for, an unqualified fact. You've found this information in an authoritative source, one that would have no reason to lie to you. The source isn't lying, but it is nevertheless wrong. In fact, what you have learned in the encyclopedia article is hooey. The first bathtub in the White House was not installed in 1851. You'll see shortly why I think so.

It is no surprise to anyone, of course, that encyclopedias and reference books are sometimes wrong. Sometimes, they are wrong because the "truth" as it was known at the time of the writing has been superceded by more, better, or different information. The author can't be blamed for not knowing that what was the case at the time of writing might turn out to be wrong in the future. But in the case of the bathtub article, the author of this "fact" has it wrong simply because he accepted it uncritically from some other source.

At some point in reading about the history of the bathtub, if you had pursued it further, you might have encountered a reference to "the infamous bathtub hoax." That might have led you in a new direction of inquiry, and sooner or later you might have come across the following essay, written for readers of a journal called *Menckeniana* for fans of an American journalist of the 1920s, H. L. Mencken. Read it through and you'll see why the encyclopedia "facts" aren't to be trusted.

THE PHILOSOPHY OF H. L. MENCKEN

P. J. Wingate

During the 1920's, when he was at the peak of his literary fame, H. L. Mencken became widely known as the "Sage of Baltimore." Mencken was busy in those days editing *The American Mercury* and preparing revised editions of his most famous book, *The American Language,* and he made no comment on being called a sage; but when some people began to call him the "Baltimore Philosopher" he objected.

In 1927 he wrote an essay called "On Metaphysicians," which was Mencken's word for philosophers, and in it made clear that he did not want to be known as a philosopher. He started his essay by saying that when Baltimore got too hot for what he called "serious mental activity," he always took a couple of weeks off for a "rereading of the so-called philosophical classics with a glance or two at the latest compositions of the extant philosophers."

He explained his annual trip into the forests of philosophy by saying,

> There is somewhere down in my recesses an obscure conviction that
> I owe a duty to my customers, who look to me to flatter them with
> occasional dark references to Aristotle, Spinoza and the categorical
> imperative. Out of this business, despite the high austerity, I always
> carry away the feeling that I have had a hell of a time. That is, I carry
> away the feeling that the art and mystery of philosophy as it is
> practiced in the world of professional philosophers, is largely moon-
> shine and wind music—or, to borrow Henry Ford's searching term,
> bunk.

"Since the dawn of time," he continued,

> they have been trying to get order and method into the thinking of Homo
> Sapiens, and Homo Sapiens, if he thinks at all, is still a brother to the
> lowly ass . . . even to the ears and the bray. I include the philosophers
> themselves unanimously and especially. True enough, one arises now
> and then who somehow manages to be charming and even plausible. I
> point to Plato, to Nietzsche, to Schopenhauer. But it is always as a poet
> or politician, not as a philosopher. The genuine professional, sticking to
> his gloomy speculations is as dull as a table of logarithms. What man in
> human history ever wrote worse than Kant?

Mencken then went on to define the problem with philosophers
this way: "What reduces all philosophers to incoherence and folly, soon
or late, is the lure of the absolute. . . . For the absolute, of course, is a
mere banshee, a concept without substance or reality. No such thing
exists."

Mencken's long experience as a reporter and editor probably was
what caused him to feel so strongly that absolute truth did not exist. He
knew from sad experience with newspapers how difficult it was to come
by the facts of events as recent as yesterday.

Mencken's own part in the history of the bathtub in America was a
case in point. A great amount had been written about bathtubs in ancient
Greece and Rome, but when Mencken became interested in them he
found that nothing at all had ever been written about bathtubs in America. So he wrote the first piece on the subject and had it published in the
New York *Evening Mail* of 28 December 1917.

He called his piece "A Neglected Anniversary" because he said no
attention had been given to the seventy-fifth anniversary of the installation of the first true bathtub—one with pipes carrying in hot and cold
water and others to carry away the spent water—ever set up in the United
States.

This bathtub, Mencken reported, had been completed on December
20, 1842, in the home of Adam Thompson, a Cincinnati grain merchant
who shipped much of his grain to England. During trips to visit customers in England Thompson became familiar with bathtubs and decided to
install one in his own home.

Thompson's tub was a large thing made of mahogany wood and lined
with lead so that it weighed 1750 pounds. It was supplied with water from

a third floor tank and some of the water was heated by running it through a long copper coil in the chimney of the fireplace. Thompson liked his new tub and invited several other wealthy Cincinnatians to try a bath in it. They liked it too and soon there were several bathtubs in Cincinnati and the newspapers there ran stories about these tubs.

Whereupon a surprising reaction to use of the bathtub occurred.

"On the one hand," Mencken wrote, "it was denounced as an epicurean and obnoxious toy from England, designed to corrupt the democratic simplicity of the republic, and on the other hand it was attacked by the medical faculty as dangerous to health."

Mencken went on to quote from the *Western Medical Repository* of April 23, 1843, which called the bathtub a certain inviter of "phthisic rheumatic fevers, inflammation of the lungs and the whole category of zymotic diseases."

Nevertheless, news about the bathtub spread and soon tubs were being installed in other cities which developed controversies of their own. Hartford, Providence, Charleston (South Carolina), and Wilmington (Delaware) all put special water taxes on homes with bathtubs, Mencken reported, and Boston in 1845 made bathing unlawful except upon medical advice. But this ordinance was never enforced and was repealed in 1862. The repeal was a slow reaction to the fact that the American Medical Association had met in Boston in 1852. A poll of the membership showed that nearly all the doctors present then thought bathing was harmless, and twenty per cent advocated it as beneficial.

However, the thing which really caused the bathtub to flourish in America, Mencken reported, was the example set by President Millard Fillmore. Fillmore had visited Cincinnati on a political tour in 1850 and had taken a bath in the original Thompson tub. To quote Mencken: "Experiencing no ill effects, he became an ardent advocate of the new invention" and when he succeeded to the Presidency, after Taylor died on July 9, 1850, he had his Secretary of War, General Conrad, install one in the White House.

"This action," Mencken reported, "revived the old controversy and its opponents made much of the fact that there was no bathtub at Mt. Vernon or Monticello, and all the Presidents and magnificos of the past had got along without such monarchial luxuries."

Nevertheless, the bathtub prospered greatly after Fillmore's term as President and by 1860, according to newspaper advertisements, every hotel in New York had a bathtub and some had two or even three.

Mencken closed his story for the *Evening Mail* this way: "So much for the history of the bathtub in America. One is astonished, on looking into it, to find that so little of it has been recorded. The literature, in fact, is almost nil. But perhaps this brief sketch will encourage other inquiries and so lay the foundation for an adequate celebration of the Centennial in 1942."

However, for the next nine years, no one wrote anything else about the bathtub, although Mencken's account was reprinted in over a hundred magazines and newspapers, and excerpts from it appeared in history books and encyclopedias. One item in particular—Fillmore's installation of the first White House bathtub—fascinated historians and it was recorded in a multitude of places. Fillmore, in fact, became known during the 1920's as "the first clean president."

Then almost a decade after he wrote his story for the New York *Evening Mail*, Mencken wrote a follow-up piece which appeared in the Chicago *Tribune* of May 23, 1926. In this new story Mencken admitted that the first piece was totally a product of his own imagination.

"This article," he wrote in the *Tribune* story, "was a tissue of absurdities, all of them deliberate and most of them obvious. If there were any facts in it they got there accidentally and against my design."

Mencken went on to say that he had liked his fabrication and was at first pleased when so many newspapers across the country reprinted it. Then he became alarmed because "I began to encounter my preposterous 'facts' in the writings of other men. They began to be used by chiropractors and other such quacks as evidence of the stupidity of medical men. They began to be cited by medical men as proof of the progress of public hygiene. They got into the learned journals. They were alluded to on the floor of Congress. They crossed the ocean and were discussed solemnly in England and on the continent. Today, I believe they are accepted as gospel everywhere on earth. To question them becomes as hazardous as to question the Norman Invasion."

This exposé, itself, was reprinted in twenty or thirty major newspapers and then a very curious situation developed. No one paid any attention to this exposé. Two weeks later the Boston *Herald* reprinted the original hoax as an interesting piece of American history. Of course, no one corrected the history books which had faithfully reproduced parts of it, particularly the item about Millard Fillmore putting in the first White House bathtub.

Mencken made one more attempt to debunk his bathtub hoax and on July 25, 1926, wrote another piece on the subject for the Chicago *Tribune*, once again calling his original story a fake.

Again, very few people apparently paid any attention to the exposé and the original story kept right on gaining credibility and acceptance. And it kept on doing so long after Mencken died.

Dr. Daniel Boorstin, Librarian of the Library of Congress, for example, included the most intriguing of Mencken's "facts" in his scholarly book *The Americans—The Democratic Experience* published by Random House in 1973. On page 353 Dr. Boorstin wrote: "In 1851 when President Millard Fillmore reputedly installed the first permanent bathtub and water closet in the White House he was criticized for doing something that was 'both unsanitary and undemocratic.'"

Dozens of other authors have done the same thing, the two most recent being Barbara Seuling in 1978 and Paul Boller in 1981. Boller's book, called *Presidential Anecdotes* was published by the Oxford University Press.

Also, all three of the national television networks reported in 1976, on January 7 the occasion of Fillmore's birthday, that he had installed the first White House bathtub.

All this has occurred despite the fact that many newspapers have exposed Mencken's fake over the years. For example, on January 4, 1977, the Washington *Post* exposed it once more but the *Post* closed its story on a note of optimism.

"Will this current account," the *Post* asked, "destroy one of the nation's most charming myths? Certainly not. It will not even slow it up any more than a single grape placed on the railroad tracks would slow up a freight train.

"So on January 7, let all true patriots retire to their bathrooms, fill up the tub with champagne, invite the neighbors in, and drink a toast to Millard Fillmore, statesman, scholar, patriot, and the finest plumber who ever lived in the White House."

The Philadelphia *Inquirer* of January 7, 1977, carried a similar story which was headlined: "A Dirty Story. Fillmore's Still in That Tub."

And so it goes. The original hoax has become indestructible while all attempts to correct it go nowhere.

Mencken explained all this in his essay which he called "Hymn To The Truth" written for the Chicago *Tribune* in 1926.

"No normal human being," he wrote, "wants to hear the truth. It is the passion of a small and aberrant minority of men, most of them pathological. They are hated for telling it while they live, and when they die are swiftly forgotten. What remains to the world, in the field of wisdom, is a series of long-tested and solidly agreeable lies."

In another essay called "The Art Eternal" Mencken stated his views in a somewhat similar manner and said that Americans were particularly resentful of the truth.

"A Galileo," he wrote, "could no more be elected President of the United States than he could be elected Pope of Rome. Both high posts are reserved for men favored by God with an extraordinary genius for swathing the bitter facts of life in bandages of soft illusion."

Mencken closed his 1927 essay on philosophers this way:

"There is no record in human history of a happy philosopher: they exist only in romantic legend. Practically all of them have turned their children out of doors and beaten their wives. And no wonder! If you want to find out how a philosopher feels when he is engaged in the practice of his profession, go to the nearest zoo and watch a chimpanzee at the weary and hopeless job of chasing fleas. Both suffer damnably and neither can win."

So it is clear why Mencken did not wish to be called a philosopher.

Nevertheless, he had a philosophy of his own. Mencken believed that the list of eternal truths is a very short one and if a man happens to come across what he believes to be one of these eternal truths he still should not take it too seriously.

As P. J. Wingate's essay makes clear, Mencken enjoyed the idea that people would believe his fictional account of the history of the bathtub. He enjoyed it because it proved that people are gullible, and Mencken, like other great cynics, thought it terribly amusing that this should be so. He poked fun at people's credulity, and by this means, perhaps, tried to make people more skeptical, like himself. Mencken lied, on purpose, in order to argue an implied thesis: that people will believe anything on the basis of authority. His lies were believed because his thesis was overlooked by uncritical readers. Their unquestioning faith in authority proved him right! (It's possible, of course, that Mencken lied when he said he lied. Why do you suppose I am rejecting that possibility here?)

The many writers of books and encyclopedia articles who repeated Mencken's fictions might have been more skeptical of the "facts" they passed along, but mere skepticism would not have been enough. If they had chosen to *disbelieve* this information, on the general principle that they would doubt everything, then they could not have written anything at all, for they would have nothing to say. The question is not whether they should or shouldn't have believed *x, y,* or *z* about bathtubs when they read it somewhere. The question is, *what kind of process did they go through as readers to measure their belief in the "facts" they read?*

What sort of process am I talking about? Not one, I assure you, that will prevent you from ever being duped or that will tell you when a thing is true. Critical reading can do no more than keep you asking about potentially good or bad reasons, so that when you face the question of whether to agree or disagree, you will be able to make a qualified decision based on your understanding of the quality of the reasons given. **Critical reading is the conscious act of adjusting the degree of one's agreement with any idea to the quality of the reasons that support that idea.** People who believe without caring about the quality of the reasons, as well as people who disbelieve without caring about the quality of the reasons, no matter *what* they believe, are, by this definition, uncritical. All of us are uncritical sometimes. We are more or less critical at different times. When we are reading, however, we should try to read as critically as we can. If we don't, we risk becoming the victims of anything a writer happens to say.

When writers write, they do not simply string together sentences that all directly assert some information. As we have seen in Chapter 1, writing takes its shape from the writer's intention. That is, writers want people to believe something. They write with an idea in mind, therefore, but their choice of things to say in addition to that idea depends on what they think people need to hear in order to believe it. Writing is purposeful and *strategic*. Writing that contains information, then, will also contain something put there in order to help you or encourage you to believe that that information is true.

A critical reader must, therefore, pay attention to more than *what* a piece of writing says. A critical reader must also consider *how* information is presented. This is because a writer who thinks strategically is mindful of the *means* that is necessary to reach the *end* that he or she has in mind. This does not mean that writers cheat or want to deceive us. It simply means that writers intuitively understand that they must convince readers to believe them, and they make use of available means of persuasion accordingly. Information by itself is rarely the *end* of a piece of writing. Information is more likely among the *means* a writer has chosen to make an idea persuasive. Or, to put this another way, writers want more than our acceptance of information as true;

they want us to adopt an attitude toward it, or to take a stance with them about the significance of the "facts."

Let me illustrate this with an example of writing that might appear at first simply to report objective information. In keeping with the theme of the bathtub hoax, here is an essay that appeared in newspapers. It repeats certain information that we have already read in Wingate's essay, but you will quickly see that this writer's purpose differs from Wingate's, and so the information is used differently.

MENCKEN AND THE GREAT "BATHTUB HOAX"

Tom Welshko

In December 1917, H. L. Mencken (we celebrated his 104th birthday Sept. 12) published an article in the New York Evening Mail titled "A Neglected Anniversary." This article purported to note the 75th anniversary of the invention of the bathtub (defined as one with pipes to carry in hot and cold water and others to carry away the spent water), and to recount the history behind its invention and how it subsequently came into common use by Americans.

According to Mencken, the bathtub was invented on Dec. 20, 1842, by one Adam Thompson of Cincinnati. It soon became popular in Ohio and the U.S. in general, we learn. Mencken also states that 19th-century physicians denounced bathing as a health hazard and several jurisdictions, on this basis, banned the tub. Millard Fillmore, Mencken notes, was the first president to install a bathtub in the White House.

The only problem with these facts is that they are totally bogus. Mencken's article has since become known as "The Bathtub Hoax." Yet, 67 years after its first publication and 28 years after Mencken's death, the article and its spurious facts are still being quoted as true.

P. J. Wingate, in the fall 1983 issue of Menckeniana (the Enoch Pratt Library's magazine dedicated to the Baltimore author), lists several references, some as late as 1981, where Millard Fillmore is credited with installing the first White House bathtub. These references are from several major U.S. newspapers and all three television networks. (It must be stressed that many of Mencken's "facts" concerning the bathtub found their way into encyclopedias during his lifetime and will remain there to be quoted for ages to come.)

Mencken himself wrote at least two articles in 1926 in which he admitted concocting the history of the bathtub, but these disclaimers seem to have done little good. He explained why he thought "The Bathtub Hoax" gained so much credibility: "No normal human being wants to hear the truth. It is the passion of a small and aberrant minority of men, most of them pathological. They are hated for telling it while they live, and when they die are swiftly forgotten. What remains to the world, in the field of wisdom, is a series of long-tested and solidly agreeable lies."

I believe this is not why Mencken's bathtub facts gained currency. People do want the truth. However, nature abhors a vacuum. Sanitation is not a polite subject; hence, there are few books or articles concerning the objects of sanitary convenience, such as the bathtub, while thousands abound regarding more polite subjects such as electric lighting, the telephone, or the computer. Mencken simply took advantage of a vacuum that existed in 1917.

Today, the vacuum still exists. The best way to combat Mencken's bogus facts about the bathtub is to recount its true history. These facts, though, are only to be found in the most dusty and obscure books. Obtaining those facts was a difficult task, and they are not as colorful, or as definitive, as Mencken's concocted history.

Of course, receptacles for bathing, where people carried water to a tub, existed from ancient times. What concerns us here is the "mechanized" bathtub. According to several sources, this process did not begin until the 19th century.

Paris was the first city to have a regular water supply, but only for well-to-do districts. This occurred in 1812. Among the earliest bathrooms in the United States were two built in the Van Ness Mansion in Washington, D.C., in 1815. The Tremont House, a Boston hotel, was said to "have an elaborate battery of water closets and bathrooms with running water in the basement" as early as 1827–29.

According to the Sept. 17, 1853, edition of The Illustrated London News, the Mount Vernon Hotel in Cape May, N.J., allowed "every guest to have his bath in his bedroom and there are hot and cold taps for his use when he pleases." As far as there being one person who can be credited with the bathtub's invention—such as Mencken's fictitious Adam Thompson—there is none.

Even as late as the 1880s, though, "5 out of every 6 dwellers in American cities had no facilities for bathing other than those provided by pail and sponge." Bathtubs were luxury items, affordable only by the rich. In fact, the Crane Co. did not begin to mass-produce copper-lined wood bathtubs until 1883 and enameled tubs until 10 years later.

Mencken, though, perpetrated one of the greatest literary hoaxes of all time. No matter what the reason, his bathtub facts will endure.

Now, what has Welshko done in this writing with the information that he seems to have derived from Wingate? In the first place, Welshko is using the information about Mencken's hoax to set up his own explanation for why people are gullible. Wingate simply presents Mencken's view of this problem by quoting or paraphrasing Mencken himself, and he seems to agree with Mencken's explanation since he does not challenge it. Welshko, on the other hand, is reporting the incident of the bathtub hoax for the purpose of *disagreeing* with Mencken's explanation, and you might observe how much of Mencken's explanation he has, therefore, left out. Welshko also skips over certain details of the bogus history of the bathtub because they do not much matter to his intention. He needs only to tell his readers enough to persuade them that there was a hoax and that "its spurious facts are still being quoted as true." Notice that Wingate goes into detail on this point; Welshko just asserts it. Welshko's purpose is to make an argument of his own, and he offers just enough information to give us a context for understanding it.

The argument that Welshko wants to make begins in the sixth paragraph. He is trying to make a case that Mencken's explanation for the success of his hoax was too harsh. Welshko does not want to blame unskeptical readers for their gullibility as much as he wants to credit some kind of universal principle, that "nature abhors a vacuum." This in turn permits him to carry his argument one more step and to say that the history of the bathtub might be set straight, not by making people more skeptical necessarily, but by recording "its true history." He seems to mean that there will be no problem once he fills the vacuum with the real facts, in place of Mencken's bogus ones. Now look at what Welshko says: "These facts . . . are only to be found in the most dusty and obscure books." He then goes on to tell us some of these facts. Does he expect us to believe him? What reasons does he give us to accept his facts? Is Welshko any more *believable* than Mencken was?

Only an uncritical reader at this point could accept Welshko's facts as true *solely on the basis of the reasons he gives*. At the same time, however, we have no solid reasons to disbelieve him. With our knowledge of Mencken's hoax in the background, we must at least acknowledge the possibility that Welshko might be perpetrating one of his own, having us on for reasons similar to Mencken's. It is possible that Welshko's reference to "dusty and obscure books," without naming them, is a hint to his ironic purpose in this context. It is possible that his reference to *The Illustrated London News* is as bogus as Mencken's reference to the *Western Medical Repository*. (Unless we did a little hunting, we couldn't say whether either reference were real or bogus.) But these are only possibilities, not certainties. In order to test Welshko's facts, to know with a greater degree of certainty that we should accept them, we would have to do some independent inquiry to confirm or to dispute them based on more reading, just as we would have to do to know whether Mencken's or the encyclopedia's facts were to be fully trusted or distrusted. Another possibility is that Welshko did not name some of his sources because he didn't think it necessary, since we would take his word for it that they say what he says they do. Yet another possibility is that Welshko did find his information in "several sources," but that these sources are themselves wrong.

These possibilities in themselves do not dispute Welshko's facts or his argument. They simply enable us to adjust the degree of acceptance we choose to give to them. We do not have to believe them. No one is compelling us by force to do so. But we must decide nevertheless how believable they are. To do this, we go through a process of weighing. We weigh our agreement, balancing it against all the other things we know and don't know, against what we know and don't know of Welshko's purpose, against what we know and don't know of Welshko's strategies, against what we know and don't know independently about the history of plumbing, and so on. The more knowledge we have, the better we are able to do this weighing, but since our judgment also involves our consciousness of what we don't know, this process can never arrive at a conclusion that does not balance belief against the possibility of being wrong.

READING AND BELIEF

Some people are accustomed to think that either facts must be believed or they must be disbelieved—as if belief were like a light switch with only two positions, on or off. My use of the bathtub hoax is intended to illustrate that belief does not have to operate as a simple yes or no choice, all or nothing. Belief can be more conditional; it can be something that we decide to have up to a point or to a degree. And so, the question we might ask ourselves while reading does not have to be "Should I believe it or not?" but instead "How much should I believe it?" This latter question implies that the belief we have in any given fact, or in any given idea, is not determined by whether it sounds right or whether the source is an authority. It means that our beliefs are determined by the reasons that justify them. Belief is not a mechanical action, brought about by invariable rules of nature. It is a human activity, the exercise of judgment. With this in mind, we might say that we perform this action better when we know what the reasons are that have led to our belief, and why they are good reasons.

The process of weighing beliefs against the quality of reasons is one that you already go through all the time, whether you are aware of it or not. We all do. The practice of critical reading is the exercise of this kind of judgment on purpose. By doing it, we protect ourselves from being led into belief for inadequate reasons, but at the same time we open up our minds to the possibility of arriving at belief for adequate ones. If we decide to grant or withhold assent based on the quality of the reasons that we are given, we admit at the same time that two things are possible: We admit that we might assent less in the future if we discover that the reasons are not so good after all; and we admit that we might assent more if we are ever presented with better reasons than we had formerly known. This attitude is not pure skepticism any more than it is pure credulity. It is somewhere in between. It is the attitude of an open-minded thinker, of someone who wishes to be responsible for deciding for herself or himself what to believe.

The practice of critical reading, then, can do more than protect us from jumping too quickly to conclusions. Because it is a process of examining reasons and measuring conclusions against them, it can provide us with a way to learn to live with uncertainty. Living with uncertainty is one of those skills we need to get along in this world, but it is also a skill that people do not talk about much. We have just seen that certainty is not easy to come by. It requires that we assume some responsibility for questioning what we read, which might entail a search for more information and better reasons than we are given in a single source. It requires independent inquiry and thought, in other words, which are carried out not only because we want to know what to believe but also because each of us alone must make up his or her own mind.

If absolute, permanent belief is not available about many matters that concern us, we must adjust to this situation and accept it. It can be a situation to be enjoyed, not lamented, because it is what makes thinking and learning an adventure. More inquiry is always possible. New ideas or new reasons may turn up. This keeps our minds alert and active. It makes us want to continue to learn because we are more able to accept new ideas. It makes us less susceptible to the tactics of people who would like to do our thinking for us. Instead of the easy convictions that come from narrow-mindedness, this process offers us the possibility of continuing to think about things that matter to us.

Critical reading, then, is something we practice in order to acknowledge that we belong to a "community of inquiring minds," as I called it earlier—a discourse community in which inquiry and argument are valued for their ability to keep us thinking and talking to each other.

SOME CONSIDERATIONS FOR CRITICAL READING

The preceding section has offered you some philosophical ideas about reading and writing, about education, on which this book is based. You are free, in fact encouraged, to question them. But now we must get practical in our thinking about critical reading.

What follows is a discussion of some questions that a critical reader might consider in order to arrive at an adequate basis for deciding how much to give or withhold assent. Asking the questions will not, of course, guarantee answers. They can only serve to guide further thinking. Perhaps you ask yourself many of these questions anyway when you read, even if you never become self-consciously deliberate about doing so. They are not intended as a checklist, to proceed through in mechanical fashion. They are not, as you will see, quite as separate as a numbered list might suggest. Nor are they equally applicable to every kind of reading; some will be more important than others, depending on the nature of the reading to which you apply them. Use them as a basis for more thought, that's all.

1. *What is the writer's purpose?* What is this writer trying to do to the reader? What is the single most important idea in the writing, the one that makes everything else in it necessary? This central idea (or thesis) may or may not be stated explicitly by the writer. It may or may not be obvious.

2. *What question does the writing answer?* The writer's intended audience is assumed to share a concern for some question, which the essay serves to answer in some way. The question may or may not be explicit or obvious. Do I share this concern? Should I?

3. *Why does the writer think this question is important?* There must be some reason the writer has chosen this question to answer. What difference does it make to the writer that the question be resolved? What about the writing tells me this?

4. *How persuadable am I?* Do I already have my mind made up on this question? How willing am I to listen to another point of view? If I agree with the author, can I maintain some critical distance and not agree with the reasons just because I already agree with the conclusion? What untested reactions do I have to the writer's thesis?

5. *What are the writer's reasons?* What ideas does the writer advance in defense of the thesis? What ideas are advanced in defense of *those* ideas?

6. *Where does the reasoning stop?* What reasons are asserted as if they are self-evident? Although some reasons are supported by a further line of reasoning, it is impossible for all of them to be. If the reasoning depends on these ideas being believed without further support, do I believe them?

7. *Are the reasons adequate?* Not all reasons actually support the conclusions they seem to support. What actually connects the reasons to the conclusions?

8. *What responsibility does the writer take for the verifiability of information?* If the writer cites facts, studies, experiences, or sources, is there an adequate basis for checking up on them, or does the writer expect us to simply take his or her word for them?

9. *What has the writer done to put the reader in a receptive frame of mind?* Not all parts of a writing have the strictly logical function of supporting a thesis. Some aspects of the composition, especially its style, will function to create confidence in the writer or a special bond between the writer and the reader. How do I react to these features?

10. *What am I going to do about it?* If a critical reader is engaged in measuring assent, then I should know how I might be changed by having read and thought about these ideas. To what extent must I adjust my thinking? Do these ideas have relevance to my thinking about other questions? Are there connections between these ideas and other things I believe?

IMPLICATIONS FOR RESEARCH

As a student—and as a voter, a consumer, a person who must decide things—you will often need to find out more than you already know about some subject before committing yourself to a conclusion or a course of action. Critical reading is necessary in order to know what to make of the knowledge that you discover when you look into some subject, but it will also help you to decide what needs looking into. When, in your further reading, you try to judge the conclusions you find against the adequacy of the reasons given for them, you will be able to isolate the particular areas in which your knowledge needs to be increased. By reading critically, you may find that you need not read further in one area, such as "anaesthesia," but do need to know more about some other, such as "sodium pentothal."

In formal research, you will be responsible for finding information to explain a phenomenon and evidence for arguing a reasonable conclusion about it. In informal research—the kind we do whenever we have unanswered questions, even if no writing will result from it—you will want to assure yourself that your ideas or actions are founded on reasons that you understand and trust. The goal of either kind of research is confidence in what you know. Critical reading will guide you in gaining that confidence, even though, as we see in this chapter, that confidence is not easy to come by.

If you are required to do formal research in connection with the writing you do while using this book in class, the "Implications for Research" sections in the next three chapters will be relevant to your assignments. But, even though no formal research is required, you will be doing a kind of informal research anyway, in the form of critical reading on subjects discussed in class. Discussion itself is like research, if it expands your understanding by confronting you with the ideas of others. Writing argumentative essays will require you to make up your own mind on issues that are open to speculation and inquiry. This involves assessing arguments that you encounter—in reading and discussion—and determining where you stand in relation to them.

Much of the writing that students do in college requires some kind of research. Because students sometimes produce writing that looks like research, but really isn't, we should consider for a moment what the term means in a college setting. Research is inquiry into the unknown. It is the pursuit of answers to questions that are yet unanswered. Research takes different forms, of course, but all research derives from a basic desire: to find out what is true.

Given these definitions, you can see why I said that the writing of college students sometimes resembles research but is, in fact, something else. The standard term paper—sometimes called a "research paper"—might not involve any genuine research at all, if, for instance, the writer only repeats information found in sources to confirm a conclusion that was never in doubt. Merely going to the library and compiling information is not research; it is more like reporting on the research of others. Thus, a "research paper" is misnamed if the writer only repeats what others have asserted, without in some way testing that knowledge or using it to solve a problem. Yet, the term paper often turns out to be just such an exercise, in which greater importance is placed on the bulk of gathered information and the formalities of footnotes and bibliographies than on the search for answers.

A long essay, with correctly documented footnotes from many bibliographic sources, is a research paper only if it results from the writer's having sought and found an answer to a question. Research writing is the process of arguing that answer in such a way that the knowledge the writer has discovered can be shared with others. Research is like learning: It proceeds from not knowing to knowing. Research writing is like argumentation: It shows why answers should be accepted.

Research is not a process that begins with complete uncertainty and ends with complete certainty; it is, therefore, not possible to become "fully" informed first and then to decide what to believe. There are always gaps in one's knowledge—even if one reaches the point, after years of research and study, of becoming an expert. One learns by doing research that there is always something more to know before absolute certainty is possible. Thus, the research writer must always argue for his or her discoveries on the basis of the best information available. The research writer, in other words, must know how to argue well and responsibly without having "all" the answers. The researcher, as a writer of argumentation, must seek clarification and belief within the limits of what it is possible to know. As a writer of argumentative essays, you should be learning to measure conclusions against the quality, not the quantity, of the available reasons. This is exactly what a good researcher also needs to know how to do.

QUESTIONS FOR THOUGHT, DISCUSSION, AND WRITING

1. Have you ever had the experience of believing something you read and then discovering later that it was not true? What did this experience teach you about reading?
2. Have you ever read something that someone told you was bad for you? Was it? How do you know? How about something that someone said would be good for you?
3. Can you think of any ideas that you agree with only to a certain degree? What has your agreement to do with the quality of the reasons you have heard in support of these ideas?
4. Do you agree or disagree with H. L. Mencken's statement that "No normal human being wants to hear the truth"? Why?
5. In general, how would you define a "good reason"? Find some examples of good reasons and bad ones to illustrate what you mean. Does everyone agree with your examples?
6. Here are three readings that contain arguments about some of the issues raised in this chapter. In each case, use the ten questions in this chapter to guide your critical reading of these essays. You might wish to write one paragraph in answer to each of the ten questions. Does your critical reading provide you with ideas for an essay of your own? Does it open up areas in which you may wish to conduct further inquiry?

◆ READINGS ◆

THE GREAT ESKIMO VOCABULARY HOAX

Geoffrey K. Pullum

Most linguistics departments have an introduction-to-language course in which students other than linguistics majors can be exposed to at least something of the mysteries of language and communication: signing apes and dancing bees; wild children and lateralization; logographic writing and the Rosetta Stone; *pit* and *spit*; Sir William Jones and Professor Henry Higgins; isoglosses and Grimm's Law; *Jabberwocky* and colourless green ideas; and of course, without fail, the Eskimos and their multiple words for snow.

Few among us, I'm sure, can say with certainty that we never told an awestruck sea of upturned sophomore faces about the multitude of snow descriptors used by these lexically profligate hyperborean nomads, about whom so little information is repeated so often to so many. Linguists have been just as active as schoolteachers or general knowledge columnists in spreading the entrancing story. What a pity the story is unredeemed piffle.

Anthropologist Laura Martin of Cleveland State University spent some of her research time during the 1980s attempting to slay the constantly changing, self-regenerating myth of Eskimo snow terminology, like a Sigourney Weaver fighting alone against the hideous space creature in the movie *Alien* (a xenomorph, they called it in the sequel *Aliens*; nice word). You may recall that the creature seemed to spring up everywhere once it got loose on the spaceship, and was very difficult to kill.

Martin presented her paper at the annual meetings of the American Anthropological Association in Washington, D.C., in December 1982, and eventually (after a four-year struggle during which bonehead reviewers cut a third of the paper, including several interesting quotes) she published an abbreviated version of it in the 'Research Reports' section of AAA's journal (Martin 1986). This ought to have been enough for the news to get out.

But no, as far as widespread recognition is concerned, Martin labored in vain. Never does a month (or in all probability a week) go by without yet another publication of the familiar claim about the wondrous richness of the Eskimo conceptual scheme: hundreds of words for different grades and types of snow, a lexicographical winter wonderland, the quintessential demonstration of how primitive minds categorize the world so differently from us.

And the alleged lexical extravagance of the Eskimos comports so well with the many other facets of their polysynthetic perversity: rubbing noses; lending their wives to strangers; eating raw seal blubber; throwing grandma out to be eaten by polar bears. "We are prepared to believe almost anything about such an unfamiliar and peculiar group," says Martin, in a gentle reminder of our buried racist tendencies.

The tale she tells is an embarrassing saga of scholarly sloppiness and popular eagerness to embrace exotic facts about other people's languages without seeing the evidence. The fact is that the myth of the multiple words for snow is based on almost nothing at all. It is a kind of accidentally developed hoax perpetrated by the anthropological linguistics community on itself.

The original source is Franz Boas' introduction to *The Handbook of North American Indians* (1911). And all Boas says there, in the context of a low-key and slightly ill-explained discussion of independent versus derived terms for things in different languages, is that just as English uses separate roots for a variety of forms of water (liquid, lake, river, brook, rain, dew, wave, foam) that might be formed by derivational morphology from a single root meaning 'water' in some other language, so Eskimo uses the apparently distinct roots *aput* 'snow on the ground', *qana* 'falling snow', *piqsirpoq* 'drifting snow', and *qimuqsuq* 'a snow drift'. Boas' point is simply that English expresses these notions by phrases involving the root *snow*, but things could have been otherwise, just as the words for lake, river, etc. could have been formed derivationally or periphrastically on the root *water*.

But with the next twist in the story, the unleashing of the xenomorphic fable of Eskimo lexicography seems to have become inevitable. What happened was that Benjamin Lee Whorf, Connecticut fire prevention inspector and weekend language-fancier, picked up Boas' example and used it, vaguely, in his 1940 amateur linguistics article 'Science and linguistics,' which was published in MIT's promotional magazine *Technology Review* (Whorf was an alumnus; he had done his B.S. in chemical engineering at MIT).

Our word *snow* would seem too inclusive to an Eskimo, our man from the Hartford Fire Insurance Company confidently asserts. With an uncanny perception into the hearts and minds of the hardy Arctic denizens (the more uncanny since Eskimos were not a prominent feature of Hartford's social scene at the time), he avers:

> We have the same word for falling snow, snow on the ground, snow packed hard like ice, slushy snow, wind-driven flying snow—whatever the situation may be. To an Eskimo, this all-inclusive word would be almost unthinkable; he would say that falling snow, slushy snow, and so on, are sensuously and operationally different, different things to contend with; he uses different words for them and for other kinds of snow. (Whorf 1940; in Carroll 1956, 216).

Whorf's article was quoted and reprinted in more subsequent books than you could shake a flame-thrower at; the creature was already loose and regenerating itself all over the ship.

Notice that Whorf's statement has illicitly inflated Boas' four terms to at least seven (1: "falling", 2: "on the ground", 3: "packed hard", 4: "slushy", 5: "flying", 6, 7, . . . : "and other kinds of snow"). Notice also that his claims about English speakers are false; I recall the stuff in question being called *snow* when fluffy and white, *slush* when partly melted, *sleet* when falling in a half-melted state, and a *blizzard* when pelting down hard enough to make driving dangerous. Whorf's remark about his own speech community is no more reliable than his glib generalizations about what things are "sensuously and operationally different" to the generic Eskimo.

But the lack of little things like verisimilitude and substantiation are not enough to stop a myth. Martin tracks the great Eskimo vocabulary hoax through successively more careless repetitions and embroiderings in a number of popular books on language. Roger Brown's *Words and Things* (1958, 234–236), attributing the example to Whorf, provides an early example of careless popularization and perversion of the issue. His numbers disagree with both Boas and Whorf (he says there are "three Eskimo words for snow", apparently getting this from figure 10 in Whorf's paper; perhaps he only looked at the pictures).[1]

After works like Brown's have picked up Whorf's second-hand misrecollection of Boas to generate third-hand accounts, we begin to get fourth-hand accounts carelessly based on Brown. For example, Martin notes that in Carol Eastman's *Aspects of Language and Culture* (1975; 3rd printing 1980), the familiar assertion that "Eskimo languages have many words for snow" is found only six lines away from a direct quote of Brown's reference to "three" words for snow.

But never mind: three, four, seven, who cares? It's a bunch, right? Once more popular sources start to get hold of the example, all constraints are removed: arbitrary numbers are just made up as the writer thinks appropriate for the readership. In Lanford Wilson's 1978 play *The Fifth of July* it is "fifty." From 1984 alone (two years *after* her 1982 presentation to the American Anthropological Association meetings on the subject—not that mere announcement at a scholarly meeting could have been expected to change anything), Martin cites the number of Eskimo snow terms given as "nine" (in a trivia encyclopedia, Adams 1984), "one hundred" (in a *New York Times* editorial on February 9), and "two hundred" (in a Cleveland TV weather forecast).

By coincidence, I happened to notice, the *New York Times* returned to the topic four years to the day after committing itself to the figure of one hundred: on February 9, 1988, on page 21, in the *Science Times*

---

[1] Murray (1987) has argued that Martin is too harsh on some people, particularly Brown, who does correctly see some English speakers also differentiate their snow terms (skiers talk of *powder*, *crust*, and *slush*). But Martin is surely correct in criticizing Brown for citing no data at all, and for making points about lexical structure, perception, and Zipf's Law that are rendered nonsense by the actual nature of Eskimo word structure (his reference to "length of a verbal expression" providing "an index of its frequency in speech" fails to take account of the fact that even with a single root for snow, the number of actual *word forms* for snow in Eskimo will be effectively infinite, and the frequency of each one approximately zero, because of the polysynthetic morphology).

section, a piece by Jane E. Brody on laboratory research into snowflake formation began: "The Eskimos have about four dozen words to describe snow and ice, and Sam Colbeck knows why." The *New York Times*, America's closest approach to a serious newspaper of record, had changed its position on the snow-term count by over 50% within four years. And in the *science* section. But hey: nine, forty-eight, a hundred, two hundred, who cares? It's a bunch, right? On this topic, no source can be trusted.

People cannot be persuaded to shut up about it, either. Attempting to slay the creature at least in my locality, I mentioned Martin's work in a public lecture in Santa Cruz in 1985, in the presence of a number of faculty, students, and members of the general public. I drove home the point about scholarly irresponsibility to an attentive crowd, and imagined I had put at least a temporary halt to careless talk about the Eskimo morpheme stock within Santa Cruz County. But it was not to be.

Within the following three months, two undergraduate students came to me to say that they had been told in class lectures about the Eskimo's highly ramified snow vocabulary, one in politics, one in psychology; my son told me he had been fed the same factoid in class at his junior high school; and the assertion turned up once again in a "fascinating facts" column in a Santa Cruz weekly paper.

Among the many depressing things about this credulous transmission and elaboration of a false claim is that even if there *were* a large number of roots for different snow types in some Arctic language, this would *not*, objectively, be intellectually interesting; it would be a most mundane and unremarkable fact.

Horsebreeders have various names for breeds, sizes, and ages of horses; botanists have names for leaf shapes; interior decorators have names for shades of mauve; printers have many different names for different fonts (Caslon, Garamond, Helvetica, Times Roman, and so on), naturally enough. If these obvious truths of specialization are supposed to be interesting facts about language, thought, and culture, then I'm sorry, but include me out.

Would anyone think of writing about printers the same kind of slop we find written about Eskimos in bad linguistics textbooks? Take a random textbook like Paul Gaeng's *Introduction to the Principles of Language* (1971), with its earnest assertion: "It is quite obvious that in the culture of the Eskimos . . . snow is of great enough importance to split up the conceptual sphere that corresponds to one word and one thought in English into several distinct classes . . . " (p. 137). Imagine reading: "It is quite obvious that in the culture of printers . . . fonts are of great enough importance to split up the conceptual sphere that corresponds to one word and one thought among non-printers into several distinct classes . . . " Utterly boring, if even true. Only the link to those legendary, promiscuous, blubber-gnawing hunters of the ice-packs could permit something this trite to be presented to us for contemplation.

And actually, when you come to think of it, Eskimos aren't really that likely to be interested in snow. Snow in the traditional Eskimo hunter's life must be a kind of constantly assumed background, like sand on the beach. And even beach bums have only one word for sand. But there you are: the more you think about the Eskimo vocabulary hoax, the more stupid it gets.

The final words of Laura Martin's paper are about her hope that we can come to see the Eskimo snow story as a cautionary tale reminding us of "the intellectual protection to be found in the careful use of sources, the clear presentation of evidence, and above all, the constant evaluation of our assumptions." Amen to that. The prevalence of the great Eskimo snow hoax is testimony to falling standards in academia, but also to a wider tendency (particularly in the United States, I'm afraid) toward fundamentally anti-intellectual "gee-whiz" modes of discourse and increasing ignorance of scientific thought.

This is one more battle that linguists must take up (like convincing people that there is no need for a law to make English the official language of Kansas, or that elementary schools shouldn't spend time trying to abolish negated auxiliary verbs). Some time in the future, and it may be soon, you will be told by someone that the Eskimos have many or dozens or scores or hundreds of words for snow. You, gentle reader, must decide here and now whether you are going to let them get away with it, or whether you are going to be true to your position as an Expert On Language by calling them on it.

The last time it happened to me (other than through the medium of print) was in July 1988 at the University of California's Irvine campus, where I was attending the university's annual Management Institute. Not just one lecturer at the Institute but two of them somehow (don't ask me how) worked the Eskimological falsehood into their tedious presentations on management psychology and administrative problem-solving. The first time I attempted to demur and was glared at by lecturer and classmates alike; the second time, discretion for once getting the upper hand over valor, I just held my face in my hands for a minute, then quietly closed my binder and crept out of the room.

Don't be a coward like me. Stand up and tell the speaker this: C. W. Schultz-Lorentzen's *Dictionary of the West Greenlandic Eskimo Language* (1927) gives just two possibly relevant roots: *qanik*, meaning 'snow in the air' or 'snowflake', and *aput*, meaning 'snow on the ground'. Then add that you would be interested to know if the speaker can cite any more.

This will not make you the most popular person in the room. It will have an effect roughly comparable to pouring fifty gallons of thick oatmeal into a harpsichord during a baroque recital. But it will strike a blow for truth, responsibility, and standards of evidence in linguistics.

References

ADAMS, CECIL: 1984, *The Straight Dope: A Compendium of Human Knowledge*, edited and with an introduction by Ed Zotti, Chicago Review Press, Chicago, Illinois.

BOAS, FRANZ: 1911, Introduction to *The Handbook of North American Indians*, *Vol. I. Bureau of American Ethnology Bulletin* 40, Part 1, Smithsonian Institution, Washington, D.C. Reprinted by Georgetown University Press, Washington D.C. (c. 1963) and by University of Nebraska Press, Lincoln, Nebraska (1966).

BROWN, ROGER: 1958, *Words and Things*, Free Press, New York.

CARROLL, JOHN B., ed.: 1956, *Language, Thought, and Reality: Selected Writings of Benjamin Lee Whorf*, MIT Press, Cambridge, Massachusetts.

EASTMAN, CAROL: 1975, *Aspects of Language and Culture*, Chandler, San Francisco, California. 3rd printing, Chandler & Sharp, Novato, California, 1980.

GAENG, PAUL A.: 1971, *Introduction to the Principles of Language*, Harper & Row, New York.

MARTIN, LAURA: 1986, ' "Eskimo words for snow": A case study in the genesis and decay of an anthropological example,' *American Anthropologist* 88, 2 (June), 418–423.

MURRAY, STEPHEN O.: 1987, 'Snowing canonical texts,' *American Anthropologist* 89, 2 (June), 443–444.

SCHULTZ-LORENTZEN, C. W.: 1927, *Dictionary of the West Greenlandic Eskimo Language, Meddelser om Grønland* 69, Reitzels, Copenhagen.

WHORF, BENJAMIN LEE: 1940, 'Science and linguistics,' *Technology Review* (MIT) 42, 6 (April), 229–231, 247–248. Reprinted in Carroll, ed., 207–219.

HOW MASQUERADERS THINK

Bamber Gascoigne

[The following essay is really two excerpts from Bamber Gascoigne's book entitled *Quest for the Golden Hare,* which is about a modern-day treasure hunt. In 1980, a British artist named Kit Williams produced an art book called *Masquerade* (published by Jonathan Cape). In his paintings Williams hid clues to the whereabouts of a golden amulet he had made in the shape of a hare and buried somewhere in England. The paintings were full of words, numbers, and tantalizing pictorial details, some of which were real clues but most of which were not. Gascoigne's book tells the story of how many "masqueraders," or people who tried to solve the puzzle and find the treasure, developed elaborate solutions that proved to be wrong. The following is the story of one masquerader, Brian, followed by some of Gascoigne's analysis of why so many people were led to believe their theories were correct.]

My first communication with Brian Pike was a letter from him saying he believed he had seen me the previous Sunday when he was hunting for the golden hare by a certain river where it was crossed by a railway bridge. A piece of green and a piece of yellow paper were enclosed. I was to return the green piece if it had indeed been me, and the yellow piece if it had not. I threw the symbolic scraps into the wastepaper basket and replied that I could not see the need for all this mystery, that I walked almost every day along the Thames and under the railway bridge at Richmond, but that the hare was not there and my advice was to stop fretting about the Masquerade puzzle because it was too difficult. He wrote back saying that the river he had been referring to was the Wey at Farnham, but that my advice not to fret had confirmed for him that he was on the right track since the lanes round Farnham were deeply 'fretted', in the sense of being rubbed or worn away.

This astonishing resilience was to prove typical of Brian, who has an ability to find what he wants in no matter how random a shred of evidence. His way into the Masquerade puzzle had been through a connection with his main hobby, sand painting. . . . Brian collects his coloured sands from a variety of pits round the country. In the top left corner of Kit's painting of a ring of animals he thought he could identify the sandpit where he goes for his greens and yellows. The pit is at Farnham, and two of the six animals shown on that page are farm animals (a cow and a ram). Brian was willing to let the phrase 'farm animals' bring Farnham to mind. He was on his way.

. . . Margaret shared Brian's excitement until the day, early on, when he found the magnet. He had told her he believed Kit had buried a magnet at the site and it would be near the railway bridge at Farnham. He set off with his 11-year-old daughter, Samantha, and later phoned in some excitement to say they had found it. Margaret was naturally impressed. But when Brian got home, the magnet turned out to be a large metal clip which had fallen or been thrown from the railway bridge above. For good measure Brian had found two. Having lived their entire professional lives supporting an electric railway system, both clips had become magnetised. For Brian they were magnets, to Margaret they were metal clips. She began to doubt his theories and was soon suggesting that he would be better spending all this time and energy actually looking for a job.

Brian had also found in the river bank at Farnham two large hemispherical plastic dishes. He assumed that Kit had left these with a purpose. They were intended, he thought, for resonating chambers, to be placed over the spot where the hare was buried. He had decided that the bells attached to the hare would vibrate when the note G was played on a tuning fork, but since their ringing would be faint in the earth these chambers were a necessary part of the discovery, amplifying the sound beneath them. The successful Masquerader would strike the note G while applying either his ear or a sounding tube, in stethoscope fashion, to the inverted plastic hemisphere.

The theories and confirmations which Brian found in *Masquerade* were legion. All were based on the slenderest of evidence, but this did nothing to diminish the conviction with which they were held. A Morris 1000 in the book was sufficient to put him in mind of Jane Austen (not even Jane Austin). Gilbert White's *Natural History of Selborne* was believed to contain some of the most important clues, partly because Selborne is in the region of Farnham but also because the shed in which Kit paints was shown in the *Sunday Times* as being white inside: moreover the shed seemed to have a series of pennants over the window, and half of Gilbert White's book is made up of letters to Thomas Pennant. It was this book which convinced Brian that the hare was buried five feet deep, not fourteen inches as Kit had misleadingly announced, because White mentions a clergyman who buried a toad in a clay pot five feet below the ground and dug him up a year later to find him still alive but somewhat larger (research for Masqueraders was full of such incidental pleasures). Gilbert White was able to provide many such revelations. Jane Austen's famous Morris 1000 has four normal car windows plus triangular push-open ones at the front. It therefore tallied perfectly with the Queen of Naples's conservatory, described by White as having sash windows on all sides except the north, which was occupied by hinged glass doors.

Brian's confidence in his theories was matched by a determination to make them widely known. As soon as the hare had been discovered, and it was revealed that the full puzzle had not yet been understood, he sprang into action. He immediately sent his 'correct solution' off to Kit, and when Cape announced a forthcoming paperback with the solution in it, assumed that it would be his. He therefore arranged for an exhibition in his local library, explaining his achievement and timed to coincide with publication of the paperback, and he wrote an article for *Hampshire, the County Magazine* announcing that 'the forthcoming paperback will include the author's model answer to the riddle' and giving *Hampshire* readers a foretaste of the truth. . . .

When the correct 'correct solution' appeared in the paperback, Brian was undaunted—though the reactions of librarian and editor are not on record. Like all other truly obsessed Masqueraders, Brian shows little interest in the undeniable elegance of the *Masquerade* riddle but instead remains convinced that another better solution, his own, is for some mysterious reason being suppressed by Kit. When I proposed myself for a visit to Brian's house, there was in no time an article in the local paper announcing my forthcoming arrival and claiming, wrongly, that I shared Brian's view that all was not yet revealed.

Brian continues, and no doubt will continue, to receive more and more confirmatory clues that he is on the right track. He told me that even Kit himself had recently conveyed this information to him through a television interview. Kit had mentioned to the interviewer that he had often imagined the hare being dug up by some north country pigeon-fancier. The phrase had been intended by Kit to mean any unexpected sort of fellow, but Brian immediately concluded that it was a personal reference to himself. 'Are you a pigeon-fancier?' I asked in some surprise. 'No, but whenever I was digging at Farnham there were always a couple of pigeons around.' 'But you come from the north?' 'No, I come from the south, but Kit always reverses things.'

'Oh dear,' said Margaret, 'there aren't many that can think like you, Brian. Just as well.'

... Tens of thousands of letters from Masqueraders have convinced me that the human mind has an equal capacity for pattern-making and for self-deception. While some addicts were busy cooking the riddle, others were more single-mindedly continuing their own pursuit of the hare quite regardless of the news that it had been found. Their own theories had come to seem so convincing that no exterior evidence could refute them. These most determined of Masqueraders may grudgingly have accepted that a hare of some sort had been dug up at Ampthill, but they believed there would be another hare, or a better solution, awaiting them at their favourite spot. Kit would expect them to continue undismayed by the much publicised diversion at Ampthill and would be looking forward to the day when he could greet them as the real discoverers of the real puzzle of *Masquerade*. Optimistic expeditions were still setting out, with shovels and maps, throughout the summer of 1982.

What made possible this amazing persistence? Certainly not just human obstinacy. The real explanation is the many coincidences which each Masquerader had stumbled upon and which seemed to confirm each theory beyond reasonable doubt. The whole Masquerade saga raises the interesting question of what does constitute a significant coincidence. My own belief is that our daily lives bristle with coincidences of all sorts, but that we only allow them particular significance, or indeed pay them more than passing attention, when they touch on a subject which is itself of importance to us. We are all aware of the odd sensation of meeting in quick succession and in two different places somebody that we have not otherwise seen for years, or of hearing again an unusual name or word very soon after hearing it for the first time. The phrase, 'It was an incredible coincidence but ... ', is so familiar in our conversation that each coincidence must in fact be less incredible than we think. While working on this book, I deliberately watched out for coincidences during one specific day. Two striking examples cropped up. My wife and I were discussing a friend called Gloria, who had recently died, when the chorus on the radio suddenly burst into the phrase 'Gloria, Gloria, Gloria' from *Aida*. My wife, not on the lookout for events of this type, did not even notice the coincidence. Later that evening I was glancing through a book on creation myths when my eye fell upon the phrase 'St John's Gospel' at exactly the moment when someone on the radio spoke those three words. To someone in a religious frame of mind, or attuned perhaps to receive voices from another world, these coincidences might well seem like confirmation of hidden and hoped-for truths. And so it was, on a different level, for Masqueraders. Their minds were absorbed by *Masquerade* in all its variety and detail. Their senses were aquiver for any echo of its themes, whether in their daily lives or in the books they were scanning to help them in the quest. Like maternal animals, whose ears pick up the faintest cry of their offspring among all other distractions, the hare-seekers were attuned to the patterns of *Masquerade* and so built every echo into a coincidence and every coincidence into a truth.

Arthur Koestler, in his book *The Roots of Coincidence*, discusses the findings of Paul Kammerer, a scientist who attempted to analyse the phenomenon of coincidence. Kammerer found so many small examples in everyday life that he was forced to reject the very idea of coincidence:

> We have found that the recurrence of identical or similar data in contiguous areas of space or time is a simple empirical fact which has to be accepted and which cannot be explained by coincidence—or, rather, which makes coincidence rule to such an extent that the concept of coincidence itself is negated.

Kammerer's conclusion from this was a surprising one. He decided that so many coincidental factors could not be chance, but must be part of some underlying and as yet unknown law or pattern in life. My own response would be the opposite—that the number of separate details impinging upon our senses as we move through the world is so great that 'surprising' pairings should not in statistical terms surprise us. This certainly rings true of the microcosm which is *Masquerade*, where the profusion of detail in Kit's paintings and text was perfectly adapted to provide hare-seekers with the coincidences which they needed to confirm their hunches. Kammerer's conclusion and mine are alike in one relevant aspect. In his view coincidences are so common that it is only in their totality that they acquire significance, in mine they are so common as not to be significant at all. Each conclusion robs the individual coincidence of meaning. As to the theories which Masqueraders believed to be confirmed by these coincidences, Koestler in the same book gives the answer to that:

> The history of science has shown over and over again that the fact that a theory 'works' and produces tangible results does not prove that the underlying assumptions are correct.

Most Masqueraders discovered their coincidences through number patterns, anagrams and word associations. The last two are particularly treacherous territories, because almost anything becomes possible. Those who worked by word association liked to have beside them a thesaurus, and such a book—offering supposed synonyms without reference to the context of the word—is the shortest possible route into the quicksands of unreality. 'Jehovah pickle our diplomatic sultana' is, for example, a version of 'God save our gracious queen' with each word strained through a thesaurus. It is not surprising that Masqueraders could arrive at any destination of their choice in such a vehicle.

At first sight number patterns appear more rigorous because of the nature of mathematics, and they have always been found a very attractive way of interpreting the universe—with good reason since much of physics is based on arithmetical and geometrical relationships. As early as the sixth century BC Pythagoras and his followers were explaining the physical world in terms of numbers (Aristotle would later accuse them of a subterfuge very similar to that of most Masqueraders—'if there was a gap anywhere they would readily make additions so as to make their whole theory coherent'), and there are still many people today who offer number patterns as a form of proof. The Pentecostal Jewish Mission distributes a pamphlet, of which I have twice received a copy in the post, attempting to prove that the Bible is the word of God on the grounds that all its verses exhibit a numerical pattern of sevens which can be found in no other body of literature. This pattern was apparently noticed early in our own century by Dr Ivan Panin, 'a former agnostic'. He and others attempted to write prose of their own with such sevenfold patterns but it is said that they failed. To be able to write in such a way thus came to seem a talent of God alone, and so his authorship of the Bible was conveniently proved. It may be so, but one wonders how many believers in the theory have tested this numerical system for themselves throughout the Hebrew Bible or have researched the equivalent incidence of patterns yielding 3, 5, or 11.

It is a fact that an exciting theory, if passionately held and passionately expounded, will often convince people who neither understand it nor are able to check it. Many Masqueraders found it easy to persuade at least some of their friends that their solutions had a good chance of being right. Jean Rachel, a keen seeker of the hare and married to a machine-setter at British Leyland, wrote on this theme:

> It has amazed me how easy it is to close your mind on to one idea, as I did, and completely deceive yourself, and how easy it is to convince other people that you're right. For my next occupation, I might start a new religion or write 'Chariots of the Gods'.

I had an interesting example of this in relation to the ideas of the delightfully eccentric Ron Fletcher. While we were talking in the Bear at Rodborough, a friend of his had expressed gentle ridicule of Ron's ideas and total scorn for *Masquerade* as a commercial gimmick. Two months later this friend rang me to say that Ron had discovered an important and unacknowledged fact, proving there was more to the *Masquerade* story than had yet been admitted. The discovery was that Kit had based his book on a minor French work called *Mascarade* by Gabriel Chevallier, better known as the author of *Clochemerle*. For a start, the friend assured me, the chapter headings were the same. I pointed out that there are no chapter headings in *Masquerade*, to which the answer was that the French chapter headings had given Kit his themes. I asked for examples. 'Tante Zoë.' But there is no Aunt Zoë. 'Le Perroquet.' There is not even a single parrot. I enquired whether Ron's friend had checked for himself in *Masquerade* and received a brusque reply: 'Certainly not. The book's complete rubbish. But Ron has given me all the details.' So the misguided enthusiasm of Ron, a man with something of the stature and cast of mind of a prophet, had been sufficient to persuade a normally rational adult to telephone me with a burning certainty for which he had no justification at all other than Ron's word. Such is the infectious power of conviction.

THE FOUR IDOLS [From *Novum Organum*, 1620.]

Francis Bacon

The idols and false notions which are now in possession of the human understanding, and have taken deep root therein, not only so beset men's minds that truth can hardly find entrance, but even after entrance obtained, they will again in the very instauration of the sciences meet and trouble us, unless men being forewarned of the danger fortify themselves as far as may be against their assaults.

There are four classes of idols which beset men's minds. To these for distinction's sake I have assigned names—calling the first class *Idols of the Tribe*; the second, *Idols of the Cave*; the third, *Idols of the Marketplace*; the fourth, *Idols of the Theater*.

The formation of ideas and axioms by true induction is no doubt the proper remedy to be applied for the keeping off and clearing away of idols. To point them out, however, is of great use; for the doctrine of idols is to the interpretation of nature what the doctrine of the refutation of sophisms is to common logic.

The *Idols of the Tribe* have their foundation in human nature itself, and in the tribe or race of men. For it is a false assertion that the sense of man is the measure of things. On the contrary, all perceptions as well of the sense as of the mind are according to the measure of the individual and not according to the measure of the universe. And the human understanding is like a false mirror, which, receiving rays irregularly, distorts and discolors the nature of things by mingling its own nature with it.

The *Idols of the Cave* are the idols of the individual man. For everyone (besides the errors common to human nature in general) has a cave or den of his own, which refracts and discolors the light of nature; owing either to his own proper and peculiar nature; or to his education and conversation with others; or to the reading of books, and the authority of those whom he esteems and admires; or to the differences of impressions, accordingly as they take place in a mind preoccupied and predisposed or in a mind indifferent and settled; or the like. So that the spirit of man (according as it is meted out to different individuals) is in fact a thing variable and full of perturbation, and governed as it were by chance. Whence it was well observed by Heraclitus that men look for sciences in their own lesser worlds, and not in the greater or common world.

There are also idols formed by the intercourse and association of men with each other, which I call *Idols of the Marketplace*, on account of the commerce and consort of men there. For it is by discourse that men associate; and words are imposed according to the apprehension of the vulgar. And therefore the ill and unfit choice of words wonderfully obstructs the understanding. Nor do the definitions or explanations wherewith in some things learned men are wont to guard and defend themselves, by any means set the matter right. But words plainly force and overrule the understanding, and throw all into confusion and lead men away into numberless empty controversies and idle fancies.

Lastly, there are idols which have immigrated into men's minds from the various dogmas of philosophies, and also from wrong laws of demonstration. These I call *Idols of the Theater*; because in my judgment all the received systems are but so many stage-plays, representing worlds of their own creation after an unreal and scenic fashion. Nor is it only of the systems now in vogue, or only of the ancient sects and philosophies, that I speak; for many more plays of the same kind may yet be composed and in like artificial manner set forth; seeing that errors the most widely different have nevertheless causes for the most part alike. Neither again do I mean this only of entire systems, but also of many principles and axioms in science, which by tradition, credulity, and negligence, have come to be received.

But of these several kinds of idols I must speak more largely and exactly, that the understanding may be duly cautioned.

The human understanding is of its own nature prone to suppose the existence of more order and regularity in the world than it finds. And though there be many things in nature which are singular and unmatched, yet it devises for them parallels and conjugates and relatives which do not exist. Hence the fiction that all celestial bodies move in perfect circles; spirals and dragons being (except in name) utterly rejected. Hence too the element of fire with its orb is brought in, to make up the square with the other three which the sense perceives. Hence also the ratio of density of the so-called elements is arbitrarily fixed at ten to one. And so on of other dreams. And these fancies affect not dogmas only, but simple notions also.

The human understanding when it has once adopted an opinion (either as being the received opinion or as being agreeable to itself) draws all things else to support and agree with it. And though there be a greater number and weight of instances to be found on the other side, yet these it either neglects and despises, or else by some distinction sets aside and rejects; in order that by this great and pernicious predetermination the authority of its former conclusions may remain inviolate. And therefore it was a good answer that was made by one who when they showed him hanging in a temple a picture of those who had paid their vows as having escaped shipwreck, and would have him say whether he did not now acknowledge the power of the gods—"Ay," asked he again, "but where are they painted that were drowned after their vows?" And such is the way of all superstition, whether in astrology, dreams, omens, divine judgments, or the like; wherein men having a delight in such vanities, mark the events where they are fulfilled, but where they fail, though this happen much oftener, neglect and pass them by. But with far more subtlety does this mischief insinuate itself into philosophy and the sciences; in which the first conclusion colors and brings into conformity with itself all that come after, though far sounder and better. Besides, independently of that delight and vanity which I have described, it is the peculiar and perpetual error of the human intellect to be more moved and excited by affirmatives than by negatives; whereas it ought properly to hold itself indifferently disposed towards both alike.

Indeed, in the establishment of any true axiom, the negative instance is the more forcible of the two.

The human understanding is moved by those things most which strike and enter the mind simultaneously and suddenly, and so fill the imagination; and then it feigns and supposes all other things to be somehow, though it cannot see how, similar to those few things by which it is surrounded. But for that going to and fro to remote and heterogeneous instances, by which axioms are tried as in the fire, the intellect is altogether slow and unfit, unless it be forced thereto by severe laws and overruling authority.

The human understanding is unquiet; it cannot stop or rest, and still presses onward, but in vain. Therefore it is that we cannot conceive of any end or limit to the world, but always as of necessity it occurs to us that there is something beyond. Neither again can it be conceived how eternity has flowed down to the present day; for that distinction which is commonly received of infinity in time past and in time to come can by no means hold; for it would thence follow that one infinity is greater than another, and that infinity is wasting away and tending to become finite. The like subtlety arises touching the infinite divisibility of lines, from the same inability of thought to stop. But this inability interferes more mischievously in the discovery of causes: for although the most general principles in nature ought to be held merely positive, as they are discovered, and cannot with truth be referred to a cause; nevertheless, the human understanding being unable to rest still seeks something prior in the order of nature. And then it is that in struggling towards that which is further off, it falls back upon that which is more nigh at hand; namely, on final causes: which have relation clearly to the nature of man rather than to the nature of the universe, and from this source have strangely defiled philosophy. But he is no less an unskilled and shallow philosopher who seeks causes of that which is most general, than he who in things subordinate and subaltern omits to do so.

The human understanding is no dry light, but receives an infusion from the will and affections; whence proceed sciences which may be called "sciences as one would." For what a man had rather were true he more readily believes. Therefore he rejects difficult things from impatience of research; sober things, because they narrow hope; the deeper things of nature, from superstition; the light of experience, from arrogance and pride, lest his mind should seem to be occupied with things mean and transitory; things not commonly believed, out of deference to the opinion of the vulgar. Numberless in short are the ways, and sometimes imperceptible, in which the affections color and infect the understanding.

But by far the greatest hindrance and aberration of the human understanding proceeds from the dullness, incompetency, and deceptions of the senses; in that things which strike the sense outweigh things which do not immediately strike it, though they be more important. Hence it is that speculation commonly ceases where sight ceases; insomuch that of things invisible there is little or no observation. Hence all the working of the spirits enclosed in tangible bodies lies hid and unobserved of men. So also all the more subtle changes of form in the parts of coarser substances (which they commonly call alteration, though it is in truth local motion through exceedingly small spaces) is in like manner unobserved. And yet unless these two things just mentioned be searched out and brought to light, nothing great can be achieved in nature, as far as the production of works is concerned. So again the essential nature of our common air, and of all bodies less dense than air (which are very many) is almost unknown. For the sense by itself is a thing infirm and erring; neither can instruments for enlarging or sharpening the senses do much; but all the truer kind of interpretation of nature is effected by instances and experiments fit and apposite; wherein the sense decides touching the experiment only, and the experiment touching the point in nature and the thing itself.

The human understanding is of its own nature prone to abstractions and gives a substance and reality to things which are fleeting. But to resolve nature into abstractions is less to our purpose than to dissect her into parts; as did the school of Democritus, which went further into nature than the rest. Matter rather than forms should be the object of our attention, its configurations and changes of configuration, and simple action, and law of action or motion; for forms are figments of the human mind, unless you will call those laws of action forms.

Such then are the idols which I call *Idols of the Tribe*; and which take their rise either from the homogeneity of the substance of the human spirit, or from its preoccupation, or from its narrowness, or from its restless motion, or from an infusion of the affections, or from the incompetency of the senses, or from the mode of impression.

The *Idols of the Cave* take their rise in the peculiar constitution, mental or bodily, of each individual; and also in education, habit, and accident. Of this kind there is a great number and variety; but I will instance those the pointing out of which contains the most important caution, and which have most effect in disturbing the clearness of the understanding.

Men become attached to certain particular sciences and speculations, either because they fancy themselves the authors and inventors thereof, or because they have bestowed the greatest pains upon them and become most habituated to them. But men of this kind, if they betake themselves to philosophy and contemplations of a general character, distort and color them in obedience to their former fancies; a thing especially to be noticed in Aristotle, who made his natural philosophy a mere bondservant to his logic, thereby rendering it contentious and well nigh useless. The race of chemists again out of a few experiments of the furnace have built up a fantastic philosophy, framed with reference to a few things; and Gilbert also, after he had employed himself most laboriously in the study and observation of the loadstone, proceeded at once to construct an entire system in accordance with his favorite subject.

There is one principal and, as it were, radical distinction between different minds, in respect of philosophy and the sciences, which is this:

that some minds are stronger and apter to mark the differences of things, others to mark their resemblances. The steady and acute mind can fix its contemplations and dwell and fasten on the subtlest distinctions: the lofty and discursive mind recognizes and puts together the finest and most general resemblances. Both kinds however easily err in excess, by catching the one at gradations, the other at shadows.

There are found some minds given to an extreme admiration of antiquity, others to an extreme love and appetite for novelty; but few so duly tempered that they can hold the mean, neither carping at what has been well laid down by the ancients, nor despising what is well introduced by the moderns. This however turns to the great injury of the sciences and philosophy; since these affectations of antiquity and novelty are the humors of partisans rather than judgments; and truth is to be sought for not in the felicity of any age, which is an unstable thing, but in the light of nature and experience, which is eternal. These factions therefore must be abjured, and care must be taken that the intellect be not hurried by them into assent.

Contemplations of nature and of bodies in their simple form break up and distract the understanding, while contemplations of nature and bodies in their composition and configuration overpower and dissolve the understanding: a distinction well seen in the school of Leucippus and Democritus as compared with the other philosophies. For that school is so busied with the particles that it hardly attends to the structure; while the others are so lost in admiration of the structure that they do not penetrate to the simplicity of nature. These kinds of contemplation should therefore be alternated and taken by turns; that so the understanding may be rendered at once penetrating and comprehensive, and the inconveniences above mentioned, with the idols which proceed from them, may be avoided.

Let such then be our provision and contemplative prudence for keeping off and dislodging the *Idols of the Cave*, which grow for the most part either out of the predominance of a favorite subject, or out of an excessive tendency to compare or to distinguish, or out of partiality for particular ages, or out of the largeness or minuteness of the objects contemplated. And generally let every student of nature take this as a rule—that whatever his mind seizes and dwells upon with peculiar satisfaction is to be held in suspicion, and that so much the more care is to be taken in dealing with such questions to keep the understanding even and clear.

But the *Idols of the Marketplace* are the most troublesome of all: idols which have crept into the understanding through the alliances of words and names. For men believe that their reason governs words; but it is also true that words react on the understanding; and this it is that has rendered philosophy and the sciences sophistical and inactive. Now words, being commonly framed and applied according to the capacity of the vulgar, follow those lines of division which are most obvious to the vulgar understanding. And whenever an understanding of greater acuteness or a more diligent observation would alter those lines to suit the true divisions of nature, words stand in the way and resist the change. Whence it comes to pass that the high and formal discussions of learned men end oftentimes in disputes about words and names; with which (according to the use and wisdom of the mathematicians) it would be more prudent to begin, and so by means of definitions reduce them to order. Yet even definitions cannot cure this evil in dealing with natural and material things; since the definitions themselves consist of words, and those words beget others: so that it is necessary to recur to individual instances, and those in due series and order; as I shall say presently when I come to the method and scheme for the formation of notions and axioms.

The idols imposed by words on the understanding are of two kinds. They are either names of things which do not exist (for as there are things left unnamed through lack of observation, so likewise are there names which result from fantastic suppositions and to which nothing in reality responds), or they are names of things which exist, but yet confused and ill-defined, and hastily and irregularly derived from realities. Of the former kind are Fortune, the Prime Mover, Planetary Orbits, Element of Fire, and like fictions which owe their origin to false and idle theories. And this class of idols is more easily expelled, because to get rid of them it is only necessary that all theories should be steadily rejected and dismissed as obsolete.

But the other class, which springs out of a faulty and unskillful abstraction, is intricate and deeply rooted. Let us take for example such a word as *humid*; and see how far the several things which the word is used to signify agree with each other; and we shall find the word *humid* to be nothing else than a mark loosely and confusedly applied to denote a variety of actions which will not bear to be reduced to any constant meaning. For it both signifies that which easily spreads itself round any other body; and that which in itself is indeterminate and cannot solidize; and that which readily yields in every direction; and that which easily divides and scatters itself; and that which easily unites and collects itself; and that which readily flows and is put in motion; and that which readily clings to another body and wets it; and that which is easily reduced to a liquid, or being solid easily melts. Accordingly when you come to apply the word—if you take it in one sense, flame is humid; if in another, air is not humid; if in another, fine dust is humid; if in another, glass is humid. So that it is easy to see that the notion is taken by abstraction only from water and common and ordinary liquids, without any due verification.

There are however in words certain degrees of distortion and error. One of the least faulty kinds is that of names of substances, especially of lowest species and well-deduced (for the notion of *chalk* and of *mud* is good, of *earth* bad); a more faulty kind is that of actions, as *to generate, to corrupt, to alter*; the most faulty is of qualities (except such as are the immediate objects of the sense), as *heavy, light, rare, dense*, and the like. Yet in all these cases some notions are of necessity a little better than others, in proportion to the greater variety of subjects that fall within the range of the human sense.

But the *Idols of the Theater* are not innate, nor do they steal into the understanding secretly, but are plainly impressed and received into the mind from the play-books of philosophical systems and the perverted rules of demonstration. To attempt refutations in this case would be merely inconsistent with what I have already said: for since we agree neither upon principles nor upon demonstrations, there is no place for argument. And this is so far well, inasmuch as it leaves the honor of the ancients untouched. For they are no wise disparaged—the question between them and me being only as to the way. For as the saying is, the lame man who keeps the right road outstrips the runner who takes a wrong one. Nay, it is obvious that when a man runs the wrong way, the more active and swift he is the further he will go astray.

But the course I propose for the discovery of sciences is such as leaves but little to the acuteness and strength of wits, but places all wits and understandings nearly on a level. For as in the drawing of a straight line or perfect circle, much depends on the steadiness and practice of the hand, if it be done by aim of hand only, but if with the aid of rule or compass, little or nothing; so is it exactly with my plan. But though particular confutations would be of no avail, yet touching the sects and general divisions of such systems I must say something; something also touching the external signs which show that they are unsound; and finally something touching the causes of such great infelicity and of such lasting and general agreement in error; that so the access to truth may be made less difficult, and the human understanding may the more willingly submit to its purgation and dismiss its idols.

Idols of the Theater, or of systems, are many, and there can be and perhaps will be yet many more. For were it not that now for many ages men's minds have been busied with religion and theology; and were it not that civil governments, especially monarchies, have been averse to such novelties, even in matters speculative; so that men labor therein to the peril and harming of their fortunes—not only unrewarded, but exposed also to contempt and envy; doubtless there would have arisen many other philosophical sects like to those which in great variety flourished once among the Greeks. For as on the phenomena of the heavens many hypotheses may be constructed, so likewise (and more also) many various dogmas may be set up and established on the phenomena of philosophy. And in the plays of this philosophical theater you may observe the same thing which is found in the theater of the poets, that stories invented for the stage are more compact and elegant, and more as one would wish them to be, than true stories out of history.

In general, however, there is taken for the material of philosophy either a great deal out of a few things, or a very little out of many things; so that on both sides philosophy is based on too narrow a foundation of experiment and natural history, and decides on the authority of too few cases. For the rational school of philosophers snatches from experience a variety of common instances, neither duly ascertained nor diligently examined and weighed, and leaves all the rest to meditation and agitation of wit.

There is also another class of philosophers, who having bestowed much diligent and careful labor on a few experiments, have thence made bold to educe and construct systems; wresting all other facts in a strange fashion to conformity therewith.

And there is yet a third class, consisting of those who out of faith and veneration mix their philosophy with theology and traditions; among whom the vanity of some has gone so far aside as to seek the origin of sciences among spirits and genii. So that this parent stock of errors—this false philosophy—is of three kinds; the sophistical, the empirical, and the superstitious. . . .

But the corruption of philosophy by superstition and an admixture of theology is far more widely spread, and does the greatest harm, whether to entire systems or to their parts. For the human understanding is obnoxious to the influence of the imagination no less than to the influence of common notions. For the contentious and sophistical kind of philosophy ensnares the understanding; but this kind, being fanciful and tumid and half poetical, misleads it more by flattery. For there is in man an ambition of the understanding, no less than of the will, especially in high and lofty spirits.

Of this kind we have among the Greeks a striking example in Pythagoras, though he united with it a coarser and more cumbrous superstition; another in Plato and his school, more dangerous and subtle. It shows itself likewise in parts of other philosophies, in the introduction of abstract forms and final causes and first causes, with the omission in most cases of causes intermediate, and the like. Upon this point the greatest caution should be used. For nothing is so mischievous as the apotheosis of error; and it is a very plague of the understanding for vanity to become the object of veneration. Yet in this vanity some of the moderns have with extreme levity indulged so far as to attempt to found a system of natural philosophy on the first chapter of Genesis, on the book of Job, and other parts of the sacred writings; seeking for the dead among the living: which also makes the inhibition and repression of it the more important, because from this unwholesome mixture of things human and divine there arises not only a fantastic philosophy but also an heretical religion. Very meet it is therefore that we be sober-minded, and give to faith that only which is faith's. . . .

So much concerning the several classes of Idols, and their equipage: all of which must be renounced and put away with a fixed and solemn determination, and the understanding thoroughly freed and cleansed; the entrance into the kingdom of man, founded on the sciences, being not much other than the entrance into the kingdom of heaven, whereinto none may enter except as a little child.

♦ *3* ♦

ASKING QUESTIONS, GENERATING IDEAS

AN IDEA WORTH WRITING ABOUT

Members of a discourse community agree about many issues but also disagree about other issues of mutual interest. When there is mutual interest, disagreement is what creates the need to find ways to cooperate and the need to reason toward the best possible answers to shared questions. You are engaged in argumentative writing whenever you use writing to respond to a difference of opinion and to support your response in some way.

So, the word *argument* in this context does not mean a fight between opponents, each of whom desires to silence the other. It means, instead, the search for reasons that will bring about cooperation among people who differ in how they view ideas but who nevertheless need to discover grounds for agreement. Argumentative writing, then, may be seen as a process of *reasonable inquiry into the best grounds for agreement between a writer and an audience who have a mutual concern to answer a question.*

This definition is not confined to the academic essay, of course. You have probably written arguments in letters or other informal situations whenever you felt the need to explain or support your ideas. The argumentative **essay** (the word comes from the French for "attempt") is a more formal composition that attempts to deal reasonably with significant ideas. It is the form that college writing usually takes, simply because in an essay a writer encounters ideas directly, for the sake of coming to a new understanding. By writing essays, you can explore significant ideas for the sake of coming to earned conclusions. But this process goes on in college for the sake of a larger aim: to help you deal reasonably with diverse ideas wherever you may encounter them.

53

A significant idea is not necessarily any idea that you happen to come up with. Some ideas are so conventional that they cannot be said to be ours. Some are trivial. Some might seem like good ideas for a moment but turn out to be silly after a bit of thought. Ideas of these kinds occur to everyone. But when we set out to *write* about an idea, it is generally not one of these. We write because we have an idea that is worth writing about. Such an idea is one that the writer thinks should matter to other people and that the writer cares enough about to discuss. This means that the writer also thinks that others can be led to share the idea and that the writer, therefore, accepts the burden of communication. If an idea is worth writing about, it must be worth communicating effectively.

WHAT A THESIS DOES

Having a significant idea confronts a writer with certain responsibilities: to be sure that sufficient reasons exist for believing the idea and to be sure that those reasons are able to be understood by others. These responsibilities are present throughout the writing process. They begin when one thinks about composing a thesis.

A thesis is an idea, stated as an assertion, that represents a reasoned response to a question at issue and that will serve as the central idea of a composition.

After the previous discussions, this definition should come as no surprise. Let's take a closer look at it, to determine what you need to think about when trying to come up with a thesis that will provide the best basis for composing an essay. Each of the terms of this definition has special significance for the process of composing a good argumentative essay.

A thesis is an idea . . . . Some people use the word *idea* to mean something like "topic" or "subject," phrases that indicate an *area* of potential interest, such as "economics," or a "cure for cancer," or "my first encounter with Professor Smith." These phrases might be said to be broad or narrow subjects, but they are not yet ideas because they do not say anything *about* economics or a cancer cure or the first time I met Smith. Perhaps you have had a teacher who was fond of telling you to narrow your subject. Such advice misses the point, unless that teacher also pushed you to come up with an idea by saying something about your subject. The noun *economics* is not an idea. The narrowed (or focused) noun phrase "economic conditions in South Africa in 1875" is still not an idea. "Economics is bull" *is* an idea—although, of course, not a very good one. The difference between noun phrases that are not ideas and statements that are ideas lies in the predication: Ideas are sentences; they complete a thought by connecting a verb to the noun phrase. Saying something *about* a subject requires making some kind of connection between it and something else. It isn't the size of the noun phrase that matters; it's what you have to say about it—and this will be found in the verb that you connect to it. Any noun phrase, no matter how broad or narrow, might become the basis of many different ideas, even totally contradictory or incompatible ones. "Economics is my best class" is a very different idea from "Economics is bull," and yet both apparently share the same subject. The difference is in the predication; that's what makes them ideas.

A thesis is . . . stated as an assertion. Not all ideas are stated with the intention of asserting something to be the case. Even though an idea must be a complete sentence, not all sentences are uttered for the purpose of asserting a proposition. "Go away" is certainly a sentence that communicates, but it does not seem to be proposing anything as true. It expresses a desire but does not put forth a claim. "I guess I'll take a walk." "What a day for baseball!" "Please tell me how to get to the geology building." "Gimme a break!" Sentences, ideas, can perform many other actions besides asserting.

To assert is to claim that some condition is the case. Each of the non-assertions above could be made into assertions by making them into such claims. "A walk would be good for me right now." "Sunny days are best for baseball." "Geology is to the left of Art." Assertions propose ideas to which one might respond, "No, that's not the case," or "Yes, that is the case." As you can see, making assertions implies that one believes in what one has just said. To seem to assert without belief would be a different kind of action: to lie or to joke. Assertions imply a willingness to defend an idea against the possibility that it might not be the case. An assertion, because it claims that something is a certain way, is an invitation to discuss the merits of an idea as an idea. Still, not all assertions make the kind of claims that we are looking for in thesis statements, so let's consider the next part of my definition.

A thesis . . . represents a reasoned response to a question at issue. An assertion is worth writing about when not everyone already believes it and when people should care whether to believe it or not. A thesis answers a question, in other words, that people are really asking because they do not already share the answer. A question **at issue** is one that people might answer in different ways, the kind of question, that is, that calls for a reasoned response. All assertions answer a question of some kind. Not all assertions answer a question at issue. Consider these assertions and the questions to which they are answers:

It's raining.	Is it raining?
Today is election day.	Is today election day?
You should vote "no" on Measure 6.	Should I vote "yes" or "no" on Measure 6?
Measure 6 will violate your constitutional right to own a handgun.	Will Measure 6 violate my constitutional right to own a handgun?
The Constitution does not make handgun ownership a right.	Does the Constitution make handgun ownership a right?

Are the questions to which these assertions respond *at issue?* You're right if you answer "it depends." It depends on who is asking them and why. It depends on the context in which the question is asked. A thesis is a response to a *situation,* which includes a community of people who, for their own reasons, are addressing certain questions. There are situations in which these questions might constitute questions at issue, and there are different situations in which they would not. The difference is whether the answer calls for argumentation. Is there some doubt whether the answer should be believed? If I assert that "It's raining" in a situation where the question is not at issue—where no one cares whether it's raining or not or where everyone is satisfied by my mere assertion—then there is no issue to be argued. If I assert that "Today is election day" in a situation where everyone already knows it, then there is no issue. In this case, however, the question at issue might become "What, then, should we do about it?" and argument might ensue over whether it's worth going out in the rain to vote. Then, again, it might not, if that question is not at issue. If I am talking to some friends who have already decided to vote against Measure 6, then my statement that "You should vote 'no' on Measure 6" would not be at issue, although my statement that "Measure 6 would violate your constitutional right to own a handgun" might be at issue if those friends were divided on *why* Measure 6 should be defeated. If I were addressing an audience of uncommitted voters, my assertion that "Measure 6 will violate your constitutional right to own a handgun" might address a question at issue. But if that audience happened to believe that the Constitution does not provide citizens with such a right, then I would have missed them with my arguments because I chose to address the wrong question. I would have to back up and address the question of whether there is, in fact, such a right. Only by finding the question at issue and arguing for an assertion that answers it do I find my audience.

The judgment of whether you have focused on such a question must be made by thinking about your audience. What do they already believe? What answers do they share with you? On what issue are you divided? To what assertions of yours will they say "Yes, but . . ."? Such questions help you decide whether to argue this assertion or that one, and the decision can change from situation to situation, from audience to audience.

This means that whatever idea you choose to argue is to some degree determined by your audience, those members of your discourse community whom you are addressing in your writing. The intention of any piece of argumentative writing combines what the writer has to say and what the audience needs to hear. What is at issue for the audience and the writer both? You are free, of course, to choose to argue anything you like, in an absolute sense, but it is only when you find your audience that you really face the necessity of reasoning well. If I were to argue that "A moon colony should be used for the purpose of manufacturing perfect golf balls" to an audience that in no way cares whether I am right or wrong, then it would hardly matter whether I based my case on good or bad reasons. (Remember Alice and the

Cheshire Cat?) But if I argue it in a situation where some people believe that moon colonies should not be used for commercial purposes or that perfect golf balls are a useless commodity, then the reasons I choose will make all the difference in whether I am listened to or not.

Your knowledge of your audience can never be complete, of course. Not only does an audience usually consist of more than one person having more than one set of interests and beliefs, but also audiences may consist of people who are entirely unknown. The question of who constitutes an audience is not a simple one, nor should it be made to seem simple. It is one of those matters about which you need to make a judgment, using whatever knowledge there is, without being able to arrive at certainty. You do not have to think of your audience as particular people with individual characteristics, nor do you have to invent imaginary readers who function as mere "straw men" to be blown over by incomplete reasoning. You can write, instead, to a more general audience, assumed to be made up of people who share your argumentative situation, who share the question at issue, and who are capable of reasoning in response to your assertions. Whether you think of this general audience as an extension of the beliefs of a particular person or as a composite of possible points of view, the relevant characteristics of that audience are characteristics that somehow make a difference for how the argument is conducted. If you were arguing about your "right to life" stance, for instance, you would probably not think about the relevant characteristics of your audience in terms of hair color or nationality, but you might think of your readers in terms of religious beliefs or social class.

As a reasoned response to a question at issue, a thesis cannot be taken for granted. It is determined by a process of inquiry into the question. A stance that does not emerge from inquiry is sometimes called a "knee-jerk response" to indicate that it is formed as a reaction without thinking. Keeping a critical reader in mind is one way to be sure that you give a thesis adequate consideration before asserting it unequivocally. And then you may find that a qualified assertion is better than an unqualified one.

A thesis . . . will serve as the central idea of a composition. This final part of the definition points us forward, toward the process of development by which a thesis becomes an essay. The last two parts of the definition, one pointing backward and one pointing forward, suggest that a thesis has two functions, which stand at the center of your thinking about what you will write. It represents the result of a process of inquiry, and it represents the beginning of a process of putting together sentences and paragraphs to make a whole. As a beginning, a thesis provides a basis for any further thinking that you must do to produce a fully developed argument. If a thesis is reasonable in the sense that it emerges from your deliberations about what assertion to argue, it should also be reason-able in the sense of being able to be supported by reasons.

We have already seen how the thesis stands for the whole composition, in a way, and represents its overall intention. This means that the parts of a composition are, in some sense, implicit parts of its thesis. As a predicated idea, a thesis will have several parts, and identifying them will become a basis of planning what the essay must say and how it must say it.

For example, suppose I have decided to argue that:

> *Hydroelectric power is an acceptable alternative to nuclear energy in supplying present power needs.*

Assuming that the assertion satisfies the definition of a thesis in other ways (although it may not), consider how it points forward to an essay. Its parts must become parts of that essay, since that essay would not be complete without satisfying certain demands that the thesis makes. The thesis calls for the essay to describe hydroelectric power and nuclear energy, and also to compare them according to how each satisfies "present power needs," which must also be described. Finally, the essay must make the essential connection that is asserted in its predication: "is an acceptable alternative to." This will necessarily entail a discussion of *how* hydroelectric power is preferable to nuclear power, probably by showing that it has some benefit that nuclear power lacks or that it avoids some risk that nuclear power creates, or maybe both. There are further parts that this essay might contain, of course, but these constitute the essential elements that an essay written from *this* thesis must contain in order to be complete.

Let's consider another example. Suppose I decide to make the following assertion my thesis:

> *The use of calculators in basic math courses results in students' lacking a fundamental understanding of number theory.*

Once again, the thesis tells me that my essay must contain certain parts, without which it would not be a complete discussion of this thesis. It must describe "the use of calculators in basic math courses," and it must describe "fundamental understanding of number theory." It must also show that an understanding of number theory is somehow part of the purpose of a basic math course, because the thesis relies on this idea. Finally, my essay must somehow make the connection between the parts that is asserted in the predication "results in." I must argue that one is the cause of the other. The *way* in which I argue that connection will depend on the reasoning that I choose to develop. (This process is the subject of Chapter 4.) But the thesis itself tells me that whatever reasoning I choose must address this connection.

These examples illustrate that any thesis statement creates responsibilities and provides the basis for fulfilling them. You are free to choose your thesis or to change it at any time, but having done so you become bound by its requirements—not strictly bound but somehow constrained. Although there will still be an incalculable range of choices that you can make, you will become responsible for somehow developing the essential parts of your thesis and for *earning* its predication. There are limitless kinds of possible thesis statements, but all will have essential parts that must be developed and connections that must be made.

Knowing precisely what your thesis is will help you think about what to include and what not to include in your essay. It will help you to distinguish between details that are necessary and those that are superfluous. Of course, no rule will tell you exactly what details are necessary and sufficient to make a complete essay, because every thesis will make its own unique demands. But a precise thesis will make the choices easier to recognize.

STASIS: KINDS OF QUESTIONS AT ISSUE

The kind of thesis that you compose and use as the basis for your essay will depend on the kind of question that is at issue for you and your audience. Whether a question is at issue or not depends on the particular situation you are in when you feel compelled to state your case. To understand this situation, it helps to know what sort of question really separates you and your audience, because if the situation calls for you to answer one kind of question and you answer another kind instead, you may not be successfully addressing the audience you mean to address.

Questions at issue may be seen as one or another of these six basic kinds:

Questions of fact *arise from the reader's need to know "Does this (whatever it is) exist?"*

Questions of definition *arise from the reader's need to know "What is it?"*

Questions of interpretation *arise from the reader's need to know "What does it signify?"*

Questions of value *arise from the reader's need to know "Is it good?"*

Questions of consequence *arise from the reader's need to know "Will this cause that to happen?"*

Questions of policy *arise from the reader's need to know "What should be done about it?"*

These are sometimes called "stasis questions." The **stasis** of any argument is the specific point on which the controversy rests, that point on which one person says "yes" but another says "no" or "I'm not sure." Such answers must be to the same question in order for inquiry between the two to go forward. You have often discovered such points when you have listened to someone else's argument and found yourself in agreement with some parts of it but not others. You might have said "Yes, but . . ." and pursued your disagreement in the context of other parts of the argument where you already agreed. The question on which you found yourself doubting was the stasis question. (The six kinds of questions above are not the only possible kinds of stasis questions, but the distinctions they imply are enough for you to inquire into the point of disagreement or uncertainty that you may wish to pursue in a thesis.)

In any particular argumentative situation, questions of one kind or another will be at issue while others may not be. In a discussion of civil disobedience, for instance, controversy may arise over the meaning of the term itself—or it may not. A writer may misjudge the issue by choosing a definitional thesis (such as "Civil disobedience applies only to laws that are unjust," or "Any law is unjust that imposes the will of a minority on the actions of another minority") in a situation where a question of consequence is what, in fact, divides the audience. In his essay "Resistance to Civil Government" Henry David Thoreau wrote:

> Unjust laws exist; shall we be content to obey them, or shall we endeavor to amend them, and obey them until we have succeeded, or shall we transgress them at once?

By putting the question in this way, Thoreau assumed that the question of definition (what makes a law unjust?) and the question of value (is an unjust law good?) were not at issue, but that the question of policy (what should we do about unjust laws?) is the one that needed his attention.

More than one kind of question may be at issue, of course, in a particular argumentative situation, and questions of one kind may have to be answered before one can ask questions of another. But the writer who wishes to make a genuine contribution to an inquiry may be aided by thinking about the kind of question that defines the situation. "What is really at issue here? Are we questioning how to *define* a concept, or whether an idea (or action) is *good,* or whether a certain consequence will *result,* or what we *should do* about it?" Trying to place the question in this way is one means by which the writer may meet the audience. Answering the wrong kind of question in any situation will lead to missing the audience—talking at cross-purposes or saying the obvious. You don't want your readers to say "Sure, but so what?"

Different kinds of stasis questions represent different argumentative situations and call for different kinds of inquiry. When questions of fact are at issue, it generally means that readers need to be given information or that they require a demonstration that some fact is "in fact" the case. The arguments of science are often of this kind. "At what temperature does water freeze?" is a question of fact, as is "Will this antifreeze work in my car over the winter?" Situations in which questions of fact are at issue are those in which there is an unknown to be discovered.

> *"When was Othello first performed?"*
> *"Who discovered X rays?"*
> *"Is it possible to build a bridge here?"*
> *"What was the final vote on Measure 6?"*

Such questions have in common the determinacy of their possible answers. In each case, the answer is a matter of verifiable fact. If the answer could not be verified somehow, then the question must remain unanswered. The answers to questions of fact are either correct or incorrect, true or false, yes or no. Such questions will be more or less interesting—either important or trivial—depending on the subject matter.

There is no absolute test of whether a question of fact is worth pursuing for its own sake. In matters of literature, say, or political science, such questions may have less inherent interest than they would in matters of, say, chemistry. I might find an answer to any of these questions and then find myself asking, "So what?" At that point I would have discovered that the question I had been pursuing was only a doorway into a question of larger significance, a question of a different sort.

When questions of definition are at issue, it generally means that readers do not accept a particular meaning for a word or concept. Although it might seem as if such questions are easily answered by consulting the dictionary, many questions of definition are not answered so easily if they are actually at issue. Definitions may separate people who know what the dictionary says but who must inquire into shared meanings that no dictionary can contain. For instance, if I do not know what *law* means, I can look it up. But if I ask "What are the different meanings of *law* in Martin Luther King Jr.'s letter?" the answer can be discovered only by examining instances of the word in the text itself, which may not define the word for us. Arguments sometimes hinge on definitions that cannot be resolved by verification in the dictionary.

> *"Is Chuck Yeager an astronaut?"*
> *"Is this film pornographic?"*
> *"Is abortion murder?"*

In such cases, the answer lies not only in the meanings of the words but also in the subtle distinctions the words may be used to imply and on whether certain circumstances match those meanings and distinctions. Such questions may hide deeper issues. Like questions of fact, questions of definition may be ends in themselves or may lead to different kinds of questions.

Questions of definition and questions of interpretation are similar and often overlap. When questions of interpretation are at issue, it means that more than the meaning of a word is in doubt but that the significance of something needs explaining. Definitions generally apply to words only, while interpretations also apply to the meaning of discourse containing many words or the significance of events, actions, structures, or concepts. Interpretations can never be answered by consulting a reference work because they refer to what something means to the interpreter.

> *"Is Othello an Aristotelian tragic hero?"*
> *"Will this new bridge represent the concern of our community for the environment or will it show others how wasteful we are?"*
> *"Does the result of this election signify a mandate for all of the candidate's policies?"*
> *"Does this film advocate the use of violence as a means of social change?"*

Questions of interpretation generally are at issue when there is a difference in point of view. Interpretations involve looking at a phenomenon from a particular perspective. Hence arguments about interpretation often require that the point of view itself be articulated or defended.

Questions of interpretation arise in most fields, especially when the subject of inquiry is discourse or human action. That Hannah Arendt called evil a "banality" is a fact I can verify by citing her work. What she meant, however, is a question with which historians and social theorists have had to struggle. Anthropologists may seek to interpret a ritual act or a social relationship. Sociologists may seek to interpret data collected in surveys. Questions of interpretation result whenever the significance of a word, an idea, an event, or a fact is not self-evident.

Does the potential uncertainty of questions of interpretation make them less important than questions of fact? We have seen just the opposite. Questions of interpretation often attempt to answer the "So what?" questions that matters of fact can raise. Yet, they seem equivocal because they cannot be established absolutely. What we know can often have more significance to our understanding as it becomes less certain. As we attempt to go beyond facts and to establish interpretations, we are dealing with our own relation to the subject matter as much as we are with the raw data. What we learn about when we interpret is twofold: We learn about the subject and we learn about ourselves. Because we must exercise interpretive judgments, applying our understanding to such questions, the facts do not speak for themselves; we must say what we understand them to signify.

Questions of value are similar to questions of interpretation. When questions of value are at issue, it generally means that people agree on the meaning of something, but differ on whether it is "good" or "bad." Like interpretation, then, value depends on one's point of view or the system of values that informs one's judgment. Some standard of "good" is used as the measure; thus arguments about questions of value often require one to articulate standards. "Is this essay worth an A?" The answer obviously depends on whose standards of judgment are being used. Yours may differ from your teacher's and each of you will judge accordingly. Any argument about the issue will have to address both those standards and the features of the essay that they apply to, a question of interpretation. Questions of value nearly always depend on answers to questions of interpretation.

Although some standard of good and bad is at issue in value questions, other words are generally used to communicate a sense of value. **Value terms** are words that already imply a judgment of good and bad. Thus, the assertion "*Huckleberry Finn* contains only racist stereotypes," although offered as a neutral interpretation, would generally imply that "racist stereotypes" are not good. The statement "This film is not pornographic, it is erotic," while seeming to answer a question of interpretation or definition, implies a distinction based on value. Questions of definition and interpretation can be questions of value in disguise.

There are those who believe that questions of value depend so much on subjective criteria that they cannot really be argued. Yet all but the most factual kinds of questions are subjective to a degree, and those kinds of questions are the very ones we do not have to argue, because we can demonstrate them. Nearly all real questions at issue require acts of judgment and interpretation, and thus subjectivity alone is not a reason to rule a question out of bounds for inquiry. If we limit argument to questions that are objective, we might find ourselves unable to decide what to do with the information we have gathered, because that decision must result from our own interests, perspectives, and concerns. We must be careful not to associate objectivity with good argument and subjectivity with bad argument. It is possible to have good or bad arguments of either kind, if that means careful or sloppy, thorough or perfunctory. The idea that objective argument is somehow better may be the result of applying the standards of scientific judgment to all realms of knowledge, but this is risky. There are many kinds of knowledge, some wholly objective, some wholly subjective, and some a mixture of the two. No one kind necessarily deserves the title *knowledge* more than another.

Questions of consequence are at issue when people find themselves disagreeing or wondering about cause and effect. Answering questions about what causes some occurrence or what result some event will have requires interpretation. "This bridge will help the economy of our city by encouraging more construction of homes across the river." This statement makes two *causal* interpretations. Causality is subject to varying degrees of certainty. "Will the bridge encourage more home building?" is a question that might not be as difficult to answer, or be as likely to be at issue, as the question "Will more homes across the river help or hurt our city's economy?" Answering either question will require argument about causes and their probabilities.

> *"Do opinion polls discourage people from voting?"*
> *"What is the effect of too much television on children?"*
> *"Will tax exemptions on capital gains stimulate investments?"*
> *"Can the slaughter of elephants be stopped by banning the sale of all ivory?"*

Speculations, rather than controlled experiments, are necessary to determine reasonable answers to such questions. Yet, like scientific experiments, those speculations must consider which variables make the difference. Thus, most speculations about cause and effect will be conditional: "It depends on . . ." or "Yes, if . . ." Arguments about probable causes generally acknowledge that certain conditions must prevail and seek to demonstrate that they do. For instance, to argue that the banning of the sale of ivory would end the slaughter of elephants, you would have to show a causal link between the sale of ivory and this slaughter. *If* ivory comes only from the illegal slaughter of elephants, and *if* that is the only reason elephants are slaughtered, then banning the sale of ivory might have this effect. In making this case, it would be your responsibility to show that these conditions were the case.

Because most questions of consequence, unless strictly scientific, can be answered only conditionally, it might seem as if they are useless to argue. Think, however, of the vast number of questions of consequence that must be argued if we are to know how to solve important problems in our lives and in society. We seek to solve such problems using the best reasoning we can construct, even if it does not constitute absolute certainty.

When questions of policy are at issue, it generally means that readers differ on whether, or how, to take a particular action. Such questions are answered with a recommendation, a prescription, or a preference for some action on someone's part. Questions of policy thus arise from situations in which alternative actions are possible, and the problem confronting those for whom such questions are at issue is which of the alternatives is best. You can see why such answers also are conditional, for they depend on acknowledging that the action will achieve its end (a question of consequence) and that the end is desirable (a question of value).

> "Should television networks voluntarily refrain from announcing voting results in the East until the polls close in the West?" "Should Congress vote to force them to do so?"
>
> "Should this bridge be built?" "Should property taxes be used to pay for it?"
>
> "Should the school board remove Huckleberry Finn from the school library?" "How should we respond to this action?"
>
> "How should AIDS prevention information be distributed to children?" "What form should it take?"

Policy questions, like questions of consequence, must be answered conditionally. If the action will bring about a specific result, and if that result is desired, then it follows that the action should take place. But it does not necessarily follow absolutely. Who should perform it? Will negative results accompany the positive one? Are there other, better, ways to achieve the same end? Such considerations always complicate policy issues.

As we have seen, questions of fact, definition, interpretation, value, consequence, and policy are interrelated. No argument is likely to be confined to only one kind of question. Arguing for an answer to one kind of question can imply that other kinds of questions are already answered. In any argumentative situation, some questions will not be at issue while others will define the stasis of the argument. This is why it is helpful to ask what *kind* of question is really at issue.

For instance, if you chose to argue that "The University should send AIDS information to all students," your thesis would answer a question of policy. But it would also presuppose that your audience shared that kind of question with you and that other kinds of questions were not at issue. The discourse community might be divided, not on the policy question, but on a question of consequence, such as "Will this particular piece of information be effective in educating students about AIDS?" You may not be in agreement with your audience on a question of interpretation, such as "Is the University responsible for AIDS education?" or of value, such as "Is AIDS education important enough to justify the expense?" Questions of fact may need to be settled first, such as "Can the University afford this?" or "Do the students already know everything the information provides?" And so forth. Knowing whether a particular kind of question is at issue requires an understanding of what the people in the discourse community are actually saying to each other, what they already agree about, and what they desire to find agreement about. The web or network of issues and stances that characterizes any real controversy is a little easier to understand by thinking about the kind (or kinds) of questions that are actually at issue.

AN EXAMPLE

A national news magazine interviewed two people who are prominent in the national debate over genetic engineering. As the opening questions in each interview reveal, the two men disagree on the question "Should there be a ban on experiments in genetic engineering?" The first, Jeremy Rifkin (President of the Foundation for Economic Trends), answers "yes" to this question. The second, Bernard Davis (a professor of bacterial physiology at Harvard Medical School), answers "no." Thus, this question of policy represents a clear stasis in the public discussion of this subject. As you read each interview, however, try to locate other kinds of questions that also are at issue and that need further discussion before Rifkin and Davis can hope to come to agreement. Do this by asking whether the statements of each person would be accepted or challenged by the other. Do some of the statements invite the other person to say "Yes, but . . ."?

INTERVIEW WITH JEREMY RIFKIN

Q Mr. Rifkin, why do you favor a ban on experiments in genetic engineering?

A My concern focuses on the release of modified genetic organisms—new forms of life—into the environment, which could trigger dangerous and irreversible problems in nature. If only a small percentage of these organisms ran amok, the long-term cumulative impact could be catastrophic.

We should take a lesson from the thousands of organisms introduced into North America from their native habitats around the world. Most were benign. But a few, such as the gypsy moth, the kudzu vine, Dutch Elm disease, and starlings, became major pests that are almost uncontrollable.

Q Many scientists insist that altering genetic material poses no hazards to humans—

A Actually, there is disagreement on that point among distinguished researchers. I would like to see the best scientific talent in the country come together to see if methods can be devised to minimize risks to the ecosystem. If they can't come up with such standards, it would be foolhardy to continue genetic-engineering research.

Q Might reliable safety tests be so costly that such projects would no longer be economically feasible?

A Perhaps, but it would be naïve to assume there are only benefits and no costs to the biological revolution. Petrochemicals brought us benefits, but they also brought economic and ecological costs. So did nuclear energy. So did the combustion engine.

We have to weigh the economic advantages of biotechnology against the possible adverse consequences for the future of civilization.

Q Haven't genetic hybrids of plants and animals been produced for hundreds of years?

A Yes, but genetic engineering opens up ominous new prospects. In nature, a sheep cannot mate with a goat. You cannot transfer genetic material from a human into the hereditary makeup of a mouse. If nature didn't provide these mating barriers, we'd have chaos.

But, using the new techniques, genetic material from any species can be stitched together on a molecular level with another species. I believe the biological integrity of species should be preserved. Science should not use these synthetic biological blueprints to create living novelties.

Q You have filed suits to stop genetic work. Are the courts suitable places to decide on scientific research?

A The biological revolution allows us to create forms of life that don't exist in nature. We'll increasingly be able to control living organisms by applying our own design principles, and that raises fundamental social, environmental, ethical and political questions unparalleled in history. Scientists should not be the only ones deciding issues that affect everyone on the planet. The courts can insure that the rest of us won't be left out of the debate.

INTERVIEW WITH BERNARD DAVIS

Q Professor Davis, why do you oppose a ban on genetic-engineering experiments?

A Because the bulk of the experiments are not dangerous. They use harmless organisms and produce harmless materials such as human insulin or growth hormone. Of course, if one aims at making a vaccine, one has to use genes from disease-producing organisms. But laboratories will then observe the same precautions that they have always used. In addition, the present governmental guidelines, as well as scientists' concern for their personal safety, provide ample further safeguards.

Q Then you believe existing safeguards are adequate—

A Yes. Genetic engineering has now been yielding increasing benefits in medicine, agriculture, and industry for six years without causing a day of illness. There is no reason to believe that the novel organisms developed for research or commerce will be more dangerous than the naturally occurring organisms from which they are derived. Conceivably, organisms might be made more dangerous for military purposes, but that is another story.

Q   Couldn't an epidemic or an ecological disaster result if new strains are released into the environment?

A   Only if the organisms were likely to spread. But that is simply not the way things work in nature, where organisms are locked in intense competition. There the jerry-built products of the laboratory are at a disadvantage—like hothouse plants competing with weeds. Any genetic modification introduced in the laboratory is infinitely more likely to impair rather than to improve an organism's ability to survive.

Q   Would no worrisome problems at all result from limitless mixing of species in the laboratory?

A   Our power is not limitless. We can only transfer very small bits of genetic material—less than one part in a thousand—between species. And if we can ever mix large amounts, they would not balance well, and the organism could not spread. You see, nature has its own self-policing process. You can cross a horse and a donkey to get a mule, for example, but the process stops there because nature doesn't allow mules to reproduce.

Finally, in bacteria bits of genetic material are being transferred between species in nature all the time: In laboratories we simply accelerate the process.

Q   Why shouldn't the concerns of critics of genetic engineering be aired in court?

A   If the courts can distinguish solid scientific evidence from demagogic appeals, fine. But, unfortunately, that is not assured by our present system. To do that, it might be desirable to set up special courts made up of judges who have expertise in science. Without such a sophisticated approach, progress will constantly be held hostage to legal interference by zealots.

What seems to be a clear choice of stances on the initial question (a question of policy) in fact reveals many shades of gray between a simple "yes" or "no." The stances taken by each of the experts on the policy question depend on answers to questions of consequence, in particular the question "Will the consequences of unintended release of genetically engineered organisms threaten humans?" Questions of value also are at issue, such as "Is the potential benefit of genetic engineering worth the risk?" Questions of interpretation remain at issue, such as "Are safeguards adequate?" or "Can the scientist create organisms that will not yield to natural processes in the environment?" And questions of fact and definition may even require answering before the policy debate can find common ground. Furthermore, there are questions that are not at issue between them (such as "Should biological experimentation be controlled?" or "Are there any benefits from genetic research?"), and these provide opportunities for them to explore further possible agreements by using reason. In a responsible discourse *between* these people (which the interview format did not allow), each would want to discover the nature of the questions at issue and try to move from agreement on some issues to achieve further agreement on others. They would otherwise be talking at cross-purposes and not addressing each other's real concerns.

THE NEED FOR PRECISION

How a question is phrased can be very important. Different ways of asking the same question can lead to different kinds of inquiry. Likewise, the way a thesis is phrased can be very important. Different ways of asserting the same stance can lead to different ways of developing an essay. Hence, you should be ready to ask yourself "Is this precisely the question?" and "Is this precisely what I want to say?" You should be concerned about the precision of your language as you think about questions at issue and thesis statements.

Let's look at a couple of the examples I used to illustrate questions of consequence and see how they might be rephrased more precisely. The question "Do opinion polls discourage people from voting?" seems very general, not because the issue itself is a large one but because the terms are imprecise. Anyone seriously asking such a question would probably intend it to refer to a specific context in which certain kinds of opinion polls occur. But it's hard to tell what is meant when the question remains so vaguely worded. Changing the wording to make it more precise would change the nature of the issue, as in the following possibilities:

> *"Does the early publishing of exit poll results discourage people from voting?"*
> *"Do people think that opinion polls accurately predict the outcome of elections?"*
> *"Do opinion polls actually change public opinion?"*
> *"Do opinion polls encourage a bandwagon effect that makes it impossible for an underdog to win?"*

Other ways of stating the question are possible. Each of them implies a different meaning for the original question. Any of them could have been intended by the original question. So, until a more precise form of the question is found, it isn't clear exactly what the issue is.

Similarly, the question "What is the effect of too much television on children?" is imprecise. Some people would call this a loaded question because the answer is implied: "Too much television" is already a bad thing, and bad effects are what "too much television" must have. But the issue probably depends instead on saying what the effect of a precise amount of television is. The inquiry might in fact need to address the kind of television and not just its sheer quantity. Also, the issue may need to be defined in terms of some children (i.e., preschoolers) and not others. It all depends on what the members of the discourse community are actually trying to decide. Thus any of these rephrasings, and others, are possible:

> *"Does lengthy exposure to violent programming cause antisocial behavior in preteens?"* (What is "lengthy exposure"? What does violent mean? What is "antisocial behavior"? Which "preteens"—in which social conditions? . . .)
> *"Do cartoons about consumer products confuse children about the difference between advertising and entertainment?"* (All such cartoons or those of a certain kind? What does confuse mean here? What is "the difference between advertising and entertainment"? . . .)

My further questions about each of these rephrasings indicate that precision is a relative matter. Readers can always ask for clarification. The wording of a question, or a thesis statement, is precise enough when both you and your reader understand it to mean the same thing. You can't know with certainty, of course, when this will be, so you have to anticipate as many questions as possible and clarify as necessary.

When you are part of an argumentative situation that will call for you to write what you think, the effort of drafting and redrafting possible questions at issue and thesis statements for precision will be worth it in helping you think clearly about your argument. You may never be completely satisfied with versions of your thesis, but trying to make the statement say precisely what you mean will move you toward greater clarity of thought and expression.

FINDING AND TESTING A THESIS

The process of rethinking and redrafting a thesis is important because it helps you to confront questions in your thinking while changes are still easily made. It is much easier to rephrase a thesis statement until it works than it is to try to revise a whole essay that has gone off in a confusing direction because it is based on a poor thesis. You cannot predict every feature of an essay in advance, of course, but you can at least have the advantage of thinking through potentially good or bad directions that an essay might take. Revising a thesis carefully can help you to avoid premature commitments to ideas that may not work out.

You can use these questions as a guide to revising possible thesis statements:

1. Is it an *idea?* Does it state, in a complete sentence, an *assertion?*
2. Does it answer a question that is really *at issue* for the audience? (What *kind* of question is it?)
3. Does the thesis say exactly what I mean? Are the terms I use precise and clear?
4. Has it developed out of a process of reasoning? Have I considered each side of the issue adequately?
5. Can it be developed reasonably?

Having a thesis that satisfies these conditions will help you to see clearly what responsibilities you must meet as you compose an essay in support of it.

At this point, let's consider a hypothetical thesis in the making. I'll climb inside the thoughts of an imaginary student and report the thoughts aloud to illustrate how these questions can be used in the discovery and testing of a thesis. If you follow the stages of my thinking in this example, you might recognize how to go through something like them yourself. No two people think in the same way, of course, and different situations and issues result in very different thought processes. My mental narrative will have to be more methodical than most thinking really is. But you too face questions and answer them somehow, as this fictional student does. What follows is but one of many possible mental stories.

Suppose I have just left a class in which we had a good discussion on the subject of the ethics of science. In class we read and analyzed some essays on different aspects of the subject (like the debate between Rifkin and Davis earlier in this chapter). The class began to disagree about whether scientists are morally responsible for the harmful effects of their research. I go back to my room after the class, vaguely troubled by the discussion, and begin to think . . .

*   *   *

. . . Whew, that was confusing! Like all our discussions, it seemed to develop in several different directions at once. It seemed as though different members of the class were discussing different things, simply because there were so many points of view. Sometimes we talked about examples, such as genetic research and nuclear weapons. One I never quite followed was experimental psychology as an example of harmful research. Sometimes we got into abstract subjects, such as the nature of objectivity and whether it is possible. Somebody said that the objectivity of science requires scientists to put their moral values aside, or else they could not search freely for the truth, but somebody else said that this is not possible because scientists make moral decisions whenever they decide what to study next. I was interested in that controversy, but I got a little lost when the class went off into the question of whether the research was sponsored by an agency that had direct application of the research as its aim.

Someone in class said that a scientist had to be paid, and if a scientist's employer intended to make weapons, for example, rather than to find a cure for cancer, that would be what determined whether the scientist had any responsibility. I could see his point, but I didn't think he was right. I even spoke up in class then and said something like, "Yes, but the same research that might lead to a cure for cancer might also get into the wrong hands and be applied later on as a weapon. Facts can be used for either good or bad. Shouldn't scientists be able to predict both kinds of applications?" Of course, after I said this someone else asked me, "Well, what would you do? Stop all research for good causes simply because someone might misuse the knowledge? We wouldn't get anywhere if we did that." Yes, I thought, she's right, too. But I still thought that maybe scientists should at least consider possible misuses. The so-called objective scientific method shouldn't stop them from thinking, after all.

But what do I think about all this? What's my thesis? "Science and morality" is a huge subject and I can't possibly handle it. I tried narrowing it down, but all the time I was nagged by the idea that it isn't how broad or narrow my subject is that matters, but what I want to say *about* it. Okay, forget narrowing and get to the point. Grab a sheet of paper and try out some thesis statements. What do I think? Well . . .

Scientists are morally responsible for the results of their research.

That seems to satisfy criterion number one, but is it what I really want to assert? It seems pretty fuzzy.

What about criterion number two? Certainly the class was divided on the general question of whether a scientist is responsible, but it was never a matter of a simple "yes" or "no" answer. No one seemed to think that the responsibility is absolute; it always seemed to depend on something. I remember that one student said something like: "How can the person who invented fire be responsible for all the arsonists? That's ridiculous." She was right. So she would think my thesis is ridiculous, too. The issue never was one of unqualified responsibility. I guess this must be a question of interpretation, but I'm not sure. I do know that my problem is to say where the responsibility starts and ends. My thesis doesn't address a question at issue, because no one in class would agree that what we need to have is an interpretation of ultimate responsibility, as in my thesis. How can I change it?

Well, what kind of responsibility do I mean? I certainly don't think every scientist who ever lived ought to be blamed for all the bad applications of their findings? But I do think that scientists at least ought to think about those possibilities, as I said in class. Maybe my thesis is:

> *Scientists are morally responsible for the results of their research if they are able to foresee those results.*

Is this what I intend? Not quite. I don't think "results of their research" makes much sense any more. It isn't precise enough to say what I really mean. I'm already thinking about criterion number three, making the terms precise so they say just what I intend. Okay, then, I'll change it:

> *Scientists are morally responsible for the harmful applications of their research if they are able to foresee those applications.*

I like that better because it answers a more specific question, one that really did concern the class. "Harmful applications" was the issue, not just "results." I thought I knew what I meant by "harmful applications," because we talked about several examples. Maybe I'll use the one about cloning as a harmful effect of genetic engineering, especially since a scientist ought to be able to foresee this result.

But, wait a minute, what do I mean by "foresee"? I can foresee a lot of things that might not happen. Scientists probably have better imaginations than I do. They might think cloning is right up there with antigravity machines. How should I know? Should their imaginations stop them from doing research? It doesn't seem like it. I remember something someone else said in class: "Don't scientists think that the risk of harmful effects is worth the potential benefit? They make a choice between probable good and improbable bad." I hadn't understood this at the time, but now I think I might. Scientists have to do more than just foresee effects; they must also think about how probable they are. What if a scientist can imagine a result but decides it isn't going to occur? If genetic research is needed to find a cure for some horrid disease, should the unlikely future of a cloned society stop the search for this cure? Well, that depends on the probability of that future occurring, as far as the scientist is able to determine it. It's a relatively sure thing against a relatively unsure one. I think I also may have to address the issue of consequence in my thesis. (I wonder if it's okay to talk about two kinds of questions at once? Why not?) Maybe now I'm getting somewhere:

> *Scientists are morally responsible for the harmful effects of their research only if those effects are highly probable in comparison to the potential good.*

Not quite. I'm still bothered by the question I just asked myself. Yes, a cure for disease is important, but a cloned society would be horrible. What troubles me is that I don't think my thesis is what I really want to argue. I think I've been sneaking up on a different idea, but my original thesis statement has been keeping me from seeing it. Since I have been thinking, I have gotten away from the scientist's responsibility for *effects,* as such, and begun to think, instead, about a different kind of responsibility. I don't want to blame scientists for anything; I just want to make them more responsible for what they do. A cloned society will be the result of many more decisions than any single scientist's. It isn't a question of who's to blame, but of what a scientist's responsibility really is. If the problem is how to make scientists responsible, then maybe the issue is: responsible for what? Back to my page, this time to make a major change:

> *Scientists are responsible for making sure that they have considered the harmful effects of their research and weighed the probability of those effects against the potential good.*

Hey, I like that. I think this idea contributes something to the discussion that answers part of the problem. The issue is not whether to blame scientists afterward, but to be sure that they think about what they're doing beforehand. In my essay I can talk about a genetic scientist's need to think about how probable cloning is, human cloning that is, the kind we don't want to see. I can begin to see my essay taking shape.

But, since I'm answering a different issue now, I should ask again whether I'm being precise enough. Well, not really. What do I mean by "responsible" now, if I don't mean "blame"? I don't mean that I want scientists to go to jail if they don't consider these things. I just think they ought to think about them as a necessary part of what they do. I have it!

> *Scientific education should include the issue of moral responsibility so that scientists will learn to consider the harmful effects of their research and weigh them against the potential good.*

I think I'm interested mainly in a policy kind of question, rather than an interpretation kind. That's a good clear stance that I think I can argue, and one that I think might help the class to clarify the issue we struggled with.

Have I satisfied criterion number four for a good thesis? Reasoning is what I've been doing all this time. Well, what about number five? Yes, I think I can develop it reasonably, because I know what I have to do to explain it. My essay will have to put the issue into a new light by explaining that scientific education might not address moral questions adequately. Then it will have to describe how a failure to address such questions can result in the failure of scientists to consider harmful effects. I think I'll have to say that this consideration cannot guarantee that those effects won't happen, to keep my reader from misunderstanding my purpose, but it might make the effects less likely because scientists would at least be weighing them against potential good effects. I'll argue that this kind of education will lead to scientific research that at least takes morality into consideration. And I'll have to make that connection. But what will I say to show that this will happen? Well, it will happen *because* . . . .

*   *   *

We'll return to this fictional mental narrative later and get into the development of that major reason. But at this point we can at least see how the result of testing an initial thesis against the five conditions might help to lead you from a loose, general, ill-considered thesis to the discovery of a thesis with much better potential to generate a good argument. Of course, I had to oversimplify and dramatize a process that will always be sloppy and unpredictable. Nothing can guarantee that you will come up with a good thesis even by working at it. Some people have no trouble coming up with good ideas, while others must struggle to find them. (Most of us experience both, at different times.) Having good ideas is simply part of the intuitive mystery of the mind, and no rules can be written to account for it. But trying out a thesis and then thinking about rewriting it—with the five criteria in mind—is one way to keep your thinking alive and focused in a productive direction. It's like giving inspiration a boost.

The hypothetical student was aided by thinking about the discussion from which the issue arose. His knowledge of how his audience (the class) had responded and might respond provoked new thoughts. He was thinking as a participant in a discourse community that will not let its members get away with mental laziness. In the illustration, the student didn't know where he was going to come out when he took the first step into his inquiry, and that, of course, was the surest sign that he was really thinking for himself, rather than simply following the road of least resistance. His ideas developed because he kept forcing himself to question. At some point, he had to call a halt to what is potentially an endless process of speculation. But at least he did it after, rather than before, doing some hard thinking.

IMPLICATIONS FOR RESEARCH

It may seem from this discussion that coming up with a reasonable thesis is a matter of thinking only about what you already know; it does not require you to become well informed before jumping off into speculation. Not so. Coming up with a reasonable thesis is *primarily* a matter of thinking hard about what you know. You will not find your thesis by going to the library in search of what to think. But in the process of thinking about potential theses you will encounter gaps in your knowledge of a subject, and if these gaps prevent you from thinking about that subject further because you do not know something that is vital to your understanding, then you should attempt to fill those gaps. There is a difference between rash speculation and honest speculation. If you are unsure of something that is crucial to your position, or if you are assuming that some part of your idea is true because you "heard it somewhere" or because "my sister told me," then you are being rash. An honest commitment to an idea should be based on your confidence that the knowledge that idea seems to assert is real knowledge.

The lesson here is simple. You must think hard about your ideas; there's no way around that, except to be irresponsible. But you might, by thinking hard, discover that you need to look something up, to find out or to verify the knowledge you want to claim. If that is the case, then finding out becomes your further responsibility.

Formulating a research question can be an aid to conducting such an inquiry. It should enable you to define the unknowns, to determine the boundaries of the inquiry, and to keep the inquiry focused as you seek to become better informed. Of course, the question starts out as a tentative formulation, subject to change. The more you discover and the more thought you give to the possible answers, the clearer you may become about the kind of question that you wish to answer. Research is seldom so straightforward that no side trips, dead ends, detours, or unexpected changes of plan happen along the road to answers. The process of becoming informed seldom follows a predictable route.

Having formulated a research question, you might ask yourself something like, "What do I need to know to answer this question?" At this point you might sketch out a plan, listing some of the specific areas you need to know more about. Any question can be broken down into constituent parts, even if the categories are temporary or turn out later to be irrelevant. You may not yet know what all of the categories are—research is, after all, exploring the unknown. Yet you are never starting out without some knowledge to begin with, since you had to understand something already in order to perceive the significance of the question you have decided to explore. Trust that knowledge and sketch out some possibilities, based on the question you have formulated, before heading off to the library.

The available resources of libraries are so vast that it is, of course, necessary to know how each library is organized and what kinds of catalogs and indexes exist to give researchers access to its holdings. If you have not become familiar with the resources of a research library, you can ask the reference staff for their advice. All good libraries have educational material available to students who wish to acquaint themselves with the basic functions of the library. Descriptions of different kinds of reference materials (subject or author/title indexes for books, indexes to periodicals, bibliographies, abstracts of research, and more) can also be found in a good college writing handbook. Rather than discuss these here, I assume you are able to look them up if you need to. Often, the best way to discover what kinds of resources the library has available in your own areas of interest is to get in there with your questions and begin to follow leads wherever they take you. It isn't efficient, of course, just to plunge in without a good idea of where to look for the information you seek. But it is often adventurous and fun to explore somewhat as a means of becoming familiar with the library at the same time that you seek to inform yourself about your subject. Doing research is often compared to the work of a detective. It's a good analogy, as far as it goes. A researcher, like a detective, has to be watchful for unexpected clues. The library is full of these, and you should be prepared to investigate any that might take you into important discoveries.

Research in the library has one crucial limitation. Only by knowing what kind of question you are researching, and what "unknowns" define the inquiry, can you know whether this limitation will apply to any particular research project you might undertake. This limitation is probably best described by distinguishing secondary research from primary research. Secondary research consists of locating and using the research that other people have already conducted and written about. One way of going about answering research questions is to read the writing of other researchers who have investigated the same or related questions. Primary research consists of investigating any phenomenon on one's own by working directly with the phenomenon rather than reading about other people's work with it. Secondary research is ordinarily conducted in the library, because that is where one usually goes to find out what others have written. Primary research is ordinarily conducted outside the library.

The distinction between primary and secondary research applies to all fields of inquiry. Science provides the most obvious examples. A biologist, for instance, may be interested in discovering how a particular species of plant reacts to changes in light. There are many things about this question that she might learn in the library. To answer it, she would have to know as much about the plant as possible and about how other species of plants react to similar changes, information that can be found in the published research of other biologists. She would also want to know whether anyone has already discovered the answer to her question or to questions that bear on it. But having informed herself in this way, the researcher would have to move from the library to the laboratory to complete the study by conducting experiments with plants and light sources. The secondary phase of the research exists as preparation for the primary phase. Depending on the kind of question under investigation, primarily research takes place in the laboratory, or in the field, or simply in the privacy of one's thoughts. An anthropologist investigating what kinds of traditions accompany marriage in urban subcultures may learn a lot by reading, but at some point he would want to go out and collect some primary information by talking to people and observing the phenomena first-hand. A sociologist studying the attitudes of teenagers toward alcohol abuse can learn much by reading in the library, but she would also have to question teenagers to find her answers. A scholar studying the possible influence of impressionist painting on the literary style of Gertrude Stein would learn much by finding sources in the library, but her research would enter its primary phase when she made careful observations about the paintings and the writing and compared them. The way in which primary research is conducted varies from discipline to discipline, depending on the kinds of questions being asked, but all research moves from the secondary collecting and assessment of others' ideas to the primary study of the phenomenon under study. Primary research *extends* secondary research. Without both, no research would be complete.

Finally, remember that the researcher enters the process of becoming informed without knowing where that process may lead. The research question, like the thesis of an argumentative essay, may change as the researcher discovers more information or complexities and continues to think about them. Further questions may arise. Answers may have to remain tentative. But just as the writer of an argumentative essay has to decide when a line of reasoning is adequate, a researcher must decide when a question can be answered reasonably. In either case, there is nothing wrong with admitting that the answer is only as good as the quality of the evidence that supports it, so that the possibility of further inquiry remains open.

QUESTIONS FOR THOUGHT, DISCUSSION, AND WRITING

1. What kind of stasis question is each of the following? How do you know? Under what circumstances might each be at issue? What related kinds of questions might also be at issue in each case?
    a. Are groups that use dangerous drugs in religious ceremonies exempt from laws against use of those drugs?
    b. Do college administrations have the right to censor the contents of student newspapers?
    c. Is marriage outmoded?
    d. Are scientific experiments that cause pain to animals necessary?
    e. Do grades inhibit learning?
    f. Does the widespread practice of repeating "urban legends" indicate that people are willing to believe anything as long as it sounds probable?
    g. Is mandatory drug testing for athletes wrong?

2. Say whether you think the following statements fit the definition of a thesis. Why or why not? If they could be improved, what would the writer have to think about?
   a. I want to write my paper about sports and society and how it should be changed.
   b. Some people just don't know how to take a joke.
   c. I wish people would stop bugging me about what I'm going to do with my life, so I can find out.
   d. The escalation of defensive weapons into space will make a nuclear war more likely.
   e. The use of *he* and *man* to refer to both men and women is sexist.
   f. *The Federalist Papers* should be read by all students before they graduate from high school.
   g. All teaching will someday be done by computers, leading to a more effective education for all students.
3. What responsibilities does a writer accept in choosing any of these statements as a thesis? What parts would an essay about each of them have to contain to be complete?
   a. Legalization of marijuana would give young people greater confidence in government.
   b. Procrastination, more than any other cause, leads good students to perform badly on assignments.
   c. Belief in a CIA conspiracy to murder President Kennedy has led critics of the Warren Report to misinterpret its findings.
   d. Overpopulation is a greater threat to world peace than nuclear proliferation.
   e. Eradicating cigarette smoking by the year 2000 should be a priority of the U.S. government.
   f. A clear conscience is not necessary for happiness.
4. Having read an essay and discussed its ideas in class, construct a thesis that represents your own response to an issue you have discovered. Test that thesis against the five criteria discussed in this chapter, and revise it until you think it will provide you with a good basis for writing an argumentative essay. Then discuss that thesis in class again to see whether the responses of others suggest the need for further thought.
5. Here are four argumentative essays. In each case:
   a. Identify the question at issue. What kind of question is it?
   b. Paraphrase the author's thesis.
   c. Make a list of unknowns about the subject that you would have to investigate if you were to conduct further research into the question in order to validate or to question the author's thesis.

◆ READINGS ◆

PEACE THROUGH STRENGTH IS A FALLACY

Mark O. Hatfield

[The following is the text of a speech delivered by Senator Hatfield, a Republican from Oregon, during the U.S. Senate's debate on the $300 million defense authorization bill of 1989.]

Mr. President, 23 years have passed since I first arrived in the Senate, a former Governor who came to Washington determined to extricate American boys from the chaos and confusion into which this country—wrongly in my view—had sent them in Southeast Asia. Those were difficult times for the Nation—and difficult times for me personally.

In the early years, I found myself in a very small minority. We would give our speeches and cast our votes—and every day, more young people were coming home in body bags and wheel chairs.

A couple years later, when the administration began to have problems getting the money it wanted from Congress to prosecute the war, people began to talk about a peace dividend. If we can just win this thing, they would say, there will be a peace dividend for the Nation—money to spend here at home, money which will help wind down the giant war economy. Victory is right around the corner. Light is at the end of the tunnel.

In 1970—before some of the interns now working in my office were even born—I rose on this floor to question this peace dividend idea, to express my doubts about this notion that we would one day begin to rechannel our resources—not away from a strong national defense, but toward a more comprehensive, more human, definition of it. Few people listened—then. People wanted to believe that victory was right around the corner, and they wanted to believe that our massive war spending would one day end. And so—at least for a couple more years—the money kept flowing into the military.

Mr. President, from the Revolutionary War to the Civil War to the Spanish-American War through World War I, through World War II, through Korea, through Vietnam, and through the cold wars in between: At no time did the spending for military purposes reduce or diminish after those wars. They reached a peak during a war, and then remained at that peak following the war. No build down—only a build up. And no peace dividend, Mr. President. None at all.

And as we entered this decade, the clarion call went out: despite one of the largest and best trained militaries in the world, despite a nuclear arsenal of unprecedented destructive power, we were—somehow—vulnerable. A spending gap is what they called it—and so we began a massive buildup; billions and billions of dollars to catch up. Nevermind that this spending gap was as phony as the bomber gap of the 1950s and the missile gap of the 1960s—Democrats and Republicans alike dutifully lined up and marched to the drummer of higher military spending.

And so it is that we have gathered here every year since only to play on the margins. Oh, we sound reasonable—and we like to think that we sound responsible. We go to hearings and briefings, we have long debates over this program and that program, this weapon or that weapon, and we cast our votes on amendment after amendment.

But when it comes right down to it, Mr. President, we are only playing on the margins. This Congress—a bipartisan majority of this Congress—has approved $2.2 trillion of the $2.3 trillion requested for defense spending during this decade alone.

We have played on the margins for so long, Mr. President, that I am afraid we do not even know what the real issues are anymore. We seem to have lost sight of the fact that many of the programs we have authorized—and are authorizing again here today—are intended for one purpose and one purpose only: mass destruction.

We seem to have lost sight of the fact that every dollar we spend on bombs and bullets means that we are underfunding programs to meet the Nation's desperate human needs: health care, education, our war on drugs, low income housing, prison construction, AIDS research—all of these things are part of our national defense.

Sometimes, Mr. President, we even lose sight of the margins. Several days ago, the Senate considered an amendment earmarking money for the development of more lethal weapons for our ground troops. More lethal? Even the words have begun to lose their meaning—what is more lethal supposed to mean when some of our troops already carry tactical nuclear weapons on their backs? But nobody else even raised an eyebrow: the vote was 98−1.

I remember, back in 1981, when 10 subcommittees of the Senate Appropriations Committee were forced to make $9.9 billion in cuts from domestic spending—so that defense spending could be increased by $7.4 billion. We can no longer afford to fool ourselves, I said in the full committee markup—but oh, how wrong I was. The Nation's defense budget has almost tripled in the past decade with our bipartisan blessing—and spending to meet the desperate human needs throughout this country has been cut and cut and cut again to pay for it—some 33 percent reduction in the nondefense discretionary programs in the last decade.

Could somebody tell me if there is some secret strategy—some finite figure that we will one day reach and then suddenly be secure? Will we ever have enough?

I do not think so. We are, Mr. President, like the thirsty man in the desert who thinks he sees an oasis ahead—but when he moves closer, it moves too. Further and further—or for us, higher and higher. And as his thirst finally kills him, our lust for bigger and better weapons of mass destruction is going to destroy us one day too.

Peace through strength is a fallacy, Mr. President, for peace is not simply the absence of a nuclear holocaust. Peace is not a nation which has seen its teenage suicide rate more than double in the past two decades. Peace is not a nation in which more people die every 2 years of gunshot wounds than died in the entire Vietnam War. Peace is not the town in Pennsylvania which last year was forced to cancel its high school graduation because officials believed that a group of students planned to commit suicide at the ceremony. And peace is not here in Washington— where after leading the Nation in murders last year, children are beginning to show the same psychological trauma as children in Belfast, Northern Ireland.

Can we really believe that the decisions we have made—and are making—do not have a direct relationship to the violence which plagues our Nation?

I suggest that we consider changing the motto on our coins, Mr. President. It now reads: In God We Trust—but by blindly pursuing the nuclear arms race, by putting the destruction of life over the preservation of life, we have foresaken our trust in God. We have shaken our fist at God—as E. B. White once put it, we have stolen God's stuff. Our motto ought to be: In Bombs We Trust. That is our national ethic—that is the example we are setting—here, on this floor.

When it comes to debating campaign finance reform and limits on honorarium, everybody seems eager to talk about ethics in government.

But is there no ethical dimension to the arms race—to our abuse of our natural and human resources, to our waste of scientific genius, to the bankrupting of the Federal Treasury to pay for weapons of mass destruction?

Is there no ethical dimension to our decision, our conscious decision, to add more and more weapons to our stockpiles, while millions of people in our own country have no roof over their heads, when we cannot fund our homeless programs, when we cannot fund our war on drugs? Is there no ethical dimension to the violent examples we are setting for our children? Is there no ethical dimension to the definition of national security that we are passing on to the developing nations of the world, where arsenals are now as bloated as the bellies of the Third World's children?

There are those who will point to the INF Treaty, the first arms control agreement between the United States and Soviet Union in 16 years, as if somehow it legitimizes everything. Never mind that these are the same people who spent almost a decade doing everything they could to sabotage arms control negotiations—never believing the Russians would agree to onsite inspection. Their message now to the millions of children of this country who do not get enough to eat, to the millions of children who have not been fully immunized, to the thousands of babies who die each year because their mothers receive no prenatal care, to the 37 million Americans who have no health insurance, their message is: See, it was worth it. These are the same people, Mr. President, who accept the twisted logic which says we must produce nerve gas to negotiate a treaty; which says we must continue nuclear testing to ensure safety. A safe nuclear weapon? Mr. President, I wish George Orwell could sit in on these debates.

The INF Treaty? Big deal. In the 6 months between the time the INF Treaty was signed here in Washington and the time it was ratified on this floor, the United States and the Soviet Union deployed more nuclear warheads than will be eliminated under the treaty. That is right. We spent and spent and spent, so that the administration could negotiate from strength. For all our money, all our weapons, the only thing we received in return was a tiny little dent in the stockpile we had just created.

And then, in an incredible display of how distorted our frame of reference has become, how low our expectations have sunk, everyone cheered as if it were the end of the nuclear arms race.

To those who may suggest that I am naive, I respond: I have been there. As a young naval officer, I walked through the rubble of Hiroshima—a month after the bomb was dropped. I saw the death—the slow, agonizing pain—and the charred bodies. As we stand here playing on the margins, Mr. President, as we stand here voting 98 to 1 for the development of more lethal weapons, the stench of death haunts me still.

Forty-five years ago, we could legitimately say that we did not know. Now we do. Let me read just a few lines of John Hershey's "Hiroshima:"

> He found about 20 men and women on the sandspit. He drove the boat onto the bank and urged them to get aboard. They did not move and he realized that they were too weak to lift themselves. He reached down and took a woman by the hands, but her skin slipped off in huge, glovelike pieces.
>
> Then he got into the water and, though a small man, lifted several of the men and women, who were naked, into his boat. Their backs and breasts were clammy, and he remembered uneasily what the great burns he had seen during the day had been like: yellow at first, then red and swollen, with the skin sloughed off, and finally, in the evening, suppurated and smelly.
>
> With the tide risen, his bamboo pole was now too short and he had to paddle most of the way across it. On the other side, at a higher spit, he lifted the slimy living bodies out and carried them up the slope away from the tide. He had to keep consciously repeating to himself:
> "These are human beings. These are human beings."

SDI, ASAT weapons, the Midgetman, the MX missile, the Stealth bomber, nerve gas, the D–5 missile, the Trident submarine: I will cast my vote against them all. Since 1980, Mr. President, I have given more than 30 speeches during our annual consideration of this bill: 7 against nerve gas production, 5 against underground testing, 3 against ASAT weapons, 3 against the MX missile, 3 against the draft, 2 against SDI—the list goes on and on. But I have felt over the years like I am speaking in a vacuum—we have approved them all. And I speak in a vacuum today—my colleagues will listen politely and then vote for it all.

I will feel that way too—as I have for many years now—when I cast my vote against final passage of this bill. For I too am playing on the margins.

In the absence of political will—on this floor and across the country—in the absence of the kind of political will we seem to be able to muster when the Department of Defense needs another increase but not when children go hungry, anything more is impossible.

Mr. President, unfortunately we only have had one President of the United States who, in my view, understood national security, national defense. He was a five-star general: Dwight David Eisenhower.

Mr. President, these are his words:

> Every gun that is made, every warship launched, every rocket fired signifies, in the final sense, a theft from those who hunger and are not fed, those who are cold and are not clothed. This world in arms is not spending money alone. It is spending the sweat of its laborers, the genius of its scientists, the hopes of its children. . . . This is not a way of life at all in any true sense. Under the cloud of threatening war, it is humanity hanging from a cross of iron.

This was the man who led the troops. This was the man who led the Allied troops in World War II—he understood war, but he also understood peace.

We are kidding ourselves, Mr. President. Today we are vulnerable. The national defense of this Nation, has left us vulnerable, but not because we lack an arsenal. The vulnerability of this Nation today is that we rank at the bottom of the list in math and science, and that at least 20 million Americans cannot read or write. The vulnerability of our Nation is the deterioration and the erosion of our infrastructure, our highways, bridges, airports, our ports. Our vulnerability today is a nonproductive economy, a noncompetitive economy. Our vulnerability is the people who are without homes, nutrition, education, health care.

Ultimately the security of the Nation is not found in its materialism. It is found in a spirit. It is found in a strength of heart and mind. It is found in its people—we the people.

We the people are vulnerable today. Let us at least be honest: we are not addressing those vulnerabilities with this bill or any other bill.

THE CAUSE OF WAR

Margaret Sanger

[The following essay is from *Woman and the New Race* (1920).]

In every nation of militaristic tendencies we find the reactionaries demanding a higher and still higher birth rate. Their plea is, first, that great armies are needed to *defend* the country from its possible enemies; second, that a huge population is required to assure the country its proper place among the powers of the world. At bottom the two pleas are the same.

As soon as the country becomes overpopulated, these reactionaries proclaim loudly its moral right to expand. They point to the huge population, which in the name of patriotism they have previously demanded should be brought into being. Again pleading patriotism, they declare that it is the moral right of the nation to take by force such room as it needs. Then comes war—usually against some nation supposed to be less well prepared than the aggressor.

Diplomats make it their business to conceal the facts, and politicians violently denounce the politicians of other countries. There is a long beating of tom-toms by the press and all other agencies for influencing public opinion. Facts are distorted and lies invented until the common people cannot get at the truth. Yet, when the war is over, if not before, we always find that "a place in the sun," "a path to the sea," "a route to India" or something of the sort is at the bottom of the trouble. These are merely other names for expansion.

The "need of expansion" is only another name for overpopulation. One supreme example is sufficient to drive home this truth. That the Great War, from the horror of which we are just beginning to emerge, had its source in overpopulation is too evident to be denied by any serious student of current history.

For the past one hundred years most of the nations of Europe have been piling up terrific debts to humanity by the encouragement of unlimited numbers. The rulers of these nations and their militarists have constantly called upon the people to breed, breed, breed! Large populations meant more people to produce wealth, more people to pay taxes, more trade for the merchants, more soldiers to protect the wealth. But more people also meant need of greater food supplies, an urgent and natural need for expansion.

As shown by C. V. Drysdale's famous "War Map of Europe," the great conflict began among the high birth rate countries—Germany, with its rate of 31.7, Austria-Hungary with 33.7 and 36.7, respectively, Russia with 45.4, Serbia with 38.6. Italy with her 38.7 came in, as the world is now well informed through the publication of secret treaties by the Soviet government of Russia, upon the promise of territory held by Austria. England, owing to her small home area, is cramped with her comparatively low birth rate of 26.3. France, among the belligerents, is conspicuous for her low birth rate of 19.9, but stood in the way of expansion of high birth rate Germany. Nearly all of the persistently neutral countries—Holland, Denmark, Norway, Sweden and Switzerland have low birth rates, the average being a little over 26.

Owing to the part Germany played in the war, a survey of her birth statistics is decidedly illuminating. The increase in the German birth rate up to 1876 was great. Though it began to decline then, the decline was not sufficient to offset the tremendous increase of the previous years. There were more millions to produce children, so while the average number of births per thousand was somewhat smaller, the net increase in population was still huge. From 41,000,000 in 1871, the year the Empire was founded, the German population grew to approximately 67,000,000 in 1918. Meanwhile her food supply increased only a very small percent. In 1910, Russia had a birth rate even higher than Germany's had ever been—a little less than 48 per thousand. When czarist Russia wanted an outlet to the Mediterranean by way of Constantinople, she was thinking of her increasing population. Germany was thinking of her increasing population when she spoke as with one voice of a "place in the sun." . . .

The militaristic claim for Germany's right to new territory was simply a claim to the right of life and food for the German babies—the same right that a chick claims to burst its shell. If there had not been other millions of people claiming the same right, there would have been no war. But there *were* other millions.

The German rulers and leaders pointed out the fact that expansion meant more business for German merchants, more work for German workmen at better wages, and more opportunities for Germans abroad. They also pointed out that lack of expansion meant crowding and crushing at home, hard times, heavy burdens, lack of opportunity for Germans, and what not. In this way, they gave the people of the Empire a startling and true picture of what would happen from overcrowding. Once they realized the facts, the majority of Germans naturally welcomed the so-called war of defense.

The argument was sound. Once the German mothers had submitted to the plea for overbreeding, it was inevitable that imperialistic Germany should make war. Once the battalions of unwanted babies came into existence—babies whom the mothers did not want but which they bore as a "patriotic duty"—it was too late to avoid international conflict. The great crime of imperialistic Germany was its high birth rate.

It has always been so. Behind all war has been the pressure of population. "Historians," says Huxley, "point to the greed and ambition of rulers, the reckless turbulence of the ruled, to the debasing effects of wealth and luxury, and to the devastating wars which have formed a great part of the occupation of mankind, as the causes of the decay of states and the foundering of old civilizations, and thereby point their story with a moral. But beneath all this superficial turmoil lay the deep-seated impulse given by unlimited multiplication."

Robert Thomas Malthus, formulator of the doctrine which bears his name, pointed out, in the closing years of the eighteenth century, the relation of overpopulation to war. He showed that mankind tends to increase faster than the food supply. He demonstrated that were it not for the more common diseases, for plague, famine, floods and wars, human beings would crowd each other to such an extent that the misery would be even greater than it now is. These he described as "natural checks," pointing out that as long as no other checks are employed, such disasters are unavoidable. If we do not exercise sufficient judgment to regulate the birth rate, we encounter disease, starvation and war.

Both Darwin and John Stuart Mill recognized, by inference at least, the fact that so-called "natural checks"—and among them war—will operate if some sort of limitation is not employed. In his *Origin of Species*, Darwin says: "There is no exception to the rule that every organic being naturally increases at so high a rate, if not destroyed, that the earth would soon be covered by the progeny of a single pair." Elsewhere he observes that we do not permit helpless human beings to die off, but we create philanthropies and charities, build asylums and hospitals and keep the medical profession busy preserving those who could not otherwise survive. John Stuart Mill, supporting the views of Malthus, speaks to exactly the same effect in regard to the multiplying power of organic beings, among them humanity. In other words, let countries become overpopulated and war is inevitable. It follows as daylight follows the sunrise.

When Charles Bradlaugh and Mrs. Annie Besant were on trial in England in 1877 for publishing information concerning contraceptives, Mrs. Besant put the case bluntly to the court and the jury:

> I have no doubt that if natural checks were allowed to operate right through the human as they do in the animal world, a better result would follow. Among the brutes, the weaker are driven to the wall, the diseased fall out in the race of life. The old brutes, when feeble or sickly, are killed. If men insisted that those who were sickly should be allowed to die without help of medicine or science, if those who are weak were put upon one side and crushed, if those who were old and useless were killed, if those who were not capable of providing food for themselves were allowed to starve, if all this were done, the struggle for existence among men would be as real as it is among brutes and would doubtless result in the production of a higher race of men.
>
> But are you willing to do that or to allow it to be done?

We are not willing to let it be done. Mother hearts cling to children, no matter how diseased, misshapen and miserable. Sons and daughters hold fast to parents, no matter how helpless. We do not allow the weak to depart; neither do we cease to bring more weak and helpless beings into the world. Among the dire results is war, which kills off, not the weak and the helpless, but the strong and the fit.

What shall be done? We have our choice of one of three policies. We may abandon our science and leave the weak and diseased to die, or kill them, as the brutes do. Or we may go on overpopulating the earth and have our famines and our wars while the earth exists. Or we can accept the third, sane, sensible, moral and practicable plan of birth control. We can refuse to bring the weak, the helpless and the unwanted children into the world. We can refuse to overcrowd families, nations and the earth. There are these ways to meet the situation, and only these three ways.

The world will never abandon its preventive and curative science; it may be expected to elevate and extend it beyond our present imagination. The efforts to do away with famine and the opposition to war are growing by leaps and bounds. Upon these efforts are largely based our modern social revolutions.

There remains only the third expedient—birth control, the real cure for war. This fact was called to the attention of the Peace Conference in Paris, in 1919, by the Malthusian League, which adopted the following resolution at its annual general meeting in London in June of that year:

> The Malthusian League desires to point out that the proposed scheme for the League of Nations has neglected to take account of the important questions of *the pressure of population*, which *causes the great international economic competition* and rivalry, and of the *increase of population*, which is put forward as a justification for *claiming increase of territory*. It, therefore, wishes to put on record its belief that the League of Nations will only be able to fulfill its aim *when it adds a clause* to the following effect:
>
> "That each Nation desiring to enter into the League of Nations shall pledge itself *so to restrict its birth rate* that its people shall be able to live in comfort *in their own dominions without need* for territorial expansion, and that it shall recognize that *increase of population shall not justify* a demand either for increase of territory or for the compulsion of other Nations to admit its emigrants; so that when all Nations in the League have shown their ability to live on their own resources without international rivalry, they will be in a position to fuse into an international federation, and territorial boundaries will then have little significance."

As a matter of course, the Peace Conference paid no attention to the resolution, for, as pointed out by Frank A. Vanderlip, the American financier, that conference not only ignored the economic factors of the world situation, but seemed unaware that Europe had produced more people than its fields could feed. So the resolution amounted to so much propaganda and nothing more.

This remedy can be applied only by woman and she will apply it. She must and will see past the call of pretended patriotism and of glory of empire and perceive what is true and what is false in these things. She will discover what base uses the militarist and the exploiter made of the idealism of peoples. Under the clamor of the press, permeating the ravings of the jingoes, she will hear the voice of Napoleon, the archtype of the militarists of all nations, calling for "fodder for cannon."

"Woman is given to us that she may bear children," said he. "Woman is our property, we are not hers, because she produces children for us—we do not yield any to her. She is, therefore, our possession as the fruit tree is that of the gardener."

That is what the imperialist is *thinking* when he speaks of the glory of the empire and the prestige of the nation. Every country has its appeal—its shibboleth—ready for the lips of the imperialist. German rulers pointed to the comfort of the workers, to old-age pensions, maternal benefits and minimum wage regulations, and other material benefits, when they wished to inspire soldiers for the Fatherland. England's strongest argument, perhaps, was a certain phase of liberty which she guarantees her subjects, and the protection afforded them wherever they may go. France and the United States, too, have their appeals to the idealism of democracy—appeals which the politicians of both countries know well how to use, though the peoples of both lands are beginning to awake to the fact that their countries have been living on the glories of their revolutions and traditions, rather than the substance of freedom. Behind the boast of old-age pensions, material benefits and wage regulations, behind the bombast concerning liberty in this country and tyranny in that, behind all the slogans and shibboleths coined out of the ideals of the peoples for the uses of imperialism, woman must and will see the iron hand of that same imperialism, condemning women to breed and men to die for the will of the rulers.

Upon woman the burden and the horrors of war are heaviest. Her heart is the hardest wrung when the husband or the son comes home to be buried or to live a shattered wreck. Upon her devolve the extra tasks of filling out the ranks of workers in the war industries, in addition to caring for the children and replenishing the war-diminished population. Hers is the crushing weight and the sickening of soul. And it is out of her womb that those things proceed. When she sees what lies behind the glory and the horror, the boasting and the burden, and gets the vision, the human perspective, she will end war. She will kill war by the simple process of starving it to death. For she will refuse longer to produce the human food upon which the monster feeds.

GOOD FENCES MAKE GOOD NEIGHBORHOODS

Fred L. Smith & Kathy H. Kushner

The collapse of socialism in Eastern Europe and the USSR, Milton Friedman recently pointed out, seems to have taught Americans nothing. Nowhere is that more true than in environmental policy. The conventional wisdom holds that the source of environmental degradation arises from self-interest, private property, and the profit motive. But because the state acts in the public interest, socialism would reverse this process and promote environmental protection. This pretty picture began to fade in the 1970s, but nothing prepared us for the unremitting, systematic devastation that we now see.

Nevertheless, in the U.S., the EPA, with wide support from almost all sectors of society, is not only being elevated to Cabinet level, but is becoming one of the most powerful economic-planning agencies in the world. It already has the power to control nearly all aspects of the U.S. economy: production processes, contents of products, the sale of goods and services, plant siting, international trade, etc. The control even extends to land-use patterns and activities on private lands, as well as consumer choices and activities, and even individual lifestyles. This enormous power over nearly every aspect of our lives has, to date, only sporadically been used. But the potential is there, and the mounting calls for tough action belie the image of a kinder and gentler America.

If we are to prove Friedman wrong, we must challenge this conventional view that while markets are vastly superior means of organizing most human activities, they cannot address environmental concerns. The allocation of rights and responsibilities that takes place in a free economy, along with the decentralization of control, the expression of diverse wishes, and the organization of vast amounts of information, could do much to reverse the environmental damage already done.

The most common cause of environmental degradation is a lack of clearly defined and transferrable property rights in the resource in question. If a thing has no owner then no one has an incentive to care for it. Few will act to safeguard or enhance the property of others. In the case of living things, no one will try to ensure that they have the necessary conditions to reproduce and thrive. These are the conditions that lead to environmental problems—disappearing species, dirty air and water, depleted aquifers, clear-cut forests. Even global warming can be traced to the fact that no one has a proprietary interest in protecting the atmosphere. If property rights were extended to resources that now enjoy no such protection, the long-term self-interest of private owners could take the place of inefficient and unpredictable bureaucratic fiat.

To see how these two different approaches to conservation work, compare redfish and catfish. In the 1980s the redfish population in the Gulf of Mexico declined alarmingly. Commercial fishermen were taken to task for their greed, and eventually a regulatory solution (a temporary banning of all commercial fishing) was imposed. Meanwhile, nearby in

Mississippi, the catfish population increased by 500 per cent during the 1980s. The difference? Redfish, like all other ocean fish, remain the property of everyone. There is no incentive for an individual to limit today's catch to increase tomorrow's harvest. Catfish, on the other hand, are farmed in ponds, where their owners diligently provide them with optimum oxygen levels, protection from disease, and whatever else catfish like.

However, if an extension of property rights is to be the basis of a new environmentalism, we must address the problems in adapting traditional legal concepts to new needs. We must in effect extend the concept of fencing from private land to public land, rivers, the sea, and even the atmosphere, and develop methods of identifying and deterring trespassers.

National parks, forests, grazing lands, wildlife refuges, and recreational areas are not in essence different from property now privately held. There are major political obstacles to privatization in these areas, but no major conceptual problems. Wildlife could be owned in the same manner as domestic livestock. In Zimbabwe, tribal communities have the right to dispose of a certain number of elephants as they see fit. Because these elephants have value to their human neighbors, they are safeguarded from poachers and tolerated in places where they would otherwise be regarded as pests. As a result, Zimbabwe's elephant population has increased by over 40 per cent in the last ten years. In Kenya, where hunting has been illegal for the same period, the elephant herds are disappearing at a rate that will bring extinction early next century. In a triumph of environmentalist rhetoric over conservation however the Convention of International Trade in Endangered Species in October 1989 declared all trade in elephant products illegal. The successful elephant-management programs of Zimbabwe and other southern-African countries are now in jeopardy as a result.

More serious problems arise with resources that have few ownership examples. Full property rights may be feasible for some of these. Consider groundwater and its similarity to subterranean oil pools. Both are underground liquid resources; both are subject to depletion and loss of quality. To address these problems, the oil industry has pioneered the concept of "unitization," which entails the assignment of all individual ownership rights to a new entity (the "unit"). The unit manager then operates the field in an integrated fashion and compensates each owner based on individual agreements. That process is complex and costly but has been used successfully by the oil industry for many years and the concept might be extended to aquifers.

Even partial property rights can play a critical role in heading off environmental problems. For example, property rights in shellfish, fish, and waterfowl would create organizations that would be concerned about deterioration in water quality. In Scotland and northern England, property rights to freshwater fish are recognized. In the 1955 *Pride of Darby* case, a fishing club successfully enjoined an upstream polluter from harming its fish, thus improving the quality of the stream as well.

An extension of the property-rights concept to protect urban air is more difficult. Conceptually, one can envision ownership of airsheds; however, we have little understanding of how such properties might be "fenced" or how "trespass" might be detected and prevented. Such problems have led most people to accept political airshed management. But political agencies charged with air-pollution control have veered from ignoring pollution in favor of growth to seeking atmospheric protection with no regard to cost.

A property-rights approach to pollution would unravel the complex sequence of events leading to environmental damage. Tracers might be added to pollutants to ensure that damage was detected early, when the costs of reduction would be lower. (Natural-gas companies employed this method decades ago by adding substances with pronounced odors to reduce the likelihood of undetected gas leaks.) With all potentially damaged resources under private ownership, such a system might even lift the smog in Los Angeles.

Once a property-rights scheme exists, then creative energies will be directed to reducing the costs of fencing and protecting property. An illustration is provided in the difficulty faced by nineteenth-century Western cattle ranchers. Neither wood nor stone fences were feasible in this area; the rancher thus used branding to distinguish their various herds and made side payments if cattle grazed too often on other ranches. Cowboys were hired to ride the perimeters and drive the cattle back within the property boundaries. The cost of these manned fences was high and their effectiveness was low. These drawbacks created a profit potential for anyone inventing a better way of protecting property, and that incentive stimulated the invention of barbed wire. Free-marketeers argue that in areas where solutions are difficult to imagine given current technology, a property-rights regime increases the prospects for better solutions.

Earth's atmosphere is the classic example. The scientific evidence on the likely magnitude of global warming is best characterized as ambiguous. If the greenhouse effect proves to be real, however it will require realistic solutions. An international treaty to reduce greenhouse emissions would not be adhered to. Since there are natural as well as man-made sources of carbon dioxide, methane, and nitrous oxides, verification would be enormously difficult. Carbon taxes and mandated emissions cutbacks would penalize the countries that now supply most of the world's wealth, while blocking an improved standard of living for the developing countries. And all the mitigation strategies so far proposed would only delay the onset of any temperature shift by a matter of years.

This suggests that a policy of resiliency and adaptation is called for. It would be better to reduce the barriers to wealth creation than to spend trillions of dollars in a doomed attempt to beat back the waves of change, whose direction is anyway unpredictable. Greater wealth would make possible many measures which would make climate change less onerous. And as we learn more about the problems, entrepreneurs would have both the knowledge and the incentive to devise imaginative solutions based on property rights.

Meanwhile, in those areas which are not readily amenable to a property-rights approach, and even in those which are, it is important to stress that there are still other approaches than bureaucratic regulation and command-and-control strategies.

For example, we should first stop the government-subsidized destruction of the environment. A good principle is: First, do no harm. For nearly a century, agricultural agencies and especially the Department of Agriculture have been subsidizing the destruction of wetlands and their conversion to croplands. Perverse incentives such as property taxes based on highest and best use have also encouraged farmers to convert wetlands and riparian areas that would be far more valuable left as they are. If taxes are the same on land yielding two hundred bushels per acre as on land producing twenty bushels, you might as well attempt to get some product from the land. Such examples are commonly used to argue against a profit-oriented agricultural system. But it is not the system that is at fault—it is the government's perverse incentives. The same holds for crop-support schemes that encourage farmers to maximize production by planting roadside-to-roadside and eliminating environmentally valuable hedgerows, windbreaks, shelterbelts, and stream buffers. If we stop encouraging the nation's farmers to destroy environmental amenities, there will be no reason to enforce national or state land-use control, or to take back wetlands through regulation, acquisition, and long prison sentences.

Another singularly important step would be to return to the polluter-pays principle, which has been increasingly abandoned as the environmentalist community has discovered the deep pockets of the Fortune 500. Why hold an individual responsible for his environmental damages, they argue, if one can force an entire well-to-do industry to pay far more? But this not only destroys the incentive for individuals and corporations to assume full responsibility for their actions, but also destroys incentives for innovation, improvements, responsibility, and stewardship by socializing costs and risks.

A striking example where this approach should be brought to bear is the EPA's ambient-air-quality standards for ozone (urban smog) and carbon monoxide. Although only a handful of urban areas still have serious ozone and carbon-monoxide problems, and although a relatively small percentage of cars produce a substantial percentage of the pollution, the regulatory approach has been to force all areas of the country, all cars, and all drivers to bear additional costs regardless of their contributions to such pollution.

Rather than identify the polluting cars and make them pay for the environmental harm they do through some form of pollution surcharge, the regulatory approach has been to force society to bear the costs by mandating the installation of on-board canisters (which pose fire risks) on all new automobiles and expensive Stage II gasoline pumps to recover vapors. What these efforts will do is to continue to waste the accumulated wealth of society, force cleanups in areas that don't need them, keep older, more pollutive cars on the road longer, and drive marginal gas stations out of business.

For a long time the USSR was superior to the U.S. in urban air pollution caused by private automobiles, because for all intents and purposes there were no private automobiles. Attempting to duplicate that dubious achievement in the U.S. today hardly seems an enlightened form of environmental protection.

People matter. Given the chance, they can and will assume stewardship over portions of the environment. In contrast, current policies assign the individual no role, save to lobby for more powers for the state, for higher taxes, and for reduced economic freedom.

In recent months, the television screens have shown dramatic scenes of environmental and economic disasters: dead elephants and fleeing East Germans. Free-marketeers note that the causes of these two disasters were the same: both the African ecology and the East German economy have been excluded from the world market. The failure of economic central planning has finally forced reform on Eastern Europe. That same inherent flaw will eventually force reform in the environmental field. Russians, Eastern Europeans, and Nicaraguans have learned that true prosperity is achieved not through the elimination, but through the encouragement, of private property. Americans, having provided the example, should not abandon the principle.

OUR SURVIVAL DEPENDS ON SAVING OTHER SPECIES

Donella Meadows

The ozone hole and the greenhouse effect have entered our public vocabulary, but we have no catchy label for the third great environmental problem of the late 20th century. It's even more diffuse than depletion of the ozone layer or global warming, harder to grasp and summarize.

The experts call it "the loss of biodiversity."

Obviously, biodiversity has something to do with pandas, tigers and tropical forests. But preserving biodiversity is a much bigger job than protecting rain forests or charismatic megafauna. It's the job of protecting all life—microscopic creepy-crawlies as well as elephants and condors—and all life's habitats—tundra, prairie and swamp as well as forests.

Why care about tundras, swamp, blue beetles or little bluestem grasses? Ecologists give three reasons, which boil down to simple self-interest on three levels of escalating importance:

• Biodiversity has both immediate and potential economic value.

This is the argument most commonly put forward to defend biodiversity, because it's the one our culture is most ready to hear. It cites the importance of the industries most directly dependent upon nature—fisheries, forestry, tourism, recreation and the harvesting of wild foods, medicines, dyes, rubber and chemicals.

Some ecologists wearily call this line of reasoning the "Madagascar periwinkle argument." That obscure plant yields the drugs vincristine and vinblastine, which have revolutionized the treatment of leukemia.

About a third of all modern medicines have been derived from molds and plants. The potential for future discoveries is astounding. The total number of species of life is somewhere between 10 million and 30 million, only 1.7 million of which we have named, only a fraction of which we have tested for usefulness.

The economic value of biodiversity is very real, but ecologists hate the argument because it is both arrogant and trivial. It assumes that the Earth's millions of species are here to serve the economic purposes of just one species. And it misses the larger and more valuable ways that nature serves us, even if we never name or harvest its millions of species.

• Biodiversity performs environmental services beyond price.

How would you like the job of pollinating all trillion or so apple blossoms in New York state some sunny afternoon in late May? It's conceivable, maybe, that you could invent a machine to do it, but inconceivable that the machine could work as elegantly and cheaply as the honeybee, much less make honey on the side.

Suppose you were assigned to turn every bit of dead organic matter, from fallen leaves to urban garbage to road kills, into nutrients that feed new life. Even if you knew how, what would it cost? A host of bacteria, molds, mites and worms do it for free. If they ever stopped, all life would stop.

We would not last long if green plants stopped turning our exhaled carbon dioxide back into oxygen. Plants would not last long if a few genera of soil bacteria stopped turning nitrogen from the air into nitrate fertilizer.

Human reckoning cannot put a value on the services performed by the ecosystems of Earth. In addition to pollination and nutrient recycling, these services include the cleansing of air and water, flood control, drought prevention, pest control, temperature regulation and maintenance of the world's most valuable library—the genes of all living organisms.

• Biodiversity contains the accumulated wisdom of nature and the key to its future.

If you ever wanted to destroy a society—not just damage it, but put it beyond hope of resuscitation—you would burn its libraries and kill its intellectuals. You would destroy its knowledge.

Nature's knowledge is contained in the DNA within living cells. The variety of that genetic information is the driving engine of evolution, the immune system for life, and the source of adaptability. This applies not just to the variety of species but also to the variety of individuals within each species.

Individuals are never quite alike. Each is genetically unique, mostly in subterranean ways that will appear only in future generations. We recognize that is true of human beings. Plant and animal breeders recognize it in dogs, cattle, wheat, roses, apples. The only reason they can bring forth bigger fruits or sweeter smells or stronger disease resistance is that those traits are already present in the genes carried by some individuals.

The amount of information in a single cell is hard to comprehend. A simple one-celled bacterium can carry genes for 1,000 traits, a flowering plant for 400,000.

Biologist E. O. Wilson says the information in the genes of an ordinary house mouse, if translated into print, would fill all the 15 editions of the Encyclopedia Britannica that have been published since 1768. And each house mouse is slightly different from all the others.

The wealth of genetic information has been selected over billions of years to fit the ever-changing necessities of the planet. As Earth's atmosphere filled with oxygen, as land masses drifted apart, as humans invented agriculture and altered the land, there were lurking within individuals pieces of genetic codes that allowed them to defend against or take advantage of the changes. These individuals were more fit for the new environment. They bred more successfully. The population began to take on their characteristics. New species came into being.

Biodiversity is the accumulation of all life's past adaptations, and it is the basis for all further adaptations (even those mediated by human genesplicers).

That's why ecologists value biodiversity as one of the Earth's great resources, as great as oil deposits or topsoils or fresh water. That's why they take seriously the loss of even the most insignificant of species; why they defend not only the preservation of species but the preservation of populations within species, and why they regard the current rate of human-induced extinctions as an unparalleled catastrophe.

We don't know how many species we are eliminating, because we don't know how many species there are. It's a fair guess that at the rate we're destroying habitat, especially but not exclusively in the tropics, we're pushing to extinction about one species every hour. That doesn't count the species whose populations are being reduced so greatly that diversity within the population is essentially gone. Earth has not seen a spasm of extinctions like this for 65 million years.

Biologists estimate that human beings usurp, directly or indirectly, about 40 percent of each year's total biological production (and our population is on its way to another doubling in 40 years). There is hardly a place on Earth where people do not log, pave, spray, drain, flood, graze, fish, plow, burn, drill, spill or dump. There is no life zone, with the possible exception of the deep ocean, that we are not degrading.

In poor countries, biodiversity is being nickeled and dimed to death; in rich countries it is being billion-dollared to death.

Biologists also call this "loss of diversity" by another name—"biotic impoverishment." What is impoverished is not just biodiversity; it is the human economy and human spirit.

Ecologist Paul Ehrlich describes biotic impoverishment this way: "Unless current trends are reversed, Americans will gradually be living in a nation that has fewer warblers and ducks and more starlings and herring gulls, fewer native wildflowers and more noxious weeds, fewer swallowtail butterflies and more cockroaches, smaller herds of elk and bigger herds of rats, less edible seafood, less productive croplands, less dependable supplies of pure fresh water, more desert wastes and dust storms, more frequent floods and more uncomfortable weather."

Biodiversity cannot be maintained by protecting a few species in a zoo, nor by preserving greenbelts or even national parks. To function properly, nature needs more room than that. It can maintain itself, however, without human expense, without zookeepers, park rangers, foresters or gene banks. All it needs is to be left alone.

To provide their priceless pollination service, the honeybees ask only that we stop saturating the landscape with poisons, stop paving the meadows where their food grows, and start leaving them enough honey to get through the winter.

To maintain our planet, our lives and our future potential, the other species have similar requests, all of which add up to this: Control yourselves. Control your numbers. Control your greed. See yourselves as what you are, part of an interdependent biological community—the most intelligent part, though you don't often act that way.

So act that way, either out of a moral respect for something magnificent that you did not create and do not understand, or out of a practical interest in your own survival.

♦ *4* ♦

GIVING REASONS

WHAT A REASON DOES

A reason is any idea that functions to support another idea. It is nothing more than the answer to an implicit question, "Why?" It invites the reader to agree with one statement by linking it to another statement that explains why it is true. A reason, then, is anything one might say after *because* or before *therefore*. Reasons, of course, do not have to be connected to conclusions by such words. They can imply such a relationship simply by being asserted along with the conclusion.

> *The present arms control negotiations do not go far enough.*
> *These negotiations do not include discussion of biological and chemical weapons.*

These two assertions are connected by an implicit "because." If they were presented in reverse order, they would seem to be connected by an implicit "therefore." Any assertion can function as a reason.

> *The current administration is not really serious about arms control.*
> *The present arms control negotiations do not go far enough.*

Here, the same assertion that functioned as a conclusion has taken on the role of a reason when put beside a different assertion.

No idea is necessarily a reason or a conclusion until it is put into relation with another idea. Reasoning is a process of creating relationships between ideas in such a way that belief in one is intended to follow as a consequence of belief in another.

Before going any further into the question of how reasons work, I want to clarify one possible confusion that results from the ambiguity of the word *reason*. The word can refer to an explanation of cause or motive, or it can refer to a statement that argues for belief. This distinction is important, because in talking about reasoning in this chapter I am focusing on the second meaning. Statements that explain "why" without actually arguing in support of another statement are also called "reasons." For instance, if I said "I want to go to the mountains for my vacation *because* I have hay fever and need to get away from the grass seed pollens," I would have explained my reason, but I would not have given a reason to believe that it is in fact the case that "I want to go the mountains." Of course, no such argument is needed in this case, an explanation will suffice. But there are many instances in which this distinction might be crucial. Here is an assertion:

> *The Supreme Court has made it harder for black citizens to achieve representation in Congress.*

If I responded to this assertion by asking "Why?" I might be asking either for an explanation or for a reason to believe the assertion. In answer to my questions, I might get answers of either sort:

> *Because the Court is inherently racist.*

or

> *Because the Court has repealed voter's rights legislation.*

The first reason answers the question "Why has the Court made it harder for black citizens to achieve representation" or "What are its motives?" The second reason answers the question "Why should I believe that assertion is true?" Both of these are reasons. Each is potentially important. But only the latter reason argues directly for the assertion to be believed. So when I said that "Reasoning is a process of creating relationships between ideas in such a way that belief in one is intended to follow as a consequence of belief in another," I did not use *reasoning* to refer to the kinds of explanations we often introduce with the word *because*. I am referring to those "because" statements that answer the implicit question, "Why should I believe that that assertion is the case?"

In this sense any assertion can function either as a conclusion or as a reason, because any assertion that is used to substantiate another (answering "Why is it true?") can also be substantiated by another reason. Here, for instance, is a paragraph in which some of the sentences seem to have this dual function:

> Ours is a paradoxical world. The achievements which are its glory threaten to destroy it. The nations with the highest standard of living, the greatest

capacity to take care of their people economically, the broadest education, and the most enlightened morality and religion exhibit the least capacity to avoid mutual destruction in war. It would seem that the more civilized we become the more incapable of maintaining civilizations we are.*

This writer has made a series of assertions, without labeling them as reasons or conclusions by adding connective phrases. But we experience the sentences as functioning logically anyway, simply by understanding what one sentence has to do with another. After analyzing these relationships, we could make them explicit (at the expense, perhaps, of the dignity of the author's prose):

> Ours is a paradoxical world. *How do I know this? Because* the achievements which are its glory threaten to destroy it. *I think this is the case because* the nations with the highest standard of living, the greatest capacity to take care of their people economically, the broadest education, and the most enlightened morality and religion exhibit the least capacity to avoid mutual destruction in war. It would, *therefore,* seem that the more civilized we become the more incapable of maintaining civilization we are.

The first sentence is supported by a reason in sentence two, which in turn becomes the conclusion of another, more detailed reason in sentence three. The last sentence is a conclusion based on the reasons offered in sentences two and three, which is itself a reason explaining the general assertion in the first sentence. People often speak of writing as having a "line of reasoning" because the sentences of prose are often held together in this way; one reason gives rise to the need for another. Reasoning is the glue that holds the ideas together.

As this example also illustrates, any reason, because it is an assertion, can be supported by another. But a writer cannot keep supporting reasons with reasons forever. This passage comes at the beginning of a book that offers much more specific support for these general claims as it goes along. But, however much support is given, it must stop somewhere. At some point, the writer must decide to stop answering the question "Why?" A line of reasoning must result from consideration of what assertions to support and what reasons to develop, because it cannot, obviously, support and develop all potential lines of reasoning that might be followed. Of all the potential reasons for asserting that "Ours is a paradoxical world," this writer had to choose those he thought best. Then he had to decide how far to pursue the line of reasoning he had chosen. Writers can make such decisions only by asking themselves what makes a good reason and how far it must be developed. In order to pursue one line of reasoning, we have to give up the pursuit of some other. Our problem as writers of arguments is to decide which of many possible lines is worth pursuing and which is not. This consideration, in relation to a thesis, will be what determines the shape, or structure, of the composition.

---

* F. S. C. Northrop, *The Meeting of East and West* (New York: Macmillan Publishers, 1946), p. 1.

THE ENTHYMEME

At this point, we need a name for the relationship created between a reason and a conclusion. I will call this combination of assertions an **enthymeme**, a term adopted from classical rhetoric. It is more open and flexible than any of the terms I might have adopted from formal logic. For many people, *logic* suggests mathematical formulas and rules that must be followed. We'll get around in this chapter to considering some logical concepts, but it is best to think about reasoning first as a natural process and not as a system of rules. We reason all the time, usually without trying to follow any rules or fit our thoughts into predefined patterns. We make connections between ideas without stopping to consider whether those connections conform to logical models. I will use the term *enthymeme* to refer to any combination of ideas in which a conclusion of any kind is supported by a reason.

Enthymemes occur throughout our discourse whenever we connect ideas in this way:

Idea 1	*because*	Idea 2

or

Idea 1	*therefore*	Idea 2

In the first case, Idea 1 is the conclusion. In the second case, Idea 2 is the conclusion. The following pairings of ideas are each enthymemes because they connect a conclusion to a reason:

> *The toxic waste disposal business is a noble career goal, because a healthy environ-*
> *ment in the future will depend on proper elimination of harmful chemicals.*
> *Free the monkeys now! (We need the laughs.)*
> *We have to win this election. So vote early and vote often!*

As the examples show, the conclusion–reason model by itself does not guarantee that an enthymeme makes connections that are reasonable. Some ideas can be put into such a relationship and seem unreasonable while others seem reasonable. What makes the difference? What makes some enthymemes seem compelling? What makes a conclusion seem to follow?

The relationship created between a reason and a conclusion is not self-contained. It makes implicit reference to other ideas that help to bind the reason to the conclusion, making it seem to follow. Before discussing serious examples of this process, let me give you a nonsense one, just to show how it works:

Suppose you walk into the room where I am studying and you say, "I saw the King walking down the street last night." My face lights up, and I shout, "I knew it! Elvis is alive." Have I jumped to a conclusion? Well, that depends. It depends on whether some other truth, which neither of us said aloud, is true. That statement is, of course: "Elvis is the King."

I used your statement as evidence, as a reason. But that reason seems like a reason only because it relies on our believing the idea that neither of us stated and applying it to the evidence. The conclusion seems to follow because an assumption connects the reason and the conclusion. In this case, the assumption is applied to the evidence in a rather strange way. If anyone heard us and said, "Elvis is not the King," then my reasoning would fall to pieces.

So, the inferential process worked something like this:

> Stated reason: *The King is alive.*
> Unstated assumption: *Elvis is the King.*
> Stated conclusion: *Elvis is alive.*

As long as this unstated assumption is a matter of agreement between us, my reason will seem like a reason. As soon as that assumption is denied, or if it is not shared at the outset, then my reason seems like no reason at all.

When enthymemes are asserted, they imply more than they say since reasons somehow appeal to assumptions that constitute the given condition behind the enthymeme's reasoning. Enthymemes therefore can be said to derive from beliefs that the particular audience is assumed already to have accepted as given. The choice of one reason or another to support a conclusion results from an understanding of what sorts of agreements can be assumed.

If I were to argue, for instance, that "America is in great shape," I could draw on a wide variety of potential reasons to use as support for this assertion. If I chose to support it by saying "because hamburger consumption grows by 10 per cent every year," I would be making a very risky assumption (as well as imagining a very uncritical reader who would share it). I would be basing my reasoning on the implied precondition that consumption of hamburgers is an index to a country's well-being. If I chose to support the assertion by arguing "because our products set the trends in international markets," I would be assuming my reader already believed that "Any country that sets the trends for other countries' markets must be in great shape," also a risky assumption. If I chose to argue the assertion by saying "because national unemployment has fallen to 6 per cent," I might be basing my reasoning on an assumption that is somewhat more likely to be acceptable to a critical audience, that falling rates of unemployment signify national health. This is not a complete argument, of course, but it is on somewhat firmer ground.

Here is an example of enthymemes used in an actual argument, a brief passage from Martin Luther King Jr.'s famous "Letter from Birmingham Jail" (1963):

> A law is unjust if it is inflicted on a minority that, as a result of being denied the right to vote, had no part in enacting or devising the law. Who can say that the legislature of Alabama which set up the state's segregation

laws was democratically elected? Throughout Alabama all sorts of devious methods are used to prevent Negroes from becoming registered voters, and there are some counties in which, even though Negroes constitute a majority of the population, not a single Negro is registered. Can any law enacted under such circumstances be considered democratically structured?

King's reasoning here supports the conclusion that Alabama's segregation laws are unjust. This conclusion is itself unstated, but we perceive it because the reasoning makes it seem to follow. That reasoning depends on enthymemes that also work on the basis of assumptions, either stated or unstated:

> Conclusion: *Alabama's segregation laws are unjust.*
> Reason: *Those laws are inflicted on a minority that had no role in enacting them.*
> Assumption: *Any law that is inflicted on a minority that had no role in enacting it is an unjust law.*

The reason here is itself the conclusion of another enthymeme:

> Conclusion: *African Americans had no role in enacting Alabama's segregation laws.*
> Reason: *African Americans were prevented from voting for the state legislature.*
> Assumption: *Anyone prevented from voting for the legislature has no role in enacting laws passed by that legislature.*

Real arguments, like King's, are often hard to reduce to the underlying enthymemes from which they derive their reasoning. But such enthymemes are there, nevertheless, providing the basis on which the argument's actual sentences are formed. The enthymemes represent the reasoning of the argument, even though that reasoning may be explicit or implicit, directly or indirectly conveyed in the language of the argument.

We have thus far talked about enthymemes as a basic structure of reasoning. We have distinguished three kinds of statements that make up enthymemes: conclusion; stated reason; and unstated reason, or assumption. There are different ways to talk about these kinds of statements and the relations among them, and none of these ways can be said to be the only correct one. In the sections that follow, I will first discuss informal, and then formal, reasoning.

INFORMAL REASONING

In our various discourse communities we rarely demand a standard of proof as rigorous as that which pertains in science and mathematics. Some people think that we ought to demand such a standard, but they are not always able to define it. The mathematical truth that $9 + 5 = 14$ is expressed in symbols that are assumed to mean exactly the same thing to everyone. The quantities referred to by the numbers and the operations referred to by the symbols are stable. But language is not like that. Some statements in plain language can be said to come very close to this degree of certainty: "Water is wet." Obviously. But the statement is self-evident; that is, it needs no evidence other than itself. It is so obvious that no one would argue with it. And if anyone did decide to argue with it, testing its self-evidence, they would begin by asking "What do these words mean?" This is one of the ways that lawyers are taught to think of the so-called self-evident in language. It seems self-evident that, if there is a law against spitting on the sidewalk, and if somebody spits on the sidewalk, he or she has broken that law. Yet this person's lawyer might ask us to ponder the unpleasant (and deceptively simple) question "What is spit?" before rendering judgment. We might, in the process, discover that what seemed obvious is not.

So when we reason about ideas that are not self-evident and when we use ordinary language (rather than mathematical symbols) to do it, we must think of reasoning as an activity *guided* by a sense of probability but not *governed* by rules of valid inference. In other words, rather than mathematical formulas to tell us whether our reasons lead to true belief in our conclusions, we rely instead on our sense that they *seem* to support conclusions with more or less certainty. Although rules guide our sense that $9 + 5 = 14$, no such rules are available to us to account fully for our belief (or disbelief) in statements about real issues, statements such as "Computer simulations can replace tests on live animals in medical research" or "The Sandinista guerrillas are justified in their actions because they are trying to achieve democracy in Nicaragua." In the world of real issues that demand real answers from us, we must settle for assent based on the best available reasons rather than absolute truth based on perfectly reliable methods of inference.

Just because real arguments are somewhat sloppy compared to the elegant and strict proofs of mathematics does not mean that we cannot talk with some precision about how they work and apply some standards to them. We have already applied one informal standard to argumentation in the last chapter, by showing how an argument must address a question at issue (or stasis question) or it will not address the concerns of the intended audience.

Another way to talk about arguments is ask whether they move from general to particular or from particular to general. It is possible for a reason to be stated in the form of a general principle from which a more specific conclusion is inferred. Or, it is possible for a reason to be stated in the form of a specific instance from which a more general conclusion is inferred. Here are some examples of each kind of enthymeme:

From general to specific:
1. *Grades should be abolished, because the purpose of education is to teach people, not to rank them.*
2. *Handguns should not be outlawed because the second amendment of the U.S. Constitution establishes the right to bear arms.*
3. *War would be less likely if women outnumbered men in the Senate, because women naturally seek compromise more readily than men.*

From specific to general:

1. *Grades do not accurately assess what students have learned because test scores reveal only a small part of the knowledge a student may have.*
2. *Handgun ownership should be unregulated because many people have protected themselves from violent assault using unlicensed handguns.*
3. *More women need to be elected to the Senate because 95 per cent of women in state legislatures voted pro-choice.*

Of course, "general" and "specific" are relative to each other. No statement is inherently either general or specific, although it may seem so when compared to another statement. Thus, the conclusion that "The Olympic Games promote world peace" could be said to be general in relation to this reason:

because countries with incompatible types of government must learn to compete in athletics using the same rules.

but specific in relation to this one:

because world peace is made more likely whenever countries cooperate to bring about international events.

Why does it matter whether an argument goes from specific to general, or from general to specific? Neither way is better nor will yield more reliable reasons. But it is important to think about when circumstances may call for one or another kind of reasoning. If general principles can be assumed to be shared, then specific arguments can proceed on that basis. But if specifics can be taken for granted, general principles may not be. It depends, like so many other rhetorical choices, on the audience.

You may already have noticed from these enthymemes that when specific reasons are stated, general principles tend to be assumed, and vice versa. Here's a simple example:

Conclusion: *Rap music is designed to shock parents . . .*
Stated reason: *. . . because its lyrics advocate teenage sexuality.*
Assumption: *Parents are shocked by lyrics that advocate teenage sexuality.*

This argument is based on the specific kinds of lyrics contained in the songs and would be developed by showing how those lyrics do in fact advocate teenage sexuality. The audience does not need any more evidence that such lyrics are shocking to parents. But this emphasis assumes a certain kind of audience. Consider the difference if the stated reason is changed from the specific one to the general one:

Conclusion: *Rap music is designed to shock parents . . .*
Stated reason: *. . . because parents are shocked by lyrics that advocate teenage sexuality.*
Assumption: *Rap lyrics advocate teenage sexuality.*

This argument assumes an audience that already knows what the lyrics advocate but does not already agree about what does and does not shock parents. Thus, some reasons might need to be developed while others can be allowed to remain undeveloped because they are assumed. This decision depends on whether the audience is most likely to agree on the general principle or on the specific facts. Of course, developing both kinds of reasons is often necessary, too.

When it is the general principle that can be assumed and the specific reason that must be developed, the reason is sometimes said to define **the burden of proof**. The term probably brings to mind a courtroom because in court settings the law itself is not on trial and forms the general principle of most arguments, so that the facts and whether they fit the general law must be argued:

> Conclusion: *Sidney S. must pay child support to Sylvia R.*
> Stated reason (burden of proof): *Sidney is the natural father of Suzie R., Sylvia's two-year-old daughter.*
> Assumption: *The law requires men to pay child support to mothers of children they father.*

If Sylvia's lawyer can establish that Sidney is the natural father, the conclusion will follow. If Sidney's lawyer can show that fact to be wrong, the conclusion will not follow. Neither spends any time arguing that the assumption is or is not true. (They will leave that argument for an appeal to the Supreme Court.*)

The concept of "burden of proof" functions in other kinds of arguments, too, even though the proof called for may not be a factual kind.

> Conclusion: *State education money should not be used to fund intercollegiate athletics . . .*
> Stated reason (burden of proof): *. . . because intercollegiate athletics has a negative effect on the education of the students.*
> Assumption: *State education money shouldn't pay for anything that has a negative effect on the education of students.*

In any real situation in which this argument would be proposed, the stated reason would have to be developed and the assumption would probably need no further explanation. (Once again, this depends, of course, on the audience.) But although this reason establishes the burden of proof, the statement cannot be proved except to offer more reasons. *Burden of proof* can simply mean *burden of development.*

So far I have used the term *enthymeme* to refer to any combination of reason and conclusion, and shown how any enthymeme necessarily relies on an assumption. From this a simple three-part model for argument has emerged.

---

* For an example of arguments about the definition of the law itself and whether it fits facts that are not themselves under dispute, see the Supreme Court decisions in the Appendix.

Any idea can function in any of these three roles in a particular argument.

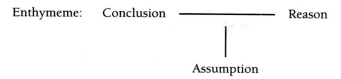

Enthymeme: Conclusion ————————— Reason

Assumption

But statements within actual arguments can have a much wider range of roles than these, causing us to need more than three terms to discuss them.

The Toulmin Model

A somewhat more complex model for informal reasoning is one developed by the twentieth-century British philosopher Stephen Toulmin. Toulmin thinks that the terms of formal logic are not flexible enough to account for the variety of actual arguments. He believes that the standards of symbolic logic do not apply very well to most arguments made in ordinary language. Consequently, Toulmin has sought to find a way to talk about the parts of all arguments (formal and informal) that is different from the models of ideal scientific logic.

Toulmin wrote of the "layout" of arguments using the following six terms:

Claim: *The idea being argued.*
Data: *The facts we appeal to as the foundation for the claim.*
Warrants: *The general, hypothetical (and often implicit) statements that serve as bridges between claim and data.*
Qualifiers: *Statements that limit the strength of the argument or that propose conditions in which it applies.*
Rebuttals: *Statements that indicate circumstances in which the argument might have to be set aside.*
Backing: *Statements that serve to support warrants.*

The terms *claim, data,* and *warrant* are very close in meaning to the terms I have been using to describe the parts of enthymemes: *conclusion, reason,* and *assumption.* The biggest difference is between *data* and *reason,* because *data* for Toulmin refers to factual statements. The addition of the other three terms as specific features of arguments clarifies the role of statements that go along with enthymemes.

Toulmin's own diagram for the relation between these features of arguments looks like this:

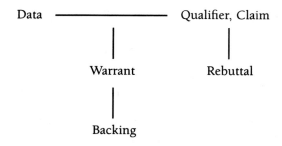

Data ————————— Qualifier, Claim

Warrant   Rebuttal

Backing

And he provides the following example:

> Harry was born in Bermuda (Data) so, presumably (Qualifier), he must be a British subject (Claim). He wouldn't be only if his parents were not themselves British subjects (Rebuttal). Otherwise, any person born in Bermuda will be considered a British subject (Warrant), according to the following statutes (Backing): . . .*

Toulmin's vocabulary can be very useful in determining the function of various statements in an argument. It also reminds us that arguments generally are expressed with qualifiers and rebuttals, rather than asserted as absolutes. These parts of the argument are necessary to let the reader know how to take the reasoning, how far it is meant to be applied, and how general it is meant to be. Here is another example of an argument analyzed in this way:

> *Congress should ban animal research (Claim) because animals are tortured in experiments that have no necessary benefit for humans, such as the testing of cosmetics (Data). The well-being of animals is more important than the profits of the cosmetics industry (Warrant). Only Congress has the authority to make such a law (Warrant) because the corporations can simply move from state to state (Backing). Of course, this ban should not apply to medical research (Qualifier). A law to ban all such research would go too far (Rebuttal).*
>
> *So the law would probably (Qualifier) have to be carefully written to define the kinds of research intended (Claim 2). . . .*

As the argument unfolds, its limits begin to appear as well as the strength of its claims. This is as it should be. No argument should pretend to be stronger or to apply further than it is meant to.

As this example shows, Toulmin's model still allows for the possibility that statements in an argument can have more than one of these roles. The Rebuttal in the example becomes the Warrant for another Claim. It is not always clear what role a given statement is playing. This terminology offers you a good way to analyze arguments by asking what role the statements play, even if the answers will sometimes seem ambiguous.

In the discussion of reasoning that follows, I will mainly be using the three-part model of the enthymeme. But Toulmin's terms will reappear when it is useful to note those other functions.

KINDS OF APPEAL

Another way to discuss reasoning informally is to distinguish reasons according to the kind of appeal that they make. I have already talked about the role

* This discussion is based on Stephen Toulmin, *The Uses of Argument* (London: Cambridge University Press, 1958), 1–20, 99–107.

of assumptions in making reasons seem like reasons. Next I want to explore what *kinds* of reasons are available to us.

In general, we can distinguish three kinds of appeal:

1. The appeal to authority.
2. The appeal to emotion.
3. The appeal to the logic of the case.

The first kind seeks to establish belief in an assertion by referring the audience to the credibility of a source. Appeals of this kind range from the writer's establishment of his or her own expertise to citations from others who are assumed to be believable on a given subject. It is a common form of reasoning, and it takes its power from our willingness to grant superior credibility to others based on their credentials. Such appeals depend on our willingness to accept an idea based on *who* says so.

The second kind of reason, the appeal to emotion, seeks to establish belief in an assertion by referring somehow to the reader's desires. Appeals of this kind can range from the writer's outright manipulation of the reader's feelings to the construction of reasons out of shared moral principles such as justice or mercy. This is also a common form of reasoning, and it takes its power from our willingness to grant superior credibility to ideas that correspond to our preference for what ought to be true.

The third kind of reason, the appeal to the logic of the case, seeks to establish belief in an assertion by showing it to be a necessary consequence of belief in some other idea or ideas. Appeals of this kind can range from the use of proven experimental data to the suggestion that one idea follows directly from the acceptance of another one. This common form of reasoning takes its power from the sense of necessity that accompanies logical inferences. Such appeals differ from the first and second kinds in that the conclusion seems to follow and to remain valid, no matter who says it or whether we wish it were true.

It might seem from this description that the third kind of reasoning is the best. To be sure, it is the "purest" kind of reasoning, insofar as it does not depend on the sometimes "irrelevant" considerations such as accepting authority or submitting to emotion. But these considerations often enter into our reasoning, to a greater or lesser degree depending on the kind of conclusion we are arguing. One could probably not persuade a mother and father that their love for a child is irrelevant to their reasoning about the child's education. An art critic could probably not be persuaded that emotion is irrelevant to his or her reasoning about the qualities of a painting. And although we all want to question authority, we all probably accept it as reasonable sometimes, as when we admit someone else's expertise. Even arguments that seem purely logical often seem to deserve more or less belief based on their source or on how well they accord with our desires. When it comes to reasoning, it is less important to try to do it "purely" than to try to do it well. All kinds of reasoning can be abused as well as used well. "Good" reasons come in all three kinds, depending on what we are reasoning about, who we are reasoning with, and who we are.

Perhaps the best way to demonstrate how these appeals work is to offer a few examples of enthymemes of each kind.

Appeals to Authority

Appeals to authority establish an idea based on the credibility of its source. Thus each of these examples, in its own way, is an appeal of this sort:

> *An exciting game of tennis relieves stress because it works for me.*
> *An exciting game of tennis relieves stress because it says so in Dr. Merit's* How to Relieve Stress.
> *An exciting game of tennis relieves stress because several studies have shown it.*

Here are three reasons put forth in support of the same assertion. These lines of reasoning might be developed further. Each suggests a different kind of discussion, however, and we must decide initially whether the basic reasoning underlying that potential development is sound. If we were to make this decision on the principle that appeals to authority are never sound, none of the examples could be said to provide a good reason for believing the conclusion. But, in fact, they provide adequate reasons for accepting the conclusion in certain circumstances.

If, for instance, the question at issue is whether tennis ever relieves stress, the testimony of a single individual that it does, as in the first example, would be one way of answering that question convincingly. Once that testimony had been given, who would dispute the fact that, for that individual, the claim holds true? This issue would be better supported by the reasoning in the first example than the reasoning established in the second example, because the best judge of whether one's own stress has been relieved is oneself, not the writer of a popular self-help book. But Dr. Merit's authority to make a general claim about the value of tennis for others may be greater than the authority of any single amateur based on a few Sundays on the court. If the issue is how best to relieve stress, the reasoning in the second example might be more adequate than in the first. This would depend, of course, on how credible Dr. Merit is. Why should I take his word for it? Because he signs himself "Dr."? Certainly not. I should only take his word for it based on what he has to say for himself. If all Merit has to say is that he has enjoyed many rousing tennis games and felt better afterward, then he could hardly be trusted as an authority on what other people ought to do. But if Merit's reasoning proceeds along the lines suggested in the third example, his authority might become more credible—as credible, at least, as the authors of the studies he cites.

Anyone can *say* that something is true "because several studies have shown it," but the speaker's authority is then only as good as the authority of those studies, whatever they are. Sloppy studies, based on inconclusive samples or weighted by inappropriate assumptions, need not *show* any such thing, even if that is what they conclude. Here, then, is an appeal to authority that is appropriate only if the studies themselves are reliable. Such an argument would have to depart from its appeal to authority and talk about the nature of the studies themselves. Studies can be used as appeals to authority or they can be used as appeals to the logic of the case. As mere authorities, studies will generally provide weak support. As a context for discussing the reasons that the studies themselves offer in support of a conclusion, their use can be quite appropriate.

The appeal to authority provides appropriate or inappropriate reasons, depending on whether someone's special knowledge, or testimony, is relevant to the issue. Some issues will call for such reasoning. It is important to consider, however, whether a conclusion would continue to be true no matter who asserted it—and if that is the case, authority might provide relevant reasons that are nevertheless insufficient. Suppose I were to argue, for instance, that

> U.S. foreign policy is inconsistent. My political science professor said so.

I could in that statement be said to have chosen a more appropriate appeal to authority than if I had chosen to argue the same conclusion by saying "Bruce Springsteen said so." My political science professor can probably be expected to know more about the subject than Bruce Springsteen does. But the appeal to authority is not my only choice, and probably not the best one. The issue underlying the assertion is not one that calls for anyone's testimony. It calls for an explanation of what it is *about* U.S. foreign policy that makes it inconsistent, independent of what my professor or anyone else might say. If I can read the newspaper, chances are I can offer this explanation without having to find an expert to agree with me.

Appeals to Emotion

Appeals to emotion can also provide appropriate reasons in certain circumstances. But, like appeals to authority, they do not generally offer the best support available unless the issue specifically makes the reader's desires relevant. Here are three examples of different reasons offered in support of a single conclusion:

> *Students should support the clerical workers' strike by boycotting classes because only scabs will go to class during the strike.*
>
> *Students should support the clerical workers' strike by boycotting classes because joining just causes shows courage.*
>
> *Students should support the clerical workers' strike by boycotting classes because the clerical workers are underpaid.*

In different ways, each of these reasons appeals to the reader's desire. The first example is a kind of threat, and it appeals to the reader's desire not to be thought of as a "scab." This kind of name-calling would probably not be effective, but there is a power nonetheless in reasons that act on the fears of the audience. "You should not go into Kasstle Park alone at night because if you do you may be a victim of a mugger." This is not an unreasonable statement, even if it uses a strategy similar to the "scab" argument. What makes that argument seem inappropriate, however, is that the issue—whether students should boycott classes—is not answered by such a threat, the way the issue of whether one should venture alone into Kasstle Park at night is answered by noting the potential danger. *Victims* is a term applied to people who are mugged, while *scab* is a label that is used to denigrate people who disagree. No one would choose to be a victim, but people can decide for reasons of their own not to participate in the boycott.

Just as the first example appeals to emotion by threatening the reader with a derogatory label, the second example works by flattering the reader with a positive image. The reasoning connects a desired image on the part of the reader with a desired action on the part of the writer. As a reason for believing that students should join a boycott of classes, however, the appeal is weak. It may flatter the reader into thinking that he or she can be a courageous defender of a just cause, but it does not provide support for the justice of the cause itself. The reader is asked to take part in a cause to be courageous, as if any cause would do. This answers the question of why students might *want* to join the clerical workers, but it does so in a way that serves the appearance of the students more than the cause itself.

In the third example, unlike the second, the reasoning answers the issue by referring to the needs of the workers. Hence, the third example seems to contain reasoning that is more relevant to the issue. The justness of the cause, not the reader's desire to escape or to acquire a particular image, is the basis of the appeal. However, that reasoning is also based on an appeal to emotion, because it arouses the reader's sympathy. Why, in other words, is the fact that the workers are underpaid a good reason to support them? It is a good reason because we desire that people should not be underpaid; we want fairness. Thus, although the reasoning seems more logical, it nevertheless depends on the reader's sense of compassion and a preference for fair treatment of the clerical workers. It may not be as blatant an appeal for sympathy as arguing that the workers cannot afford to feed their families, but it is the same kind of appeal.

The emotional appeal is often ridiculed as illogical—as in the joke about the man accused of killing his mother and father who asks the court for mercy because he is an orphan—but it is nevertheless an honest form of reasoning. In the case of issues having to do with what is right and just, such appeals are unavoidable, because our feelings inevitably, and properly, enter into our sense of what we *should* believe and do. In the example, the reason "because the workers are underpaid" is a value statement that functions to arouse our consciences. Some emotional appeals attempt to play on our feelings at the expense of reason, but others result from attempts to find reasons that are not "cold and objective," or devoid of human feeling.

Appeals to the Logic of the Case

Appeals to the logic of the case derive one idea from another independent of the writer's authority and the reader's sympathy. The use of this kind of reason does not guarantee that the specific reason chosen will be appropriate, of course. Here are some examples in which the reasoning is not always well chosen:

> *Commercial television threatens to diminish the intellectual standards of American society because most people would rather watch television than read.*
> *Commercial television threatens to diminish the intellectual standards of American society because it portrays people who value only money and status.*
> *Commercial television threatens to diminish the intellectual standards of American society because it demands no thought from the viewer.*

All of these enthymemes in some way draw inferences about television's threat from some alleged fact, but they provide more or less adequate answers to the question of why we should believe that threat exists. In the first example, even if it may be the case that many people would rather watch television than read, this in itself does not seem to address the question of why commercial television threatens intellectual standards. The reason seems somewhat remote from the conclusion. That reason is certainly *related to the topic,* but it does not seem directly *relevant to the issue.* After all, if these same people read nothing but trashy magazines, their intellectual standards might be as low or lower than if they watched television. It is the sort of reason that makes us want to respond with a "So what?"

The second example does address the nature of television and, therefore, has more relevance to the issue. But the way in which it attempts to make that connection is nevertheless inadequate. If it is the case that television portrays people who value only money and status (and, of course, such a generalization is itself too sweeping), this by itself has little relevance to television's threat to intellectual standards, unless viewers are assumed to hold the same values as the characters portrayed. It seems that the reasoning, although less remote, still is not complete.

Of the three examples, the third uses a line of reasoning that has the most potential to explain why the effect of television on the viewer is a threat to intellectual standards; it seeks to connect the conclusion not only to the nature of television but also to the nature of television's audience. It thus provides a better reason than the first two because its relevance is direct and apparent. If it were to be developed by showing *how* television places no demand on thought (the burden of proof) and by showing how this affects intellectual standards (whatever they are), then this reason might provide the basis for a fairly good, although not airtight, argument about the effects of television on society. It is an argument that you may have heard in one form or another. It is one that a few authorities have used to convince people, emotionally, of television's dangerous qualities. It may be an argument that contributes to making television better. At any rate, although it may have all of these functions, it is an argument based on the logic of the case, independent of who says it or whether we want to believe it. This argument will be convincing or not depending on how well each of the aspects of its logic can be supported.

FORMAL REASONING: SOME ELEMENTS OF LOGIC

Logic is often taught by using symbols and formulas that have little relation to the way actual arguments are formed. Because logic is the study of what makes valid inferences, it also often includes abstract models for valid and invalid logical forms. As interesting as all of that can be, it is not my concern in this book. Logic relates to argumentative writing only insofar as it helps you to understand how reasons work and how enthymemes necessarily derive from the beliefs of the audience. To be useful in argumentative writing, logic must be related to the beliefs of writers and readers and not simply serve to display abstract models of reasoning.

One useful distinction made in formal logic is the difference between induction and deduction. **Induction** is a process of inference by means of examples. **Deduction** is a process of inference by means of the syllogism.

Induction moves from the observations of specific instances to some kind of conclusion based on what they have in common. Thus, if I were to set a steel ball on an inclined plane and watch it roll down, and then if I were to do it again, I might conclude from these observations that it would happen the same way again. Induction results from observing similarities among instances and then forming hypotheses based on those similarities. Sometimes those general hypotheses can be fully tested, as in the following induction:

> Instance 1: *Your mother has green eyes.*
> Instance 2: *Your father has green eyes.*
> Instance 3: *Your sister has green eyes.*
> Instance 4: *So do you.*
> Conclusion: *Everyone in your family has green eyes.*

This conclusion has been fully tested by inductive means only if there are no other members of your family, of course. If there are, then the conclusion is not certain. Most often, inductions result in hypotheses that cannot be fully tested and that are not, therefore, certain. That is, only a sampling of the instances is available, and all instances cannot therefore be observed:

> Instance 1: *My math teacher is Armenian.*
> Instance 2: *My Spanish teacher is Portuguese.*
> Instance 3: *My economics teacher is Taiwanese. . . .*
> Conclusion: *This university must hire only foreign teachers.*

It is for this reason that induction is said to form probable inferences only. The degree of probability may be said to increase with the size of the sample, but even this is not a very reliable guide. Consider, for instance, this example:

> Instance 1: *Forty-three people sent back the questionnaire and all said that they had had a "religious experience" in their lives.*
> Instance 2: *Thirty-five said that they go to church "regularly."*
> Instance 3: *Twenty-nine said they were "born again."* . . .
> Conclusion: *America is made up of religious people.*

What is the size of the sample? Is it representative? Who is left out of the study? Inductive inferences must often be qualified. Of the two inferences drawn from these data, which is the more reasonable conclusion?

> Instance 1: *My health class is too easy.*
> Instance 2: *My psych class is too easy.*
> Instance 3: *My history class is too easy.* . . .
> Conclusion 1: *All classes at this university are too easy.*
> Conclusion 2: *I seem to get a lot of classes at this university that are too easy.*

Not enough data exist to draw the first inference, while enough might be said to exist for the second, less absolute, claim.

One of the risks of induction is that it can easily lead to overgeneralization. The conclusions of inductive reasoning may need to be phrased with qualifiers like *many, often, most,* and so on. As imprecise as such words are, they at least inform the reader that the conclusion is not meant to go beyond the evidence. Scientific inductions can be stated with more precision: In my experiment involving one hundred instances, Y occurred seventy-eight times. There is therefore a 78 percent probability that Y will occur under the same circumstances." In most other inductions, however, some kind of qualifier is needed to avoid overgeneralization: "Because all of the protesters I observed at the rally appeared to be over sixty-five, I'd say that young people do not seem to be interested in this issue." Does this conclusion seem like a hasty overgeneralization to you? Why or why not?

But even if an inductive conclusion is sufficiently qualified, it is still only as good as the observations that it is based on. In the "easy class" example above, for instance, one might object to my conclusion by saying that I am not a good judge of what is or is not an easy class, because I hardly ever bother to attend my classes. My logic might be sound, but my observations are flawed.

This means that logical conclusions can seem to follow and still be wrong or unworthy of assent. Logic as an abstract system does not concern itself with the truths of observations, but only with whether they are derived by valid means. The following is a valid induction:

> Instance 1: *Green M&Ms contain chloroform.*
> Instance 2: *Yellow M&Ms contain lye.*
> Instance 3: *Brown M&Ms contain strychnine.* . . .
> Conclusion: *This M&M is probably poisonous.*

But just being valid does not make it true. The instances from which the conclusion is derived are themselves false. Remembering that valid logic and truth are very different can keep you from jumping to conclusions that seem temptingly "logical." If you know people who are bigoted about race, gender, or religion, for instance, you might have heard them utter statements that were perfectly "logical," yet also quite wrong. Prejudice can be reinforced by inductions that adhere to valid logic but that derive from badly judged or misinterpreted observations. Prejudicially interpreted observations lead to pejudicial conclusions. Try listening, inductively, to examples of inductions by people who you think are sexist or racist to hear if their observations support their conclusions. (Then ask yourself about the prejudice of your own observations of them!)

Nearly any conclusion that can be justified by induction also can be justified by deduction, a different logical process. Deduction moves from general statements about the properties of some category to specific statements about other things in that category. If I wanted to argue that steel balls will roll down inclined planes, I would not need to use inductive means. I could make the case deductively:

> *Any object that is not obstructed in its movement along a plane surface will move in the direction of gravity, if friction is minimal. A steel ball has minimal friction. It will therefore roll down an inclined plane.*

Unlike an inductive argument, this one works by postulating a general principle and making a conclusion about a specific case that fits the principle. This process is most often described as a **syllogism**. We often construct syllogisms when we reason whether we know what they are or not. There are many kinds of syllogism that we might discuss, but it is enough, I think, to consider briefly its general form.

The categorical syllogism has three parts (in any order): a major premise, a minor premise, and a conclusion. To be put into the form of a syllogism, an argument needs to be restated so that these three parts are present. The nonsense dialogue we imagined earlier can be restated as a syllogism:

> Major premise: *Elvis is the King.*
> Minor premise: *I saw the King last night.*
> Conclusion: *I saw Elvis last night.*

(Notice that the conclusion can follow only if the word *King* means the same thing in each premise.) The conclusion follows as a consequence of the two linked premises. They are called "major" and "minor" because they refer to larger and smaller categories, as in this example:

> Major premise: *All sports have rules.*
> Minor premise: *Baseball is a sport.*
> Conclusion: *Baseball has rules.*

The conclusion here states a specific instance of the general principle asserted in the major premise, and it is connected to that premise by a minor premise that states that the specific subject is a member of the class referred to by the generalization in the major premise. That's a complicated way of saying a fairly simple thing—the mental process is easier to do than it is to describe. Why does the conclusion seem inescapable? Let's analyze this simple syllogism another way, in graphic form:

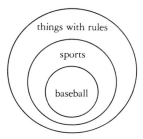

What these circles picture are categories defined by certain qualities. The category "sports" is shown to be a subcategory of "things with rules," and "baseball" is shown to be a subcategory of "sports." If these relations apply, then baseball is also necessarily a subcategory of "things with rules." Now, all that a syllogism does is to put these relations into words by asserting the conditions that apply to the categories. The conclusion asserts the relationship between the category "baseball" and the category "things with rules," a relationship that follows from those already established in the major and minor premises. In other words, any relation between "sports" and "things with rules" must be shared by "baseball" and "things with rules."

The three circles contain three "terms," as I call them, which the statements of the syllogism relate in different ways. Each of the three statements of a syllogism shares two of the three terms, and no two statements share the same two terms. These facts about the syllogism make it possible to reconstruct a complete syllogism from any two of its statements. From the conclusion and one of the premises, one can easily recreate the missing premise, because that premise must relate the two terms that are unshared by the conclusion and the stated reason. (See the following diagram.) This shows

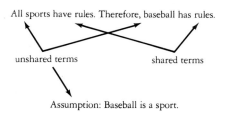

why any one reason and a conclusion imply the presence of another reason (the logical assumption).

In actual discourse, logical assumptions may be fully stated, but if not, they are always implied. Implied or unstated assumptions may be reconstructed by using the syllogism as a model, by looking for the relationship between the terms that are unshared by the conclusion and the stated reason. But remember that actual discourse rarely comes in the neat categorical statements of syllogisms (even though such logic may underlie the reasoning), so that the task of reconstructing unstated assumptions can become complex and unguidable by rules and formulas. In Toulmin's vocabulary for talking about these relationships (see page 105), such logical assumptions are called "warrants." But because it does not depend on the syllogism, his model leaves the reconstruction of such warrants, if they are unstated in the argument, up to the reader's intuition. This is probably how we, as readers and as arguers, understand such assumptions; they simply operate as givens based on our intuitive sense that our conclusions are connected to our reasons by the bridge of obvious truths. One reason to be more conscious of what the implied assumptions of our own and others' arguments are, however, is that those truths may not turn out to be so obvious after all.

Any enthymeme can be understood by using either the model of Toulmin's *claim/qualifier/data/warrant* or the model of the syllogism. Here is an example of a somewhat complex enthymeme:

> *Smoking should be banned from all campus offices, unless an office is not accessible to the public and all users of the office are themselves smokers*

> *Because*

> *Several studies have shown that nonsmokers who habitually breathe air polluted by secondary smoke face the same risk of lung disease as smokers.*

It is easy to see what the claim, qualifier, and data of this reasoning are. But the warrant is not so readily apparent, and we can understand it only by forming a hunch about what it might be. If the warrant consists of general statements that serve as a bridge between claim and data, then perhaps the reasoning may rely on more than one warrant. Several warrants seem to be operating here, such as:

> *The results of the cited studies are valid.*
> *Anyone who uses an office occupied by smokers habitually breathes air polluted by secondary smoke.*
> *Nonsmokers have a right to be free of the risk of lung disease.*
> *Banning smoking protects that right.*
> *Banning smoking will eliminate air polluted by secondary smoke.*
> *It is fair to smokers to prevent them from smoking in offices.*

All of these, and others, constitute the givens that must be accepted for the reasoning to work. As you can see, some of these givens are more assumable than others, and challenging any of them might provide a way for someone to challenge the whole argument.

Arguments often depend on what we might call "presumptions"— conditions in the real world that must be accepted for the reasoning to work. But not all presumptions form the logical assumption that functions as the major premise of the underlying syllogism. To separate the presumptions from the logical premises requires putting the reasoning into the form of a syllogism for the sake of analysis, and this seems difficult because the shared terms here are not obvious. To isolate the terms of the syllogism requires paraphrasing the argument so that the unshared and shared terms are more evident, an act of interpretation. The following is what I come up with when I try to paraphrase the above enthymeme as a syllogism:

> Major premise: *All people have the right to be protected from the risk of lung disease.*
> Minor premise: *Nonsmokers risk lung disease by breathing secondary smoke.*
> Conclusion: *Nonsmokers have the right to be protected from breathing secondary smoke.*

Such a paraphrase has the advantage of sorting out the one logical premise that governs the whole argument. It has the disadvantage of leaving many parts of the argument unstated. But this disadvantage is overcome by realizing that those parts of the argument may themselves be paraphrased as syllogisms for the purpose of finding the logical assumptions that govern their logic. For instance, another syllogism that is operating in the above enthymeme is:

> Major premise: *Any activity that causes risks to others should be banned.*
> Minor premise: *Smoking in public offices is an activity that causes risks to nonsmokers.*
> Conclusion: *Smoking in public offices should be banned.*

Thus, complex enthymemes may depend on several underlying syllogisms at the same time. The potential benefit of paraphrasing those syllogisms is that it reveals the logical assumptions.

Logical assumptions, as I said, may be challenged, primarily because they seem to function as universal truths. Does the major premise of the above syllogism seem to you to be universally true? If you can think of other instances of "activities that cause risk to others" that should not be banned, then perhaps that major premise is not one that you can automatically share. Finding logical assumptions by rephrasing arguments as syllogisms (as well as uncovering all the implicit warrants) can be an aid to measuring the degree to which you will assent to any argument. Here, for instance, is a simple enthymeme I once read in a campus newspaper:

> *Beer should be allowed to be sold in our student union because it will provide additional revenue for the student body.*

The underlying syllogism seems to be:

> Major premise: *Anything that will provide additional revenue for the student body should be allowed.*
> Minor premise: *Selling beer in the student union will provide additional revenue for the student body.*
> Conclusion: *Selling beer in the student union should be allowed.*

The writer of the enthymeme seems to have committed herself or himself to an untenable assumption, because the universal warrant provided by the major premise is not as universal as the enthymeme seems to suggest. Should selling cocaine be allowed for the same reason? If not, then the writer needs to be clearer about the boundaries of the argument. Qualifiers are needed.

Making logical assumptions that go too far is a risk in using deductive reasoning. Using the syllogism as an analytical tool can be one way of looking at the reasoning for the possibility of such overgeneralized assumptions. Another risk, which the syllogism can help to isolate, is the risk of circular reasoning.

The baseball syllogism I employed to illustrate the concept of "shared terms" uses the verb *is* as the predication of its statements. Syllogisms may be made from sentences that use any kind of predication, as long as it connects the terms. Any of these sentences could be parts of syllogisms:

> *Dragons* smell *like cinnamon and sludge.*
> *Dennis* has *a vast wardrobe.*
> *Sylvia* will vote *in tomorrow's election.*
> *Peace* cannot be achieved *without communication.*
> *The dollar* rose in value *against the yen.*

Each has a different predication. In any syllogism in which one of these statements might be used (as the major or minor premise or as the conclusion), that predication would have to be repeated.

> *All students who have signed this letter* will vote *in tommorrow's election.*
> *Sylvia* has signed this letter.
> *Therefore, Sylvia* will vote *in tomorrow's election.*

The verbs in syllogisms express the relations between the terms. Forms of the verb *to be* (called the copula) are quite troublesome in syllogisms, simply because the kind of relation they assert is one of equivalence, and this can often lead to reasoning that is circular.

Circular reasoning is called **tautology**. Tautology is a kind of logic that appears to be reasoning when it is actually not. Rather than an inference, it is a repetition of the same idea. Tautological inquiries end up exactly where they started, usually because of forms of the verb *to be*. The following are two syllogisms using *is* verbs, one of which is tautological and the other of which is not:

Abortion is killing babies.
Killing babies is murder.
Therefore, abortion is murder.

Anything prohibited by the church is wrong.
Abortion is prohibited by the church.
Therefore, abortion is wrong.

Is the difference obvious to you? If not, it is because each of the syllogisms has the same form: A is B, B is C, therefore A is C. But the difference is that the first syllogism does not place its terms into categories. Instead it *redefines* each of the terms to mean the same thing as the others. The first syllogism is a tautology: A is B, B is A, therefore A is B. Or: A is A, therefore A is A. The second syllogism, which comes to a similar conclusion, is not a tautology because it does not simply redefine the terms to mean the same thing.

One final caution about deduction: Valid syllogisms do not, as I have already illustrated, require true premises. A deduction in the real world of reasoning is only as good as the premises it asserts, just as the conclusion of an induction is only as good as the observations from which it derives. Logical validity by itself is not the way we know what to believe. The following syllogism is valid, but none of its premises is true:

All sports require a catcher's mitt.
Embroidery is a sport.
Therefore, embroidery requires a catcher's mitt.

A true conclusion can even be derived from a syllogism with false premises, as in this example:

Vegetables make good pack animals.
Burros are a kind of vegetable.
Therefore, burros make good pack animals.

Again, valid logical form alone does not provide sufficient reason to trust a conclusion. Valid logical form can be used to mislead, or to lead to (or from) absurdities.

The fact that a valid deduction is not necessarily true (or believable) means that deduction in actual arguments is somehow always *conditional*. Acceptable conclusions follow from premises only *if* those premises are accepted. The premises of syllogisms assert conditions about the nature of things, and if those conditions are not acceptable the conclusions are not acceptable, even though they may result from valid syllogistic relationships.

Thus, in practical reasoning, those premises that are implied when reasons are offered must constitute acceptable conditions on which to base an appeal. If not, the reasons will not support the conclusions. Suppose, for instance, that I were to assert the following enthymeme (based on a categorical syllogism):

The use of biological warfare is moral because it is an effective means of defeating an enemy.

You might respond that I am being logical or that I am being irrational. The difference will be whether you accept the assumption I have relied on as an appropriate condition. Whether I am aware of it or not, if I make that argument I necessarily commit myself to the implied condition that

Anything that effectively defeats an enemy is moral.

It is the acceptability of this condition, this major premise, that will determine how good my stated reason seems. Those who accept this assumption will be inclined to see my reason as supportive of the conclusion. Those who refuse to accept that assumption will not accept the reason as offering support. Thus, although logic itself is no guarantee that an argument will be reasonable, understanding how logic works can be one way of seeing more deeply into how practical arguments work in relation to their intended audience.

ENTHYMEMES AND LOGIC

All the enthymemes we have looked at resemble syllogisms, whether they are expressed in the form of a syllogism or whether they only imply such a form. We have seen that any combination of a reason and a conclusion will imply a logical assumption (the missing premise), as well as a variety of possible presumptions. The enthymeme works a lot like the syllogism does. In fact, the enthymeme is sometimes said to be a kind of syllogism. But there are differences between syllogisms and enthymemes that are just as important as their similarities. These differences are:

1. An enthymeme may be either inductive or deductive.
2. An enthymeme derives one of its premises (the implied or stated assumption) from the audience to whom it is addressed, in order to help create agreement with a conclusion that the audience may not accept. That is, an enthymeme is tied to inquiry and to persuasion. A syllogism, however, may be made of statements that no one believes, or that everyone believes and no one cares about. Thus, a syllogism as an abstract form stays the same from one audience to another, while enthymemes are formed in response to situations.
3. An enthymeme may appeal to authority and emotion as well as to the logic of the case. A syllogism generally appeals only to the logic of the case. In formal logic, appeals to authority and emotion are considered fallacies of reasoning. In actual argument, they often form the basis of our agreements.

4. An enthymeme is judged to be good or bad, valid or invalid, or adequate or inadequate, based on the response of the desired audience. The validity test for an enthymeme is "Does my audience understand what I am offering as justification for my conclusion?" A syllogism, however, must be judged by how well it conforms to the model for a valid syllogism. This is why perfect syllogisms either tend to be about inconsequential issues (like whether baseball has rules) or are expressed by symbolic formulas instead of words. Syllogisms about real issues expressed in ordinary language are often imperfect because the issues are complex and words can be ambiguous. In contrast, enthymemes always are expressed in ordinary language. They concern real issues.

5. Enthymemes do not, therefore, attempt to express permanent, stable, unambiguous truths. They attempt to say what we believe, here and now, and why we think so. Syllogisms are sometimes advocated for the sake of methodological rigor, especially in math and science, where fixed truths might be available to us. But enthymemes express the reasoning we do concerning issues of interpretation, value, consequence, and policy, where no exact method is available to us. They express the kind of knowledge that we use to solve most of life's problems: not permanent truth but contingent belief.

6. An enthymeme, then, is a dynamic form, the natural expression of practical reasoning. The syllogism can be a static form, into which our practical reasonings often do not fit. Syllogisms reduce the complexity of our reasoning (often helpfully), but enthymemes more often attempt to express that complexity.

These differences are underscored by the simple fact that you can talk about enthymemes (and reason) without ever using the concept of the syllogism or the vocabulary of formal logic. The terms *conclusion, reason,* and *assumption* are enough, or, alternatively, Toulmin's *claim, data, warrant, backing,* and so on, may suffice. But understanding the ways in which induction and deduction work can nevertheless help you to gain insights into the reasoning in your own and others' enthymemes. It helps you to be clear about what the assumptions are. It helps you to see implied logical connections and to test their universality. It helps you to see, and if possible to avoid, circular reasoning.

IMPLICATIONS FOR RESEARCH

Reasons are assertions and therefore subject to verification if they rely on information that the writer is not absolutely confident about. In that case, everything I said at the end of Chapter 3 about the possible need to inform yourself before making rash statements in your thesis applies to the claims you decide to use as reasons. Your reasoning does not depend solely on the validity of your logic. It depends equally on the dependability of your information. Hence, my advice now as before is: When in doubt, look it up. But you know by now that looking it up is not sufficient. How do you know whether to trust what you find? By thinking about logic in this chapter, you have refined the kinds of critical questions you can apply to the information you might discover as you seek to inform yourself. As you read, for instance, consider the *kind of appeal* that the writer is making. Does this give you more or less confidence in the source? As you read, isolate the enthymemes and reconstruct the warrants and assumptions that you are expected to accept as self-evident. What does this say about the writer's view of his or her reader? How does this affect your understanding of the subject?

There is no foolproof way to know whether one's sources can be trusted. An open mind is necessary to ensure that you discover adequate information. A critical mind is necessary to ensure that you assess that information well. Rather than try to offer a dependable procedure for knowing when a source is right or wrong, let me describe the worst kind of uncritical research and see what it tells us about our responsibilities as critical readers. I have seen student term papers in which many sources were cited to support the writer's idea, but in each case those sources consisted exclusively of the conclusions of studies that agree with the writer. In other words, the writer's thesis is argued by constructing a list of authorities all saying the same thing, as if such a list alone proved the point. This catalog of authorities does not constitute an argument, however, because the *reasons* that these sources give for their conclusions are not explored. Such a writer has located many sources and found their conclusions, but he or she has not tried to assess those conclusions according to the process by which they were derived. The resulting "research paper" does not discriminate between conclusions derived by adequate means and conclusions derived by inadequate ones. As an argument, it is weak. As research, it is useless.

Clearly, then, anyone conducting serious research has the responsibility of doing more than skimming through sources to find conclusions. Once you have found a source that seems relevant, you must know not only what its conclusions are but also how those conclusions have been derived. In other words, you must consider the arguments that have been presented in support of those conclusions and assess the conclusions accordingly.

> *What does it claim?*
> *By what process have the conclusions been derived? What data and backing are presented? What qualifiers?*
> *On what assumptions or warrants do the reasons depend?*
> *How valid is the logic?*

Your answers to these questions are just as important to your research as the conclusions themselves. Your own presentation of the results of your research must demonstrate that your inquiry has included such questions. Your reader, after all, can be assumed to be capable of asking them about your own conclusions.

It is also the researcher's responsibility to have located and considered studies that do not support whatever potential conclusion he or she may intend to reach. Research questions are open-ended, but researchers often work from a hypothesis, whether it is defined early in the study or late. Whenever answers begin to emerge, it is essential to know which reasons may contradict those answers as well as which reasons support them. This way of looking at arguments, whether others' or one's own, is called **falsification**.

The process of falsifying ideas is an important mental exercise, involving seriously trying to answer questions like:

What if this idea is wrong?
What kinds of reasons could be used to argue against it?
What would have to be true for those reasons to be valid?
What assumptions are available to support those reasons?

To be able to consider such questions seriously, a researcher must have the mental agility to shift points of view. (We all probably increase our mental agility simply by trying to answer such questions.) It helps to see the weakness in a given line of reasoning to know how a different conclusion might be argued. To learn this requires that we be able to imagine how someone who holds a different view might defend it. No harm is done if by this means we come to question our ideas, or even to change our minds.

QUESTIONS FOR THOUGHT, DISCUSSION, AND WRITING

1. In the following passages, which sentences are reasons and which are conclusions? Do some sentences have both functions? Which ones that you describe as reasons offer explanations of the conclusion, and which offer justifications for believing the conclusion?

   a. I like reading detective novels. They keep me looking for interesting possibilities, like a game of chess. I never can guess the right solution, though. The writers are clever. I'm also too gullible. But it's fun to be fooled. It wouldn't be a challenge if I always knew "whodunnit."

   b. The narrator of "The Turn of the Screw" is unreliable. It isn't possible to tell whether to trust what we are told. Henry James seems to want his reader to wonder whether the events really happened or whether they occur only in the minds of the characters. But which characters? The reader must be meant to wonder which of the characters can trust their own impressions. I think it's a story about the ambiguity of appearance and reality.

   c. Sixty-seven per cent of the people surveyed said that they are not influenced by advertising with irrelevant sexual content. This does not, however, mean that such an influence is not more common. If we accept the possibility that there is a subliminal appeal in advertising, some of those who say that they are not influenced might be influenced without knowing it. Survey techniques alone cannot test hypotheses about subconscious knowledge.

2. What kinds of appeal are being made in each of the reasons offered here? How appropriate is the choice of each kind of appeal? Why?

   a. Salaries for state employees should be based on comparable worth, since women workers on the average earn lower wages than men.

   b. A recent study showed that cocaine users are no more likely than anyone else to experiment with heroin. But only a fool would accept this as a "green light" to use coke.

   c. When you consider the extent to which the computer will be used in all parts of our lives in the near future, it becomes obvious that computer literacy should be taught in elementary grades.

   d. We need leaders who are not afraid to tell the truth. Without them, this country is doomed.

   e. The newspaper decided to print pictures of men who went into adult book-stores in our town, hoping to humiliate them into staying away and by this means force the stores to close. The question is whether the newspaper is guilty of invasion of privacy or whether freedom of the press can include this kind of action. I think the paper has the right but would be wise not to use it. The public's trust in the press is undermined when it abuses its freedoms, just as the booksellers lose respect when they take the First Amendment too far. In both cases, the First Amendment is pushed far enough to risk a backlash that could destroy it.

3. Reconstruct the logical assumptions that connect the following reasons and con-clusions.

   a. The student union should be allowed to sell beer because this would create more revenue to support student activities.

   b. Boxers frequently suffer permanent injury as a result of the impact of brain tissue hitting the inside of the skull. Yet some people continue to call this a "sport." It's not a sport, it's a brutal entertainment spectacle. It should be outlawed.

   c. As long as the nation's laws are written and voted on by a majority of whites, the laws that send minorities to prison in greater numbers than whites are political laws. This makes political prisoners out of people who have done no more than follow their consciences in matters that they have not been able to change with their votes.

   d. The only way a politician can get elected is by telling people what they want to hear. No honest person can win enough votes to get into office.

   e. If the Constitution hadn't guaranteed people the right to pursue happiness, Americans might not be as selfish as they are.

4. Having decided on a thesis for your next essay, turn it into an enthymeme by adding a "because clause" that you might offer as a major reason for justifying that thesis. If, in the process of doing so, you find that you need to revise the thesis itself, go ahead. After you have composed this enthymeme, bring it to class for a discussion of the reasoning it uses, according to any of the concepts in this chapter.

5. Here are three essays, two of which were written in response to the first one. As you read them and analyze them according to the reasoning they develop, consider the following questions:

   a. What enthymemes does the writer use?

   b. Can you identify appeals to authority, emotion, and the logic of the case? Does the reasoning tend to move from specific to general or from general to specific, or does it stay on the same level? How are these kinds of reasoning combined?

c. Can you identify aspects of the essay that function as claim, qualifier, data, warrant, or rebuttal?

d. Can you identify aspects of the essay that function as unstated presumptions or as logical assumptions? Can you paraphrase the arguments of the case in the logical forms of induction or deduction? Has the author overgeneralized from the evidence, made use of overly general assumptions, or fallen into circular reasoning?

e. What do such analyses tell you about the author's view of the audience for which the essay is composed?

f. Finally, how do the two responses differ from each other in their attempts to rebut the first argument? Which of the responses do you find to be more persuasive? fairer? more reasonable? Why?

◆ READINGS ◆

MANAGEMENT WOMEN AND THE NEW FACTS OF LIFE

Felice N. Schwartz

The cost of employing women in management is greater than the cost of employing men. This is a jarring statement, partly because it is true, but mostly because it is something people are reluctant to talk about. A new study by one multinational corporation shows that the rate of turnover in management positions is 2½ times higher among top-performing women than it is among men. A large producer of consumer goods reports that one half of the women who take maternity leave return to their jobs late or not at all. And we know that women also have a greater tendency to plateau or to interrupt their careers in ways that limit their growth and development. But we have become so sensitive to charges of sexism and so afraid of confrontation, even litigation, that we rarely say what we know to be true. Unfortunately, our bottled-up awareness leaks out in misleading metaphors ("glass ceiling" is one notable example), veiled hostility, lowered expectations, distrust, and reluctant adherence to Equal Employment Opportunity requirements.

Career interruptions, plateauing, and turnover are expensive. The money corporations invest in recruitment, training, and development is less likely to produce top executives among women than among men, and the invaluable company experience that developing executives acquire at every level as they move up through management ranks is more often lost.

The studies just mentioned are only the first of many, I'm quite sure. Demographic realities are going to force corporations all across the country to analyze the cost of employing women in managerial positions, and what they will discover is that women cost more.

But here is another startling truth: The greater cost of employing women is not a function of inescapable gender differences. Women *are* different from men, but what increases their cost to the corporation is principally the clash of their perceptions, attitudes, and behavior with those of men, which is to say, with the policies and practices of male-led corporations.

It is terribly important that employers draw the right conclusions from the studies now being done. The studies will be useless—or worse, harmful—if all they teach us is that women are expensive to employ. What we need to learn is how to reduce that expense, how to stop throwing away the investments we make in talented women, how to become more responsive to the needs of the women that corporations *must* employ if they are to have the best and the brightest of all those now entering the work force.

The gender differences relevant to business fall into two categories: those related to maternity and those related to the differing traditions and expectations of the sexes. Maternity is biological rather than cultural. We can't alter it, but we can dramatically reduce its impact on the workplace and in many cases eliminate its negative effect on employee development. We can accomplish this by addressing the second set of differences, those between male and female socialization. Today, these differences exaggerate the real costs of maternity and can turn a relatively slight disruption in work schedule into a serious business problem and a career derailment for individual women. If we are to overcome the cost differential between male and female employees, we need to address the issues that arise when female socialization meets the male corporate culture and masculine rules of career development—issues of behavior and style, of expectation, of stereotypes and preconceptions, of sexual tension and harassment, of female mentoring, lateral mobility, relocation, compensation, and early identification of top performers.

The one immutable, enduring difference between men and women is maternity. Maternity is not simply childbirth but a continuum that begins with an awareness of the ticking of the biological clock, proceeds to the anticipation of motherhood, includes pregnancy, childbirth, physical recuperation, psychological adjustment, and continues on to nursing, bonding, and child rearing. Not all women choose to become mothers, of course, and among those who do, the process varies from case to case depending on the health of the mother and baby, the values of the parents, and the availability, cost, and quality of child care.

In past centuries, the biological fact of maternity shaped the traditional roles of the sexes. Women performed the home-centered functions that related to the bearing and nurturing of children. Men did the work that required great physical strength. Over time, however, family size contracted, the community assumed greater responsibility for the care and education of children, packaged foods and household technology reduced the work load in the home, and technology eliminated much of the need for muscle power at the workplace. Today, in the developed world, the only role still uniquely gender related is childbearing. Yet men and women are still socialized to perform their traditional roles.

Men and women may or may not have some innate psychological disposition toward these traditional roles—men to be aggressive, competitive, self-reliant, risk taking; women to be supportive, nurturing, intuitive, sensitive, communicative—but certainly both men and women are capable of the full range of behavior. Indeed, the male and female roles have already begun to expand and merge. In the decades ahead, as the socialization of boys and girls and the experience and expectations of young men and women grow steadily more androgynous, the differences in workplace behavior will continue to fade. At the moment, however, we are still plagued by disparities in perception and behavior that make the integration of men and women in the workplace unnecessarily difficult and expensive.

Let me illustrate with a few broadbrush generalizations. Of course, these are only stereotypes, but I think they help to exemplify the kinds of preconceptions that can muddy the corporate waters.

Men continue to perceive women as the rearers of their children, so they find it understandable, indeed appropriate, that women should renounce their careers to raise families. Edmund Pratt, CEO of Pfizer, once asked me in all sincerity, "Why would any woman choose to be a chief financial officer rather than a full-time mother?" By condoning and taking pleasure in women's traditional behavior, men reinforce it. Not only do they see parenting as fundamentally female, they see a career as fundamentally male—either an unbroken series of promotions and advancements toward CEOdom or stagnation and disappointment. This attitude serves to legitimize a woman's choice to extend maternity leave and even, for those who can afford it, to leave employment altogether for several years. By the same token, men who might want to take a leave after the birth of a child know that management will see such behavior as a lack of career commitment, even when company policy permits parental leave for men.

Women also bring counterproductive expectations and perceptions to the workplace. Ironically, although the feminist movement was an expression of women's quest for freedom from their home-based lives, most women were remarkably free already. They had many responsibilities, but they were autonomous and could be entrepreneurial in how and when they carried them out. And once their children grew up and left home, they were essentially free to do what they wanted with their lives. Women's traditional role also included freedom from responsibility for the financial support of their families. Many of us were socialized from girlhood to expect our husbands to take care of us, while our brothers were socialized from an equally early age to complete their educations, pursue careers, climb the ladder of success, and provide dependable financial support for their families. To the extent that this tradition of freedom lingers subliminally, women tend to bring to their employment a sense that they can choose to change jobs or careers at will, take time off, or reduce their hours.

Finally, women's traditional role encouraged particular attention to the quality and substance of what they did, specifically to the physical, psychological, and intellectual development of their children. This traditional focus may explain women's continuing tendency to search for more than monetary reward—intrinsic significance, social importance, meaning—in what they do. This too makes them more likely than men to leave the corporation in search of other values.

The misleading metaphor of the glass ceiling suggests an invisible barrier constructed by corporate leaders to impede the upward mobility of women beyond the middle levels. A more appropriate metaphor, I believe, is the kind of cross-sectional diagram used in geology. The barriers to women's leadership occur when potentially counterproductive layers of influence on women—maternity, tradition, socialization—meet management strata pervaded by the largely unconscious preconceptions, stereotypes, and expectations of men. Such interfaces do not exist for men and tend to be impermeable for women.

One result of these gender differences has been to convince some executives that women are simply not suited to top management. Other executives feel helpless. If they see even a few of their valued female employees fail to return to work from maternity leave on schedule or see one of their most promising women plateau in her career after the birth of a child, they begin to fear there is nothing they can do to infuse women with new energy and enthusiasm and persuade them to stay. At the same time, they know there is nothing they can do to stem the tide of women into management ranks.

Another result is to place every working woman on a continuum that runs from total dedication to career at one end to a balance between career and family at the other. What women discover is that the male corporate culture sees both extremes as unacceptable. Women who want the flexibility to balance their families and their careers are not adequately committed to the organization. Women who perform as aggressively and competitively as men are abrasive and unfeminine. But the fact is, business needs all the talented women it can get. Moreover, as I will explain, the women I call career-primary and those I call career-and-family each have particular value to the corporation.

Women in the corporation are about to move from a buyer's to a seller's market. The sudden, startling recognition that 80% of new entrants in the work force over the next decade will be women, minorities, and immigrants has stimulated a mushrooming incentive to "value diversity."

Women are no longer simply an enticing pool of occasional creative talent, a thorn in the side of the EEO officer, or a source of frustration to corporate leaders truly puzzled by the slowness of their upward trickle into executive positions. A real demographic change is taking place. The era of sudden population growth of the 1950s and 1960s is over. The birth rate has dropped about 40%, from a high of 25.3 live births per 1,000 population in 1957, at the peak of the baby boom, to a stable low of a little more than 15 per 1,000 over the last 16 years, and there is no indication of a return to a higher rate. The tidal wave of baby boomers that swelled the recruitment pool to overflowing seems to have been a one-time phenomenon. For 20 years, employers had the pick of a very large crop and were able to choose males almost exclusively for the executive track. But if future population remains fairly stable while the economy continues to expand, and if the new information society simultaneously creates a greater need for creative, educated managers, then the gap between supply and demand will grow dramatically and, with it, the competition for managerial talent.

The decrease in numbers has even greater implications if we look at the traditional source of corporate recruitment for leadership positions— white males from the top 10% of the country's best universities. Over the past decade, the increase in the number of women graduating from leading universities has been much greater than the increase in the total number of graduates, and these women are well represented in the top 10% of their classes.

The trend extends into business and professional programs as well. In the old days, virtually all MBAs were male. I remember addressing a meeting at the Harvard Business School as recently as the mid-1970s and looking out at a sea of exclusively male faces. Today, about 25% of that audience would be women. The pool of male MBAs from which corporations have traditionally drawn their leaders has shrunk significantly.

Of course, this reduction does not have to mean a shortage of talent. The top 10% is at least as smart as it always was—smarter, probably, since it's now drawn from a broader segment of the population. But it now consists increasingly of women. Companies that are determined to recruit the same number of men as before will have to dig much deeper into the male pool, while their competitors will have the opportunity to pick the best people from both the male and female graduates.

Under these circumstances, there is no question that the management ranks of business will include increasing numbers of women. There remains, however, the question of how these women will succeed—how long they will stay, how high they will climb, how completely they will fulfill their promise and potential, and what kind of return the corporation will realize on its investment in their training and development.

There is ample business reason for finding ways to make sure that as many of these women as possible will succeed. The first step in this process is to recognize that women are not all alike. Like men, they are individuals with differing talents, priorities, and motivations. For the sake of simplicity, let me focus on the two women I referred to earlier, on what I call the career-primary woman and the career-and-family woman.

Like many men, some women put their careers first. They are ready to make the same trade-offs traditionally made by the men who seek leadership positions. They make a career decision to put in extra hours, to make sacrifices in their personal lives, to make the most of every opportunity for professional development. For women, of course, this decision also requires that they remain single or at least childless or, if they do have children, that they be satisfied to have others raise them. Some 90% of executive men but only 35% of executive women have children by the age of 40. The *automatic* association of all women with babies is clearly unjustified.

The secret to dealing with such women is to recognize them early, accept them, and clear artificial barriers from their path to the top. After all, the best of these women are among the best managerial talent you will ever see. And career-primary women have another important value to the company that men and other women lack. They can act as role models and mentors to younger women who put their careers first. Since upwardly mobile career-primary women still have few role models to motivate and inspire them, a company with women in its top echelon has a significant advantage in the competition for executive talent.

Men at the top of the organization—most of them over 55, with wives who tend to be traditional—often find career women "masculine" and difficult to accept as colleagues. Such men miss the point, which is not that these women are just like men but that they are just like the *best* men in the organization. And there is such a shortage of the best people that gender cannot be allowed to matter. It is clearly counterproductive to disparage in a woman with executive talent the very qualities that are most critical to the business and that might carry a man to the CEO's office.

Clearing a path to the top for career-primary women has four requirements:

1. Identify them early.

2. Give them the same opportunity you give to talented men to grow and develop and contribute to company profitability. Give them client and customer responsibility. Expect them to travel and relocate, to make the same commitment to the company as men aspiring to leadership positions.

3. Accept them as valued members of your management team. Include them in every kind of communication. Listen to them.

4. Recognize that the business environment is more difficult and stressful for them than for their male peers. They are always a minority, often the only woman. The male perception of talented, ambitious women is at best ambivalent, a mixture of admiration, resentment, confusion, competitiveness, attraction, skepticism, anxiety, pride, and animosity. Women can never feel secure about how they should dress and act, whether they should speak out or grin and bear it when they encounter discrimination, stereotyping, sexual harassment, and paternalism. Social interaction and travel with male colleagues and with male clients can be charged. As they move up, the normal increase in pressure and responsibility is compounded for women because they are women.

Stereotypical language and sexist day-to-day behavior do take their toll on women's career development. Few male executives realize how common it is to call women by their first names while men in the same group are greeted with surnames, how frequently female executives are assumed by men to be secretaries, how often women are excluded from all-male social events where business is being transacted. With notable exceptions, men are still generally more comfortable with other men, and as a result women miss many of the career and business opportunities that arise over lunch, on the golf course, or in the locker room.

The majority of women, however, are what I call career-and-family women, women who want to pursue serious careers while participating actively in the rearing of children. These women are a precious resource that has yet to be mined. Many of them are talented and creative. Most of them are willing to trade some career growth and compensation for freedom from the constant pressure to work long hours and weekends.

Most companies today are ambivalent at best about the career-and-family women in their management ranks. They would prefer that all employees were willing to give their all to the company. They believe it is in their best interests for all managers to compete for the top positions so the company will have the largest possible pool from which to draw its leaders.

"If you have both talent and motivation," many employers seem to say, "we want to move you up. If you haven't got that motivation, if you want less pressure and greater flexibility, then you can leave and make room for a new generation." These companies lose on two counts. First, they fail to amortize the investment they made in the early training and experience of management women who find themselves committed to family as well as to career. Second, they fail to recognize what these women could do for their middle management.

The ranks of middle managers are filled with people on their way up and people who have stalled. Many of them have simply reached their limits, achieved career growth commensurate with or exceeding their capabilities, and they cause problems because their performance is mediocre but they still want to move ahead. The career-and-family woman is willing to trade off the pressures and demands that go with promotion for the freedom to spend more time with her children. She's very smart, she's talented, she's committed to her career, and she's satisfied to stay at the middle level, at least during the early child-rearing years. Compare her with some of the people you have there now.

Consider a typical example, a woman who decides in college on a business career and enters management at age 22. For nine years, the company invests in her career as she gains experience and skills and steadily improves her performance. But at 31, just as the investment begins to pay off in earnest, she decides to have a baby. Can the company afford to let her go home, take another job, or go into business for herself? The common perception now is yes, the corporation can afford to lose her unless, after six or eight weeks or even three months of disability and maternity leave, she returns to work on a full-time schedule with the same vigor, commitment, and ambition that she showed before.

But what if she doesn't? What if she wants or needs to go on leave for six months or a year or, heaven forbid, five years? In this worst-case scenario, she works full-time from age 22 to 31 and from 36 to 65 — a total of 38 years as opposed to the typical male's 43 years. That's not a huge difference. Moreover, my typical example is willing to work part-time while her children are young, if only her employer will give her the opportunity. There are two rewards for companies responsive to this need: higher retention of their best people and greatly improved performance and satisfaction in their middle management.

The high-performing career-and-family woman can be a major player in your company. She can give you a significant business advantage as the competition for able people escalates. Sometimes too, if you can hold on to her, she will switch gears in mid-life and reenter the competition for the top. The price you must pay to retain these women is threefold: you must plan for and manage maternity, you must provide the flexibility that will allow them to be maximally productive, and you must take an active role in helping to make family supports and high-quality, affordable child care available to all women.

The key to managing maternity is to recognize the value of high-performing women and the urgent need to retain them and keep them productive. The first step must be a genuine partnership between the woman and her boss. I know this partnership can seem difficult to forge. One of my own senior executives came to me recently to discuss plans for her maternity leave and subsequent return to work. She knew she wanted to come back. I wanted to make certain that she would. Still, we had a somewhat awkward conversation, because I knew that no woman can predict with certainty when she will be able to return to work or under what conditions. Physical problems can lengthen her leave. So can a demanding infant, a difficult family or personal adjustment, or problems with child care.

I still don't know when this valuable executive will be back on the job full-time, and her absence creates some genuine problems for our organization. But I do know that I can't simply replace her years of experience with a new recruit. Since our conversation, I also know that she wants to come back, and that she *will* come back—part-time at first—unless I make it impossible for her by, for example, setting an arbitrary date for her full-time return or resignation. In turn, she knows that the organization wants and needs her and, more to the point, that it will be responsive to her needs in terms of working hours and child-care arrangements.

In having this kind of conversation it's important to ask concrete questions that will help to move the discussion from uncertainty and anxiety to some level of predictability. Questions can touch on everything from family income and energy level to child care arrangements and career commitment. Of course you want your star manager to return to work as soon as possible, but you want her to return permanently and productively. Her downtime on the job is a drain on her energies and a waste of your money.

For all the women who want to combine career and family—the women who want to participate actively in the rearing of their children and who also want to pursue their careers seriously—the key to retention is to provide the flexibility and family supports they need in order to function effectively.

Time spent in the office increases productivity if it is time well spent, but the fact that most women continue to take the primary responsibility for child care is a cause of distraction, diversion, anxiety, and absenteeism—to say nothing of the persistent guilt experienced by all working mothers. A great many women, perhaps most of all women who have always performed at the highest levels, are also frustrated by a sense that while their children are babies they cannot function at their best either at home or at work.

In its simplest form, flexibility is the freedom to take time off—a couple of hours, a day, a week—or to do some work at home and some at the office, an arrangement that communication technology makes increasingly feasible. At the complex end of the spectrum are alternative work schedules that permit the woman to work less than full-time and her employer to reap the benefits of her experience and, with careful planning, the top level of her abilities.

Part-time employment is the single greatest inducement to getting women back on the job expeditiously and the provision women themselves most desire. A part-time return to work enables them to maintain responsibility for critical aspects of their jobs, keeps them in touch with the changes constantly occurring at the workplace and in the job itself, reduces stress and fatigue, often eliminates the need for paid maternity leave by permitting a return to the office as soon as disability leave is over, and, not least, can greatly enhance company loyalty. The part-time solution works particularly well when a work load can be reduced for one individual in a department or when a full-time job can be broken down by skill levels and apportioned to two individuals at different levels of skill and pay.

I believe, however, that shared employment is the most promising and will be the most widespread form of flexible scheduling in the future. It is feasible at every level of the corporation except at the pinnacle, for both the short and the long term. It involves two people taking responsibility for one job.

Two red lights flash on as soon as most executives hear the words "job sharing": continuity and client-customer contact. The answer to the continuity question is to place responsibility entirely on the two individuals sharing the job to discuss everything that transpires—thoroughly, daily, and on their own time. The answer to the problem of client-customer contact is yes, job sharing requires re-education and a period of adjustment. But as both client and supervisor will quickly come to appreciate, two contacts means that the customer has continuous access to the company's representative, without interruptions for vacation, travel, or sick leave. The two people holding the job can simply cover for each other, and the uninterrupted, full-time coverage they provide together can be a stipulation of their arrangement.

Flexibility is costly in numerous ways. It requires more supervisory time to coordinate and manage, more office space, and somewhat greater benefits costs (though these can be contained with flexible benefits plans, prorated benefits, and, in two-paycheck families, elimination of duplicate benefits). But the advantages of reduced turnover and the greater productivity that results from higher energy levels and greater focus can outweigh the costs.

A few hints:

☐ Provide flexibility selectively. I'm not suggesting private arrangements subject to the suspicion of favoritism but rather a policy that makes flexible work schedules available only to high performers.

☐ Make it clear that in most instances (but not all) the rates of advancement and pay will be appropriately lower for those who take time off or who work part-time than for those who work full-time. Most career-and-family women are entirely willing to make that trade-off.

☐ Discuss costs as well as benefits. Be willing to risk accusations of bias. Insist, for example, that half time is half of whatever time it takes to do the job, not merely half of 35 or 40 hours.

The woman who is eager to get home to her child has a powerful incentive to use her time effectively at the office and to carry with her reading and other work that can be done at home. The talented professional who wants to have it all can be a high performer by carefully ordering her priorities and by focusing on objectives rather than on the legendary 15-hour day. By the time professional women have their first babies—at an average age of 31—they have already had nine years to work long hours at a desk, to travel, and to relocate. In the case of high performers, the need for flexibility coincides with what has gradually become the goal-oriented nature of responsibility.

Family supports—in addition to maternity leave and flexibility—include the provision of parental leave for men, support for two-career and single-parent families during relocation, and flexible benefits. But the primary ingredient is child care. The capacity of working mothers to function effectively and without interruption depends on the availability of good, affordable child care. Now that women make up almost half the work force and the growing percentage of managers, the decision to become involved in the personal lives of employees is no longer a philosophical question but a practical one. To make matters worse, the quality of child care has almost no relation to technology, inventiveness, or profitability but is more or less a pure function of the quality of child care personnel and the ratio of adults to children. These costs are irreducible. Only by joining hands with government and the public sector can corporations hope to create the vast quantity and variety of child care that their employees need.

Until quite recently, the response of corporations to women has been largely symbolic and cosmetic, motivated in large part by the will to avoid litigation and legal penalties. In some cases, companies were also moved by a genuine sense of fairness and a vague discomfort and frustration at the absence of women above the middle of the corporate pyramid. The actions they took were mostly quick, easy, and highly visible—child care information services, a three-month parental leave available to men as well as women, a woman appointed to the board of directors.

When I first began to discuss these issues 26 years ago, I was sometimes able to get an appointment with the assistant to the assistant in personnel, but it was only a courtesy. Over the past decade, I have met with the CEOs of many large corporations, and I've watched them become involved with ideas they had never previously thought much about. Until recently, however, the shelf life of that enhanced awareness was always short. Given pressing, short-term concerns, women were not a front-burner issue. In the past few months, I have seen yet another change. Some CEOs and top management groups now take the initiative. They call and ask us to show them how to shift gears from a responsive to a proactive approach to recruiting, developing, and retaining women.

I think this change is more probably a response to business needs—to concern for the quality of future profits and managerial talent—than to uneasiness about legal requirements, sympathy with the demands of women and minorities, or the desire to do what is right and fair. The nature of such business motivation varies. Some companies want to move women to higher positions as role models for those below them and as beacons for talented young recruits. Some want to achieve a favorable image with employees, customers, clients, and stockholders. These are all legitimate motives. But I think the companies that stand to gain most are motivated as well by a desire to capture competitive advantage in an era when talent and competence will be in increasingly short supply. These companies are now ready to stop being defensive about their experience with women and to ask incisive questions without preconceptions.

Even so, incredibly, I don't know of more than one or two companies that have looked into their own records to study the absolutely critical issue of maternity leave—how many women took it, when and whether they returned, and how this behavior correlated with their rank, tenure, age, and performance. The unique drawback to the employment of women is the physical reality of maternity and the particular socializing influence maternity has had. Yet to make women equal to men in the workplace we have chosen on the whole not to discuss this single most significant difference between them. Unless we do, we cannot evaluate the cost of recruiting, developing, and moving women up.

Now that interest is replacing indifference, there are four steps every company can take to examine its own experience with women:

1. Gather quantitative data on the company's experience with management-level women regarding turnover rates, occurrence of and return from maternity leave, and organizational level attained in relation to tenure and performance.

2. Correlate this data with factors such as age, marital status, and presence and age of children, and attempt to identify and analyze why women respond the way they do.

3. Gather qualitative data on the experience of women in your company and on how women are perceived by both sexes.

4. Conduct a cost-benefit analysis of the return on your investment in high-performing women. Factor in the cost to the company of women's negative reactions to negative experience, as well as the probable cost of corrective measures and policies. If women's value to your company is greater than the cost to recruit, train, and develop them—and of course I believe it will be—then you will want to do everything you can to retain them.

We have come a tremendous distance since the days when the prevailing male wisdom saw women as lacking the kind of intelligence that would allow them to succeed in business. For decades, even women themselves have harbored an unspoken belief that they couldn't make it because they couldn't be just like men, and nothing else would do. But now that women have shown themselves the equal of men in every area of organizational activity, now that they have demonstrated that they can be stars in every field of endeavor, now we can all venture to examine the fact that women and men are different.

On balance, employing women is more costly than employing men. Women can acknowledge this fact today because they know that their value to employers exceeds the additional cost and because they know that changing attitudes can reduce the additional cost dramatically. Women in management are no longer an idiosyncrasy of the arts and education. They have always matched men in natural ability. Within a very few years, they will equal men in numbers as well in every area of economic activity.

The demographic motivation to recruit and develop women is compelling. But an older question remains: Is society better for the change? Women's exit from the home and entry into the work force has certainly created problems—an urgent need for good, affordable child care; troubling questions about the kind of parenting children need; the costs and difficulties of diversity in the workplace; the stress and fatigue of combining work and family responsibilities. Wouldn't we all be happier if we could turn back the clock to an age when men were in the workplace and women in the home, when male and female roles were clearly differentiated and complementary?

Nostalgia, anxiety, and discouragement will urge many to say yes, but my answer is emphatically no. Two fundamental benefits that were unattainable in the past are now within our reach. For the individual, freedom of choice—in this case the freedom to choose career, family, or a combination of the two. For the corporation, access to the most gifted individuals in the country. These benefits are neither self-indulgent nor insubstantial. Freedom of choice and self-realization are too deeply American to be cast aside for some wistful vision of the past. And access to our most talented human resources is not a luxury in this age of explosive international competition but rather the barest minimum that prudence and national self-preservation require.

BLOWING THE WHISTLE ON THE "MOMMY TRACK"

Barbara Ehrenreich and Deirdre English

When a feminist has something bad to say about women, the media listen. Three years ago it was Sylvia Hewlett, announcing in her book *A Lesser Life* that feminism had sold women out by neglecting to win childcare and maternity leaves. This year it's Felice Schwartz, the New York-based consultant who argues that women—or at least the mothers among us—have become a corporate liability. They cost too much to employ, she argues, and the solution is to put them on a special lower-paid, low-pressure career track—the now-notorious "mommy track."

The "mommy track" story rated prominent coverage in the New York *Times* and *USA Today*, a cover story in *Business Week*, and airtime on dozens of talk shows. Schwartz, after all, seemed perfectly legitimate. She is the president of Catalyst, an organization that has been advising corporations on women's careers since 1962. She had published her controversial claims in no less a spot than the *Harvard Business Review* ("Management Women and the New Facts of Life," January–February 1989). And her intentions, as she put it in a later op-ed piece, seemed thoroughly benign: "to urge employers to create policies that help mothers balance career and family responsibilities."

Moreover, Schwartz's argument seemed to confirm what everybody already knew. Women haven't been climbing up the corporate ladder as fast as might once have been expected, and women with children are still, on average, groping around the bottom rungs. Only about 40 percent of top female executives have children, compared to 95 percent of their male peers. There have been dozens of articles about female dropouts: women who slink off the fast track, at age 30-something, to bear a strategically timed baby or two. In fact, the "mommy track"—meaning a lower-pressure, flexible, or part-time approach to work—was neither a term Schwartz used nor her invention. It was already, in an anecdotal sort of way, a well-worn issue.

Most of the controversy focused on Schwartz's wildly anachronistic "solution." Corporate employers, she advised, should distinguish between two categories of women: "career-primary" women, who won't interrupt their careers for children and hence belong on the fast track with the men, and "career-and-family" women, who should be shunted directly to the mommy track. Schwartz had no answers for the obvious questions: how is the employer supposed to sort the potential "breeders" from the strivers? Would such distinction even be legal? What about *fathers?* But in a sense, the damage had already been done. A respected feminist, writing in a respected journal, had made a case that most women can't pull their weight in the corporate world, and should be paid accordingly.

Few people, though, actually read Schwartz's article. The first surprise is that it contains *no* evidence to support her principal claim, that "the cost of employing women in management is greater than the cost of employing men." Schwartz offers no data, no documentation at all—except for two unpublished studies by two *anonymous* corporations. Do these studies really support her claim? Were they methodologically sound? Do they even exist? There is no way to know.

Few media reports of the "mommy track" article bothered to mention the peculiar nature of Schwartz's "evidence." We, however, were moved to call the *Harvard Business Review* and inquire whether the article was representative of its normal editorial standard. Timothy Blodgett, the executive editor, defended the article as "an expression of opinion and judgment." When we suggested that such potentially damaging "opinions" might need a bit of bolstering, he responded by defending Schwartz: "She speaks with a tone of authority. That comes through."

(The conversation went downhill from there, with Blodgett stating sarcastically, "I'm sure your article in *Ms.* will be *very* objective." Couldn't fall much lower than the *Harvard Business Review,* we assured him.)

Are managerial women more costly to employ than men? As far as we could determine—with the help of the Business and Professional Women's Foundation and Women's Equity Action League—there is no *published* data on this point. A 1987 government study did show female managerial employees spending less time with each employer than males (5 years compared to 6.8 years), but there is no way of knowing what causes this turnover or what costs it incurs. And despite pregnancy, and despite women's generally greater responsibility for child-raising, they use up on the average only 5.1 sick days per year, compared to 4.9 for men.

The second surprise, given Schwartz's feminist credentials, is that the article is riddled with ancient sexist assumptions—for example, about the possibility of a more androgynous approach to child-raising *and* work. She starts with the unobjectionable statement that "maternity is biological rather than cultural." The same thing, after all, could be said of paternity. But a moment later, we find her defining maternity as ". . . a continuum that begins with an awareness of the ticking of the biological clock, proceeds to the anticipation of motherhood, includes pregnancy, childbirth, physical recuperation, psychological adjustment, and continues on to nursing, bonding, and childrearing."

Now, pregnancy, childbirth, and nursing do qualify as biological processes. But slipping childrearing into the list, as if changing diapers and picking up socks were hormonally programmed activities, is an old masculinist trick. Child-raising is a *social* undertaking, which may involve nannies, aunts, grandparents, day-care workers, or, of course, *fathers*.

Equally strange for a "feminist" article is Schwartz's implicit assumption that employment, in the case of married women, is strictly optional, or at least that *mothers* don't need to be top-flight earners. The "career-and-family woman," she tells us, is "willing" and "satisfied" to forgo promotions and "stay at the middle level." What about the single mother, or the wife of a low-paid male? But Schwartz's out-of-date—and class-bound—assumption that every woman is supported by a male breadwinner fits in with her apparent nostalgia for the era of the feminine mystique. "Ironically," she writes, "although the feminist movement was an expression of women's quest for freedom from their home-based lives, *most women were remarkably free already* [emphasis added]."

But perhaps the oddest thing about the "mommy track" article—even as an "expression of opinion and judgment"—is that it is full of what we might charitably call ambivalence or, more bluntly, self-contradictions. Take the matter of the "glass ceiling," which symbolized all the barriers, both subtle and overt, that corporate women keep banging their heads against. At the outset, Schwartz dismisses the glass ceiling as a "misleading metaphor." Sexism, in short, is not the problem.

Nevertheless, within a few pages, she is describing the glass ceiling (not by that phrase, of course) like a veteran. "Male corporate culture," she tells us, sees both the career-primary and the career-and-family woman as "unacceptable." The woman with family responsibilities is likely to be seen as lacking commitment to the organization, while the woman who *is* fully committed to the organization is likely to be seen as "abrasive and unfeminine." She goes on to cite the corporate male's "confusion, competitiveness," and his "stereotypical language and sexist . . . behavior," concluding that "with notable exceptions, men are still more comfortable with other men."

And we're supposed to blame *women* for their lack of progress in the corporate world?

Even on her premier point, that women are more costly to employ, Schwartz loops around and rebuts herself. Near the end of her article, she urges corporations to conduct their own studies of the costs of employing women—the two anonymous studies were apparently not definitive after all—and asserts confidently ("of course I believe") that the benefits will end up outweighing the costs. In a more recent New York *Times* article, she puts it even more baldly: "The costs of employing women pale beside the payoffs."

Could it be that both Felice Schwartz and the editors of the *Harvard Business Review* are ignorant of that most basic financial management concept, the cost-benefit analysis? If the "payoffs" outweigh the costs of employing women—runny noses and maternity leaves included—then the net cost may indeed be *lower* than the cost of employing men.

In sum, the notorious "mommy track" article is a tortured muddle of feminist perceptions and sexist assumptions, good intentions and dangerous suggestions—unsupported by any acceptable evidence at all. It should never have been taken seriously, not by the media and not by the nation's most prestigious academic business publication. The fact that it was suggests that something serious *is* afoot: a backlash against America's high-status, better paid women, and potentially against all women workers.

We should have seen it coming. For the past 15 years upwardly mobile, managerial women have done everything possible to fit into an often hostile corporate world. They dressed up as nonthreatening corporate clones. They put in 70-hour workweeks; and of course, they postponed childbearing. Thanks in part to their commitment to the work world, the birthrate dropped by 16 percent since 1970. But now many of these women are ready to start families. This should hardly be surprising; after all, 90 percent of American women do become mothers.

But while corporate women were busily making adjustments and concessions, the larger corporate world was not. The "fast track," with its macho camaraderie and toxic work load, remains the only track to success. As a result, success is indeed usually incompatible with motherhood—as well as with any engaged and active form of fatherhood. The corporate culture strongly discourages *men* from taking parental leave even if offered. And how many families can afford to have both earners on the mommy track?

Today there's an additional factor on the scene—the corporate women who *have* made it. Many of them are reliable advocates for the supports that working parents need. But you don't have to hang out with the skirted-suit crowd for long to discover that others of them are impatient with, and sometimes even actively resentful of, younger women who are trying to combine career and family. Recall that 60 percent of top female executives are themselves childless. Others are of the "if I did it, so can you" school of thought. Felice Schwartz may herself belong in this unsisterly category. In a telling anecdote in her original article, she describes her own problems with an executive employee seeking maternity leave, and the "somewhat awkward conversations" that ensued.

Sooner or later, corporations will have to yield to the pressure for paid parental leave, flextime, and child care, if only because they've become dependent on female talent. The danger is that employers—no doubt quoting Felice Schwartz for legitimation—will insist that the price for such options be reduced pay and withheld promotions, i.e., consignment to the mommy track. Such a policy would place a penalty on parenthood, and the ultimate victims—especially if the policy trickles down to the already low-paid female majority—will of course be children.

Bumping women—or just fertile women, or married women, or whomever—off the fast track may sound smart to cost-conscious CEOs, but eventually it is the corporate culture itself that needs to slow down to a human pace. No one, male or female, works at peak productivity for 70 hours a week, year after year, without sabbaticals or leaves. Think of it this way. If the price of success were exposure to a toxic chemical, would we argue that only women should be protected? Work loads that are incompatible with family life are themselves a kind of toxin—to men as well as women, and ultimately to businesses as well as families.

HOW TO GET 'EM ON TRACK

Carol Kleiman

It's hard to take seriously Felice Schwartz's proposition in the *Harvard Business Review* that some women are career-minded, some are family-minded, and the two should be identified and separated, as the wheat from the chaff, by employers at the onset of women's professional lives.

But, suppose for one minimum-$4.65-an-hour moment that there really are such differences among the paid labor market's 53 million women (a figure that's going to climb onward and upward in the next decade; despite Catalyst's dire prediction of an erosion in women's commitment to the workplace, women continue to swell managerial ranks—which will, in fact, be swell for business). Good executives, even the few women among them, know that identifying work characteristics is a management job. So the smart ones probably are busily working on how to figure out which women are destined to be chief honchos and which—in their eyes—couch potatoes.

It's obvious that the best way to approach the problem is by giving a series of entry-level tests to all women applicants, from clerks to MBAs. It's too late to do anything about the Superwomen—the millions of working mothers who are at this very moment rushing frantically from home to work to family, trying to be all things to all people except themselves; they're much too busy to be tested anyway.

From now on, though, a blood test should be given the minute a woman walks into the personnel office. The blood analysis should be used to eliminate women with a high hormone count: clearly, when hormones rage, women will want to have sex, fulfill their biological destinies, and stay at home with them after they're born. No one would want to hire anyone so decadent, anyway.

Women with high levels of testosterone, the male hormone, should be given A-pluses for strong career tracks. Obviously, they will eschew feminine ways; even if they do have babies, they will leave them alone at home and continue a vigorous climb up the corporate ladder—just like men.

Of course, the fact that women have very little testosterone in their blood should not hinder such a serious researcher as Schwartz in identifying her victims.

Brain tests are another source of information. The usual examination of which side dominates, the right or left, and whether or not you can do math doesn't add up here. The criterion should be weight. Women whose brains are extremely heavy probably have heads filled with grand ideas of being treated equally, getting promotions they deserve, and never being sexually harassed. A few may even envision a workplace that accommodates the real responsibilities of working women, rather than disregarding almost half the labor force. These women should be dropped now to save a lot of trouble later, whether they ever have a family or not. Instead, lighter-brained women should be given every affirmative action opportunity: they're less likely to complain about the burden of having too much to do.

But workplace tests are not enough. Women should do self-examination on a monthly basis, preferably in the shower. They should check for any signs of biological destiny erupting on their bodies—scar tissue from worrying about quality care for their families; dark shadows under their eyes from staying late at work to finish the annual report. Women who find such symptoms should be honorable enough to turn themselves in to their supervisors as counterproductive to the male corporate culture. They should, as decent human beings, eliminate themselves from the workplace. These are likely candidates for disappearance behind 1950s' picture-frame windows to bolster the diminishing numbers of traditional U.S. nuclear families—now at an all-time low of only 9 percent.

Probably no one will institute these serious tests; instead, management will just let women plod along, with yearnings for both family and career dogging them every step of the way. But the "mommy" joke ultimately is on management, which, in the next decade, will be pursuing women vigorously whether or not they pass the critical devotion-to-duty test. Demographics show that women will make up 51 percent of new entrants to the labor force, and 65 percent of employees filling new jobs, by the year 2000; employers will be competing for their services—by offering, among other things, child care, flexible hours, and paid maternity leave.

The genie is out of the bottle: women are going to work, blood-screening notwithstanding. Perhaps Catalyst's Schwartz could devote future efforts to ascertaining which male executives are good bets for top management spots in a more family-oriented workplace—and to eliminating early on those who are not.

By blood-testing their estrogen levels, of course.

◆ 5 ◆

DEVELOPING STRUCTURES

THE STRUCTURAL ENTHYMEME

A thesis statement in the form of an enthymeme can provide you with a bridge between the process of thinking about your argument and the process of developing it into the parts of an essay. It can help you to think about and to revise the whole argument in advance. An enthymeme composed to represent the whole argument (the conclusion and the major reason chosen to argue it) will not only help to ensure that the reasoning is adequate to your argumentative situation, but also point the way toward structural possibilities in the essay itself.

Once you have discovered a thesis that respresents the conclusion of your essay, you can begin to think about potential reasons. Obviously, many reasons are possible. What you seek at this point is a reason that might function as the central or main rational basis for arriving at the conclusion. Putting that reason together with the thesis will make the whole thesis statement into an enthymeme. So now, the whole essay, rather than being based on an assertion alone, can be said to be based on an enthymeme, a line of reasoning.

This means that the reason you choose will be derived in part from the potential assumptions that you expect your reader to accept without further argument. This will be the shared ground for the reasoning in your essay. You will be searching, in other words, for a line of reasoning that can be used to establish your conclusion by starting with an assumable condition.

The thesis statement asserted as an enthymeme will have the following basic, but very open, form:

144

| Assertion 1 | *because* | Assertion 2 |
| (thesis) | | (reason) |

Each of these assertions will be a complete idea. The first one will be your conclusion and the second one will be the main reason you have chosen in support of that conclusion. I will call Assertion 2 a "because clause" since together the two assertions can be phrased as a single sentence. If the thesis statement is in this form, you should be able to reconstruct the assumption (or missing premise that may complete a syllogism) and by that means ensure that you have thought about the potential connection that your reasoning makes to the beliefs of your readers. It isn't necessary to write that assumption out as a part of the thesis statement. As we have seen in the previous chapter, that assumption will be there anyway, whether you write it out or not. But it is necessary for you to know what it is if you want to be sure that your reasoning, as well as the issue, finds the audience.

The task, simply stated, is to find the best reason you can to support your idea. I don't mean that there is only one "best" reason for every idea. But the choice of reasons is crucial. Reasons determine the directions in which our thoughts go. The because clause, then, should provide a clear direction, in answer to the question, "Why should my reader believe that my thesis is true?" (Of course, an honest search for such an answer might result in the need to rethink the thesis itself. In fact, it often does. We view our ideas more critically when we carry out a sincere search for good reasons.)

The task can be guided by some criteria for an adequate because clause, like those presented in Chapter 3 to help guide the search for an adequate thesis (see page 69). Once you have used those criteria to help you decide on a thesis, the following considerations can guide your search for a because clause:

1. Is the because clause a complete, precisely stated idea?
2. Does it represent a central reason for answering the question "What makes the thesis true?"
3. Does it share one logical term with the thesis?
4. Is the implied assumption one that my audience can be expected to accept without further argument? (This means, of course, the same audience for whom the question answered by the thesis is at issue.)
5. Have I avoided using "unshared terms" that mean the same thing? (If I haven't, my reasoning may be circular.)

If these five criteria are satisfied, the thesis statement as a whole will be an enthymeme that you can rely on to provide an adequate line of reasoning for a good argumentative essay. Such an enthymeme provides the logical direction for the essay to take.

To illustrate how the search for an adequate enthymeme can entail a process of discovery, guided—but not governed—by these criteria, let's go back inside the head of that student, the one who came up with the thesis about ethics and scientific education in Chapter 3. In that anecdotal narrative, the student had just arrived at what he considered to be a pretty good idea for an essay, in response to a class discussion about science and morality. Once he had found this thesis, however, he faced the question of how to earn it.

*   *   *

Well, it will happen because. . . . Let's see, I'm going to make a case for the idea that

> *Scientific education should include the issue of moral responsibility so that scientists will learn to consider the harmful effects of their research and weigh them against the potential good.*

I have to decide on a reason. Why is this class always making me think? Oh, well. I got this far, didn't I? I guess I can keep going. Anyway, why should I bother to think so hard about my position if I'm not willing to think about why I hold it? Some classes will let a person get away with just reporting what other people think. I suppose I could write an essay based on all the sources that agree with me—but I've found an idea of my own and I don't know if I can find anyone else who has argued it. "Because Einstein said so"—wouldn't that be great? But the appeal to authority won't work in this case and I know it. I have to think about why it's true.

Why, then, should scientific education include the issue of moral responsibility? Well, if it didn't, we all know what might happen. Scientists could get so caught up in their experiments and their data that they might not stop and think how horrible their ideas might be in the hands of immoral—or even amoral—technocrats. Look what happened at Los Alamos. So, what if I tried to make an enthymeme by adding

> *because harmful effects are always possible.*

Anyone who is concerned about the possibility of harmful effects should be willing to accept that reason for making scientists think about them. And we're all concerned with that possibility; we live in fear of what might be done with scientific knowledge. Of course, I'd be appealing to the reader's fears, but so what? Okay. Now, what's the assumption? Let's see, the shared term must be "harmful effects of science," so the assumption must relate the unshared terms. I think it must be something like this:

> *Education should prepare one for whatever is possible.*

That seems to be assumable. Or is it? Something bothers me about my reasoning, but I don't know what. My enthymeme is this:

> *Scientific education should include the issue of moral responsibility so that scientists will learn to consider the harmful effects of their research and weigh them against the potential good, because harmful effects are always possible.*

I wonder if it fulfills all the criteria? The because clause is a complete idea. Does it answer the question "What makes it true?" I think that's my problem. My emotional appeal to the reader's fears that something might go wrong have directed my attention away from the real issue. Sure, that's a reason that scientific education *should* include ethics, but my reasoning has nothing to do with why such an education would make scientists "weigh" potential effects, and so on. When I asked myself for a reason earlier, I asked, "Why will it happen?" What I need is a reason that addresses the question of consequence, that moral education will do what I say it will. But that means that my thesis itself may not say what I want it to. It seems to contain two ideas: one is what should happen, the other is what will happen as a result. My because clause addressed only the "should" statement, not the other one. I think I'm going to have to make the thesis more precise after all:

> *Ethics classes for scientists will teach them to weigh the potentially harmful effects of their research against the potential good, because. . .*

Yes, that's better. The "should" part of my thesis really isn't necessary, because what I need to address is the reason that such an education will have this result. If I can say that, well, the "should" part ought to take care of itself. What seemed to be a question of policy turns out to be a question of consequence. But where does that leave me for a reason? I know one thing, I can't appeal to fear any more. I've stated the issue now in such a way that I have to appeal to the logic of the case.

Why, then, will ethics classes teach scientists to weigh harmful effects? Hey, that's easy:

> *because such classes would raise questions of right and wrong about science, which a purely scientific education would ignore.*

Now I can sneak in that "pure science" definition after all. But maybe that's too easy. It seems that I may have just repeated what an ethics class *is* and made a circular argument. What's my implied assumption? Something like:

> *Weighing harmful effects against potential good is a question of right and wrong.*

Sure, but that *is* a circular syllogism. It just says the same thing over again. Ethics is ethics. I can do better than that. Scrap that because clause and try again. Let's see:

> *because raising questions of right and wrong in relation to science will provide a new perspective.*

I like that a little better. But what's my assumption now? Let's see, do I have a shared term? Well, if my reasoning was circular before because "ethics" and "questions of right and wrong" were really the same thing, then I guess that those are my shared terms now. They don't have the same words, but the concept is the same: "Ethics classes for scientists" is simply redefined as "raising questions of right and wrong about science." So, my assumption must be

> *Learning to weigh harmful effects against potential good effects requires a new perspective.*

That sounds assumable to me, and it seems to make a syllogism. But have I satisfied all the criteria? That because clause is a complete idea, but is it precise? I guess not, since "new perspective" could mean a lot of different things. There I go again, thinking that something clear to me is clear in the words I use! Because I'm going to have to say what this "new perspective" is anyway, I ought to be able to say it here. What *do* I mean by it?

I guess I must be thinking about the perspective of the scientist as being restricted to empirical proofs, while the perspective of morality allows for human feeling. Didn't one of our readings say something like this? Scientists can study the phenomenon of pain, somebody wrote, but they won't understand it until they feel it. I guess I mean that the new perspective will be one of feeling. But is that precise? Do I really mean something like "compassion"? Let me try it out in my because clause:

> *because raising questions of right and wrong in relation to science will require compassion.*

Not quite. Maybe it would be better if I said

> *because raising questions of right and wrong in relation to science requires actively confronting one's compassionate feelings for other people.*

That seems precise, and it also seems to say something that supports the thesis well. "Actively confronting" seems necessary because everybody has feelings, but not everyone bothers to think about them. I still have to test the implied assumption, which now is something like this:

> *Weighing potentially harmful effects of scientific research against potentially good effects requires one to confront actively one's compassionate feelings for other people.*

Is that assumable? Well, maybe not, since it's very general. But I think I can explain what I mean by it, and if I can make it clear I don't think I will have to argue for it. It seems assumable in that sense. Yes. I think I can do that. So here's my basic argument:

> Assumption: *Learning to weigh potentially harmful effects of scientific research against potentially good effects requires one to confront actively one's compassionate feelings for other people.*

Reason: *Ethics classes for scientists (that is, raising questions of right and wrong in relation to science) will confront them with their compassionate feelings for other people.*

Conclusion: *Ethics classes for scientists will teach them to weigh the potential effects of their research against the potential good.*

Well, that may not be the best syllogism in the world (I think there may be an extra assumption in there), but at least it's a case I can make reasonably. And I think it's worth making. It helps me to understand what I think we can learn from the issue of science and morality and maybe even what we can do about it. So, now maybe I'm ready to write the essay. I've got a lot of ideas to develop and a line of reasoning to hang them on as I go along. But where do I start?

*   *   *

Once more, we leave this student in midthought. Let me stress again that the process just portrayed is only an illustration of the need for thinking and not a model of exactly the steps that anyone must or will follow. The point is not that the fictional student does everything systematically and comes up with a good result (you may have thought the resulting enthymeme was not logical or not worth arguing), but that the *task* of finding a thesis and a because clause that satisfies the criteria placed on them will be a stimulus to thought.

The criteria can't guarantee any result; they can merely keep you from being too easily satisfied with your thinking until you have taken it through some active stages to a conclusion. If this student seems to you to be too simple-minded or too abstract, remember that the same general process of discovery must go on no matter how simple or complex, abstract or concrete, the ideas are. The general process need follow no prescribed order. It won't be a conscious process at every stage. But it must contain, as this student's thinking did, certain considerations that are prompted by the five criteria. Once again, such considerations are more likely to be serious if you *write down* successive drafts of the because clause.

FROM ENTHYMEME TO STRUCTURE

A thesis statement, in the form of a well-thought-out enthymeme, provides you with the major parts that will need to be present in your essay and the connections between them that will hold the structure of your composition together. By thinking through the enthymeme, you will have given yourself a basis for thinking about structure. The shape that your essay will take will, therefore, be the shape of your reasoning, a structure that you have generated to fit the argument that you have chosen to develop. You need rely on no "model" essay form to find that shape. Your reasoning will generate the shape of your essay.

In the broadest sense, the parts of the enthymeme can be thought of as the largest units of an essay's structure. They can be diagrammed as follows:

Enthymeme		*Structure*
(question at issue)	→	beginning
(assumption) ⎫	→	middle
because clause ⎭		
assertion	→	end

The enthymeme, having emerged from thinking about your ideas and reasons, can now be looked at as the source for the specific functions of these large structural parts—"specific" because each enthymeme will have its own requirements. These requirements can be understood by thinking of the structure of an essay as the fulfillment of the logical relationships in the enthymeme:

> Beginning: *The reader is introduced to a problem that is of interest because it requires a solution.* The question at issue.
> Middle: *The solution to the problem depends on the reader and writer sharing a common understanding.* The assumption.
> *Given this understanding, an answer to the problem can be developed if a condition can be shown to be the case.* The because clause; the burden of proof.
> End: *Given the assumption and the condition just developed, the solution follows.* The assertion; the thesis.

Needless to say, these parts can be as long or as short as the specific case requires. They do not correspond to paragraphs; this could be the structure of an essay, a chapter, or a book. And within these parts, many kinds of sentences and transitions can occur, as they are called for. But these basic functions are common to essays that *take a reader through a developing line of reasoning toward an earned conclusion.* These elements will in turn help you select and order other elements of thought.

The actual order of these elements will grow out of what you have to say. The enthymeme can therefore help to guide this growth, but it does not determine what form the essay must take. The enthymeme suggests structural possibilities because it connects ideas through reasoning and concepts through predications. Consequently, any enthymeme that seems to satisfy the criteria listed at the beginning of this chapter can give rise to different structures for essays, depending on the writer's choices and how the writer sees those connections. In each case, the writer can use the thinking in the enthymeme to create larger structures of thought.

Any actual essay will have many more parts than the enthymeme from which its structure derives. This is because as the essay moves through the reasoning of the enthymeme other things must happen. Terms may need to be explained. Distinctions may need to be offered. Further reasons may need to be gone into. Examples may need to be used for clarity. Transitions may need to be composed. At any point that a reader may be expected to question, to object, or to be confused, the writer may find a way to help the reader along. Such considerations arise when the writer attempts to develop the basic reasoning of the enthymeme in such a way that a reader will be able to follow it clearly.

An enthymeme can help you to guide the development of your essay's structure by suggesting an outline of ideas. I do not mean an outline having blank spaces with labels such as I.A.b. and to be filled in with a few words—an outline with subdivisions and brief headings. I mean, rather, a sequence of fully predicated sentences that represents the progress of thought in the essay, the ideas in the order in which they will arise in the essay. Having produced such an outline of ideas, you can use it to help define further responsibilities that you might face as the essay unfolds.

There is no single way of generating a structure of ideas from the parts of an enthymeme, and there is no formula that tells you how to do it. You can learn it only by doing it. But to help make this process clearer, I will give some examples of possible structures that might be generated from an enthymeme. This will also help to give you some sense of the range of possibilities implicit in the enthymeme. The enthymeme is not meant to restrict thought to a narrow linear chain, but to help stimulate thought. In each case, I will illustrate the structure of the essay as an outline of ideas.

Suppose I have composed the following structural enthymeme to represent my argument:

> *The study of myths helps us to understand the social roles of women in history*
>
> *because*
>
> *it reveals how the myths of the past have molded the attitudes of successive generations and preserved social order.* *

This reasoning implies a question at issue and an assumption, both of which connect it to its intended audience. The question at issue (a question of consequence) might be stated this way:

> *Can the study of myths help us to understand the social roles of women in history?*

The assumption that holds the reasoning together might be stated like this:

> *The study of whatever has molded the attitudes of successive generations and preserved social order will be helpful in understanding the social role of women in history.*

---

* This basic reasoning, though not the structures or examples that follow, has been adapted from Sarah B. Pomeroy, *Goddesses, Whores, Wives, and Slaves* (New York: Shocken Books, 1975).

Writing out the enthymeme, the question at issue, and the assumption is useful in trying to make decisions about structure. Having written them out, I can ask myself: "Does the assumption need to be included and explained or can it remain unstated?" In the present case, I might well decide that the assumption does not need to be put into the essay at all. I can also ask myself: "Should the question at issue be stated? Should it be developed? Is it obvious to the reader why it is at issue? Should I start with it?" In this case, I might think that it needs to be explained and that it might make a good place to start. Furthermore, I can (and should) ask myself: "What parts does an essay need to have in order to earn this thesis by means of this reasoning?" In this case I might make a small list.

> *The essay must*
> *—show some myths.*
> *—show how those myths molded the attitudes of successive generations.*
> *—show how those myths preserved social order.*
> *—connect those attitudes to the social role of women in history.*
> *—show that those attitudes are preserved as part of the social order.*

My choice to argue this enthymeme and not some other has made me responsible to do these things. Of course, my list of responsibilities might be longer. But any structural enthymeme will contain such responsibilities, and they will consist of explaining the parts of the enthymeme and connecting them according to the predications. Furthermore, I can ask myself: "Should I put the conclusion at the beginning of the essay or should I save it for later?"

Considerations of this sort will enable me to make some structural decisions. I can see that several potential structures are implicit in this enthymeme. The following three outlines of ideas that might result from such considerations:

Structure 1

Our understanding of the social roles of women in history can be enhanced by the study of myth.

. . .

How? By seeing first that myths of the past molded the attitudes of successive generations.

. . .

For example, in the myth of Atalanta, her father abandoned her in the forest because he wanted a son.

. . .

This myth suggested that female children were less desirable than male children.

. . .

Also, in Homer, female goddesses direct the actions of the men at war.

. . .

These stories allow men to blame their actions on women.

. . .

These attitudes are reflected in the historical role of women as both socially inferior to men and the cause of men's misfortunes.

. . .

Second, we can see that myths of the past also preserved the social order that such attitudes created.

. . .

For example, Athena was the goddess of wisdom, peace, and war. She was worshiped, and the city of Athens was dedicated to her.

. . .

She was part of the religion, and civil order was seen as part of a sacred order.

. . .

Social roles could not be questioned without questioning sacred order.

. . .

Consequently, we can see how the social role of women in history was so difficult to escape. It was seen as divinely ordered. Men had an excuse to maintain the role of female inferiority and did not have to take the blame themselves.

Structure 2

Women feature prominently in ancient myths.

. . .

For example, the myth of Atalanta. . .

. . .

The goddesses in Homer. . .

. . .

The worship of Athena. . .

. . .

What attitudes toward women do these myths teach?

. . .

That they are inferior to men.

. . .

That they are to blame for men's actions.

. . .

That the civil order was seen as part of a sacred order.

. . .

What do these myths have to do with the continuation of social roles for women in later history?

. . .

They serve to instill these attitudes.

. . .

They preserved the social role of women by connecting those roles to religious beliefs.

. . .

From this we see that the study of myth can help us to understand the social roles of women in history.

Structure 3

In history women were held in high esteem, but they also were kept in subordinate social roles.

. . .

This is a paradox that is hard to understand.

. . .

Perhaps one way to understand it is to look at the function of myth in creating and preserving those roles.

. . .

Myths mold the attitudes of successive generations.

. . .

They do this by giving examples of people that one is supposed to admire.

. . .

The heroes of Greek legends, for instance, illustrate the virtues of brave and noble behavior.

. . .

Myths also preserve social order.

. . .

They do this not only by defining roles according to the attitudes they create about virtuous behavior, but also by suggesting that these roles in civil society fit into a divine plan.

. . .

Myths about the gods show them to be very human in their actions, and they not only control but also model how human mortals should behave in society.

. . .

How do these observations about myth help us to understand the social roles of women in history? Let's look at some myths about women in these terms.

. . .

Myths that molded attitudes toward women include the myth of Atalanta and the myths of Homeric goddesses.

. . .

These suggest the attitudes that women are inferior to men and that they control men's actions.

. . .

Myths that preserve social order include the worship of Athena in Greek society.

. . .

This myth suggests that attitudes toward women in society are in accord with divine order and cannot change.

. . .

Therefore, we can see that the study of myths can help us to understand the social roles of women in history and why those roles have been hard to change.

. . .

Perhaps by understanding how myth functions to create and perpetuate women's roles in history we can begin to see how those roles can change in the future.

The basic reasoning in the enthymeme has been used to generate each of these structural outlines, and others could be generated from that same reasoning. None of these outlines is complete, of course. Each of the ideas that will make up parts of the essay must themselves be developed further, as the ellipses indicate. But each of these outlines might form the basis of a well-structured essay, one in which the structure develops out of the reasoning.

If the basic reasoning is the same in each case, then how do these three structures differ? Structure 1 starts out with the thesis itself. Next it asserts and illustrates the first part of the because clause, and then the second part, using each example to explain the implications of the because clause. When the explanation of the reasoning is complete, so is the essay, because the conclusion has already been asserted at the outset.

Structure 2, however, does not assert the conclusion until the end of the essay. It begins, instead, with the examples, as if teasing the reader with these interesting details but not saying what their significance is until the reader is well into the essay. After the examples have gotten the reader's interest, the essay asks a question about them that is designed to lead into the reasoning of the because clause. The question at issue is then posed, and the reasoning that has been developed is used to answer it in the form of a concluding assertion.

Structure 3 begins with statements that are intended to show why the question at issue is important, to raise the issue in such a way that the problem being solved is immediately clear. The essay then explains each part of the because clause, and only after that does it go into any examples. The examples are used to further explain the because clause, and the conclusion is asserted. A further consequence of the reasoning (one that was not necessarily explicit in the enthymeme but may have been in the writer's mind anyway) is then asserted, as a way of ending the essay on a strong note.

In addition to dealing with the specific parts of the enthymeme and their connections, each of these structures necessarily contains elements that are not explicitly part of the enthymeme. That is to be expected because the enthymeme represents the basic reasoning of the argument, which only the essay itself can fully explain and support. Each of them would do justice to the reasoning, then, while also necessarily going beyond it. My choice of which structure to use, or whether to think of another, would depend on which parts of the reasoning needed the most emphasis, on what kinds of information I wanted to include, on what I imagine to be my reader's needs and interests in this issue, and on what kind of effect I wanted to create for the reader. Any essay structured in each of the above ways would differ slightly in emphasis, in detail, and in both its initial impact and its final effect on the reader.

In each of the structures, the enthymeme also led me into further reasoning. Not only did the parts of the essay need to explain the parts of the enthymeme, but often new reasons had to be developed to support those parts. In this case some of those reasons were inductive (the actual myths that enabled conclusions to be drawn about the function of myth in general). As in any inductive argument, the number of examples was limited somewhat arbitrarily. Any of these structures could have contained further examples. The adequacy of the examples, the amount of development each one needs, and the range of my knowledge or research could affect the decision to use more or fewer examples. The idea outline generated by the enthymeme acts like an accordion file: It expands to fit what needs to go into it at any point. If details or examples are added to such a structure, the writer knows where they belong.

As the reasoning of the enthymeme expands to become a structure, further needs arise. In the example, the reasoning depended on assertions which themselves required reasons. This is why an essay often develops into a more complex line of reasoning than that contained in the initial enthymeme. One reason becomes a "mini-thesis" that requires support in the form of another enthymeme. This is why I call the thesis statement a "structural enthymeme," to distinguish it from all the other enthymemes that any essay might contain as parts of its reasoning. The structural enthymeme contains the whole argument and consequently generates the needs for subarguments; mini-theses; and other, local enthymemes. The result is a patchwork of reasons, stitched together to form the overall design sketched by the thesis statement.

Among the needs that may arise as an enthymeme is expanded into a structure are the need for examples (which we have already encountered), the need for definitions, the need for qualifications, the need for factual evidence, the need for explanations (perhaps by way of analogy or anecdote), the need for authoritative testimony, and the need to acknowledge or to refute potential counterarguments. It is impossible to say in advance whether an essay must respond to any of these needs, because they arise as the essay unfolds in relation to the nature of the case being made and the audience.

I will illustrate how another enthymeme may generate different structures, this time showing how such needs might be addressed in their proper place. Suppose I have drafted this enthymeme to represent the argument I wish to make:

> *Education about date rape would reduce the incidence of rapes on college campuses*
>
> *because*
>
> *informing students that all forced sex is rape would make them less likely to force an acquaintance or date to have sex against her will.*

I have based my reasoning on an assumption something like this:

> *Anything that would make students less likely to force an acquaintance or date to have sex against her will would reduce the incidence of rapes on college campuses.*

That assumption is one that I may or may not be able to take for granted, depending on my audience.

Here is one way I might develop this reasoning into a structure:

Structure 1

What is rape?

. . .

The law defines it as "the forcing of sexual intercourse upon a person against that person's will or without that person's permission."

. . .

The law does not say that it's a rape only if there is a gun or knife, or a threat of physical violence. It does not limit rape to the case of a deranged pervert breaking into a stranger's apartment.

. . .

The law does not say that it isn't rape if the man is the woman's husband, or if he has bought her dinner, or if he has been to bed with her in the past.

. . .

In fact, as many as 80 percent of the rapes reported to police have been committed by someone the woman knows, often someone whom she knows very well. Experts call this "date rape" or "acquaintance rape."

. . .

But many women do not report such rapes because they do not believe that what their friend or lover has done is the same as rape. They suffer in silence and do not get help.

. . .

And many men say they do not believe that the use of some force with a woman who says "no," or sex with a woman who has had so much to drink that she cannot resist is rape.

. . .

This ignorance—of the law and of what women and men should expect from each other as equal partners in sexual decisions—is the cause of many rapes.

. . .

These are rapes that could be avoided if education informed people of the law and changed people's way of thinking about sexual relationships.

Here is a structure that begins with a question of definition that is part of the overall attempt to answer a question of policy. The definition is needed because it is what the "education" term in the thesis refers to. The essay need not have started with that definition, but it is an effective way to work into the development of the because clause. The structure also incorporates several other parts that do not belong to the enthymeme but turn out to be needed as the reasoning develops. Facts, of course, are introduced to support and to clarify the premise asserted in the because clause. Authorities are cited to add credibility to the facts. When the essay turns toward showing that women and men are ignorant of those facts, further opportunities arise. To show that the assertions are true, the writer could add the authority of surveys or more experts. Or, to give the reader a sense of the immediacy of the assertions and to illustrate just how often women or men misunderstand what rape is, the writer could add anecdotes or examples of events that illustrate rapes of these kinds.

In a different argumentative situation (as perceived by the writer), the same enthymeme could generate a very different structure and a very different kind of essay.

Structure 2

We have a serious problem on this campus.

. . .

Here are some documented cases of rape on this campus in the previous two months, told to me by the head counselor.

. . .

Tell about Bud expecting to have sex with Miriam because he bought her an expensive dinner. She said "no," but he convinced her that she "owed" it to him. She blames herself.

. . .

Tell about Jesse getting drunk and passing out at the party, when five house members then had sex with her. She is about to sue the fraternity and the University.

. . .

Tell about Edna who has finally sought counseling to get out of an abusive marriage. Her husband frequently threatens her with more violence if she does not have sex, but she says she doesn't think this is rape.

. . .

Tell about Teri who resisted when her date got a little rough and who was then raped. She didn't seek help for three weeks because her friends told her it happens all the time and she should toughen up. But she was too distressed about it to study.

. . .

These are just four of ten similar instances.

. . .

Here are statistics showing that for every rape reported to anyone, ten go unreported.

. . .

That means that there were probably twenty such rapes on this campus in the last two months.

. . .

So, as college deans, you must begin the date rape education campaign now or you will not be acting responsibly toward our women students.

Here is a situation (an exhortation to the college deans) in which all that needs to be done in the essay is to demonstrate the enormity of the problem and its seriousness. Most of the actual reasoning, which is implicit, is undeveloped in relation to the citation of case histories and expert testimony. The deans do not have to be told that these are cases of rape according to the law's definition. They are presumed to know that. They do not need to be told that education is needed to overcome the ignorance of those who commit such rapes or fall victim to them. But they do need to be exhorted to act, and the structure is designed to have that effect.

A third possible structure based on the reasoning of this enthymeme follows.

Structure 3

In a recent case reported in the news, a jury acquitted a man of rape on the grounds that the woman was dressed provocatively and was therefore "asking for it."

. . .

Such a case illustrates that attitudes toward rape are slow to change. Even in the 1990s some people think that a woman can be blamed when a man forces her to have sex.

. . .

Even the widespread success of the feminist movement has not changed many people's minds.

. . .

This is clear from the fact that most rapes are committed by acquaintances, and even dates. Contrary to public opinion, rapes are most likely to be committed by the nice young man next door and not the armed stranger in the night. Attitudes in society, not deranged individuals, seem to be the cause.

. . .

One reason seems to be that young men and women practice courtship in ways that enforce the attitude that rape is an accepted form of sex.

. . .

Men are the aggressors in courtship situations, while women are passive.

. . .

Men spend their money while women are supposed to be grateful.

. . .

Men believe that women who say they do not want sex don't really mean it.

. . .

Of course, it is true that not all men believe such things. But enough do to make the problem widespread, and even those who don't often find that peer pressure to "score" is too strong to resist.

. . .

Such beliefs result in some men forcing women to have sex because the men think it is consistent with male/female roles.

. . .

Beliefs are not inevitable. They can be changed.

. . .

College is one place where young men and women can be asked to confront their attitudes and change them.

. . .

Therefore, our campus is an appropriate place to conduct an educational campaign to reduce the number of rapes committed by men who do not believe that forced sex in some circumstances is rape.

. . .

Maybe then some of society's attitudes will change more quickly than they seem to have done.

Because this essay plan develops the idea of attitudes (or the "belief" term of the because clause), it can begin with a more indirect anecdote and it need not offer as many examples. Other ways of raising the issue of people's attitudes are possible. The essay will also contain one section that qualifies its statements about the beliefs of men, to try to answer a potential reader's objection that the generalizations are too large and sweeping. The essay later raises the issue of education (and college) to offer a positive solution to the problem.

The purpose of these examples is to show how an enthymeme can guide the writer in developing a structure for an essay. But the enthymeme does not predetermine the structure. As the essay must somehow fulfill the basic reasoning of the enthymeme, it must make certain moves and have certain parts. But the order they come in and anything else the writer might choose to include to develop the reasoning are still up to the writer, based on the perceived needs of the audience and the desired effect. Such decisions will differ from argument to argument. No model can tell you in advance what parts your essay must have and what order they must go in. Since the enthymeme stands for the specific argument you wish to make, you can use it to guide your thinking about the specific decisions you face when structuring the parts of an essay. A structure generated by the conditions of a well-reasoned enthymeme will be more likely to move the reader from beginning to end than one that is based on a prefabricated form or one that develops aimlessly.

FROM STRUCTURE TO ESSAY: AN ANALYSIS

I am not able to offer you much advice about the actual drafting of the prose of your essay. I think that if you have come this far you don't need such advice anyway. The kind of inquiry that has enabled you to compose a sound enthymeme that represents what you want to say will also enable you to generate an adequate structure for the essay. The same inquiry will have provided you with many ideas for your essay, and those ideas will find a place within the structure you have generated. The words of the sentences also will follow from the clear sense of purpose and structure that you have discovered in this process, although you may sometimes have to struggle to find them. No principles or rules can account for how the right word suddenly enters your mind. If your mind is focused on what you want to say at any given point of your essay, you will find the words.

Rather than tell you any more about how to compose your essay, I will give a final example showing the enthymeme, the structure, and the essay that results. The process is one of moving from a clear sense of what the argument is, to considering the sequence or design of ideas that the argument requires and that will help it along, to writing the sentences that will bring your reader through those ideas most effectively. To show this, let's return to the argument developed by the fictional student we have been following as he moved from class discussion to thesis to enthymeme.

> *Ethics classes for scientists will teach them to weigh the potential effects of their research against the potential good*
>
> *because*
>
> *raising questions of right and wrong in relation to science will confront them with their compassionate feelings for other people.*

An essay structured according to the logic of this enthymeme might begin by conveying to the reader that there is a problem to be solved. The question at issue is implicit in the thesis, but it requires explanation nonetheless. What makes the issue an issue? Such a consideration seems to provide the best place to start. Thus, the first thing the essay might do is to state the problem in such terms:

> *The problem of whether scientists should be ethically responsible for the harmful applications of their research is one that concerns us all.*

. . .

Even if someone else makes the application, the scientist is responsible to some degree if he or she is aware of the possibility of harmful effects. Thus, one aspect of the problem is to find a way for scientists to consider their options by weighing harmful effects against beneficial ones.

. . .

It should not be assumed that scientists, schooled in objective methods of research, necessarily know how to do this.

. . .

Thus, it may be a question of how scientists are taught. Might the addition of ethics classes for scientists enable them to learn how to weigh harmful and good effects, as a way of thinking about their responsibilities?

. . .

As part of the introduction to an essay (we don't know yet how many sentences or even paragraphs that introduction might take), these ideas function to develop the need for the writer's thesis and to promise an answer. To continue, this line of reasoning might next develop a connection to the terms of the because clause:

The answer depends on understanding what kind of knowledge is required to be able to weigh harmful effects against good ones.

. . .

What does harmful *mean in this case? It means effects that hurt people.*

. . .

Thus, if scientists are to weigh the harm done to other human beings, they must be able to feel compassion for others' suffering. Feeling compassion is what makes it possible for one to know how harmful an effect might be.

At this point, the assumption implicit in the enthymeme has been proposed. The structure now requires linking this assumption with the remaining terms of the because clause. The essay's structure now enters the crucial burden of proof phase of the reasoning in the enthymeme.

How do people become aware of their compassionate feelings for others? If people are confronted with their feelings about the welfare of others, they cannot help but think about the extent of their compassion. What kind of activities bring about this confrontation?

. . .

Asking questions of right and wrong. Questions that require a choice between a right course of action and a wrong one will involve one in examining compassionate interest in the welfare of others.

. . .

At this point, the major and minor premises of the logic have both been asserted, but a redefinition of the terms of the because clause is needed to bring the logic of the enthymeme to its conclusion.

Raising such questions of right and wrong about matters of science would be the aim of an ethics class for scientists.

. . .

Such a class would, therefore, enable scientists to learn to weigh potential harmful effects against potential benefits of their research and help to make them see their responsibilities.

The enthymeme has helped the writer to generate a progression of ideas from problem to solution. This basic line of reasoning resulted from introducing the terms of the enthymeme and making connections among them, in an order that the reader might be expected to follow.

These statements do not yet constitute the prose of an essay. They merely represent a rational backbone for an essay. We have been concerned only with finding a structure that will unfold according to the logic of the case, so that the parts of the essay will follow each other and move toward the conclusion. The statements constitute an outline that has yet to be fleshed out with further connections, further development, and further support. The outline of ideas that is generated by the enthymeme must now generate an even more thorough treatment, in the actual prose of the essay, according to the needs of the reader.

What does the reader need to know at each point in order to understand, to follow, and to agree? The writer must provide the answers—by guessing, of course, since the actual responses of readers can't be predicted with much certainty. A writer might decide to provide a definition, to explain a concept, to provide an illustrative example, to cite the writing of others, or to bring in additional reasons in support of some claim. All such additions to the basic structure might be provided in response to a reader's potential needs, at points where the reader might be imagined to ask "What's that mean?" or "Can you show me an example?" or "Why should I believe that?" Anticipating such questions, when they are reasonable, is one way in which the writer can decide whether any of the innumerable "things to be said" should be said in *this* essay, and if so, where those things should go. The writer is responsible to try to see his or her own argument from the point of view of a reader who may not already agree with it and to consider whether good reasons may also be found to support opposing ideas. This consideration helped the writer to develop a reasonable thesis in the first place. It can now help the writer to develop a better essay, by enabling him or her to deal with objections as they arise within the essay's developing structure.

Based on such considerations, and following the outline of ideas generated by the enthymeme, the next essay might have been written by our fictional student. As you read it, ask what needs of the reader (as the writer imagined them) led to each decision the writer made.

*   *   *

THE NEED FOR AN ETHICAL EDUCATION
FOR SCIENTISTS

Scientists are taught to discover "truth" by conducting experiments in an objective manner, without allowing personal feelings to affect the outcome. Yet this view of science has often come under attack, when the possibility exists that objectivity may do more harm than good. When the application of scientific knowledge creates harm, many are willing to blame the scientists, or at least to argue that the scientist shares in the ethical responsibility for these applications.

It would be ridiculous to assume that all scientists share in this responsibility equally. Sir Isaac Newton, for instance, cannot be blamed for the applications that the scientists and technicians who developed the first atomic weapon made of his basic laws of physics. It is interesting, though, that Albert Einstein, who built his theories on the basis of Newton's, expressed regret about his contribution to the atomic age. The scientists who worked on the Manhattan project have recently expressed even more sense of responsibility for their more direct contributions to atomic weaponry. Thus, the question of responsibility seems to be a matter of degree, depending on the closeness of the scientist to the application itself. It seems reasonable to think that scientists share a greater burden of ethical responsibility if they are more able to predict the specific harmful application and its likelihood. Newton thought he was disclosing the wonders of God's creation. But the Los Alamos scientists were fully aware that they were working on a bomb.

These scientists faced a choice. They could contribute their knowledge to uncovering the secrets of the atom, or they could withhold their support for this project. Some chose to participate because, as scientists, they desired to increase knowledge, while others were motivated by the patriotic goal of winning the war by any means. Some chose to stay home, or even to protest the activities of the Los Alamos scientists. These scientists all made ethical decisions because they knew that their research could lead to specific harmful applications.

Although responsibility must be shared with those who choose to make the application, it does seem that scientists who make a choice to conduct research in full knowledge of the potential beneficial and harmful applications have accepted some ethical responsibility for themselves. They have made their choice by weighing the beneficial applications against the harmful ones, by deciding to risk the possibility of one outcome against the likelihood of another. This kind of decision does not depend on how much one understands about science—although scientific knowledge does help one to predict the likelihood of a result—as much as it depends on being able to determine right and wrong. Scientists have ethical responsibility not as scientists, but as human beings with consciences. They are no more or less able to know what is morally right than anyone else. Yet, because of the power given to scientists by virtue of their ability to create knowledge, they seem to have a special obligation to choose whether to conduct certain kinds of research.

Modern society invests scientists with this power, yet it does not seem to do anything special to teach them how to exercise it conscientiously. Vast resources are used to ensure that scientists are good at practicing science, but very little is done to ensure that they become better at making ethical choices. In a world in which the impact of science on the quality of people's lives is enormous, and especially after recent history has shown us how scientists do make ethical choices, it seems obvious that thought should be given to how a scientific education might prepare future scientists for making ethical decisions.

Although ethics classes for scientists seems like a good idea, it isn't necessarily clear how such classes might actually make scientists better able to decide whether or not to conduct research based on weighing potentially harmful effects against beneficial ones. A commitment to the idea of adding ethics classes to the scientific curriculum would be easier to make if we were sure that such classes would succeed in making future scientists more capable of thinking about their ethical responsibilities. The question then becomes how such classes would make a difference: Would ethics classes for scientists teach them to make ethical choices?

To answer this question, we might consider what kind of knowledge is required by anyone who is able to weigh harmful effects against beneficial ones. How does one learn to think about the relative importance of good and bad outcomes, when both might result? This is a difficult problem, and I cannot solve it to my own complete satisfaction. I think there is a way to begin thinking about it, however, by asking what we mean in this case by *harmful* and *beneficial*.

Harmful and *beneficial* must refer to effects that hurt or benefit people. They are terms that refer to what people feel about their own conditions. Now, it may be possible to try to measure those conditions by some scientific means, but such efforts will always impose an outside view on feelings that only an individual can really know. What I mean is that *harmful* and *beneficial* could be defined so that they refer to statistical conditions: Society is harmed if unemployment rates rise, or society is benefited if the gypsy moth is eradicated. These are ways of thinking about harm and benefit as objectively measured characteristics, and by using such definitions, people's actual feelings are abstracted out of the picture. But another way of approaching *harm* and *benefit* is to see them as matters of personal suffering or personal satisfaction. Each person's actual suffering as a result of unemployment will be different; each person's actual benefit as a result of employment will be different, too. Eradicating the gypsy moth may save an industry, but the degree of actual suffering caused by the elimination of that industry is different from the amount of money gained or lost in the process.

This distinction helps us to see that scientific methods, such as the study of gain and loss in statistical terms, might provide one way of weighing harm and benefit, but this way does not necessarily produce the ability to measure harm in terms of human suffering. The way in which suffering is really known is not through statistics and balance sheets, but through compassion. Compassion—perhaps an old-fashioned-sounding word to some—is the ability to feel another's hurt or pleasure and to understand it from the inside. If an action results in suffering for individuals, the actual degree of its harmfulness will be unknown to anyone who cannot feel that suffering by empathizing compassionately with the victim.

If scientists are to learn to weigh the harm done to other human beings as a foreseeable result of the application of their research, they must be able to feel other's suffering compassionately. This sounds self-evident, but it is easy to forget that scientists may be more inclined than others to view suffering from the objective, "bottom line" perspective. But they need not be. Scientists can become aware of their compassionate feelings for others in the same way other people do, by being confronted directly with their feelings for others. Science education doesn't necessarily create this kind of confrontation, but other kinds of learning situations do. This sort of confrontation exists whenever students are asked to choose between right and wrong actions in particular situations where harm and benefit would result. In such situations, more than the likelihood of a specific outcome is at stake; one must also determine how much suffering one is willing to tolerate in exchange for how much benefit.

Consider this example: If I am invited to go cycling with a friend, I might object to her refusal to wear a protective helmet. I would face an ethical decision. Should I refuse to go along unless she agrees to wear one? It's her own business to make up her mind, but it's my business whether to encourage her to risk hurting herself. She might say that the risk of having an accident is very slight. That's true, but the suffering that might result for her could be horrible. I have read about such accidents. My ethical responsibility, if that suffering were to result, would be great, I feel, because the suffering would be great. Thus, my decision would be based on three factors—my ability to foresee the possibility of an accident, the likelihood of that possibility, *and* my compassionate understanding of the potential suffering. We all face similar decisions all the time—whether to let a friend drive drunk, for example, or whether to insist that passengers use seat belts.

An education in science would presumably enable scientists to consider the first two factors, since scientific thinking can be applied to predicting effects and their likelihood. But an ethical education of some kind is necessary to enable one to consider the third.

Ethics classes for scientists could present such choices in relation to actual kinds of research. Issues in medicine, for instance, such as whether certain kinds of human experimentation should be used, or issues in genetic engineering, would present students with the kinds of confrontation that I have described. Presented with a choice of actions, students would have to examine their own compassionate feelings in order to answer the question of whether the suffering would be worth the benefits. Scientists would not learn that the answers are easy, but they might come to a greater understanding of the kinds of ethical choices they will face in their research careers. This may not prevent harmful effects from occurring, but it might enable scientists to recognize their individual ethical responsibilities. In a society in which scientific knowledge is necessary to solve problems created by science, this is the least that we must hope for.

You may think this is a good argument or a poor one, but at this point let's suspend that judgment and ask *how* this student got from the sketchy structure generated earlier to this more fully developed essay.

Writing is a process of discovery, and discovery happens within constraints. Writing combines freedom and control. The draft essay above illustrates this, even though we do not see what actually went on as the drafting progressed. As the student's thinking developed from enthymeme to structure and from structure to essay, new discoveries resulted at each stage, and they were prompted by the new kinds of questions that each new task presented. In the process of trying to develop the smaller units of the composition out of a clear understanding of the larger units (what I earlier called moving from whole to parts), the writer discovers new possibilities, new requirements, and new challenges. This is inevitable, because a writer cannot conceive of a complete, fully developed essay all at once; an essay must be built up part by part. The process of determining the logic and the structure before drafting is not meant to reduce the writer's freedom. Nothing could do that; there are always new possibilities to be discovered. It is meant to direct the necessary choices toward a consistent and intelligent end.

In going over the essay, in comparison with the student's structural plan, we can see where some of these challenges occurred and how the student responded to them. Notice first of all that the student takes four paragraphs at the beginning to get through the first two structural steps, introducing the problem of whether scientists should be ethically responsible as a subject for inquiry. Why? The writer probably had to back up so far because the *nature* of that problem has to be understood in a certain way in order to prepare for later elements of the essay. The first paragraph not only introduces and explains the general problem, but also speaks of it in terms of what the scientist is "taught," which will be a matter of concern later in the essay, as will the idea of "objectivity." The second paragraph attempts to clarify the kind of responsibility under discussion by using examples that also serve to introduce the need to solve the general problem. A new idea is introduced into this paragraph, one the outline had not specifically required, but that the progression of the prose now seems to call for: Not only is responsibility said to be a matter of degree, as in the second step of the structural plan, but degree itself is determined by the scientist's "closeness" to the application. This detail occurs, we presume, to explain why the writer thinks it is a matter of degree, but also to answer a potential objection, which the writer has anticipated: How can a scientist like Newton be responsible at all, even if he could imagine some kinds of applications?

Certain details of these paragraphs are included to clarify the writer's purpose to the reader. The whole of the third paragraph seems to have resulted from the writer's sense that the idea of ethical choice may not be clear to the reader. Thus, the writer feels a need to expand on the example of scientists who did know what the consequences of their research might be. This example demonstrates for the reader that the problem is not a simple one of choosing between good and evil, because it involves scientists who had to weigh their choice between conflicting goods. Thus, the writer has prepared the reader to accept the next part of the structure, the idea that a way must be found for scientists to "consider their options by weighing harmful effects against beneficial ones." This idea is made explicit in paragraph five, but is implicit nonetheless in three and four. The writer has, in fact, departed from the order of the ideas in the outline, because new relationships among thoughts developed as the writing unfolded. The outline would call for saying at this point that "objective methods of research" do not necessarily teach scientists how to make this choice, but the writer has already made us aware of this and, in paragraph four, the writer goes into a variation on this idea:

This kind of decision does not depend on how much one understands about science—although scientific knowledge does help one to predict the likelihood of a result—as

much as it depends on being able to determine right and wrong. Scientists have
ethical responsibility not as scientists, but as human beings with consciences. . . . Yet,
because of the power given to scientists by virtue of their ability to create knowledge,
they seem to have a special obligation to choose whether to conduct certain kinds of
research.

Here, the writer has developed new ideas, within the structure as planned and
even *because* of the demands created by that structure. The writer is still
thinking about the argument, and these new ideas emerge as a result. The
distinction between using scientific knowledge to determine the likelihood of
a result and using some other kind of knowledge to weigh good and harmful
results is not part of the logic of the enthymeme, and it is not an element in
the idea outline. But it is to become a major feature of the essay as it
progresses, one that supports the line of reasoning.

In the fifth paragraph, the idea of the scientist's "power" becomes a transition to the need for education, returning to the structure of the idea outline.
This helps the writer make a transition from the question at issue to the
writer's initial discussion of the thesis, but it also functions to add an emotional appeal. Note the special appeal to the quality of our lives and how that
appeal is strengthened by the writer's understated return to the earlier example
of "recent history," reminding us of the nuclear threat without hitting us over
the heads with it.

The sixth and seventh paragraphs follow the structural outline and move
the argument forward. In explaining the next stages of the line of reasoning,
these paragraphs also attempt to respond to a critical reader's potential doubts.
They are functional paragraphs, leading the reader to the next crucial step in
the logic, but they also defend the need for going on to that step. "A commitment
to the idea of adding ethics classes to the scientific curriculum would be easier
to make if. . . ." This prepares the reader for an answer at the same time that
it asks the reader to speculate along with the writer before rejecting the possibility. In the seventh paragraph, the writer sees a need to make a confession.

This is a difficult problem, and I cannot solve it to my own complete satisfaction. I
think there is a way to begin thinking about it, however, by. . . .

The writer has become aware of the possibility that a reader might say something like this: "Who are you to be answering a question that has confused
people for centuries? It's not as simple as you think." And the writer wants the
reader to know that he is speculating, not trying to cram his belief down
anyone's throat.

It is in paragraphs eight and nine that the new distinction between what
can and cannot be known by scientific means becomes part of the writer's
logic. (A reader of the essay would be surprised to learn that this distinction
was not planned, but emerged during the composition, as the necessity for it
arose.) The distinction works within the writer's logic by helping to explain
what *harmful* and *beneficial* mean—a predetermined move on the writer's part,

but not fully thought out when the structural outline was written. It also smooths the way for the introduction of an important term in the logic: *compassion*. The structural outline introduced this term abruptly; the essay makes its introduction seem more natural. The distinction between what scientific methods can teach and what they cannot is brought forward again, in paragraph ten, as a way of returning to the question of education, and the next term in the logical structure, *confrontation*, is addressed.

When paragraph ten ends, the writer seems to sense the reader's potential confusion. *Confrontation* is a pretty abstract word here, and the reader may feel that it needs clarification. Paragraph eleven attempts to bring the essay back down to earth a bit and to make the meaning of *confrontation* come alive. The writer creates a believable example of everyday confrontation with a question of right and wrong. The bicycle example also clarifies the writer's earlier distinction between scientific and ethical ways of knowing.

> *Thus, my decision would be based on three factors: my ability to foresee the possibility of an accident, the likelihood of that possibility,* and *my compassionate understanding of the potential suffering.*

The example also takes us back to earlier parts of the essay. It reminds us that in being able to predict the outcome, we are more like the Los Alamos scientists than we are like Newton—"closer" to the outcome and hence responsible to a greater degree. In being able to calculate the likelihood of an accident, we are thinking like a scientist. In having compassion, we are able to confront the ethical nature of the decision most fully. Paragraph twelve explicitly connects the example with those principles. Thus, the writer's case has been well served by an example at this point. It adds reality to the abstract reasoning.

The last paragraph completes the logic of the enthymeme and the structure of the argument. Further examples are brought in to show the reader that the thesis is applicable to a variety of specific issues. The logic is summarized, but in the process the writer introduces a qualification that is once again not present in the structural outline. The writer is again reminding readers of the complexity of the issue and putting the thesis into that context: "This is not the final solution," it seems to say, "but a path to follow." To prevent the reader from leaving the essay with a false impression, the writer adds a final sentence that goes beyond the thesis and yet shows how the thesis might apply to our thinking about the issue. "Don't get me wrong," it seems to say, "I don't think science is bad. We need science. But we need ethics, too, if we are to make science succeed." The writer's final idea—thought up in the process of composing—helps to make the thesis believable, not by continuing to give reasons for believing it, but by relating it to the hope for a better future that the writer and the reader are assumed to share.

This analysis isn't meant to explain why the writer included every sentence or every word. No analysis could explain how a writer makes such decisions. Sometimes the answer to why a writer has done it one way and not another is simply "because it felt right." But that does not mean that you can use that reason for an excuse; a decision, after it is made, either will work together with all other elements of the writing or it won't. The best basis for making such a judgment, as this book has argued, is your own clear sense of your intention: what you want to say and how you plan to support it; what you want the reader to understand and how you plan to take the reader there. The thesis, the enthymeme, and the structure that you work out for this purpose will not guarantee answers or make composing easier. But they will bring the process under greater control than would otherwise be the case.

One serious matter that this analysis has not addressed is in what ways this essay may fail to earn its conclusion. It is not a perfect argument, nor is it written in very eloquent style. But in the process of composing it, the writer's thinking progressed to a stage it had not before reached, and that is a significant achievement. It leaves room for further growth, of course. But without the attempt to make the argument as good as possible, this writer would not have achieved even this much. Although we could measure the success of this essay according to some absolute scale of quality and find it lacking, we can also see it as the result of a writer's struggle to come to a significant understanding and to structure and clarify that understanding for others. We can measure only what the writer achieved according to what level of thinking and composing he was capable of before and is now capable of a result of making this attempt. From here, two directions are possible: The writer might reconsider the issue, rethink the thesis, restructure the argument, or simply revise the prose, and produce a better essay on the same subject; or, the writer might use everything learned in the process of writing this essay—much of it unconsciously—to face the challenges of a new one.

IMPLICATIONS FOR RESEARCH

Every researcher is also a communicator. Since the progress of research goes from formulating a question and becoming informed to drawing and testing conclusions, these same elements constitute the essence of what the researcher must communicate. These, of course, are the elements of an argumentative essay. Formulating a thesis, developing a principle line of reasoning, structuring the reasoning into major parts of the composition, revising the argument, generating a structure, and drafting the essay do not change for the researcher. The research paper adds to these responsibilities certain others that follow from having used secondary sources and conducted primary research of some kind.

The researcher, in the process of gathering information and discovering reasons to support a hypothesis, has amassed much information and tested its relevance and validity. Not everything that the inquiry has turned up will necessarily be relevant, and the writer may eventually use only a portion of the actual information he or she has discovered. The writer should include whatever is necessary and sufficient to lead to a conclusion, as well as whatever may need to be said to refute the arguments of others or suggest limitations on one's own. To do this requires planning, along the lines discussed in this chapter. The writer can perceive the necessary structure of the essay by analyzing the parts of the whole argument, which can be summarized in an enthymeme. It is important to remember here that the order in which the research findings appear in the essay will not necessarily be the same as the order in which the researcher discovered them. The structure of the final essay is not a narrative of what happened to the researcher during the inquiry. The structure of the final argument is made up of ideas discovered during research, in whatever logical order binds those ideas into a whole, developing argument.

The structure of research writing in some disciplines is determined in part by conventional formats. It may or may not be necessary for you to follow them in writing for college courses, because the formats generally derive from the conventions of publication in different fields. Thus, an academic journal of research in psychology may specify that papers submitted for publication have a certain form. Articles in the social sciences often follow the conventional divisions of scientific reports, with all the material organized under headings, such as:

Problem and hypothesis
Review of relevant literature
Experiment design
Results
Analysis
Conclusion and discussion

The specific headings differ from discipline to discipline, and even from publication to publication, so you should not try to reproduce a standard format of this kind unless you are fulfilling an assignment that specifically calls for one, or writing for a publication that does. If your audience expects to find your research organized in such a way, then your use of a conventional format will make their reading easier. If not, you should be guided only by the ideas you present. Do not confuse structure with format. You are no less responsible for structuring your ideas *within* each of these conventional sections, if you use them.

As a research writer you have a special obligation to provide whatever the reader needs to know to assess the validity of your findings. Remember that you are interested in finding the best possible reasons for drawing a conclusion, not in bullying the reader into believing some idea that you haven't adequately supported. This means that you should consider including a description of the methods that you have used in your study and any limitations imposed by those methods. In some cases, this may mean a description of an experiment, a survey, or some other form of primary research, together with a description of the sorts of conclusions that such methods are not able to support. Or it may mean that you should inform the reader about any prior assumptions or perspectives that have guided your inquiry. If you have doubts about any of your sources, you can say so. If you think there are weaknesses in your conclusions, qualify them accordingly. If you have discovered reasons against your case (by reading sources that disagree or by falsifying your conclusions), present them fairly and let the reader assess them as you have done. Be sure that your reason for leaving anything out is that it isn't relevant or necessary, not that you wish to hide anything. Honest research, like honest argumentative writing, is intended to put the whole case forward, as you see it, so that the reader's understanding and agreement are *earned*.

QUESTIONS FOR THOUGHT, DISCUSSION, AND WRITING

1. If you have written a structural enthymeme to use as the basis for your next essay, use the criteria on p. 145 to revise it, if necessary.
2. Having done so, list some of the things that an essay written for this enthymeme makes you responsible to do. Then write an outline of ideas that develops the reasoning contained in the enthymeme. The sentences in this outline should represent the stages in the reasoning suggested by your enthymeme, covering the terms and the relationships you have asserted among them.
3. Where in the developing reasoning might your argument require, or be improved by, any of the following?
   a. further reasons
   b. examples/illustrations
   c. data
   d. qualifications
   e. acknowledgments of counterarguments
   f. analogies
   g. descriptions
   h. anything else?
4. Based on this planning, draft your essay. Don't be afraid to change any part of the plan if you discover a better way while you are composing. Don't be afraid to try out anything that seems right; you can scratch out, tear up, rewrite, or move anything you want to.
5. Here are two argumentative essays. After reading each one, try to compose an enthymeme that represents the major line of reasoning developed in the argument. Based on that, analyze the structure of the essay according to how the author has chosen to develop that reasoning. What makes each of its parts necessary? Why are they presented in this order? Are there unnecessary parts? Are there missing parts?

◆ **READINGS** ◆

LETTER TO THE PULITZER PRIZE COMMITTEE

Sinclair Lewis

Sirs:—I wish to acknowledge your choice of my novel *Arrowsmith* for the Pulitzer Prize. That prize I must refuse, and my refusal would be meaningless unless I explained the reasons.

All prizes, like all titles, are dangerous. The seekers for prizes tend to labor not for inherent excellence but for alien rewards: they tend to write this, or timorously to avoid writing that, in order to tickle the prejudices of a haphazard committee. And the Pulitzer Prize for novels is peculiarly objectionable because the terms of it have been constantly and grievously misrepresented.

Those terms are that the prize shall be given "for the American novel published during the year which shall best present the wholesome atmosphere of American life, and the highest standard of American manners and manhood." This phrase, if it means anything whatever, would appear to mean that the appraisal of the novels shall be made not according to their actual literary merit but in obedience to whatever code of Good Form may chance to be popular at the moment.

That there is such a limitation of the award is little understood. Because of the condensed manner in which the announcement is usually reported, and because certain publishers have trumpeted that any novel which has received the Pulitzer Prize has thus been established without qualification as *the best* novel, the public has come to believe that the prize is the highest honor which an American novelist can receive.

The Pulitzer Prize for novels signifies, already, much more than a convenient thousand dollars to be accepted even by such writers as smile secretly at the actual wording of the terms. It is tending to become a sanctified tradition. There is a general belief that the administrators of the prize are a pontifical body with the discernment and power to grant the prize as the ultimate proof of merit. It is believed that they are always guided by a committee of responsible critics, though in the case both of this and other Pulitzer Prizes, the administrators can, and sometimes do, quite arbitrarily reject the recommendations of their supposed advisers.

If already the Pulitzer Prize is so important, it is not absurd to suggest that in another generation it may, with the actual terms of the award ignored, become the one thing for which any ambitious novelist will strive; and the administrators of the prize may become a supreme court, a college of cardinals, so rooted and so sacred that to challenge them will be to commit blasphemy. Such is the French Academy, and we have had the spectacle of even an Anatole France intriguing for election.

Only by regularly refusing the Pulitzer Prize can novelists keep such a power from being permanently set up over them.

Between the Pulitzer Prizes, the American Academy of Arts and Letters and its training-school, the National Institute of Arts and Letters, amateur boards of censorship, and the inquisition of earnest literary ladies, every compulsion is put upon writers to become safe, polite, obedient, and sterile. In protest, I declined election to the National Institute of Arts and Letters some years ago, and now I must decline the Pulitzer Prize.

I invite other writers to consider the fact that by accepting the prizes and approval of these vague institutions we are admitting their authority, publicly confirming them as the final judges of literary excellence, and I inquire whether any prize is worth that subservience.

I am, Sirs,
Yours sincerely,
(Signed) Sinclair Lewis

THE CULTURE WAR

Henry J. Hyde

[The author is the congressman for the Sixth District of Illinois.]

I'm not quite sure what it says about America that one of the most intense public controversies in the months between the Tiananmen Square massacre and the breaching of the Berlin Wall had to do with homoerotic photographs and a crucifix suspended in a vat of urine.

My formulation is deliberately provocative. While Central and Eastern Europe were giving birth, in joy and pain, to the Revolution of 1989, Americans were transfixed by an argument over, let me say it again, homoerotic photographs and a crucifix suspended in a vat of urine. One might have been tempted to think that Oswald Spengler was right, and Francis Fukuyama wrong: the West was indeed headed down the slippery slope to decadence and irrelevance; but the "end of history" wouldn't be so much boring as appalling.

Whatever else can be said for or against our national media, their attention span is short: and so public life moves on. But we shouldn't be quite so eager to leave the debate over Mapplethorpe and Serrano behind us. For the Great Arts Controversy demonstrated that America is, in truth, involved in a *Kulturkampf*—a culture war, a war between cultures and a war about the very meaning of "culture."

Many people would prefer to deny this. But the conscientious public servant and the thoughtful citizen cannot afford to miss the full truth of our situation, for politics is, at its deepest level, a function of culture. The American *Kulturkampf* may be understood, to paraphrase Clausewitz, as civil war by other means.

It is best to be precise about the terminology here. By "culture war," I don't mean arguments over the relative merits of Mozart and Beethoven, *Henry V* on stage and *Henry V* on screen, Eliot and Auden, Tom Wolfe and E. L. Doctorow, the Chicago Symphony Orchestra and the New York Philharmonic. Nor do I mean the tensions between highbrows and lowbrows, between sports fans and opera buffs, between people who think Bruce Springsteen is the greatest artist alive and people who wouldn't know Bruce Springsteen if he rang their doorbell and asked to use the telephone.

No, by "culture war" I mean the struggle between those who believe that the norms of "bourgeois morality" (which is drawn in the main from classic Jewish and Christian morality) should form the ethical basis of our common life, and those who are determined that those norms will be replaced with a radical and thoroughgoing moral relativism. That the "relativism" in question is as absolutist and as condescendingly self-righteous as any sixteenth-century inquisitor is a nice irony. But that is the division in our house.

Whose Money?

The public-policy issue is, to my mind, not all that difficult to resolve. Public funds, in a democracy, are to be spent for public purposes, not for the satisfaction of individuals' aesthetic impulses. And if the impulse in question produces a work which is palpably offensive to the sensibilities of a significant proportion of the public, then that work ought not to be supported by public funds.

Ideally, the funding agencies would understand this principle and abide by it. Legislatures and courts are ill suited to setting the boundaries in an area such as this, as we should have learned from the days of Anthony Comstock and the Boston Watch and Ward Society. But when the funding agencies do not set the boundaries in a way that maintains public confidence, then the legislature must act.

To do so is not an act of censorship, *pace* President Bush. In announcing his support for continued federal funding of the National Endowment for the Arts, the President stated he didn't "know of anybody in the government . . . that should be set up to censor what you write or what you paint or how you express yourself." However, the President went on to say: "I am deeply offended by some of the filth that I see into which federal money has gone, and some of the sacrilegious, blasphemous depictions that are portrayed as art."

Congressman Dana Rohrabacher (R., Calif.), while cheered by the fact that the President doesn't like pornography any better than he likes broccoli, points out that "We're talking about sponsorship, not censorship." If the NEA were prohibited from funding certain types of work, no artist's right to create his work and display it would have been infringed. Censorship and refusal to subsidize are two very different things. All that a legislature would be saying is that the public has no responsibility to pay for a work that would give deep offense to a significant proportion of that public. One would hope that the artist, out of self-respect if nothing else, would agree.

There are those who argue that these kinds of entanglements are unavoidable and that we should therefore extract the Federal Government from the business of funding the arts. It may, over time, come to that. But I would hope not. It would be bad (although certainly not fatal) for the arts. But it would also say something deeply saddening about America: it would tell us that we simply can't reach agreement on a reasonable approach to issues at the intersection of politics and culture. And that is not the situation of choice for the American experiment in ordered liberty.

Negotiating the Kulturkampf

How might we craft an approach to the American *Kulturkampf* that would at least begin a civilized conversation about our differences? How do we argue these issues within the bounds of democratic tolerance: not the false tolerance that glosses over differences, but the true tolerance that engages differences forthrightly but civilly? Here are some themes that may be worth exploring.

1. *On the freedom of the artist:* Artists should, of course, be free from political coercion in their work. Those of us who have celebrated the triumph of Vaclav Havel have no desire to shackle the poet, the composer, the painter, the dramatist, or the photographer.

The key question for the cultural debate, however, is: Freedom *for what*? The artist's purpose is surely not fulfilled in mere self-expression;

for if self-expression were all there is to art, then a puppy chasing kittens would be as much an artist as Raphael, Vermeer, or Bach. Rather, as Thomas Aquinas wrote in the *Summa*, "The test of the artist does not lie in the will with which he goes to work, but in the excellence of the work he produces."

So the purpose of the artist's freedom is to help him and us to a fuller apprehension of, and delight in, the three transcendentals—the good, the true, and the beautiful. Lord Acton got it quite right: "Freedom is not the power to do what you want, but rather the right to do what you ought." Art detached from the quest for truth and goodness is, to repeat, simply self-expression and ultimately self-absorption. It is narcissism, and, like Narcissus, it inevitably destroys itself.

I am aware that this understanding of the purpose of artistic freedom can be dismissed as hopelessly provincial. But "art for art's sake" presents a serious problem to legislators who are expected at least to explain, if not to justify, their expenditure of tax dollars. We are now told that "great art forces us to abandon our most cherished values," but most people aren't pleased to have their most cherished values challenged, much less to pay for the experience. Franklin W. Robinson, director of a museum attached to the Rhode Island School of Design, has been quoted as saying: "Among the many things that art does for us all is that it challenges us, it demands that we rethink our assumptions about every issue in life, from religion to politics, from love to sex to death and afterlife." Thus the twentieth-century artist has changed the object of art from the three transcendentals to challenge and revolution.

The congressional reaction to what Carol Iannone calls "the insistent and progressive artistic exploration of the forbidden frontiers of human experience" was predictable, but at least has drawn attention to the "works of art" involved and to the difficult issues of artistic freedom and congressional accountability. Censorship, discrimination—these words have unpleasant connotations. But when a limited amount of money must be distributed among a large number of applicants, some form of discrimination is inevitable. I was interested in a case of curatorial discretion written up in the October 1989 *Arts Journal.* Mr. Ted Potter, the director of the Southeastern Center for Contemporary Art, is quoted as explaining why he refused to display a videotape that was "grossly racist" as to both the black and the Jewish populations. Mr. Potter said: "It was just a straightforward case of racial slurs and bigotry, and I'm not interested in that, so we didn't show it."

Justice Potter Stewart once said that he couldn't define pornography, but he knew it when he saw it. I suggest that where racism and bigotry are present, most people, even congressmen, are capable of exercising curatorial discretion.

Modern artists also demean the memory of their predecessors when they suggest that any boundary-setting by public authorities is a threat to art itself. Evelyn Waugh was indulging in characteristic exaggeration when he wrote in 1939 that "most of the greatest art has appeared under systems of political tyranny." But there is something there to think about. Great art may have been created because it enjoyed the financial favor of public authorities at the time (whether the public authority in question was a prince or a president); but it endures because it enables men and women to discern the true and the good in fuller proportion than before.

2. *On democratic civility:* Public opinion cannot be the final touchstone of artistic merit. That, too, should go without saying. While it certainly would not be accurate to suggest that virtually all great artists experienced public rejection before they enjoyed (sometimes posthumous) acceptance—Haydn, Bach, and Brahms, to choose from just one art, were quite comfortably secure in public esteem—it is also true that public opinion can be slow to recognize artistic genius, particularly when that genius is consciously striving to break new aesthetic ground.

But there is a converse truth that is rarely acknowledged. Gratuitous insults to the religious sensibilities of fellow citizens, by artists or by anyone else, are damaging to civil comity and democratic tolerance. Whatever the art world may think, Americans remain an incorrigibly religious people. Happily for the Republic, the growth of American religiosity has, over the past two generations, bred an even greater religious tolerance: the overwhelming majority of Americans believe it to be the will of God that we not kill each other over what constitutes the will of God. One wonders, though, if the democratic courtesy of tolerance is always reciprocated.

Let me take the obvious example. Whatever ex-post-facto rationalizations Andres Serrano may have constructed, I cannot believe that his *Piss Christ* was anything other than a deliberate attempt to provoke: in this case, to provoke Christians. Suppose Mr. Serrano's work had involved suspending a Torah scroll in a vat of urine; would any reasonable person have doubted that this was a gross act of anti-Semitism? Or, at an entirely different level, suppose that Mr. Serrano had suspended a peace symbol in a vat of urine and labeled it *Piss Peace*? Can you believe that this would have been defended as legitimate artistic endeavor by the same people who defended the funding of *Piss Christ*? Whatever else it was, *Piss Christ* was a vicious violation of democratic civility.

The artist may well have a gift of insight that transcends the capabilities of less aesthetically endowed citizens. But that insight confers no right to indulge oneself in thoughtless—or, worse, deliberate—trashing of others' deepest convictions.

3. *Provocative or evocative?* Some people, in fact some quite distinguished people, seem to think that any expression issuing from an artist is art. Robert McCormick Adams, secretary of the Smithsonian Institution, has even argued that graffiti are art. Would that include, I'm immediately tempted to ask, graffiti spray-painted onto the East Building of the National Gallery of Art in Washington, of which Mr. Adams is a trustee? After all, the East Building provides a much more inviting canvas for the graffiti-ist than a New York subway car, and ever so many more people would have the opportunity to see the "artist's" work if it weren't buried underground and whisked away from the viewer within a minute or so.

My argument is not against provocation per se. The first two crashing chords (indeed the entire first movement) of Beethoven's Third Symphony were a deliberate provocation: a challenge to the genteel limits which had characterized earlier uses of the symphonic form. But this was provocation in the service of a larger end. It was not provocation for its own sake.

I am no philosopher of aesthetics, but I would suggest that we ought to consider the possibility that good art is evocative rather than provocative, although the evocative quality can sometimes involve the artist in provocative expressions. Provocation, in short, should be at the service of evocation.

Which immediately raises the question, Evocative of what? Again, with the caution of a philosophical amateur, I would suggest: evocative of man's highest and noblest aspirations, our aspirations for the good, the true, and the beautiful. Put another way, art as evocation is neither art at the service of some political program nor art as an ideological instrument, but art as one means by which man gains a glimpse of the transcendent dimension of the human experience.

Beyond the Neural Itch

I suppose this returns me, in a roundabout way, to my first point: that art is not, and must not be, mere self-indulgent self-expression. If we can agree on that—if we can agree that discipline, craftsmanship, and a purpose transcending the mere satisfying of a neural itch are of the essence of the truly artistic act—then we have marked off the ground on which we can intelligibly debate questions of boundary-setting, funding, and all the rest of the public-policy arts agenda.

And that would be no small accomplishment.

◆ 6 ◆

REVISING AND EDITING

REVISION AND STYLE AS RETHINKING

All writers revise. If writing is a process of discovering ideas, then we change what we have written for the same reasons that we sometimes change our minds: New ideas alter our way of thinking about old ideas. But even if a draft of an essay does not lead to different ways of viewing the subject, revision is still necessary because, after honest reflection, the way in which our writing emerges is not necessarily the way we would like it to appear. But it is probably misleading to think of revision as the last stage of the writing process, because writers revise continuously. Revision takes place whenever a writer replaces one phrase or sentence with another, adds a word or phrase or sentence or paragraph, cuts out some part of a composition, or moves writing from one part of an essay to another. These actions can take place at any time during composing, or as a separate activity after a draft is completed. Revision is recomposing, and as such it is simply a matter of changing one's mind about any aspect of the writing. There is no "right" time for changing one's mind; it can happen at any time the writer discovers a better way.

Rethinking your choices may lead to the discovery of new ones. If writing is an act of taking responsibility for ideas, then revising acknowledges that responsibility as an ongoing obligation. Once a word, or sentence, or whole essay is committed to paper, you assume the responsibility of reassessing, and changing if necessary, what is written.

When is writing ever finished? A time must come when a deadline is reached, an assignment is due, a final draft is abandoned. In that sense, writing is finished when it is submitted to its intended audience. Often, someone has imposed a deadline or a due date. Of course, the final product ought to be as good as you can make it, given the time available, but this does not mean that the final product is finished, in the sense of no longer having room for improvement. Writing may never reach that mythical point of perfection, simply because it is always subject to change. Thus, the decision to stop revising may be somewhat arbitrary, based on your sense that further change would not substantially improve the writing. There comes a time when it is more important to get the writing into the hands of its audience than to continue to tinker with it.

Since any aspect of writing can be revised, a full discussion of revision would take us back to the beginning of this book. It is possible to reconsider your thesis statement, to change your mind not only about the phrasing but also about the stance or the question at issue. In the earlier example of a student's composing a thesis statement, we saw revision taking place at this early stage. It is even possible to revise your attitude toward a writing situation—to decide to take it as a serious challenge, for instance, after having started to approach it as a perfunctory exercise. It is possible to revise your reasoning—to change your mind about the kinds of premises you will develop—or to revise your structure—to decide that an idea should go earlier or later, or that there should be a new transition between two parts of an argument.

As I said earlier, writing itself encourages discoveries. This means that revision is necessary to be sure that all parts of a composition continue to work together, to satisfy your purpose, as that purpose refines itself during writing. Writers frequently discover that after they have finished a draft of a composition, they must return to the beginning, to change aspects of the writing to fit a new sense of purpose that has evolved. This does not necessarily mean that the thesis itself has changed, but that the writer's attitude, or even degree of conviction, may have changed the writer's approach to that thesis. Revision enables you to consider whether the whole essay, as written, consistently satisfies the needs of its thesis.

OBSTACLES TO REVISION

Revision is difficult without **critical distance**, the perspective required to see writing *as writing* and separate from one's self. Revising may sometimes seem harder than writing because we cannot separate ourselves from our thoughts enough to know whether they would be clear to someone who encounters them only through the words that we have written. Our own words seem clear to us because they are intimately related to the thoughts we had while composing them. We may miss many faults of our own writing simply because as we reread it we are engaged in the same mental process we went through as we wrote it. Yet a reader lacks this intimacy with the mental process that led to those words. Therefore, it is necessary to achieve distance from the writing, somehow, to see it *as if* for the first time. Of course, our own words can never be entirely new to us as we reread them. What, then, can you do to achieve as much distance as possible?

The best source of distance is time. If it is possible to return to a piece of writing after a long period of time, its faults become more obvious. Allowing yourself the leisure to forget how the sentences sound, to let the words slip out of the mental grooves that they have forged in the short-term memory, enables you to read them more critically. There is no better source of critical distance than a desk drawer, where a draft can be put away and returned to after enough time has gone by. But no one has enough time, of course, to make this practical. There is a lesson in this, however, that all writers can apply, even when the time available for composing is short: Don't procrastinate. No matter how much time is available, you should take advantage of all of it, and this means a certain amount of time between drafts to let the distance between you and your words increase. Returning to a draft of an essay after having done something else for a day or two—or a week or two, if possible—can provide just enough critical distance to make revision effective.

Lacking time, you can create other sources of distance. Writers are known to do some wacky things just to alienate themselves from their own prose so that they can revise it from a new point of view. I heard about one writer who tapes his manuscript to a distant wall and revises while reading it through binoculars. A friend of mine revises by turning her manuscript upside-down to read it. Another reads her writing in a mirror. I don't advise any of these tactics; these writers obviously worked them out to suit their own needs. But I can suggest two practices that are less "far out" but effective: First, *read your writing to yourself out loud.* Just the sound of the words is often enough to reveal flaws that you might otherwise miss. The rhythm and balance of your sentences can often be improved after you have heard them. Second, *have someone else read your writing out loud while you listen.* This will not only allow you to hear what you have written, but it will reveal trouble spots wherever the reader stumbles or gets the intonation of your meaning wrong.

A second obstacle to revision is an unwillingness to allow anyone to see our writing until it is finished. Perhaps we fear the possibility of negative judgments. Perhaps we want others to read what we have written only so that they will praise us. But such attitudes are not helpful to a writer. It is especially important to develop a positive attitude toward the honest criticism of others. By seeking this criticism, we learn new things about our writing, and thereby learn how to make it better.

Most writers rely on a circle of trusted readers who will comment on their drafts. These test readers can often ask questions or make observations that the writer had not thought about. To have the benefit of a critical reader's response is enormously helpful to writers who wish to revise thoughtfully. Choose your readers carefully, therefore. Friends who will only flatter you or readers who do not know how to read critically will be of no help. This raises a third potential obstacle to effective revision.

To revise well you must be able to take criticism without offense and be willing to make critical judgments about your own writing without damage to your ego. Yes, writing does come from the depths of our minds and hearts, but it is also separate from ourselves once it is on the page, and we can attack it *as writing,* without attacking our own souls in the process. Thus, to revise well, you must be able to separate the personality in your writing from your own personality. This is especially important in college, and in a writing class in particular, because teachers and other members of the class must be able to talk about your writing without making judgments about you as a person.

In reading others' writing, and in accepting the comments of others about your own, the golden rule should apply: Comment about others' writing as you would have them comment about your own; accept the comments of others as you would have them accept yours. If we could accept all advice about our own writing as if it were given solely for the purpose of helping us to write better, we would be fortunate. But advice, like other aspects of human relations, can come with hidden intentions and can be defended against by rationalization—sometimes beyond our conscious control. It is necessary, therefore, to make a real effort to accept criticism gladly and to respond to it thoughtfully.

RESPONDING TO YOUR TEACHER'S CRITICISM

It's one thing to revise in response to the criticisms of a friend, classmate, or peer, but responding to the criticism of your teacher is more difficult. Your teacher is indeed a member of your intended audience, and should therefore function as a critical reader, responding to your ideas just as she or he might respond to the ideas in others' writing. But, let's face it, your teacher is also the person who will judge your performance and whom you would like to please. More importantly, as the person whose responsibility is to help you become a better writer, your teacher will comment on your writing with that end in view. Because you may often be revising your writing in response to your teacher's comments, or writing new essays with those comments in mind, the question of how to take them is worth considering at this point.

Students are certainly justified in their concern for the grade that each assignment receives, but if this concern overshadows their assessment and application of the teacher's critical comments, they have not learned all that they can from the teacher. Although a grade determines what kind of credit you receive for the assignment, it says nothing about how you have written, or might write again. A grade is a kind of conclusion, and comments are the reasons that support it. Like any conclusion, a grade is only as good as the line of reasoning that justifies it. To understand the grade, you must understand the basis on which the teacher determined it. For this reason, many teachers, especially writing teachers, choose not to include a final grade on the returned essay itself, but to communicate the grade separately later. This is an attempt to ensure that students will not read the comments in a defensive or perfunctory way, as they sometimes do when their knowledge of the grade may already have prejudiced their reaction to the comments, for better or worse.

Many students do not respond to grades in this way, of course. You will have to examine your own experience to know whether any such "typical" way of responding applies to you. Whether it does or not, some considerations about how to apply critical comments can lead to making the best use of them.

Although it seems obvious, it is helpful to remember that a teacher's comments on an essay may be intended for a variety of responses. The way in which you should respond to comments will differ, for instance, depending on whether the teacher expects the essay to be revised or not. Some teachers like to comment on drafts of a composition and require a revision. Other assignments are, in effect, finished after the teacher has evaluated them. If a teacher expects revision, the student has an opportunity to respond *directly* to the comments, by applying the teacher's specific advice about a particular essay to continued work on that same essay. If no revision is required, however, the teacher's comments can be applied only *indirectly* to future essays. The direct application of comments is perhaps the easiest kind. If the teacher has pointed out stylistic infelicities, you can follow the teacher's specific advice. If the teacher has commented that a particular passage is unclear or in need of further support, you can attempt to clarify or explain or add reasons to that portion of the essay. And, if the teacher has made general comments about the logic or the structure of the argument, you can rethink those aspects of the essay.

Direct responses to comments in revision, because they are guided by the teacher's observations, can also be the most perfunctory kind—for the student who is content to do the minimum that a teacher asks for. It is always tempting to respond to a teacher's specific comments without understanding fully why those comments are there or what difference the revisions actually make to the quality of the essay. It is too easy, in other words, to make changes just to satisfy the teacher, but not to improve the essay in any way that also satisfies you. A teacher's comments are meant to guide you in rethinking what you have done, and if you respond by automatically doing whatever the teacher asks for you have not taken the opportunity to use those comments to your best advantage. A teacher's comment is not a commandment; it is a suggestion. Only you can decide whether the comment will lead to a better way of writing, and only the thoughtful application of that suggestion can produce a change that will benefit you in the future.

So, if revision is required based on your teacher's comments on a draft of an essay, you are not meant to change the essay only in ways that the teacher has suggested and in no other, nor are you meant to adopt the teacher's suggestions without thinking about their effect on the rest of the essay. Comments are meant to nudge you into further thought. The outcome of that thought should be a revision that goes beyond the teacher's suggestions. It may even be a revision in which some of those suggestions are not adopted. The important thing is not to make every change the teacher says, but to know why such changes are necessary. At times, they may not be. Teachers are human; as they read your essays, they respond in different ways, just as any member of your audience might. This doesn't mean that teachers are "unfair" if you disagree with them. If you choose not to follow a teacher's specific advice— assuming you have understood both that advice and your own reasons for doing it your way—you might want to explain why to your teacher, who may be more impressed finally by how thoughtfully you approach writing than by how slavishly you follow instructions.

It is important, therefore, that you read the comments carefully and attempt to see what has elicited them. Rereading your essay along with the comments will often make otherwise cryptic comments clear. If a teacher's comments are expressed in ways that you do not understand, it becomes your responsibility to consult with the teacher, to be sure that you and the teacher are reading your essay in the same way. I'm not talking about arguing with the teacher over your grade, but seeking to understand the intention and the source of whatever troublesome comments the teacher may have made. Most teachers respond positively to this kind of inquiry, even if they may not, understandably, respond favorably to complaints about grades. Make it clear that what you want is a genuine understanding of your own writing. A good deal of the learning that takes place in a writing course can happen in the teacher's office during such conferences.

It helps, further, to remember that comments differ in degree of importance. Typically, a teacher's comments will follow the structure of the essay, usually because it is most convenient to write them in the margins alongside the relevant passage in the essay. (Some teachers have their own methods of making comments, such as putting them all at the end of the composition, or using one form of comment to talk about mechanics and another form to talk about ideas.) Comments that appear side by side are not necessarily equally significant. A teacher may mark a split infinitive in one of your sentences and observe that the logic of the next sentence is not valid. Your response to those comments would necessarily be of a different order. On the one hand you need only make a simple correction. On the other hand you would have to reconsider what you mean and how you might best argue it. The change you are expected to make in the first instance is predictable, but in the second case the teacher has no "right response" in mind other than that you should look critically at your reasoning. The first is a mechanical correction and relatively trivial; the second may be crucial to the success of your argument.

In revising an essay, it would be pointless to make all the minor corrections the teacher has marked at the same time that you attempt to respond to comments about the structure and the argument. As in the case of original composition, your attention should be on the nature of the case you are trying to make and the structure of the argument first, letting matters of lesser significance have your attention only when those are under control. You should determine which of the teacher's comments address the most basic aspects of the essay—its reasoning and structure—so that you can respond to those comments before editing the essay.

It may be that a teacher's comments suggest problems with the thesis itself or with the general approach you have taken in arguing it. In that case, an appropriate response would lead you to reconsider the thesis and the logic, which might result in a revised essay that has a different argument and structure from the original. If what is most in need of revision is the thesis of your essay, your revision may well turn out to be a wholly new composition based on a revised intention.

Some students assume that writing teachers should respond only to form and have no right to criticize students' ideas. A writing teacher is not simply an editor, whose job is to make sure that all formal aspects of the writing are under control. He or she is also part of the community of critical, inquiring minds to which your essay is addressed. As an expert on matters of usage and structure, a writing teacher may help you to learn about writing from a formal point of view. But as a critical reader, one who responds intelligently to ideas and their support, a teacher also helps you to learn about your thinking. The two are inseparable, and it is unreasonable to expect a writing teacher, as a thinking person, to ignore ideas for the sake of teaching form alone. If a teacher makes a comment about an idea that he or she thinks is not well argued, it isn't because he or she disagrees with that idea but because it needs further thinking. Your teacher cannot ignore that good writing requires well-reasoned ideas as much as it requires effective and correct composition.

If a teacher's comments refer to form, consider that your teacher is someone well experienced in English composition who wants to help you understand the intricacies of writing. If the comments refer to your ideas, your teacher's expertise may be limited to that of any other member of your intended audience. You might, in some cases, feel that your idea is better than your teacher thinks it is. But in that case, you have not managed to make your idea understandable or persuasive for a reader whose basic intelligence enables him or her to think about what you have to say. A critical comment from such a reader can only help you in the attempt to further clarify and justify your ideas.

If you are not required to revise an essay based on the teacher's comments, you will still benefit from analyzing those comments in all the ways I just discussed. It isn't necessary to revise each essay in order to get the benefit of a teacher's evaluation. But a somewhat different strategy for applying comments is necessary, if you aren't going to revise, because you have to apply concepts that you derive from the comments to new writing situations. In other words, although comments that refer to particular aspects of one essay may not apply to another essay, *principles* derived from those comments can still be applied to any new composition. It is necessary for you to derive those principles yourself.

One specific practice may help you to do this most effectively. When you read a teacher's comments, keep notes to yourself of any problems your teacher has found in your writing, so that you can keep track of them apart from the context of any given essay. Say, for instance, that your teacher has marked sentence fragments or suggested that in several places in your essay you have not supplied a clear transition. On a separate page, in a note intended only for yourself, you might write: "Watch for fragments," or "Concentrate on clear transitions." (It would be best to have separate pages for different kinds of problems—one for words you have misspelled, another for grammar, another for more general concepts—tailored to your own needs.) These notes, no matter what kinds of advice they contain, will be invaluable to you as you revise your next essay by providing a guide for focusing on problems that you especially need to work on. You can add new features to the list as you receive comments on each essay you hand in, and over the course of time you will find yourself gaining more control of most of the writing problems that your teacher has pointed out to you. If you simply read comments once and make no such attempt to remember and apply them, you risk repeating mistakes or getting yourself into the same logical or structural problems.

STYLE AND ATTITUDES

Up to this point we have discussed revision in general as applying to any aspect of the writing, at any stage. One aspect of writing that we haven't discussed is style. Anything you write will have some kind of style, and paying too much attention to it as you compose may result in distracting you from your ideas. But paying attention to style during revision is very important.

Style is the "texture" of the writing, the way it sounds and the kinds of words and sentences it uses to communicate to the reader. Qualities of style contribute to the **tone** of a piece of writing, which refers to the mood or attitude that the reader *hears* in the words. Behind the silent words on a page, we are able to hear a voice, not necessarily the real voice of the flesh-and-blood writer, whom we may not know, but that of a possible or apparent speaker of the words. If we judge a writer to be condescending or patronizing, angry or deeply moved, open-minded or intolerant, sincere or hypocritical, we do so in part because the writer *sounds* that way. Sometimes these impressions result from the writer's ideas, but they often come from the way the writer's voice comes across.

If style communicates the writer's attitude to the reader, then a consideration of attitude might be a useful place to begin thinking about stylistic choices. Attitude is a combination of the writer's feelings toward the subject, toward the intended audience, and toward the writer's self. These feelings change from situation to situation, and even from time to time as the writer works on a composition. To discuss them requires oversimplification, but the purpose of this discussion is not to provide definitions of all possible attitudes. It is to give you some basis for thinking about your own attitudes and how they are reflected in the stylistic choices that you make.

The first consideration is that the self reflected in your writing is not necessarily the same self that you reflect in other situations. Even in different pieces of writing, depending on their purpose, you construct an image of yourself that may be different. The aspects of our personalities that we present to others at different times reflect the circumstances within which we act and the purposes behind our actions. There are times when it is appropriate for us to emphasize one aspect of ourselves while making certain to de-emphasize other aspects. We do this not because we are dishonest, but because we are adaptable. In writing, this means that we choose how we wish to appear to our reader, based on who the reader is and what we wish our writing to accomplish. I may come across as an entirely different sort of person when I write a letter to my parents, or to my former professor, or to my senator. I may seem like an angry person if I am writing to complain about something, or a tolerant person if I am writing to defend someone, or a serious-minded person if I am writing to express my concern over an injustice, or a clown if I am writing to get people to see something in a comical light. All of these are aspects of my true self, but I may choose from them to fit my purpose and my reader. Human personalities contain within them a wide range of possible selves that add up to who we are, even if some of them might seem contradictory. It is a sign of health, not of inconsistency, to be able to respond with different sides of ourselves to different situations.

How well you are able to find the right self for your writing depends on how well you judge the situation, how clearly you understand your own purposes, how you view the subject, and how you wish the reader to view it. As you think about the ideas you wish to present to the reader and the reasons you wish to offer in support of those ideas, you are engaged in defining all of those attitudes at once, and you will already have done most of the work of adapting the right style. It is not necessary to do all the thinking first, and then to make all of the decisions about how to present yourself, because by doing the thinking you will have already been working on this presentation. You have been adjusting your attitude to fit the subject simply by giving it your best thinking in the first place.

All of us have probably encountered writing that we thought was somehow flawed in its tone and have judged it accordingly. Whether we accepted the ideas in spite of this or not, we could characterize our response to the writer's way of presenting himself or herself to us by using adjectives that otherwise would apply to personality: This writer is childish, we might say, or self-indulgent, or selfish, or dishonest, or conceited, or petty, or condescending, or closed-minded. All such adjectives, when applied to writing, are responses to the writer's failure to control the tone of the writing in relation to its purposes. They reflect our judgment of the writer's attitude toward the subject, toward us, or toward himself or herself. Thus, the writer's tone is determined by how well those attitudes are shaped in the writing and kept in harmony with one another. Let's take a closer look at those attitudes and see how they may work for or against the writer's purpose.

When we are led to characterize a writer's style by using adjectives such as *pedantic,* or *lifeless,* or *monotonous,* or even *trivial,* we are probably responding to our feeling that the writer has taken the subject more seriously than it deserves, by neglecting to consider the needs of the reader who must be helped to understand it.

Here, for instance, is an example of writing that is serious about its subject but contains inappropriate stylistic choices:

> It is often contended that the citizens who protested this nation's involvement in the conflict in Vietnam during the anti-Vietnam demonstrations of the 1960s did so out of an abiding sense of patriotism for the country. Indeed, it is so often said by those who have not thoroughly analyzed the conflict that to suggest otherwise is to make one vulnerable to the charge that one believes in the slogan "My Country Right or Wrong." It is the case, however, that one can come to the inevitable conclusion that the protesters acted out of treasonous motives, in sufficient numbers of cases to warrant a skeptical attitude toward the protest movement in general, without becoming guilty oneself of any rashly suspect form of blind patriotic fervor. . . .

What about this writing gives us the impression that the writer has neglected to consider the needs of the reader? It is enough, perhaps, to hear the writer's sneering tone and to conclude that he has no respect for the opinions of any reader who does not already agree with his stance. This blindness to other potential points of view emerges as disrespect; any reader who might entertain another opinion has been labeled as someone who has "not thoroughly analyzed the conflict." His attitude of superiority makes the prose sound pompous. His contempt for the audience is evident also in the kind of appeal he makes in his reasoning; he asserts his own invulnerability to emotional stereotyping while engaging in the same tactic himself. He calls others names while attempting to defend himself against name calling used against his own position.

The style of the paragraph contributes to this impression. Notice that the writer has tried to stay aloof from the discussion by making the prose impersonal. The paragraph contains three long sentences, each of which starts with the vague "it is" construction. The structures of these sentences make them unnecessarily difficult to read. The first one contains wordy repetitions ("who protested this nation's involvement in the conflict in Vietnam during the anti-Vietnam demonstrations of the 1960s," "patriotism for the country"). The second one has an awkward word order, forcing the reader to have to reconstruct its meaning after reaching the conclusion. The third is interrupted by a distracting subordinate clause, one that makes a new point worth a sentence of its own. Notice too that the writer's diction is inflated. He uses "citizens" because it seems to sound more high-toned than "people," and it may seem to the writer that he is being scornfully ironic to call them "citizens" rather than "protesters." Likewise, the words "involvement" and "conflict" are chosen to make the role of the United States sound innocent; they are euphemisms. Some of the language is loaded; the writer uses "inevitable" and "treasonous" in ways that implicitly threaten the reader who might not accept them. The phrase "rashly suspect" is simply a clumsy oratorical flourish that makes no sense, and "blind patriotic fervor" is a bumbled cliché.

The subject matter of this paragraph is not so unfamiliar or complex that it can't be communicated plainly and inoffensively. There are subjects, however, that may seem to call for writing that the reader will find difficult, simply because they are complex or unfamiliar. If you have a specialized knowledge that your reader is assumed to lack, your writing may contain concepts or vocabulary that make the reader's task difficult. If the ideas you are trying to communicate are especially complicated, it won't help to translate them into baby talk just to satisfy the reader's need for simplicity. You must use your best judgment about the appropriateness of stylistic choices; it is as easy to insult the reader's intelligence by condescending as it is by obfuscating simple concepts.

Style, in this sense, is like logic: Its clarity and effectiveness depend not only on what is said, but on what assumptions about the reader are appealed to in the saying. Stylistic choices, like logical connections, are often neither good nor bad in an absolute sense, but only in their appropriateness to the knowledge shared by the reader and the writer. What appears obscure to one reader is clear to another. It is your task to adjust the style, as well as the reasoning, to the audience. But just as reasoning cannot be reduced to saying always what the reader wants to hear, styles cannot always be chosen for their simplicity, when the ideas call for a certain degree of sophistication. The writer who tries to sound intelligent or educated by adding stylistic flourishes— complex sentences and inflated diction—will not fool the careful reader. But the writer whose style makes appropriate assumptions about the reader's knowledge and reflects a shared understanding and respect for the subject will have earned the reader's goodwill.

Writers who believe that they can improve their image by inflating their diction sometimes turn to a thesaurus in search of synonyms. This misuse of an otherwise useful resource generally results in stylistic problems. The writer who tries to substitute a high-falutin' word for a simple one, consulting the thesaurus for a better-sounding word, risks two undesirable effects. The first is the possibility of misusing a word that sounds better but that doesn't quite mean what the writer wishes the word to say. If a word is not part of a writer's working vocabulary, if he or she never would have thought of it without looking in a thesaurus, then chances are the writer doesn't really understand what the word means. It is better to let the meaning choose the word for you than to let some unfamiliar word alter your meaning. The second potential effect is that the writer's tone will become pompous as a result of putting long or fancy words in place of simple, direct ones. When Mark Twain said, "I never use *metropolis* when I can get the same price for *city*," he was exaggerating.

Metropolis has some appropriate uses, or it wouldn't be in the language. But *city* will do in most situations where *metropolis* would be phony. So the principle behind Twain's rule is a good one.

Writers may pay too much attention to the reader and too little to the subject, producing styles that are inappropriate because they suggest an attitude of someone who would rather conform to the reader's tastes than tell the truth. If a writer's tone sounds condescending or patronizing, it is because the style is out of control somehow; the balance between respect for the subject, respect for the reader, and respect for the self has somehow been lost. Student writers who first become conscious of the need to consider the audience often make the mistake of trying to bring the reader into the writing and end up producing sentences that are as much about the reader as anything else. Here is an extreme example of this sort of mistake:

> *In this essay, I will try to persuade you that college athletic programs benefit all students. As a fellow student at this college, you are aware of this controversy, so I need not explain to you why it is important. You have heard that the college pays too much attention to sports, and perhaps you agree that the college could pay more attention to your education if sports programs were eliminated or cut back. As I discuss this issue, I will begin by describing the sports programs and their relation to academics, and then I will list the benefits that you receive as a student from the existence of these programs. I will also attempt to refute whatever objections you may have to my reasoning, as I argue that athletics is indeed a benefit to you, whether you realize it or not.*

All this talk addressed to the reader is unnecessary. It seems to imply, although inadvertently, that the writer thinks the reader is unable to understand the writer's purpose without this "hand-holding." The writer also makes assumptions about the reader's beliefs that may or may not be shared with actual readers, and the essay further insults the reader's intelligence, therefore, by pretending that the writing is addressed only to those readers who need the writer's superior guidance. Even though there is nothing wrong with refuting potential objections in a persuasive essay, this writer gives the reader no credit for having any objections that are valid.

The paragraph actually says very little. It announces its stance and refers to a controversy. The first three sentences contain information that could be communicated quite efficiently in a single sentence introducing the issue. Then the last two sentences explain what the essay will proceed to do. These are also unnecessary; if the essay is well organized, there is no reason to provide the reader with these advance clues to the transitions that will come later. Sentences of this sort often find their way into writing, unnecessarily.

> *I am now going to take up the second part of my topic . . . .*
> *At this point, let us look at the related question of . . . .*
> *I will now begin the discussion of my reasons . . . .*

Such road signs are seldom necessary, but writers often include them out of a sense that the reader needs help. These transitional markers do not make the structure easier to follow, as they may intend, but in fact bring unnecessary attention to the structure and distract the reader's attention from the content. If you construct a clear transition from a given discussion to a related question, showing what the relation is, there should be no need to say "At this point, let us look at the related question of . . . ." It will go without saying. Too many such phrases, meant to help the reader through the structure, can seem like condescension. They should be used sparingly. (Sparingly does not mean never. Do you think I have overused such phrases in this book?)

An inappropriate kind of attention to the reader may also result when the writer is tempted to define words that do not really require definition. In some situations an initial definition of a technical term will prevent the reader from being confused, or an operational definition—a special use of a common term—may prevent misunderstanding. You must decide when including a definition will contribute to the clarity of your prose or when it might get in the way or insult the reader.

One further result of paying too much attention to the needs of the reader is the impression that the writer cares more about pleasing the reader than about telling the truth. In other words, a writer's failure to find a stance—to write from a point of view that does justice to the writer's thoughts on an issue—can result in a desire to entertain that overwhelms any desire to find good reasons. Thus, the writing can take the form of an elaborate bluff. This is likely to be the case if we detect in the writer's style some attempt to use language to draw attention away from the subject and to the style itself. Here's an example from an essay on evolution:

> *What's all the trouble about anyway? If our grand-daddies and grand-mommies got created in one big bang (no pun intended), or if they crawled out of the water, shook off their feathers and said, "where's the exit of this zoo?", it really can't make much difference to us. We all have to get born, whether the chicken came first or the egg. But, you know, some people are never satisfied with not knowing something, so they feel like they have to invent an answer or bust. So the scientists, who could be trying to cure cancer, put their big brains to work theorizing about "evil-lution," while the glory brigade sing hallelujah to a creator who didn't have to make cancer in the first place.*

This clever style has some interesting and original turns of phrase, and even some sophisticated uses of sentence structure (such as the parallel clauses about cancer in the last sentence). But are we amused, as the writer clearly intends that we should be? Maybe, but also puzzled. What's the point of this glib talk? There's nothing wrong with a sense of humor, and most of us would like to see a spark of wit in the things we read rather than an unremitting glumness. But wit can be purposeful or it can be a way of thumbing one's nose at ideas in order to avoid having to think about them. That's the impression I get from this writer, who clowns at the expense of confronting the questions that his own writing raises. Clowning can be a way of answering questions sometimes, but it can also be a way of avoiding having to come up with something to say about them. Thus, the impulse to entertain can become an excuse for not thinking.

The issue of whether to use humor, like other stylistic questions, cannot be answered with a rule. The only rule is: It depends. It would be as mistaken to take everything more seriously than it deserves to be taken as it would be to take nothing seriously enough. A balance, some kind of golden mean, is the best answer, and it is found when the writer is conscious of having a choice and of making it on the basis of careful considerations. How do I want to sound in this essay? What attitude do I want to reflect, given my stance and my readers' attitudes? What kind of style does my subject and my audience deserve? These considerations do not guarantee that the style will be appropriate in every case, but without them a writer may fall back on convenient habit, sheer clumsiness, or bluff.

STYLE AND CLEAR THINKING

It is important to pay attention to style in order to be sure that your writing says what you want it to say, that it is readable, and that it conveys an attitude that is appropriate to the reasoning. There is another reason that paying attention to style is important. We not only write in words and sentences, but think in them as well. The thoughts we think can be affected by any habits that we may have in the use of words. Thus, style, when we lose control of it, can influence how we think. This is not a reason to use any particular style in a particular piece of writing. It is a reason to remain conscious of the possibility of being controlled by stylistic habits.

The potential effect of stylistic habits on mental habits is discussed in a famous essay by George Orwell, the British author whose novels include *Animal Farm* and *Nineteen Eighty–Four*. As you know if you have read these novels, Orwell was keenly interested in "groupthink," or the control of how and what people think by totalitarian regimes. He showed how language can be a powerful tool to suppress freedom of thought, open-mindedness, and independent judgment. The control of language by the state, he believed, was the same as the power to control thinking. Similarly, he believed that control of language by the individual was the same as freedom of thought, and that consciousness of style could, therefore, help the individual remain free of the unwarranted power of others' uncritical ideas.

Orwell's argument, in his essay "Politics and the English Language,"* goes something like this: It is easy for people to imitate stylistic habits that become

---

* See page 209 for the complete essay.

conventional in the language they hear all around them. Some of these habits have their origins in uses of language that are deceptive, such as the euphemisms, half-truths, or misleading expressions that may be found in some political writing, advertising, or journalism. Some may be caused by simple neglect: Sloppy and inaccurate thinking has given rise to sloppy and inaccurate expressions. Whatever the origin of such habits, they can in turn become the cause of poor thinking. The English language, Orwell wrote, "becomes ugly and inaccurate because our thoughts are foolish, but the slovenliness of our language makes it easier for us to have foolish thoughts." Thus, failure to pay attention to style can produce unclear thinking, without our being aware of it. But, Orwell believed, "if one gets rid of these habits one can think more clearly."

Thus, although Orwell believed that language can have an insidious effect on our thinking, we can prevent this effect by taking the trouble to choose our manner of expression carefully. In what is to me the most powerful part of his essay, Orwell put it this way:

> *A scrupulous writer, in every sentence that he writes, will ask himself at least four questions, thus: What am I trying to say? What words will express it? What image or idiom will make it clear? Is the image fresh enough to have an effect? And he will probably ask himself two more: Can I put it more shortly? Have I said anything that is avoidably ugly? But you are not obliged to go to all this trouble. You can shirk it simply by throwing your mind open and letting the ready-made phrases come crowding in. They will construct your sentences for you—even think your thoughts for you, to a certain extent—and at need they will perform the important service of partially concealing your meaning even from yourself.*

It is that closing irony that makes this passage most effective, I think. Orwell has reminded us that life would be simpler if we did not have to think for ourselves, and we are often ready to give up freedom of thought for the comfort of conformity. But the price we pay for this comfort is self-deception.

Orwell supported his argument with many examples drawn from contemporary writing. It is amazing how many of his examples continue to be found in popular language habits of today. Language, like other fashions, has fads and trends, some of which last longer than others. If you read Orwell's essay, you will be able to think of many expressions in fashion today that could be added to his list of examples. Many language habits may change over time, but the principles that Orwell argued have stayed valid. Based on his examples, Orwell devised six general rules of style, which he said could be relied on "when instinct fails." His rules are:

1. Never use a metaphor, simile or other figure of speech which you are used to seeing in print.
2. Never use a long word when a short one will do.

3. If it is possible to cut a word out, always cut it out.
4. Never use the passive when you can use the active.
5. Never use a foreign phrase, a scientific word or a jargon word if you can think of an everyday English equivalent.
6. Break any of these rules sooner than say anything outright barbarous.

Do these rules seem consistent with some of the advice I have already given about style? They are another way of saying some of the same things that I have discussed, without Orwell's gift for precision. His rule number six is another reminder that when it comes to style there are no real "rules," in the sense of laws that cannot be broken. Style serves a purpose. The purpose must determine the validity of the rule. It depends.

As a writer, you could probably not keep these rules in mind all of the time while you are composing. Worrying too much about rules, whether they are grammar rules or stylistic rules or rules for organization, can distract you from the most important consideration, which is the careful scrutiny of what you believe about an issue and why you believe it. The point at which you ought to think about such rules consciously is during revision. Rules, as Orwell said, are at our service when instinct fails. Applying them thoughtfully, as a means of revising, can help to make them instinctive. If you revise carefully, with such principles in mind, eventually you will not have to revise as much as before, because the old, sloppy habits of composition will be replaced by new, sound habits. But habits of any kind are potentially dangerous in writing. It always helps to remember the importance of being in control of the stylistic choices faced at every phase of writing, from the drafting of a thesis statement, through the structuring of an argument, to the editing and proofreading of the final draft.

EDITING AS RETHINKING

Editing a rough draft is a process of looking at the words and sentences with the intention of making them express just what you mean and do just what you want them to do. It might include moving parts of the writing around, restructuring, or adding or deleting parts. But mainly, editing concerns word choice and sentence structure. As you edit your writing, you are necessarily engaged in a kind of analysis of how it sounds. It is always helpful, therefore, to read it aloud. Deliberately editing according to certain principles can also provide you with a source of critical distance. By looking for particular features, perhaps those that someone has made you aware of by offering you criticism, you can separate yourself somewhat from the flow of your thoughts about the content and look at the writing as writing. But since the question of whether any specific editing change actually improves the essay will depend on the purpose of the writing and the context of the whole argument, editing in this way leads to rethinking the ideas.

Because I have already cited Orwell's "rules," let's look at them in more detail, as principles that can be used in editing.

Using Figurative Language

Orwell's first rule refers to the use of figurative language: "*Never use a meta-phor, simile, or other figure of speech which you are used to seeing in print.*" Notice that Orwell is not telling us to avoid figurative language, but cautioning us against using it thoughtlessly. When certain figures of speech become over-used, they lose their power to communicate and become clichés. Because such phrases are overused, they often cease to convey a precise idea and reflect instead the writer's disregard for precision.

A figure of speech is simply a means by which words are able to say one thing while communicating something else. From this fact comes the power of figurative language—its novelty and ability to suggest unique connections—but this is also the source of its potential imprecision. For example, the phi-losopher Aristotle took advantage of the suggestive power of language when he wrote, "Poverty is the parent of revolution." He assumed that his readers would know that he did not mean "parent" literally and that they would understand him to mean something by it other than "parent" in the dictionary sense. He assumed that they would associate the relation between poverty and revolu-tion with the relation between parent and child. If he could not assume these things, he would have risked being misunderstood. Because figurative lan-guage works by suggestion, one must be especially careful to control figurative language to get just the right effect from it.

When writers use figures of speech that have become clichés, this control is surrendered. Consider this passage:

> The administration is grasping at straws in its policy toward apartheid in South Africa. We hear harsh words being spoken about racial segregation on the one hand, and on the other we hear glowing praise of the South African government. Our waffling Congress should get its act together and tell the White House to get off its horse. The bottom line is whether we are going to support any government that condones the moral blood-bath taking place in the name of economic necessity.

The only clear idea being communicated here is that the writer wishes the Congress to impel the Administration to condemn apartheid. The overuse of figures of speech makes the meaning harder to find than necessary. "Straws" and "waffles" clash in meaning, "house" and "horse" in sound. Some of the phrases are simply not clear. This writer blurts out commonplace sentiments without giving them much thought—an impression that does not depend on whether the reader agrees with the stance. A few of this writer's phrases might survive careful editing, but most of them should be axed.

Figures of speech and clichés are not always easy to find, because some "dead" metaphors seem to have become literal. You probably identified the following as clichés:

grasping at straws
waffling Congress

get its act together
get off its horse
moral blood-bath

But other figurative phrases are more subtle:

harsh words
glowing praise
on the one hand . . . on the other hand
White House
bottom line
in the name of

These phrases have become so common that we can easily forget they are metaphors. Whether a metaphor communicates the writer's meaning precisely is a question that must be asked of all such phrases, no matter how literal they may sound. This is why a careful assessment of one's own metaphors as Orwell prescribed is important.

Figurative language nearly always works by means of comparison. A simile ("He worked on that project like a fiend") is a direct comparison. A metaphor ("He sweat blood to get it done") is an implied comparison. Figurative language thus gets its power from its ability to relate one realm of experience to another, usually in a way that suggests unstated connections. The reader associates qualities of the metaphoric subject with those of the literal subject, even though those qualities are left unstated. Figurative speech is so common that readers perform this act of interpretation without hesitation. In the Declaration of Independence, Thomas Jefferson wrote, "When, in the course of human events, it becomes necessary for one people to dissolve the political bands which have connected them to another . . . ." As we read those words, we associate qualities that we understand "dissolve" and "bands" to have in their literal sense with the new context in which Jefferson used them. Bands do not literally connect people, nor was Jefferson calling for bands to be literally dissolved. But because we know that to dissolve something is to dilute its power, and that bands can inhibit freedom, we are not confused by his meaning. We understand it all the more powerfully because it is communicated in well-chosen figures.

Forgetting that figurative language draws on one aspect of experience in order to describe another can lead to losing control of its use. As in the example from Jefferson, there must be an appropriate connection between the kinds of experiences being associated. Examples of experiences inappropriately connected may be found today in the popular application of metaphors deriving from computers. For instance, consider these phrases:

I will provide my input to our discussion of Plato's concept of beauty.
Abusive parents have difficulty interfacing with their children.

The metaphors here seem inappropriate to the subject matter because there is no reason to compare the experiences under discussion to associations that we have with computers. *Input* was originally technical jargon for entering data into machines but it has now become a common metaphor for thoughts, opinions, or ideas. Similarly, *interface* is jargon for the capacity of computers to combine functions, but it is often used to refer to human relations as well—such as *talking* or *understanding*. As these terms lose their metaphoric power through overuse, it becomes easier to apply them to experiences for which they are inappropriate. It is not part of the purpose of these writers to say that Plato's concept of beauty is able to be calculated by machine, according to the manipulation of bits of data, or that the relationship between parents and children ought to be machinelike. Yet the sentences contain these unintended implications. The popular overuse of this kind of language to refer to human actions or problems (as well as other metaphors taken from business or military or education jargon, such as *bottom line, window of opportunity,* or *gifted*) can change the way we think about people or issues, if we do not remember that they are metaphors. You probably have your own favorite examples of metaphors that affect how people perceive reality when they are taken too literally.

It is not possible, and certainly not necessary, to write without ever using expressions that are commonplace. Avoiding all such phrases could produce a style that is sterile and officious, lacking a human voice. Figurative expressions give our speech color and liveliness, they suggest the personality of the writer, and they communicate special meanings. Orwell's rule cautions us against using worn-out and commonplace figures of speech, but it does not prevent us from using occasional figures that contribute to the effectiveness of the writing.

Inflated Diction

Orwell's second rule, *"Never use a long word when a short one will do,"* returns us to the caution against inflated diction. It is worth going into further. Don't assume that long words will make you sound more intelligent or that short ones will make you sound simple-minded. Let the meaning choose the right word and length will take care of itself. What Orwell is getting at is the habit common to many writers of substituting polysyllabic monstrosities(!) for the simple, direct terms of everyday English. As an editing technique, Orwell's rule would lead us to examine the long words we use, to see whether we have chosen them because they are right or simply because they are long.

The way some writers try to imitate a "learned" style, editing for precision can seem like translating from one variety of English to another. Here's an extreme case:

> *Utilizing civil disobedience methodologies pursuant to the conceptualizations of Thoreau facilitated the efficacious attainment of the primary objective of civil rights activists, namely the modification of statutory prohibitions deleterious toward racial minorities.*

Translated into plain English, this means:

> *Using civil disobedience according to the ideas of Thoreau made it easier for civil rights activists to reach their goal of changing laws harmful to racial minorities.*

Although the meaning is much the same, the effect on the reader is much different.

Notice that the goal of the editor of this sentence was not to get rid of all words over two syllables long. That would be silly. Rather, the goal was to get rid of long words for which perfectly good short ones exist. Thus, the phrase "civil disobedience" remained, because no shorter phrase could be substituted for it without changing the meaning. The same is true for "activists" and "minorities." But because all of the other monstrosities found in the sentence have simple equivalents, they are easily replaced.

utilizing	=	using
pursuant to	=	according to
conceptualization	=	idea
facilitate	=	make easy
efficacious attainment	=	reaching
objective	=	goal
modification	=	change
statutory prohibitions	=	laws
deleterious	=	harmful

Some long words are perfectly appropriate in some contexts, but they are misused by writers who habitually prefer the puffed-up to the plain. Orwell blames politicians for overusing such words, which are parroted by others— those who can be fooled into thinking that "selective disinformation" means something other than "lying." Many long words cannot and should not be avoided. But the English vocabulary is so vast that many words have become popular whose only function is to bedevil those who wish to express themselves clearly. Remember that you aren't trying to achieve the fewest possible number of syllables. You are trying to avoid the ponderous effect of wordiness. This brings us to Orwell's next rule.

Cutting

"If it is possible to cut a word out, always cut it out." Clumsy writers not only use longer words than necessary, they also crowd their writing with empty words and roundabout phrases. Empty words contribute no meaning to the sentence in which they occur. Roundabout phrases are those that substitute several words for one.

Almost any word can be an empty word if it contributes no additional meaning to a sentence. Here are some examples:

Her decision was painful in nature.
I am majoring in the field of accounting.
Despite various minor flaws, the essay shows a good reasoning process.

Each of these sentences could be made more economical by cutting words that have no function, thus:

Her decision was painful.
I am majoring in accounting.
Despite minor flaws, the essay shows good reasoning.

No reader would respond to these sentences by wondering, "Do you mean painful *in nature?*" or "Do you mean the *field* of accounting?" or "Do you mean a good reasoning *process?*" or "Are the flaws *various?*" These words contribute nothing essential. Yet they are all words that in other contexts might have a specific function:

By nature, people question authority.
You have to choose one field for your major.
Writing is a process, leading to a product.
The same end can be reached by various means.

The words that were not contributing meaning before are doing so here. Thus it isn't the word itself that is empty; it depends on the role it plays. The context of a sentence within the whole composition will determine if any words are superfluous. Editing for economy thus requires a writer to re-examine the meaning carefully and to ask what each word adds and whether that addition is necessary.

Here's a passage in which the writer would face many such considerations as he or she edited for economy. I have exaggerated the wordiness on purpose to illustrate several different ways that language can be inflated.

The question to pose now is whether or not the acceptance of the basic concept of renewable energy resource production is justified at this time. Each and every kind of nonfossil fuel energy source, such as hydroelectric, nuclear, solar, and wind, etc., has recognized advantages over fossil fuels, but due to the fact that each also has unsolved problems attendant with its use, there is no consensus of opinion up to this point in time that the various benefits tend to outweigh the actual costs. Hydroelectric power resources make use of abundantly available supplies of water, but nevertheless there is opposition against their use from many who view the protection of lakes and streams from negative effects as a higher priority than meeting the energy needs of this nation. The reason why nuclear power is a controversial issue is that the extent to which nuclear waste materials will have lasting effects on the surrounding environment cannot be determined at the present time. Notwithstanding the fact that wind power is a feasible approach technologically, it is not practical from the standpoint of cost-effectiveness. Solar power is dependent on the climate situation to a large degree, and in consequence its maximum possible potential may be viewed as restricted to certain regions of the country. But yet it is the one other alternative that does not have drawbacks sufficient enough to prevent us from directing our efforts toward its further development on a widespread scale.

Get out the blue pencil. Let's start cutting words. (In the following discussion, be prepared to refer to this passage, since I will make lists of words from it, out of context.) This gassy writer has used more than twice the number of words necessary. Does anybody really write this badly? Maybe not, but many writers slip into one or another kind of wordiness, all of which are illustrated. Some of the gas results from the kind of empty words we have already discussed. These phrases add no meaning to the passage, in context:

> *to pose*   (What other kinds of questions are there?)
> *basic*   (The word is just noise.)
> *the concept of*   (More noise.)
> *attendant*   (Can problems ever not be attendant?)
> *various*   (Sheer humbug.)
> *situation*   (More noise.)

Getting rid of those is a start, but the writing still overflows with other kinds of waste. It is polluted by many other phrases that are simply redundant.

> *now . . . at this time*
> *whether or not*
> *each and every*
> *such as . . . ,etc.*
> *unsolved problems*
> *consensus of opinion*
> *this point in time*
> *but nevertheless*
> *opposition against*
> *reason why*
> *controversial issue*
> *surrounding environment*
> *possible potential*
> *but yet*
> *other alternative*
> *sufficient enough*
> *further development*

Eliminate half the words and they say the same thing.

Another kind of redundancy persists in the passage (not "continues to persist"). It results from including words that refer to concepts already clear from the context, as in these cases:

> *resource production*   ("Production" is understood in context.)
> *energy source*   (In context, "source" is redundant.)

recognized advantages   (If they were unrecognized, would we be describing them?)

problems . . . with its use   (More empty words.)

up to this point   (Implied by the use of the present tense.)

tend to outweigh   (Either they do or they don't.)

available   (How could they be abundant but not available?)

protection . . . from negative effects   (Who protects anything from positive effects?)

the energy needs of this nation   (We weren't thinking of any other nation.)

nuclear waste materials   (What else could the wastes be if not materials?)

at the present time   (We weren't thinking of any other time.)

feasible . . . approach   (Just wind.)

practical . . . cost-effectiveness   (Cost is practical by definition.)

maximum . . . potential   (A useless modifier.)

regions of the country   (Could it be regions of anything else?)

Practice the art of not saying the obvious by eliminating such repetitions. The paragraph is shrinking before our very eyes.

The passage contains yet another kind of wordiness. Many of its phrases consist of strings of words that can be replaced by one word that means the same thing. These stringy roundabout expressions should be translated into their economical equivalents:

due to the fact that	=	because or since
not withstanding the fact that	=	although
from the standpoint of	=	in
to a large degree	=	largely
in consequence	=	so
may be viewed as	=	may be (or is)
directing our efforts toward	=	trying
on a widespread scale	=	widely

With these changes, the passage is really shaping up. It may even be starting to sound human.

But before we finish with it, we still have to attack one last source of wordiness, the extended noun phrases that hide verbs. One way in which writers unknowingly add extra words is to transform verbs into nouns by attaching suffixes and auxiliary words to them, as in these examples from the paragraph:

the acceptance of	=	accept
make use of	=	use
there is opposition to	=	(someone) opposes
the protection of	=	protect

is dependent on	=	depends on
directing our attention toward its development	=	trying to develop

When you edit your writing for economy, then, look for verbs hidden inside noun phrases. The offending nouns often contain these suffixes:

-ive	(*is indicative of* instead of *indicates*)
-sion	(*made a decision* instead of *decided*)
-tion	(*gave consideration to* instead of *considered*)
-ment	(*made an improvement* instead of *improved*)
-ance	(*has the appearance of* instead of *appears*)
-al	(*made an arrival* instead of *arrived*)

Sometimes no suffix is needed to turn a verb into a noun, although it does require adding words, as in

do harm to instead of *harm*
is in need of instead of *needs*
effect a change in instead of *change*

None of these phrases by itself will make your writing clumsy, and there may be times when any such phrase is more appropriate than its shorter equivalent. But the habit of substituting noun phrases for verbs will result in wordiness if it is not kept under control.

It may seem that editing for economy is fairly mechanical: Remove empty words, cut redundancy, transform hidden verbs. These are good principles, but they do not automatically result in a neat, economically worded product without further editing. Applying the blue pencil to our long passage of overwritten prose might result in some sentences that are still in need of polishing. The result of cutting—or of any revision—can be quite messy, as in the illustration on page 193. Editing like this is not intended for your readers' eyes. A rough draft is like a sketchbook, a record of your thoughts-in-process.*

Having edited the passage for each kind of wordiness, we may still have to touch up the prose. When you cut words from a sentence, you will often have to rephrase some parts of the sentence to make it sound right. Now that we have cut out the verbal fat and put the sentences back together, here is the result:

---

* Of course, if you edit on a word processor, the result won't look like this; it will always look tidy. But don't be fooled by the finished appearance that the word processor seems to give to prose; you will have to reread it to hear how it sounds. (I've been surprised to find that some students who edit on word processors make more mistakes than those who edit by hand on paper, possibly because they do not feel the same necessity to reread their prose as those who must recopy it.)

The question to pose now is whether or not the acceptance of the basic concept of renewable energy resource production is justified at this time. Each and every kind of nonfossil fuel energy source, such as hydroelectric, nuclear, solar, and wind, etc., has recognized advantages over fossil fuels, but [due to the fact that] because each also has unsolved problems attendant with its use, there is no consensus of opinion up to this point in time that the various benefits tend to outweigh the [actual] costs. Hydroelectric power resources make use of abundantly available supplies uses of water, but

The question is whether using renewable energy resources is justified. Each alternative to fossil fuels has advantages, but since each also has problems there is no consensus that the benefits outweigh the costs. Hydroelectric power uses abundant supplies of water, but many oppose it who view protecting lakes and streams as a higher priority than more energy. Nuclear power is controversial because the extent of lasting effects on the environment from nuclear waste cannot be determined. Although wind power is feasible technologically, it is not cost-effective. Solar power depends largely on climate, so its potential is restricted regionally. Yet it is the one alternative that does not have drawbacks sufficient to prevent us from developing it further.

The edited version of the paragraph could probably be reduced still further, although not much would be accomplished by cutting alone at this point. It now has 117 words, compared with the 243 of the original version. That's a "flab factor" of 52 per cent. I don't recommend that you literally count your words, because there is no formula for the right number of words for any idea. You should edit for economy of expression, not because there is some ideal numerical goal but because you do not want the reader to think you are padding.

The Passive Voice

Orwell's next rule is "*Never use the passive where you can use the active.*" Some writers overuse the passive voice out of habit, and the result is confusion. The passive voice can result in unclear statements or in deceptive ones. A simple example shows how it works. Here's a sentence in the active voice:

The chicken crossed the road.

In this sentence the **agent** of the action is "the chicken"; that's what's doing whatever the verb indicates is happening. The **object** of the action is "the road." In the passive voice, the agent and the object change places, thus:

The road was crossed by the chicken.

These two sentences describe the same action, but the change from active to passive changes the emphasis, from the chicken to the road. Both sentences are clear, although the second one is wordier. What makes the passive voice potentially unclear is that it permits a writer to ignore the agent, as in:

The road was crossed.

This is a grammatical sentence, whereas if we tried to get rid of the agent while keeping the verb in the active voice we would not have a complete sentence: ". . . crossed the road." This is what makes the passive risky, or convenient, depending on how you look at it: It permits you to get rid of the chicken! Actions take place in the passive, but nobody *does* them.

> *The need for higher standards is established.*
> *It is believed that the strike should be canceled.*
> *The new theory is regarded as practical, but it has not yet been tried.*

Because they eliminate the agent, these sentences also hide information. The reader is left to wonder what that information is: "Is established" by whom? "Is believed" by whom? "Should be canceled" by whom? "Is regarded" by whom? "Hasn't been tried" by whom? When writers habitually use the passive voice, they seem to be hiding something. In fact, the passive voice has gotten its bad reputation because it is often used when people do have something to hide: "A decision was made to cut your budget," an administrator might say, so that he or she can avoid having to admit that he or she decided it. The deliberate use of the passive to deceive is probably rare, but unintended deceptions happen frequently when writers habitually use passive verbs and fail to ask whether the excluded information is relevant. In editing, you should first identify the passive verbs and then ask whether the information they exclude is necessary for honesty, clarity, or completeness.

Jargons

A long discussion of Orwell's next rule would repeat much of what I covered earlier. It too concerns diction: "*Never use a foreign phrase, a scientific word or a jargon word if you can think of an everyday English equivalent."* This rule hardly needs much explaining. Jargon words and scientific words belong to the specialized vocabulary shared by a specific group. If you are writing for an audience that cannot be expected to share such terms, avoid them. If a jargon term or a scientific term is more convenient because it is precise and eliminates the need to repeat a string of plainer, explanatory words, use it, but not without being sure that your audience will understand it. If your motive for using jargon or scientific language is to impress the reader with your knowledge or to make your ideas sound more important than they really are, forget it.

The same might be said for foreign expressions, if their meaning would be obscure to the intended audience, unless there is some particular reason for using another language. If you were writing an essay about the way in which American tourists use foreign idioms, for instance, you could hardly do the subject justice without giving examples in the foreign languages. Or, if you were arguing that a translation of a poem sacrificed emotional intensity for literal meaning, you would want to use examples to clarify and support your thesis. In such cases, you would have to depend on your knowledge of the audience to decide what examples to use and whether to provide translations. If you are unreasonable in your expectation that a reader knows the meaning of foreign expressions, then those expressions may be functioning, like some jargon and scientific terminology, to bluff rather than to communicate.

Rules Are Not Laws

Orwell's final rule is the least specific and the most interesting. *"Break any of these rules sooner than say anything outright barbarous."* What Orwell is saying, perhaps, is that rules can take you only so far, and if you rely on them slavishly, they might result in making your writing worse instead of better. Rules are for convenience, but they cannot replace good sense. Applying editing rules can help you gain control over your writing. To be in control of your writing means that *you* decide how to phrase what *you* have to say; it is not control to let rules decide for you. But you earn the right to break rules when you know your options and have good reasons for choosing one way instead of another.

What does Orwell mean by "barbarous"? I'm not sure I know. I think he chose the word on purpose to make us think about what it means to be educated and civil, or whatever we think of as the opposite of "barbarous." Although the word is usually applied to behavior in general, it has special connotations when it is applied to language. To write barbarously is to write without care, without respect for the reader or the subject. It is to mimic the prevailing style of others without thinking. But, ironically, to write in an "educated" way can often mean the same thing, when the writer uses big words or padding or passive verbs to bluff and bluster and impress rather than to speak honestly and clearly. The "educated" writer may be the most barbarous of all, if he or she has learned how to imitate official-sounding prose without at the same time learning how to think more responsibly. Thus, once again, ideas come first. The educated writer should be one for whom reasoning well is the most important goal. Editing well is a responsibility that follows from this goal and that helps the writer achieve it. It can't be faked.

PROOFREADING

Revision generally occurs in rough draft, when a piece of writing is meant to be recopied. The final draft is the actual manuscript that a writer recopies and submits. The reader of this version assumes that the writer intends no further changes. Proofreading refers to the limited kind of revising that a writer does to a final draft. Proofreading appears to the reader as last-minute changes that the writer has made, usually to correct typographical or spelling or grammatical errors, or to make minor stylistic changes overlooked in earlier drafts.

Careful proofreading is a sign that the writer has said exactly what he or she intended to say. If it matters to a writer that his or her ideas are communicated, the burden of making all parts of the writing work—from the reasoning and structure to the style and finally to the correctness of mechanics and grammar—is assumed by the writer. Proofreading is the final check that what the reader actually sees is what the writer intends.

It is during the proofreading stage that writers must think about aspects of grammar that may not have occurred to them earlier. Most of the time, grammatical errors will be caught and corrected during revision, so the following advice applies to revision and to proofreading. If there is any aspect of grammar that you are uncertain about, take the trouble to look it up or ask someone who knows the answer, like your teacher. You may make some mistakes in English usage that you do not know are mistakes—and you shouldn't be afraid to make them because you should hope to learn from having them pointed out to you. But at this point in your education, you probably know those areas of grammar that give you trouble. When in doubt, find out. Not knowing when to use *who* and *whom,* for instance, is not a sign of stupidity or of moral negligence, but such a mistake may distract your reader from your ideas. You can avoid such errors and learn the grammatical principle involved by consulting a good handbook. The conscientious writer will keep such a reference handy to consult when any question of grammar arises.

Proofreading consists merely of neat, legible corrections added to the final draft. Your reader should not be distracted by such corrections. Too many of them might mean that you should consider recopying, but it is better to include all necessary corrections than to give the reader the impression that you did not see errors or did not care whether they existed. The example on page 207 shows part of a manuscript that has been carefully proofread and corrected. Notice that most of the changes are minor. A stylistic change here and there does not detract from the writer's credibility; it suggests that the writer is still thinking.

Be sure that you understand any particular kinds of proofreading marks that your teacher may prefer or require, because there are many ways of indicating such changes. A good handbook will describe specific proofreading conventions. The main objective of careful proofreading is to make sure that the final manuscript says exactly what you want it to say.

Teachers appreciate careful proofreading because it tells them exactly what the student understands about his or her own writing. A writing teacher is justified in thinking that any error you leave in your writing is the result of your ignorance of some aspect of English usage, and the teacher will therefore mark your errors for you in order to teach you. Sometimes uncorrected errors can affect the reader's judgment of your credibility. If you allow errors to go uncorrected in your writing when you do understand the correct way, you are not getting credit for what you know and you may be putting an unnecessary obstacle between your reader and your meaning.

```
The film attepmted to explore the question of what is

"normal" behavior in our society by having the main

characters reverse roles and putting them in situations

where their otherwise "abnormal" attributes make them more

able to cope.  Tom, the radical drop out, does not suffer
                                              not
the anxietes of his fellow workers because he does take the

business world all that seriously.  And Sarah, who is
                         her
equally fanatic in desire to be upwardly mobile, is never

persuaded that the revolution is just, but she makes it more

efficient with her businesslike approach to organizing

people.  As light farce, the film leaves too many issues
                      )              I
unexplored, however and this reviewer missed the depth of

questioning found in films like One Flew Over the Cuckoo's

Nest or King of Hearts.  Compared to these, this film

suffers from myopia.  It cannot see beyond the narrow
```

QUESTIONS FOR THOUGHT, DISCUSSION, AND WRITING

1. Analyze the style of a piece of argumentative writing that you think is effectively written. What stylistic choices seem to be present in order to make the sentences more readable? What choices seem to be present in order to make the writer sound more reasonable, credible, honest, sincere? What choices may hinder the writer's credibility?

2. Analyze a piece of your own writing in this same way.

3. After looking carefully for features that characterize the texture of your prose, make a list of any stylistic *habits* that you find in it.

4. Read George Orwell's "Politics and the English Language," and discuss these questions:
   a. Orwell admits that he has violated his own rules in his essay. Can you find some examples? Why does Orwell do so, and what does this tell you about the nature of language and rules for its use?
   b. Find examples from present-day political language that illustrate Orwell's principles, and say how you think their use has affected political thinking.
   c. Look carefully at an example of your own previous writing to find usages of which Orwell would disapprove. How might you change them? Do the same kind of analysis of the writing of a friend, a political columnist, or other writer.

5. A literary critic once said that "Every change in style is a change in meaning." Do you agree with this claim? Why or why not?

6. In your outside reading, locate several examples of figurative language used effectively and ineffectively. What reasons do you have for judging the examples in these ways?

7. Find examples of metaphors common in speech and writing that have the power to affect how people perceive reality. What gives them this power?

8. Find a piece of writing that you completed some time ago for a different class. Then:
   a. Locate and list all the metaphors. Do they work? Would you want to eliminate them? Why?
   b. Edit the writing by looking carefully at the diction, cutting unnecessary words, changing passive verbs to active ones in appropriate cases, changing the length and shape of your sentences, and trying to find effective, honest transitional phrases where they might be needed.

9. Once you have completed a rough draft of an essay for class, revise it according to principles discussed in this chapter. Try first to get someone to read it to you aloud. Listen carefully. By hearing it read, what do you learn?

10. After you receive an essay back from your teacher, analyze the comments according to the advice in this chapter. Reread your essay. What do the comments *teach* you as you think about applying them?

11. Following the essay by George Orwell discussed in the chapter are two more recent essays that also deal with the issue of the relationship between language and our thinking or the way in which we perceive the world. Do you think that the writers of the other essays view this relationship in the same way that Orwell does or do you think they view it differently? What are the differences and similarities among all three essays? Based on these arguments, how do you think language is formed by culture and culture by language?

◆ READINGS ◆

POLITICS AND THE ENGLISH LANGUAGE

George Orwell

Most people who bother with the matter at all would admit that the English language is in a bad way, but it is generally assumed that we cannot by conscious action do anything about it. Our civilization is decadent and our language—so the argument runs—must inevitably share in the general collapse. It follows that any struggle against the abuse of language is a sentimental archaism, like preferring candles to electric light or hansom cabs to aeroplanes. Underneath this lies the half-conscious belief that language is a natural growth and not an instrument which we shape for our own purposes.

Now, it is clear that the decline of a language must ultimately have political and economic causes: it is not due simply to the bad influence of this or that individual writer. But an effect can become a cause, reinforcing the original cause and producing the same effect in an intensified form, and so on indefinitely. A man may take to drink because he feels himself to be a failure, and then fail all the more completely because he drinks. It is rather the same thing that is happening to the English language. It becomes ugly and inaccurate because our thoughts are foolish, but the slovenliness of our language makes it easier for us to have foolish thoughts. The point is that the process is reversible. Modern English, especially written English, is full of bad habits which spread by imitation and which can be avoided if one is willing to take the necessary trouble. If one gets rid of these habits one can think more clearly, and to think clearly is a necessary first step towards political regeneration: so that the fight against bad English is not frivolous and is not the exclusive concern of professional writers. I will come back to this presently, and I hope that by that time the meaning of what I have said here will have become clearer. Meanwhile, here are five specimens of the English language as it is now habitually written.

These five passages have not been picked out because they are especially bad—I could have quoted far worse if I had chosen—but because they illustrate various of the mental vices from which we now suffer. They are a little below the average, but are fairly representative samples. I number them so that I can refer back to them when necessary:

(1) I am not, indeed, sure whether it is not true to say that the Milton who once seemed not unlike a seventeenth-century Shelley had not become, out of an experience ever more bitter in each year, more alien [*sic*] to the founder of that Jesuit sect which nothing could induce him to tolerate.

Professor Harold Laski (Essay in *Freedom of Expression*).

(2) Above all, we cannot play ducks and drakes with a native battery of idioms which prescribes such egregious collocations of vocables as the Basic *put up with* for *tolerate* or *put at a loss* for *bewilder*.

Professor Lancelot Hogben (*Interglossa*).

(3) On the one side we have the free personality: by definition, it is not neurotic, for it has neither conflict nor dream. Its desires, such as they are, are transparent, for they are just what institutional approval keeps in the forefront of consciousness; another institutional pattern would alter their number and intensity; there is little in them that is natural, irreducible, or culturally dangerous. But *on the other side*, the social bond itself is nothing but the mutual reflection of these self-secure integrities. Recall the definition of love. Is not this the very picture of a small academic? Where is there a place in this hall of mirrors for either personality or fraternity?

Essay on psychology in *Politics* (New York).

(4) All the "best people" from the gentlemen's clubs, and all the frantic fascist captains, united in common hatred of Socialism and bestial horror of the rising tide of the mass revolutionary movement, have turned to acts of provocation, to foul incendiarism, to medieval legends of poisoned wells, to legalize their own destruction of proletarian organizations, and rouse the agitated petty-bourgeoisie to chauvinistic fervor on behalf of the fight against the revolutionary way out of the crisis.

Communist pamphlet.

(5) If a new spirit *is* to be infused into this old country, there is one thorny and contentious reform which must be tackled, and that is the humanization and galvanization of the B.B.C. Timidity here will bespeak cancer and atrophy of the soul. The heart of Britain may be sound and of strong beat, for instance, but the British lion's roar at present is like that of Bottom in Shakespeare's *Midsummer Night's Dream*—as gentle as any sucking dove. A virile new Britain cannot continue indefinitely to be traduced in the eyes or rather ears, of the world by the effete languors of Langham Place, brazenly masquerading as "standard English." When the Voice of Britain is heard at nine o'clock, better far and infinitely less ludicrous to hear aitches honestly dropped than the present priggish, inflated, inhibited, schoolma'amish arch braying of blameless bashful mewing maidens!

Letter in *Tribune*.

Each of these passages has faults of its own, but, quite apart from avoidable ugliness, two qualities are common to all of them. The first is staleness of imagery: the other is lack of precision. The writer either has a meaning and cannot express it, or he inadvertently says something else, or he is almost indifferent as to whether his words mean anything or not. The mixture of vagueness and sheer incompetence is the most marked characteristic of modern English prose, and especially of any kind of political writing. As soon as certain topics are raised, the concrete melts into the abstract and no one seems to think of turns of speech that are not hackneyed: prose consists less and less of *words* chosen for the sake of their meaning, and more and more of *phrases* tacked together like the sections of a prefabricated hen-house. I list below, with notes and examples, various of the tricks by means of which the work of prose-construction is habitually dodged:

Dying Metaphors

A newly invented metaphor assists thought by evoking a visual image, while on the other hand a metaphor which is technically "dead" (e.g., *iron resolution*) has in effect reverted to being an ordinary word and can generally be used without loss of vividness. But in between these two classes there is a huge dump of worn-out metaphors which have lost all evocative power and are merely used because they save people the trouble of inventing phrases for themselves. Examples are: *Ring the changes on, take up the cudgels for, toe the line, ride rough-shod over, stand shoulder to shoulder with, play into the hands of, no axe to grind, grist to the mill, fishing in troubled waters, on the order of the day, Achilles' heel, swan song, hotbed.* Many of these are used without knowledge of their meaning (what is a "rift," for instance?), and incompatible metaphors are frequently mixed, a sure sign that the writer is not interested in what he is saying. Some metaphors now current have been twisted out of their original meaning without those who use them even being aware of the fact. For example, *toe the line* is sometimes written *tow the line.* Another example is *the hammer and the anvil,* now always used with the implication that the anvil gets the worst of it. In real life it is always the anvil that breaks the hammer, never the other way about: a writer who stopped to think what he was saying would be aware of this, and would avoid perverting the original phrase.

Operators or Verbal False Limbs

These save the trouble of picking out appropriate verbs and nouns, and at the same time pad each sentence with extra syllables which give it an appearance of symmetry. Characteristic phrases are: *render inoperative, militate against, make contact with, be subjected to, give rise to, give grounds for, have the effect of, play a leading part (role) in, make itself felt, take effect, exhibit a tendency to, serve the purpose of, etc., etc.* The keynote is the elimination of simple verbs. Instead of being a single word, such as *break, stop, spoil, mend, kill,* a verb becomes a *phrase,* made up of a noun or adjective tacked on to some general-purpose verb such as *prove, serve, form, play, render.* In addition, the passive voice is wherever possible used in preference to the active, and noun constructions are used instead of gerunds (*by exami-nation of* instead of *by examining*). The range of verbs is further cut down by means of the *-ize* and *de-* formation, and the banal statements are given an appearance of profundity by means of the *not un-* forma-tion. Simple conjunctions and prepositions are replaced by such phrases as *with respect to, having regard to, the fact that, by dint of, in view of, in the interests of, on the hypothesis that;* and the ends of sentences are saved from anticlimax by such resounding common-places as *greatly to be desired, cannot be left out of account, a devel-opment to be expected in the near future, deserving of serious consid-eration, brought to a satisfactory conclusion,* and so on and so forth.

Pretentious Diction

Words like *phenomenon, element, individual* (as noun), *objective, categorical, effective, virtual, basic, primary, promote, constitute, ex-hibit, exploit, utilize, eliminate, liquidate,* are used to dress up simple statements and give an air of scientific impartiality to biased judgments. Adjectives like *epoch-making, epic, historic, unforgettable, triumphant, age-old, inevitable, inexorable, veritable,* are used to dignify the sordid processes of international politics, while writing that aims at glorifying war usually takes on an archaic color, its characteristic words being: *realm, throne, chariot, mailed fist, trident, sword, shield, buckler, ban-ner, jackboot, clarion.* Foreign words and expressions such as *cul de sac, ancien régime, deus ex machina, mutatis mutandis, status quo, gleichshaltung, weltanschauung,* are used to give an air of culture and elegance. Except for the useful abbreviations *i.e., e.g.,* and *etc.,* there is no real need for any of the hundreds of foreign phrases now current in English. Bad writers, and especially scientific, political and sociological writers, are nearly always haunted by the notion that Latin or Greek words are grander than Saxon ones, and unnecessary words like *expe-dite, ameliorate, predict, extraneous, deracinated, clandestine, sub-aqueous* and hundreds of others constantly gain ground from their Anglo-Saxon opposite numbers.[1] The jargon peculiar to Marxist writing (*hyena, hangman, cannibal, petty bourgeois, these gentry, lackey, flun-key, mad dog, White Guard,* etc.) consists largely of words and phrases translated from Russian, German or French; but the normal way of coining a new word is to use a Latin or Greek root with the appropriate affix and, where necessary, the *-ize* formation. It is often easier to make up words of this kind (*deregionalize, impermissible, extramarital, non-fragmentatory* and so forth) than to think up the English words that will cover one's meaning. The result, in general, is an increase in slovenli-ness and vagueness.

---

[1] An interesting illustration of this is the way in which the English flower names which were in use till very recently are being ousted by Greek ones, *snapdragon* becoming *antirrhinum, forget-me-not* becoming *myosotis,* etc. It is hard to see any practical reason for this change of fashion: it is probably due to an instinctive turning-away from the more homely word and a vague feeling that the Greek word is scientific.

Meaningless Words

In certain kinds of writing, particularly in art criticism and literary criticism, it is normal to come across long passages which are almost completely lacking in meaning.[2] Words like *romantic, plastic, values, human, dead, sentimental, natural, vitality,* as used in art criticism, are strictly meaningless in the sense that they not only do not point to any discoverable object, but are hardly ever expected to do so by the reader. When one critic writes, "The outstanding feature of Mr. X's work is its living quality," while another writes, "The immediately striking thing about Mr. X's work is its peculiar deadness," the reader accepts this as a simple difference of opinion. If words like *black* and *white* were involved, instead of the jargon words *dead* and *living,* he would see at once that language was being used in an improper way. Many political words are similarly abused. The word *Fascism* has now no meaning except in so far as it signifies "something not desirable." The words *democracy, socialism, freedom, patriotic, realistic, justice,* have each of them several different meanings which cannot be reconciled with one another. In the case of a word like *democracy,* not only is there no agreed definition, but the attempt to make one is resisted from all sides. It is almost universally felt that when we call a country democratic we are praising it: consequently the defenders of every kind of regime claim that it is a democracy, and fear that they might have to stop using the word if it were tied down to any one meaning. Words of this kind are often used in a consciously dishonest way. That is, the person who uses them has his own private definition, but allows his hearer to think he means something quite different. Statements like *Marshal Pétain was a true patriot, The Soviet Press is the freest in the world, The Catholic Church is opposed to persecution,* are almost always made with intent to deceive. Other words used in variable meanings, in most cases more or less dishonestly, are: *class, totalitarian, science, progressive, reactionary, bourgeois, equality.*

Now that I have made this catalogue of swindles and perversions, let me give another example of the kind of writing that they lead to. This time it must of its nature be an imaginary one. I am going to translate a passage of good English into modern English of the worst sort. Here is a well-known verse from *Ecclesiastes:*

> I returned and saw under the sun, that the race is not to the swift, nor the battle to the strong, neither yet bread to the wise, nor yet riches to men of understanding, nor yet favor to men of skill; but time and chance happeneth to them all.

[2] Example: "Comfort's catholicity of perception and image, strangely Whitmanesque in range, almost the exact opposite in aesthetic compulsion, continues to evoke that trembling atmospheric accumulative hinting at a cruel, an inexorably serene timelessness. . . . Wrey Gardiner scores by aiming at simple bull's-eyes with precision. Only they are not so simple, and through this contented sadness runs more than the surface bitter-sweet of resignation." (*Poetry Quarterly.*)

Here it is in modern English:

> Objective consideration of contemporary phenomena compels the conclusion that success or failure in competitive activities exhibits no tendency to be commensurate with innate capacity, but that a considerable element of the unpredictable must invariably be taken into account.

This is a parody, but not a very gross one. Exhibit (3), above, for instance, contains several patches of the same kind of English. It will be seen that I have not made a full translation. The beginning and ending of the sentence follow the original meaning fairly closely, but in the middle the concrete illustrations—race, battle, bread—dissolve into the vague phrase "success or failure in competitive activities." This had to be so, because no modern writer of the kind I am discussing—no one capable of using phrases like "objective consideration of contemporary phenomena"—would ever tabulate his thoughts in that precise and detailed way. The whole tendency of modern prose is away from concreteness. Now analyze these two sentences a little more closely. The first contains forty-nine words but only sixty syllables, and all its words are those of everyday life. The second contains thirty-eight words of ninety syllables: eighteen of its words are from Latin roots, and one from Greek. The first sentence contains six vivid images, and only one phrase ("time and chance") that could be called vague. The second contains not a single fresh, arresting phrase, and in spite of its ninety syllables it gives only a shortened version of the meaning contained in the first. Yet without a doubt it is the second kind of sentence that is gaining ground in modern English. I do not want to exaggerate. This kind of writing is not yet universal, and outcrops of simplicity will occur here and there in the worst-written page. Still, if you or I were told to write a few lines on the uncertainty of human fortunes, we should probably come much nearer to my imaginary sentence that to the one from *Ecclesiastes*.

As I have tried to show, modern writing at its worst does not consist in picking out words for the sake of their meaning and inventing images in order to make the meaning clearer. It consists in gumming together long strips of words which have already been set in order by someone else, and making the results presentable by sheer humbug. The attraction of this way of writing is that it is easy. It is easier—even quicker once you have the habit—to say *In my opinion it is a not unjustifiable assumption that* than to say *I think*. If you use ready-made phrases, you not only don't have to hunt about for words; you also don't have to bother with the rhythms of your sentences, since these phrases are generally so arranged as to be more or less euphonious. When you are composing in a hurry—when you are dictating to a stenographer, for instance, or making a public speech—it is natural to fall into a pretentious, Latinized style. Tags like *a consideration which we should do well to bear in mind* or *a conclusion to which all of us would readily assent* will save many a sentence from coming down with a bump. By using stale metaphors, similes and idioms, you save much mental effort, at the cost of leaving your meaning vague, not only for your reader but for yourself. This is the significance of mixed metaphors. The sole aim of a metaphor is to call up a visual image. When these images clash—as in *The Fascist octopus has sung its swan song, the jackboot is thrown into the melting pot*—it can be taken as certain that the writer is not seeing a mental image of the objects he is naming; in other words he is not really thinking. Look again at the examples I gave at the beginning of this essay. Professor Laski (1) uses five negatives in fifty-three words. One of these is superfluous, making nonsense of the whole passage, and in addition there is the slip *alien* for akin, making further nonsense, and several avoidable pieces of clumsiness which increase the general vagueness. Professor Hogben (2) plays ducks and drakes with a battery which is able to write prescriptions, and, while disapproving of the every-day phrase *put up with*, is unwilling to look *egregious* up in the dictionary and see what it means. (3), if one takes an uncharitable attitude towards it, is simply meaningless: probably one could work out its intended meaning by reading the whole of the article in which it occurs. In (4), the writer knows more or less what he wants to say, but an accumulation of stale phrases chokes him like tea leaves blocking a sink. In (5), words and meaning have almost parted company. People who write in this manner usually have a general emotional meaning—they dislike one thing and want to express solidarity with another—but they are not interested in the detail of what they are saying. A scrupulous writer, in every sentence that he writes, will ask himself at least four questions, thus: What am I trying to say? What words will express it? What image or idiom will make it clearer? Is this image fresh enough to have an effect? And he will probably ask himself two more: Could I put it more shortly? Have I said anything that is avoidably ugly? But you are not obliged to go to all this trouble. You can shirk it by simply throwing your mind open and letting the ready-made phrases come crowding in. They will construct your sentences for you—even think your thoughts for you, to a certain extent—and at need they will perform the important service of partially concealing your meaning even from yourself. It is at this point that the special connection between politics and the debasement of language becomes clear.

In our time it is broadly true that political writing is bad writing. Where it is not true, it will generally be found that the writer is some kind of rebel, expressing his private opinions and not a "party line." Orthodoxy, of whatever color, seems to demand a lifeless, imitative style. The political dialects to be found in pamphlets, leading articles, manifestos, White Papers and the speeches of under-secretaries do, of course, vary from party to party, but they are all alike in that one almost never finds in them a fresh, vivid, home-made turn of speech. When one watches some tired hack on the platform mechanically repeating the familiar phrases— *bestial atrocities, iron heel, bloodstained tyranny, free peoples of the world, stand shoulder to shoulder*—one often has a curious feeling that one is not watching a live human being but some kind of dummy; a feeling which suddenly becomes stronger at moments when the light catches the speaker's spectacles and turns them into blank discs which seem to have no eyes behind them. And this is not altogether fanciful. A speaker who uses that kind of phraseology has gone some distance towards turning himself into a machine. The appropriate noises are coming out of his larynx, but his brain is not involved as it would be if he were choosing his words for himself. If the speech he is making is one that he is accustomed to make over and over again, he may be almost unconscious of what he is saying, as one is when one utters the responses in church. And this reduced state of consciousness, if not indispensable, is at any rate favorable to political conformity.

In our time, political speech and writing are largely the defense of the indefensible. Things like the continuance of British rule in India, the Russian purges and deportations, the dropping of the atom bombs on Japan, can indeed be defended, but only by arguments which are too brutal for most people to face, and which do not square with the professed aims of political parties. Thus political language has to consist largely of euphemism, question-begging and sheer cloudy vagueness. Defenseless villages are bombarded from the air, the inhabitants driven out into the countryside, the cattle machine-gunned, the huts set on fire with incendiary bullets: this is called *pacification*. Millions of peasants are robbed of their farms and sent trudging along the roads with no more than they can carry: this is called *transfer of population* or *rectification of frontiers*. People are imprisoned for years without trial, or shot in the back of the neck or sent to die of scurvy in Arctic lumber camps: this is called *elimination of unreliable elements*. Such phraseology is needed if one wants to name things without calling up mental pictures of them. Consider for instance some comfortable English professor defending Russian totalitarianism. He cannot say outright, "I believe in killing off your opponents when you can get good results by doing so." Probably, therefore, he will say something like this:

"While freely conceding that the Soviet régime exhibits certain features which the humanitarian may be inclined to deplore, we must, I think, agree that a certain curtailment of the right to political opposition is an unavoidable concomitant of transitional periods, and that the rigors which the Russian people have been called upon to undergo have been amply justified in the sphere of concrete achievement."

The inflated style is itself a kind of euphemism. A mass of Latin words fall upon the facts like soft snow, blurring the outlines and covering up all the details. The great enemy of clear language is insincerity. When there is a gap between one's real and one's declared aims, one turns as it were instinctively to long words and exhausted idioms, like a cuttlefish squirting out ink. In our age there is no such thing as "keeping out of politics." All issues are political issues, and politics itself is a mass of lies, evasions, folly, hatred and schizophrenia. When the general atmosphere is bad, language must suffer. I should expect to find—this is a guess which I have not sufficient knowledge to verify—that the German, Russian and Italian languages have all deteriorated in the last ten or fifteen years, as a result of dictatorship.

But if thought corrupts language, language can also corrupt thought. A bad usage can spread by tradition and imitation, even among people who should and do know better. The debased language that I have been discussing is in some ways very convenient. Phrases like *a not unjustifiable assumption, leaves much to be desired, would serve no good purpose, a consideration which we should do well to bear in mind*, are a continuous temptation, a packet of aspirins always at one's elbow. Look back through this essay, and for certain you will find that I have again and again committed the very faults I am protesting against. By this morning's post I have received a pamphlet dealing with conditions in Germany. The author tells me that he "felt impelled" to write it. I open it at random, and here is almost the first sentence that I see: "(The Allies) have an opportunity not only of achieving a radical transformation of Germany's social and political structure in such a way as to avoid a nationalistic reaction in Germany itself, but at the same time of laying the foundations of a co-operative and unified Europe." You see, he "feels impelled" to write—feels, presumably, that he has something new to say—and yet his words, like cavalry horses answering the bugle, group themselves automatically into the familiar dreary pattern. This invasion of one's mind by ready-made phrases (*lay the foundations, achieve a radical transformation*) can only be prevented if one is constantly on guard against them, and every such phrase anaesthetizes a portion of one's brain.

I said earlier that the decadence of our language is probably curable. Those who deny this would argue, if they produced an argument at all, that language merely reflects existing social conditions, and that we cannot influence its development by any direct tinkering with words and constructions. So far as the general tone or spirit of a language goes, this may be true, but it is not true in detail. Silly words and expressions have often disappeared, not through any evolutionary process but owing to the conscious action of a minority. Two recent examples were *explore every avenue* and *leave no stone unturned,* which were killed by the jeers of a few journalists. There is a long list of flyblown metaphors which could similarly be got rid of if enough people would interest themselves in the job; and it should also be possible to laugh the *not un-* formation out of existence,[3] to reduce the amount of Latin and Greek in the average sentence, to drive out foreign phrases and strayed scientific words, and, in general, to make pretentiousness unfashionable. But all these are minor points. The defense of the English language implies more than this, and perhaps it is best to start by saying what it does *not* imply.

To begin with it has nothing to do with archaism, with the salvaging of obsolete words and turns of speech, or with the setting up of a "standard English" which must never be departed from. On the contrary, it is especially concerned with the scrapping of every word or idiom which has outworn its usefulness. It has nothing to do with correct grammar and syntax, which are of no importance so long as one makes one's meaning clear, or with the avoidance of Americanisms, or with having what is called a "good prose style." On the other hand it is not concerned with fake simplicity and the attempt to make written English colloquial. Nor does it even imply in every case preferring the Saxon word to the Latin one, though it does imply using the fewest and shortest words that will cover one's meaning. What is above all needed is to let the meaning choose the word, and not the other way about. In prose, the worst thing one can do with words is to surrender to them. When you think of a

---

[3] One can cure oneself of the *not un-* formation by memorizing this sentence. *A not unblack dog was chasing a not unsmall rabbit across a not ungreen field.*

concrete object, you think wordlessly, and then, if you want to describe the thing you have been visualizing you probably hunt about till you find the exact words that seem to fit. When you think of something abstract you are more inclined to use words from the start, and unless you make a conscious effort to prevent it, the existing dialect will come rushing in and do the job for you, at the expense of blurring or even changing your meaning. Probably it is better to put off using words as long as possible and get one's meaning as clear as one can through pictures or sensations. Afterwards one can choose—not simply *accept*—the phrases that will best cover the meaning, and then switch round and decide what impression one's words are likely to make on another person. This last effort of the mind cuts out all stale or mixed images, all prefabricated phrases, needless repetitions, and humbug and vagueness generally. But one can often be in doubt about the effect of a word or phrase, and one needs rules that one can rely on when instinct fails. I think the following rules will cover most cases:

(i)   Never use a metaphor, simile or other figure of speech which you are used to seeing in print.
(ii)   Never use a long word where a short one will do.
(iii)   If it is possible to cut a word out, always cut it out.
(iv)   Never use the passive where you can use the active.
(v)   Never use a foreign phrase, a scientific word or a jargon word if you can think of an everyday English equivalent.
(vi)   Break any of these rules sooner than say anything outright barbarous.

These rules sound elementary, and so they are, but they demand a deep change in attitude in anyone who has grown used to writing in the style now fashionable. One could keep all of them and still write bad English, but one could not write the kind of stuff that I quoted in those five specimens at the beginning of this article.

I have not here been considering the literary use of language, but merely language as an instrument for expressing and not for concealing or preventing thought. Stuart Chase and others have come near to claiming that all abstract words are meaningless, and have used this as a pretext for advocating a kind of political quietism. Since you don't know what Fascism is, how can you struggle against Fascism? One need not swallow such absurdities as this, but one ought to recognize that the present political chaos is connected with the decay of language, and that one can probably bring about some improvement by starting at the verbal end. If you simplify your English, you are freed from the worst follies of orthodoxy. You cannot speak any of the necessary dialects, and when you make a stupid remark its stupidity will be obvious, even to yourself. Political language—and with variations this is true of all political parties, from Conservatives to Anarchists—is designed to make lies sound truthful and murder respectable, and to give an appearance of solidity to pure wind. One cannot change this all in a moment, but one can at least change one's own habits, and from time to time one can even, if one jeers loudly enough, send some worn-out and useless phrase—some *jackboot, Achilles' heel, hotbed, melting pot, acid test, veritable inferno* or other lump of verbal refuse—into the dustbin where it belongs.

FROM OUTSIDE, IN

Barbara Mellix

Two years ago, when I started writing this paper, trying to bring order out of chaos, my ten-year-old daughter was suffering from an acute attack of boredom. She drifted in and out of the room complaining that she had nothing to do, no one to "be with" because none of her friends were at home. Patiently I explained that I was working on something special and needed peace and quiet, and I suggested that she paint, read, or work with her computer. None of these interested her. Finally, she pulled up a chair to my desk and watched me, now and then heaving long, loud sighs. After two or three minutes (nine or ten sighs), I lost my patience. "Looka here, Allie," I said, "you too old for this kinda carryin' on. I done told you this is important. You wronger than dirt to be in here haggin' me like this and you know it. Now git on outta here and leave me off before I put my foot all the way down."

I was at home, alone with my family, and my daughter understood that this way of speaking was appropriate in that context. She knew, as a matter of fact, that it was almost inevitable; when I get angry at home, I speak some of my finest, most cherished black English. Had I been speaking to my daughter in this manner in certain other environments, she would have been shocked and probably worried that I had taken leave of my sense of propriety.

Like my children, I grew up speaking what I considered two distinctly different languages—black English and standard English (or as I thought of them then, the ordinary everyday speech of "country" coloreds and "proper" English)—and in the process of acquiring these languages, I developed an understanding of when, where, and how to use them. But unlike my children, I grew up in a world that was primarily black. My friends, neighbors, minister, teachers—almost everybody I associated with every day—were black. And we spoke to one another in our own special language: *That sho is a pretty dress you got on. If she don' soon leave me off I'm gon tell her head a mess. I was so mad I could'a pissed a blue nail. He all the time trying to low-rate somebody. Ain't that just about the nastiest thing you ever set ears on?*

Then there were the "others," the "proper" blacks, transplanted relatives and one-time friends who came home from the city for weddings, funerals, and vacations. And the whites. To these we spoke standard English. "Ain't?" my mother would yell at me when I used the term in the presence of "others." "You *know* better than that." And I would hang my head in shame and say the "proper" word.

I remember one summer sitting in my grandmother's house in Greeleyville, South Carolina, when it was full of the chatter of city relatives who were home on vacation. My parents sat quietly, only now and then volunteering a comment or answering a question. My mother's face took on a strained expression when she spoke. I could see that she was being careful to say just the right words in just the right way. Her voice sounded thick, muffled. And when she finished speaking, she would lapse into silence, her proper smile on her face. My father was more articulate, more aggressive. He spoke quickly, his words sharp and clear. But he held his proud head higher, a signal that he, too, was uncomfortable. My sisters and brothers and I stared at our aunts, uncles, and cousins, speaking only when prompted. Even then, we hesitated, formed our sentences in our minds, then spoke softly, shyly.

My parents looked small and anxious during those occasions, and I waited impatiently for our leave-taking when we would mock our relatives the moment we were out of their hearing. "Reeely," we would say to one another, flexing our wrists and rolling our eyes, "how dooo you stan' this heat? Chile, it just too hyooo-mid for words." Our relatives had made us feel "country," and this was our way of regaining pride in ourselves while getting a little revenge in the bargain. The words bubbled in our throats and rolled across our tongues, a balming.

As a child I felt this same doubleness in uptown Greeleyville where the whites lived. "Ain't that a pretty dress you're wearing!" Toby, the town policeman, said to me one day when I was fifteen. "Thank you very much," I replied, my voice barely audible in my own ears. The words felt wrong in my mouth, rigid, foreign. It was not that I had never spoken that phrase before—it was common in black English, too—but I was extremely conscious that this was an occasion for proper English. I had taken out my English and put it on as I did my church clothes, and I felt as if I were wearing my Sunday best in the middle of the week. It did not matter that Toby had not spoken grammatically correct English. He was white and could speak as he wished. I had something to prove. Toby did not.

Speaking standard English to whites was our way of demonstrating that we knew their language and could use it. Speaking it to standard-English-speaking blacks was our way of showing them that we, as well as they, could "put on airs." But when we spoke standard English, we acknowledged (to ourselves and to others—but primarily to ourselves) that our customary way of speaking was inferior. We felt foolish, embarrassed, somehow diminished because we were ashamed to be our real selves. We were reserved, shy in the presence of those who owned and/or spoke *the* language.

My parents never set aside time to drill us in standard English. Their forms of instruction were less formal. When my father was feeling particularly expansive, he would regale us with tales of his exploits in the outside world. In almost flawless English, complete with dialogue and flavored with gestures and embellishment, he told us about his attempt to get a haircut at a white barbershop; his refusal to acknowledge one of the town merchants until the man addressed him as "Mister"; the time he refused to step off the sidewalk uptown to let some whites pass; his airplane trip to New York City (to visit a sick relative) during which the stewardesses and porters—recognizing that he was a "gentleman"—addressed him as "Sir." I did not realize then—nor, I think, did my father—that he was teaching us, among other things, standard English and the relationship between language and power.

My mother's approach was different. Often, when one of us said, "I'm gon wash off my feet," she would say, "And what will you walk on if you wash them off?" Everyone would laugh at the victim of my mother's "proper" mood. But it was different when one of us children was in a proper mood. "You think you are so superior," I said to my oldest sister one day when we were arguing and she was winning. "Superior!" my sister mocked. "You mean I am acting 'biggidy'?" My sisters and brothers sniggered, then joined in teasing me. Finally, my mother said, "Leave your sister alone. There's nothing wrong with using proper English." There was a half-smile on her face. I had gotten "uppity," had "put on airs" for no good reason. I was at home, alone with the family, and I hadn't been prompted by one of my mother's proper moods. But there was also a proud light in my mother's eyes; her children were learning English very well.

Not until years later, as a college student, did I begin to understand our ambivalence toward English, our scorn of it, our need to master it, to own and be owned by it—an ambivalence that extended to the public-school classroom. In our school, where there were no whites, my teachers taught standard English but used black English to do it. When my grammar-school teachers wanted us to write, for example, they usually said something like, "I want y'all to write five sentences that make a statement. Anybody git done before the rest can color." It was probably almost those exact words that led me to write these sentences in 1953 when I was in the second grade:

> The white clouds are pretty.
> There are only 15 people in our room.
> We will go to gym.
> We have a new poster.
> We may go out doors.

Second grade came after "Little First" and "Big First," so by then I knew the implied rules that accompanied all writing assignments. Writing was an occasion for proper English. I was not to write in the way we spoke to one another: The white clouds pretty; There ain't but 15 people in our room; We going to gym; We got a new poster; We can go out in the yard. Rather I was to use the language of "other": clouds *are*, there *are*, we *will*, we *have*, we *may*.

My sentences were short, rigid, perfunctory, like the letters my mother wrote to relatives:

> Dear Papa,
> How are you? How is Mattie? Fine I hope. We are fine. We will come to see you Sunday. Cousin Ned will give us a ride.
>
> > Love,
> > Daughter

The language was not ours. It was something from outside us, something we used for special occasions.

But my coloring on the other side of that second-grade paper is different. I drew three hearts and a sun. The sun has a smiling face that radiates and envelops everything it touches. And although the sun and its world are enclosed in a circle, the colors I used—red, blue, green, purple, orange, yellow, black—indicate that I was less restricted with drawing and coloring than I was with writing standard English. My valentines were not just red. My sun was not just a yellow ball in the sky.

By the time I reached the twelfth grade, speaking and writing standard English had taken on new importance. Each year, about half of the newly graduated seniors of our school moved to large cities—particularly in the North—to live with relatives and find work. Our English teacher constantly corrected our grammar: "Not 'ain't', but 'isn't.' " We seldom wrote papers, and even those few were usually plot summaries of short stories. When our teacher returned the papers, she usually lectured on the importance of using standard English: "I *am;* you *are;* he, she, or it *is,*" she would say, writing on the chalkboard as she spoke. "How you gon git a job talking about 'I is,' or 'I isn't' or 'I ain't'?"

In Pittsburgh, where I moved after graduation, I watched my aunt and uncle—who had always spoken standard English when in Greeleyville—switch from black English to standard English to a mixture of the two, according to where they were or who they were with. At home and with certain close relatives, friends, and neighbors, they spoke black English. With those less close, they spoke a mixture. In public and with strangers, they generally spoke standard English.

In time, I learned to speak standard English with ease and to switch smoothly from black to standard or a mixture, and back again. But no matter where I was, no matter what the situation or occasion, I continued to write as I had in school:

> Dear Mommie,
> How are you? How is everybody else? Fine I hope. I am fine. So are Aunt and Uncle. Tell everyone I said hello. I will write again soon.
> > Love,
> > Barbara

At work, at a health insurance company, I learned to write letters to customers. I studied form letters and letters written by co-workers, memorizing the phrases and the ways in which they were used. I dictated:

> Thank you for your letter of January 5. We have made the changes in your coverage you requested. Your new premium will be $150 every three months. We are pleased to have been of service to you.

In a sense, I was proud of the letters I wrote for the company: they were proof of my ability to survive in the city, the outside world—an indication of my growing mastery of English. But they also indicate that writing was still mechanical for me, something that didn't require much thought.

Reading also became a more significant part of my life during those early years in Pittsburgh. I had always liked reading, but now I devoted more and more of my spare time to it. I read romances, mysteries, popular novels. Looking back, I realize that the books I liked best were simple, unambiguous: good versus bad and right versus wrong with right rewarded and wrong punished, mysteries unraveled and all set right in the end. It was how I remembered life in Greeleyville.

Of course I was romanticizing. Life in Greeleyville had not been so very uncomplicated. Back there I had been—first as a child, then as a young woman with limited experience in the outside word—living in a relatively closed-in society. But there were implicit and explicit principles that guided our way of life and shaped our relationships with one another and the people outside—principles that a newcomer would find elusive and baffling. In Pittsburgh, I had matured, become more experienced: I had worked at three different jobs, associated with a wider range of people, married, had children. This new environment with different prescripts for living required that I speak standard English much of the time, and slowly, imperceptibly, I had ceased seeing a sharp distinction between myself and "others." Reading romances and mysteries, characterized by dichotomy, was a way of shying away from change, from the person I was becoming.

But that other part of me—that part which took great pride in my ability to hold a job writing business letters—was increasingly drawn to the new developments in my life and the attending possibilities, opportunities for even greater change. If I could write letters for a nationally known business, could I not also do something better, more challenging, more important? Could I not, perhaps, go to college and become a school teacher? For years, afraid and a little embarrassed, I did no more than imagine this different me, this possible me. But sixteen years after coming north, when my younger daughter entered kindergarten, I found myself unable—or unwilling—to resist the lure of possibility. I enrolled in my first college course: Basic Writing, at the University of Pittsburgh.

For the first time in my life, I was required to write extensively about myself. Using the most formal English at my command, I wrote these sentences near the beginning of the term:

> One of my duties as a homemaker is simply picking up after others. A day seldom passes that I don't search for a mislaid toy, book, or gym shoe, etc. I change the Ty-D-Bol, fight "ring around the collar," and keep our laundry smelling "April fresh." Occasionally, I settle arguments between my children and suggest things to do when they're bored. Taking telephone messages for my oldest daughter is my newest (and sometimes most aggravating) chore. Hanging the toilet paper roll is my most insignificant.

My concern was to use "appropriate" language, to sound as if I belonged in a college classroom. But I felt separate from the language—as if it did not and could not belong to me. I couldn't think and feel genuinely in that language, couldn't make it express what I thought and felt about being a housewife. A part of me resented, among other things, being judged by such things as the appearance of my family's laundry and toilet bowl, but in that language I could only imagine and write about a conventional housewife.

For the most part, the remainder of the term was a period of adjustment, a time of trying to find my bearings as a student in a college composition class, to learn to shut out my black English whenever I composed, and to prevent it from creeping into my formulations; a time for trying to grasp the language of the classroom and reproduce it in my prose; for trying to talk about myself in that language, reach others through it. Each experience of writing was like standing naked and revealing my imperfection, my "otherness." And each new assignment was another chance to make myself over in language, reshape myself, make myself "better" in my rapidly changing image of a student in a college composition class.

But writing became increasingly unmanageable as the term progressed, and by the end of the semester, my sentences sounded like this:

> My excitement was soon dampened, however, by what seemed like a small voice in the back of my head saying that I should be careful with my long awaited opportunity. I felt frustrated and this seemed to make it difficult to concentrate.

There is a poverty of language in these sentences. By this point, I knew that the clichéd language of my Housewife essay was unacceptable, and I generally recognized trite expressions. At the same time, I hadn't yet mastered the language of the classroom, hadn't yet come to see it as belonging to me. Most notable is the lifelessness of the prose, the apparent absence of a person behind the words. I wanted those sentences—and the rest of the essay—to convey the anguish of yearning to, at once, become something more and yet remain the same. I had the sensation of being split in two, part of me going into a future the other part didn't believe possible. As that person, the student writer at that moment, I was essentially mute. I could not—in the process of composing—use the language of the old me, yet I couldn't imagine myself in the language of "others."

I found this particularly discouraging because at midsemester I had been writing in a much different way. Note the language of this introduction to an essay I had written then, near the middle of the term:

> Pain is a constant companion to the people in "Footwork." Their jobs are physically damaging. Employers are insensitive to their feelings and in many cases add to their problems. The general public wounds them further by treating them with disgrace because of what they do for a living. Although the workers are as diverse as they are similar, there is a definite link between them. They suffer a great deal of abuse.

The voice here is stronger, more confident, appropriating terms like "physically damaging," "wounds them further," "insensitive," "diverse"—terms I couldn't have imagined using when writing about my own experience—and shaping them into sentences like "Although the workers are as diverse as they are similar, there is a definite link between them." And there is the sense of a personality behind the prose, someone who sympathizes with the workers. "The general public wounds them further by treating them with disgrace because of what they do for a living."

What caused these differences? I was, I believed, explaining other people's thoughts and feelings, and I was free to move about in the language of "others" so long as I was speaking *of* others. I was unaware that I was transforming into my best classroom language my own thoughts and feelings about people whose experiences and ways of speaking were in many ways similar to mine.

The following year, unable to turn back or to let go of what had become something of an obsession with language (and hoping to catch and hold the sense of control that had eluded me in Basic Writing), I enrolled in a research writing course. I spent most of the term learning how to prepare for and write a research paper. I chose sex education as my subject and spent hours in libraries, searching for information, reading, taking notes. Then (not without messiness and often-demoralizing frustration) I organized my information into categories, wrote a thesis statement, and composed my paper—a series of paraphrases and quotations spaced between carefully constructed transitions. The process and results felt artificial, but as I would later come to realize I was passing through a necessary stage. My sentences sounded like this:

> This reserve becomes understandable with examination of who the abusers are. In an overwhelming number of cases, they are people the victims know and trust. Family members, relatives, neighbors and close family friends commit seventy-five percent of all reported sex crimes against children, and parents, parent substitutes and relatives are the offenders in thirty to eighty percent of all reported cases.[12] While assault by strangers does occur, it is less common, and is usually a single episode.[13] But abuse by family members, relatives and acquaintances may continue for an extended period of time. In cases of incest, for example, children are abused repeatedly for an average of eight years.[14] In such cases, "the use of physical force is rarely necessary because of the child's trusting, dependent relationship with the offender. The child's cooperation is often facilitated by the adult's position of dominance, an offer of material goods, a threat of physical violence, or a misrepresentation of moral standards."[15]

The completed paper gave me a sense of profound satisfaction, and I read it often after my professor returned it. I know now that what I was pleased with was the language I used and the professional voice it helped me maintain. "Use better words," my teacher had snapped at me one day after reading the notes I'd begun accumulating from my research, and slowly I began taking on the language of my sources. In my next set of notes, I used the word "vacillating"; my professor applauded. And by the time I composed the final draft, I felt at ease with terms like "overwhelming number of cases," "single episode," and "reserve," and I shaped them into sentences similar to those of my "expert" sources.

If I were writing the paper today, I would of course do some things differently. Rather than open with an anecdote—as my teacher suggested—I would begin simply with a quotation that caught my interest as I was researching my paper (and which I scribbled, without its source, in the margin of my notebook): "Truth does not do so much good in the world as the semblance of truth does evil." The quotation felt right because it captured what was for me the central idea of my essay—an idea that emerged gradually during the making of my paper—and expressed it in a way I would like to have said it. The anecdote, a hypothetical situation I invented to conform to the information in the paper, felt forced and insincere because it represented—to a great degree—my teacher's understanding of the essay, *her* idea of what in it was most significant. Improving upon my previous experiences with writing, I was beginning to think and feel in the language I used, to find my own voices in it, to sense that how one speaks influences how one means. But I was not yet secure enough, comfortable enough with the language to trust my intuition.

Now that I know that to seek knowledge, freedom, and autonomy means always to be in the concentrated process of becoming—always to be venturing into new territory, feeling one's way at first, then getting one's balance, negotiating, accommodating, discovering one's self in ways that previously defined "others"—I sometimes get tired. And I ask myself why I keep on participating in this highbrow form of violence, this slamming against perplexity. But there is no real futility in the question, no hint of that part of the old me who stood outside standard English, hugging to herself a disabling mistrust of a language she thought could not represent a person with her history and experience. Rather, the question represents a person who feels the consequence of her education, the weight of her possibilities as a teacher and writer and human being, a voice in society. And I would not change that person, would not give back the good burden that accompanies my growing expertise, my increasing power to shape myself in language and share that self with "others."

"To speak," says Frantz Fanon, "means to be in a position to use a certain syntax, to grasp the morphology of this or that language, but it means above all to assume a culture, to support the weight of a civilization."[1] To write means to do the same, but in a more profound sense. However, Fanon also says that to achieve mastery means to "get" in a position of power, to "grasp," to "assume." This, I have learned both as a student and subsequently as a teacher—can involve tremendous emotional and psychological conflict for those attempting to master academic discourse. Although as a beginning student writer I had a fairly good grasp of ordinary spoken English and was proficient at what Labov calls "code-switching" (and what John Baugh in *Black Street Speech* terms "style shifting"), when I came face to face with the demands of academic writing, I grew increasingly self-conscious, constantly aware of my status as a black and a speaker of one of the many black English vernaculars—a traditional outsider. For the first time, I experienced my sense of doubleness as something menacing, a built-in enemy. Whenever I turned inward for salvation, the balm so available during my childhood, I found instead this new fragmentation which spoke to me in many voices. It was the voice of my desire to prosper, but at the same time it spoke of what I had relinquished and could not regain: a safe way of being, a state of powerlessness which exempted me from responsibility for who I was and might be. And it accused me of betrayal, of turning away from blackness. To recover balance, I had to take on the language of the academy, the language of "others." And to do that, I had to learn to imagine myself a part

---

[1] *Black Skin, White Masks* (1952; rpt. New York: Grove Press, 1967), pp. 17–18.

of the culture of that language, and therefore someone free to manage that language, to take liberties with it. Writing and rewriting, practicing, experimenting, I came to comprehend more fully the generative power of language. I discovered—with the help of some especially sensitive teachers—that through writing one can continually bring new selves into being, each with new responsibilities and difficulties, but also with new possibilities. Remarkable power, indeed. I write and continually give birth to myself.

SEXISM IN ENGLISH: A 1990s UPDATE

Aileen Pace Nilsen

Twenty years ago I embarked on a study of the sexism inherent in American English. I had just returned to Ann Arbor, Michigan, after living for two years (1967–1969) in Kabul, Afghanistan, where I had begun to look critically at the role society assigned to women. The Afghan version of the *chaderi* prescribed for Moslem women was particularly confining. Few women attended the American-built Kabul University where my husband was teaching linguistics because there were no women's dormitories, which meant that the only females who could attend were those whose families happened to live in the capital city. Afghan jokes and folklore were blatantly sexist, for example this proverb, "If you see an old man, sit down and take a lesson; if you see an old woman, throw a stone."

But it wasn't only the native culture that made me question women's roles; it was also the American community. Nearly six hundred Americans lived in Kabul, mostly supported by U.S. taxpayers. The single women were career secretaries, school teachers, or nurses. The three women who had jobs comparable to the American men's jobs were textbook editors with the assignment of developing reading books in Dari (Afghan Persian) for young children. They worked at the Ministry of Education, a large building in the center of the city. There were no women's restrooms, so during their two-year assignment whenever they needed to go to the bathroom they had to walk across the street and down the block to the Kabul Hotel.

The rest of the American women were like myself—wives and mothers whose husbands were either career diplomats, employees of USAID, or college professors who had been recruited to work on various contract teams including an education team from Teachers College, Columbia University and an agricultural team from the University of Wyoming. These were the women who were most influential in changing my way of thinking. We were suddenly bereft of our traditional roles; some of us became alcoholics; others got very good at bridge, while others searched desperately for ways to contribute either to our families or to the Afghans. The local economy provided few jobs for women and certainly none for foreigners; we were isolated from former friends and the social goals we had grown up with. Most of us had three servants (they worked for $1.00 a day) because the cook refused to wash dishes and the dishwasher refused to water the lawn or sweep the sidewalks—it was their form of unionization. Occasionally, someone would try to get along without servants, but it was impossible because the houses were huge and we didn't have the mechanical aids we had at home. Drinking water had to be brought from the deep well at the American Embassy, and kerosene and wood stoves had to be stocked and lit. The servants were all males, the highest-paid one being the cook who could usually speak some English. Our days revolved around supervising these servants. One woman's husband got so tired of hearing her complain about such annoyances as the *bacha* (the housekeeper) stealing kerosene and needles and batteries, and about the cook putting chili powder instead of paprika on the deviled eggs, and about the gardener subcontracting his work and expecting her to pay all his friends that he scheduled an hour a week for listening to complaints. The rest of the time he wanted to keep his mind clear to focus on his important work with his Afghan counterparts and with the president of the university and the Minister of Education. What he was doing in this country was going to make a difference! In the great eternal scheme of things, of what possible importance could be his wife's trivial troubles with the servants?

These were the thoughts in my mind when we finished our contract and returned in the fall of 1969 to the University of Michigan in Ann Arbor. I was surprised to find that many other women were also questioning the expectations that they had grown up with. In the spring of 1970, a women's conference was announced. I hired a babysitter and attended, but I returned home more troubled than ever. Now that I knew housework was worth only a dollar a day, I couldn't take it seriously, but I wasn't angry in the same way these women were. Their militancy frightened me. Since I wasn't ready for a revolution, I decided I would have my own feminist movement. I would study the English language and see what it could tell me about sexism. I started reading a desk dictionary and making notecards on every entry that seemed to tell something about male and female. I soon had a dog-eared dictionary, along with a collection of notecards filling two shoe boxes.

Ironically, I started reading the dictionary because I wanted to avoid getting involved in social issues, but what happened was that my notecards brought me right back to looking at society. Language and society are as intertwined as a chicken and an egg. The language that a culture uses is telltale evidence of the values and beliefs of that culture. And because there is a lag in how fast a language changes—new words can easily be introduced, but it takes a long time for old words and usages to disappear—a careful look at English will reveal the attitudes that our ancestors held and that we as a culture are therefore predisposed to hold. My notecards revealed three main points. Friends have offered the opinion that I didn't need to read the dictionary to learn such obvious facts. Nevertheless, it was interesting to have linguistic evidence of sociological observations.

Women Are Sexy; Men Are Successful

First, in American culture a woman is valued for the attractiveness and sexiness of her body, while a man is valued for his physical strength and accomplishments. A woman is sexy. A man is successful.

A persuasive piece of evidence supporting this view are the eponyms—words that have come from someone's name—found in English. I had a two-and-a-half-inch stack of cards taken from men's names, but less than a half-inch stack from women's names, and most of those came from Greek mythology. In the words that came into American English since we separated from Britain, there are many eponyms based on the names of famous American men: bartlett pear, boysenberry, diesel engine, franklin stove, ferris wheel, gatling gun, mason jar, sideburns, sousaphone, schick test, and winchester rifle. The only common eponyms taken from American women's names are *Alice blue* (after Alice Roosevelt Longworth), *bloomers* (after Amelia Jenks Bloomer), and *Mae West jacket* (after the buxom actress). Two out of the three feminine eponyms relate closely to a woman's physical anatomy, while the masculine eponyms (except for *sideburns* after General Burnsides) have nothing to do with the namesake's body, but instead honor the man for an accomplishment of some kind.

Although in Greek mythology women played a bigger role than they did in the biblical stories of the Judeo-Christian cultures and so the names of goddesses are accepted parts of the language in such place names as Pomona from the goddess of fruit and Athens from Athena and in such common words as *cereal* from Ceres, *psychology* from Psyche, and *arachnoid* from Arachne, the same tendency to think of women in relation to sexuality is seen in the eponyms *aphrodisiac* from Aphrodite, the Greek name for the goddess of love and beauty, and *venereal disease*, from Venus, the Roman name for Aphrodite.

Another interesting word from Greek mythology is *Amazon*. According to Greek folk etymology, the *a* means "without" as in *atypical* or *amoral* while *mazon* comes from *mazos*, meaning *breast* as still seen in *mastectomy*. In the Greek legend, Amazon women cut off their right breasts so that they could better shoot their bows. Apparently, the storytellers had a feeling that for women to play the active, "masculine" role that the Amazons adopted for themselves, they had to trade in part of their femininity.

This preoccupation with women's breasts is not limited to ancient stories. As a volunteer for the University of Wisconsin's *Dictionary of American Regional English (DARE)*, I read a western trapper's diary from the 1830s. I was to make notes of any unusual usages or language patterns. My most interesting finding was that he referred to a range of mountains as *The Teats*, a metaphor based on the similarity between the shapes of the mountains and women's breasts. Because today we use the French wording, *The Grand Tetons*, the metaphor isn't as obvious, but I wrote to mapmakers and found the following listings: *Nippletop* and *Little Nipple Top* near Mt. Marcy in the Adirondacks, *Nipple Mountain* in Archuleta County, Colorado, *Nipple Peak* in Coke County, Texas, *Nipple Butte* in Pennington, South Dakota, *Squaw Peak* in Placer County, California (and many other locations), *Maiden's Peak* and *Squaw Tit* (they're the same mountain) in the Cascade Range in Oregon, *Mary's Nipple* near Salt Lake City, Utah, and *Jane Russell Peaks* near Stark, New Hampshire.

Except for the movie star Jane Russell, the women being referred to are anonymous—it's only a sexual part of their body that is mentioned. When topographical features are named after men, it's probably not going to be to draw attention to a sexual part of their bodies but instead to honor individuals for an accomplishment. For example, no one thinks of a part of the male body when hearing a reference to Pike's Peak, Colorado, or Jackson Hole, Wyoming.

Going back to what I learned from my dictionary cards, I was surprised to realize how many pairs of words we have in which the feminine word has acquired sexual connotations while the masculine word retains a serious businesslike aura. For example, a *callboy* is the person who calls actors when it is time for them to go on stage, but a *callgirl* is a prostitute. Compare *sir* and *madam*. *Sir* is a term of respect while *madam* has acquired the specialized meaning of a brothel manager. Something similar has happened to *master* and *mistress*. Would you rather have a painting by *an old master* or *an old mistress*?

It's because the word *woman* had sexual connotations, as in "She's his woman," that people began avoiding its use, hence such terminology as *ladies room, lady of the house*, and *girls' school* or *school for young ladies*. Feminists, who ask that people use the term *woman* rather than *girl* or *lady*, are rejecting the idea that *woman* is primarily a sexual term. They have been at least partially successful in that today *woman* is commonly used to communicate gender without intending implications about sexuality.

I found two hundred pairs of words with masculine and feminine forms, e.g., *heir–heiress, hero–heroine, steward–stewardess, usher–usherette*, etc. In nearly all such pairs, the masculine word is considered the base with some kind of a feminine suffix being added. The masculine form is the one from which compounds are made, e.g., from *king–queen* comes *kingdom* but not *queendom*, from *sportsman–sportslady* comes *sportmanship* but not *sportsladyship*. There is one—and only one—semantic area in which the masculine word is not the base or more powerful word. This is in the area dealing with sex and marriage. When someone refers to a *virgin*, a listener will probably think of a female unless the speaker specifies *male* or uses a masculine pronoun. The same is true for *prostitute*.

In relation to marriage, there is much linguistic evidence showing that weddings are more important to women than to men. A woman cherishes the wedding and is considered a bride for a whole year, but a man is referred to as a groom only on the day of the wedding. The word *bride* appears in *bridal attendant, bridal gown, bridesmaid, bridal shower*, and even *bridegroom*. *Groom* comes from the Middle English *grom*, meaning "man," and in this sense is seldom used outside of a wedding. With most pairs of male/female words, people habitually put the masculine word first—*Mr. and Mrs., his and hers, boys and girls, men and women, kings and queens, brothers and sisters, guys and dolls*, and *host and hostess*—but it is the *bride and groom* who are talked about, not the *groom and bride*.

The importance of marriage to a woman is also shown by the fact that when a marriage ends in death, the woman gets the title of *widow*. A man gets the derived title of *widower*. This term is not used in other phrases or contexts, but *widow* is seen in *widowhood, widow's peak*, and *widow's walk*. A *widow* in a card game is an extra hand of cards, while in typesetting it is an extra line of type.

How changing cultural ideas bring changes to language is clearly visible in this semantic area. The feminist movement has caused the differences between the sexes to be downplayed, and since I did my dictionary study two decades ago, the word *singles* has largely replaced such sex-specific and value-laden terms as *bachelor, old maid, spinster, divorcee, widow*, and *widower*. And in 1970 I wrote that when a man is called *a professional* he is thought to be a doctor or a lawyer, but when people hear a woman referred to as *a professional* they are likely to think of a prostitute. That's not as true today because so many women have become doctors and lawyers that it's no longer incongruous to think of women in those professional roles.

Another change that has taken place is in wedding announcements. They used to be sent out from the bride's parents and did not even give the name of the groom's parents. Today, most couples choose to list either all or none of the parents' names. Also it is now much more likely that both the bride and groom's picture will be in the newspaper, while a decade ago only the bride's picture was published on the "Women's" or the "Society" page. Even the traditional wording of the wedding ceremony is being changed. Many officials now pronounce the couple "husband and wife" instead of the old "man and wife," and they ask the bride if she promises "to love, honor, and cherish," instead of "to love, honor, and obey."

Women Are Passive; Men Are Active

The wording of the wedding ceremony also relates to the second point that my cards showed, which is that women are expected to play a passive or weak role while men play an active or strong role. In the traditional ceremony, the official asks, "Who gives the bride away?" and the father answers, "I do." Some fathers answer, "Her mother and I do," but that doesn't solve the problem inherent in the question. The idea that a bride is something to be handed over from one man to another bothers people because it goes back to the days when a man's servants, his children, and his wife were all considered to be his property. They were known by his name because they belonged to him and he was responsible for their actions and their debts.

The grammar used in talking or writing about weddings as well as other sexual relationships shows the expectation of men playing the active role. Men *wed* women while women *become* brides of men. A man *possesses* a woman; he *deflowers* her; he *performs*; he *scores*; he *takes away* her virginity. Although a woman can *seduce* a man, she cannot offer him her virginity. When talking about virginity, the only way to make the woman the actor in the sentence is to say that "She lost her virginity," but people lose things by accident rather than by purposeful actions, and so she's only the grammatical, not the real-life, actor.

The reason that women tried to bring the term *Ms.* into the language to replace *Miss* and *Mrs.* relates to this point. Married women resented being identified only under their husband's names. For example, when Susan Glascoe did something newsworthy, she would be identified in the newspaper only as Mrs. John Glascoe. The dictionary cards showed what appeared to be an attitude on the part of editors that it was almost indecent to let a respectable woman's name march unaccompanied across the pages of a dictionary. Women were listed with male names whether or not the male contributed to the woman's reason for being in the dictionary or in his own right was as famous as the woman. For example, Charlotte Bronte was identified as Mrs. Arthur B. Nicholls, Amelia Earhart as Mrs. George Palmer Putnam, Helen Hayes as Mrs. Charles MacArthur, Jenny

Lind as Mme. Otto Goldschmit, Cornelia Otis Skinner as the daughter of Otis Skinner, Harriet Beecher Stowe as the sister of Henry Ward Beecher, and Edith Sitwell as the sister of Osbert and Sacheverell. A very small number of women got into the dictionary without the benefit of a masculine escort. They were rebels and crusaders: temperance leaders Frances Elizabeth Caroline Willard and Carry Nation, women's rights leaders Carrie Chapman Catt and Elizabeth Cady Stanton, birth control educator Margaret Sanger, religious leader Mary Baker Eddy, and slaves Harriet Tubman and Phyllis Wheatley.

Etiquette books used to teach that if a woman had *Mrs.* in front of her name then the husband's name should follow because *Mrs.* is an abbreviated form of *Mistress* and a woman couldn't be a mistress of herself. As with many arguments about "correct" language usage, this isn't very logical because *Miss* is also an abbreviation of *Mistress.* Feminists hoped to simplify matters by introducing *Ms.* as an alternative to both *Mrs.* and *Miss,* but what happened is that *Ms.* largely replaced *Miss* to become a catch-all business title for women. Many married women still prefer the title *Mrs.,* and some resent being addressed with the term *Ms.* As one frustrated newspaper reporter complained, "Before I can write about a woman, I have to know not only her marital status but also her political philosophy." The result of such complications may contribute to the demise of titles which are already being ignored by many computer programmers who find it more efficient to simply use names; for example in a business letter: "Dear Joan Garcia," instead of "Dear Mrs. Joan Garcia," "Dear Ms. Garcia," or "Dear Mrs. Louis Garcia."

The titles given to royalty provide an example of how males can be disadvantaged by the assumption that they are always to play the more powerful role. In British royalty, when a male holds a title, his wife is automatically given the feminine equivalent. But the reverse is not true. For example, a *count* is a high political officer with a *countess* being his wife. The same is true for a *duke* and a *duchess* and a *king* and a *queen.* But when a female holds the royal title, the man she marries does not automatically acquire the matching title. For example, Queen Elizabeth's husband has the title of *prince* rather than *king,* but if Prince Charles should become king while he is still married to Lady or Princess Diana, she will be known as the queen. The reasoning appears to be that since masculine words are stronger, they are reserved for true heirs and withheld from males coming into the royal family by marriage. If Prince Phillip were called *King Phillip,* it would be much easier for British subjects to forget where the true power lies.

The names that people give their children show the hopes and dreams they have for them, and when we look at the differences between male and female names in a culture we can see the cumulative expectations of that culture. In our culture girls often have names taken from small, aesthetically pleasing items, e.g., *Ruby, Jewel,* and *Pearl. Esther* and *Stella* mean "star," *Ada* means "ornament," and *Vanessa* means "butterfly." Boys are more likely to be given names with meanings of power and strength, e.g., *Neil* means "champion," *Martin* is from Mars, the god of war, *Raymond* means "wise protection," *Harold* means "chief of the army," *Ira* means "vigilant," *Rex* means "king," and *Richard* means "strong king."

We see similar differences in food metaphors. Food is a passive substance just sitting there waiting to be eaten. Many people have recognized this and so no longer feel comfortable describing women as "delectable morsels." However, when I was a teenager, it was considered a compliment to refer to a girl (we didn't call anyone a *woman* until she was middle-aged) as *a cute tomato, a peach, a dish, a cookie, honey, sugar,* or *sweetie-pie.* When being affectionate, women will occasionally call a man *honey* or *sweetie,* but in general, food metaphors are used much less often with men than with women. If a man is called *a fruit,* his masculinity is being questioned. But it's perfectly acceptable to use a food metaphor if the food is heavier and more substantive than that used for women. For example, pin-up pictures of women have long been known as *cheesecake,* but when Burt Reynolds posed for a nude centerfold, the picture was immediately dubbed *beefcake,* c.f. *a hunk of meat.* That such sexual references to men have come into the general language is another reflection of how society is beginning to lessen the differences between their attitudes toward men and women.

Something similar to the *fruit* metaphor happens with references to plants. We insult a man by calling him *a pansy,* but it wasn't considered particularly insulting to talk about a girl being a *wallflower,* a *clinging vine,* or a *shrinking violet,* or to give girls such names as *Ivy, Rose, Lily, Iris, Daisy, Camellia, Heather,* and *Flora.* A plant metaphor can be used with a man if the plant is big and strong, for example Andrew Jackson's nickname of *Old Hickory.* Also, the phrases *blooming idiots* and *budding geniuses* can be used with either sex, but notice how they are based on the most active thing a plant can do which is to bloom or bud.

Animal metaphors also illustrate the different expectations for males and females. Men are referred to as *studs, bucks,* and *wolves* while women are referred to with such metaphors as *kitten, bunny, beaver, bird, chick,* and *lamb.* In the 1950s we said that boys went *tomcatting,* but today it's just *catting around* and both boys and girls do it. When the term *foxy,* meaning that someone was sexy, first became popular, it was used only for girls, but now someone of either sex can be described as *a fox.* Some animal metaphors that are used predominantly with men have negative connotations based on the size and/or strength of the animals, e.g., *beast, bullheaded, jackass, rat, loanshark,* and *vulture.* Negative metaphors used with women are based on smaller animals, e.g., *social butterfly, mousy, catty,* and *vixen.* The feminine terms connote action, but not the same kind of large-scale action as with the masculine terms.

Women Are Connected with Negative Connotations, Men with Positive Connotations

The final point that my notecards illustrated was how many positive connotations are associated with the concept of masculine, while there are either trivial or negative connotations connected with the corresponding feminine concept. An example from the animal metaphors makes a good illustration. The word *shrew* taken from the name of a small but especially vicious animal was defined in my dictionary as "an ill-tempered scolding woman," but the word *shrewd* taken from the same root was defined as "marked by clever, discerning awareness" and was illustrated with the phrase "a shrewd businessman."

Early in life, children are conditioned to the superiority of the masculine role. As child psychologists point out, little girls have much more freedom to experiment with sex roles than do little boys. If a little girl acts like a *tomboy*, most parents have mixed feelings, being at least partially proud. But if their little boy acts like a *sissy* (derived from *sister*), they call a psychologist. It's perfectly acceptable for a little girl to sleep in the crib that was purchased for her brother, to wear his hand-me-down jeans and shirts, and to ride the bicycle that he has outgrown. But few parents would put a boy baby in a white and gold crib decorated with frills and lace, and virtually no parents would have their little boy wear his sister's hand-me-down dresses, nor would they have their son ride a girl's pink bicycle with a flower-bedecked basket. The proper names given to girls and boys show this same attitude. Girls can have "boy" names—*Cris, Craig, Jo, Kelly, Shawn, Teri, Toni*, and *Sam*—but it doesn't work the other way around. A couple of generations ago, *Beverley, Frances, Hazel, Marion*, and *Shirley* were common boys' names. As parents gave these names to more and more girls, they fell into disuse for males, and some older men who have these names prefer to go by their initials or by such abbreviated forms as *Haze* or *Shirl*.

When a little girl is told to *be a lady*, she is being told to sit with her knees together and to be quiet and dainty. But when a little boy is told to *be a man*, he is being told to be noble, strong, and virtuous—to have all the qualities that the speaker looks on as desirable. The concept of manliness has such positive connotations that it used to be a compliment to call someone a *he-man*, to say that he was doubly a man. Today many people are more ambivalent about this term and respond to it much as they do to the word *macho*. But calling someone a *manly man* or a *virile man* is nearly always meant as a compliment. *Virile* comes from the Indo-European *vir* meaning "man," which is also the basis of *virtuous*. Contrast the positive connotations of both *virile* and *virtuous* with the negative connotations of *hysterical*. The Greeks took this latter word from their name for *uterus* (as still seen in *hysterectomy*). They thought that women were the only ones who experienced uncontrolled emotional outbursts and so the condition must have something to do with a part of the body that only women have.

Differences between positive male and negative female connotations can be seen in several pairs of words which differ denotatively only in the matter of sex. *Bachelor* as compared to *spinster* or *old maid* has such positive connotations that women try to adopt them by using the term *bachelor-girl* or *bachelorette*. *Old maid* is so negative that it's the basis for metaphors: pretentious and fussy old men are called *old maids*, as are the leftover kernels of unpopped popcorn and the last card in a popular children's game.

Patron and *matron* (Middle English for *father* and *mother*) have such different levels of prestige that women try to borrow the more positive masculine connotations with the word *patroness*, literally "female father." Such a peculiar term came about because of the high prestige attached to *patron* in such phrases as *a patron of the arts* or *a patron saint. Matron* is more apt to be used in talking about a woman in charge of a jail or a public restroom.

When men are doing jobs that women often do, we apparently try to pay the men extra by giving them fancy titles; for example, a male cook is more likely to be called a *chef*, while a male seamstress will get the title of *tailor*. The armed forces have a special program in that they recruit under such slogans as "The Marine Corps Builds Men!" and "Join the Army! Become a Man." Once the recruits are enlisted, they find themselves doing much of the work that has been traditionally thought of as "women's work." The solution to getting the work done and not insulting anyone's masculinity was to change the titles as shown below:

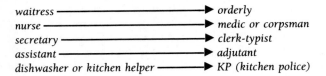

waitress	*orderly*
nurse	*medic or corpsman*
secretary	*clerk-typist*
assistant	*adjutant*
dishwasher or kitchen helper	*KP (kitchen police)*

Compare *brave* and *squaw*. Early settlers in America truly admired Indian men and hence named them with a word that carried connotations of youth, vigor, and courage. But they used the Algonquin's name for "woman," and over the years it developed almost opposite connotations to those of *brave*. *Wizard* and *witch* contrast almost as much. The masculine *wizard* implies skill and wisdom combined with magic, while the feminine *witch* implies evil intentions combined with magic. Part of the unattractiveness of both *witch* and *squaw* is that they have been used so often to refer to old women, something with which our culture is particularly uncomfortable, just as the Afghans were. Imagine my surprise when I ran across the phrases *grandfatherly advice* and *old wives' tales* and realized that the underlying implication is the same as the Afghan proverb about old men being worth listening to while old women talk only foolishness.

Other terms which show how negatively we view old women as compared to young women are *old nag* as compared to *filly*, *old crow* or *old bat* as compared to *bird*, and being *catty* as compared to being *kittenish*. There is no matching set of metaphors for men. The chicken metaphor tells the whole story of a woman's life. In her youth she is a *chick*. Then she marries and begins *feathering her nest*. Soon she begins feeling *cooped up*, so she goes to *hen parties* where she *cackles* with her friends. Then she has her *brood*, begins to *henpeck* her husband, and finally turns into *an old biddy*.

I embarked on my study of the dictionary not with the intention of prescribing language change but simply to see what the language would tell me about sexism. Nevertheless I have been both surprised and pleased as I've watched the changes that have occurred over the past two decades. I'm one of those linguists who believes that new language customs will cause a new generation of speakers to grow up with different expectations. This is why I'm happy about people's efforts to use inclusive language, to say *he or she* or *they* when speaking about individuals whose names they do not know. I'm glad that leading publishers have developed guidelines to help writers use language that is fair to both sexes, and I'm glad that most newspapers and magazines list women by their own names instead of only by their husbands' names and that educated and thoughtful people no longer begin their business letters with "Dear Sir" or "Gentlemen," but instead use a memo form or begin with such salutations as "Dear Colleagues," "Dear Reader," or "Dear Committee Members." I'm also glad that such words as *poetess, authoress, conductress,* and *aviatrix* now sound quaint and old fashioned and that *chairman* is giving way to *chair* or *head, mailman* to *mail carrier, clergyman* to *clergy,* and *stewardess* to *flight attendant.* I was also pleased when the National Oceanic and Atmospheric Administration bowed to feminist complaints and in the late '70s began to alternate men's and women's names for hurricanes. However, I wasn't so pleased to discover that the change did not immediately erase sexist thoughts from everyone's mind as shown by a headline about Hurricane David in a 1979 New York tabloid, "David Rapes Virgin Islands." More recently a similar metaphor appeared in a headline in the *Arizona Republic* about Hurricane Charlie: "Charlie Quits Carolinas, Flirts with Virginia."

What these incidents show is that sexism is not something existing independently in American English or in the particular dictionary that I happened to read. Rather, it exists in people's minds. Language is like an x-ray in providing visible evidence of invisible thoughts. The best thing about people being interested in and discussing sexist language is that as they make conscious decisions about what pronouns they will use, what jokes they will tell or laugh at, how they will write their names, or how they will begin their letters, they are forced to think about the underlying issue of sexism. This is good, because as a problem that begins in people's assumptions and expectations, it's a problem that will be solved only when a great many people have given it a great deal of thought.

◆ APPENDIX ◆

ARGUMENTS FOR DISCUSSION AND ANALYSIS

The readings in this section are simply meant to offer you more examples of arguments, so that you can apply the principles in this book when you read them critically and so that you can respond to them in discussion and writing. I have chosen these particular arguments because they are interesting, complex, and rich in possibilities for exploring ideas. They are about issues that concern us in our daily lives, as students, as private individuals, and as citizens. They also exemplify argumentative writing at its best: when it is designed to earn our assent by means of reasoning. That does not mean, of course, that it necessarily succeeds. The final selections, written by Justices of the Supreme Court, may seem to depend on special knowledge of the law. But you will notice that the argumentative appeals are no different from those of other writers, despite the technical language and citations. And in the law, as in other things, we agree to disagree about what ideas mean.

TALKING IN CLASS

Dale Spender

Women don't talk as much as men in mixed company and girls don't talk as much as boys in mixed classrooms. These facts, which have been provided by numerous research findings, appear to conflict with a stereotyped image of the female as an excessive talker (Kramer et al, 1978). However, like many other stereotypes, it can be demonstrated that not only does the stereotype bear little resemblance to empirical reality, but it also serves a particular purpose. Before analysing the reasons for female non-participation in verbal activities in the classroom it can be quite enlightening to take a closer look at the 'chattering female' stereotype to see the way it has been constructed and used.

Behind the constantly reiterated assertion that females are the talkative sex an implicit comparison is being made against some standard or norm. It has been generally accepted that females talk more than males but it is only necessary to tape a conversation at a social gathering, a trade union meeting or in a classroom to find that it is males who do the talking. The yardstick against which women's talk is, in fact, measured is that of SILENCE. 'Silence gives the proper grace to women', wrote Sophocles in *Ajax* and his sentiments are still echoed in today's image of the desirable woman. When silence is considered the appropriate behaviour for women then, quite conveniently in a sexist society, almost any talk a woman engages in can be considered too much!

Although we have evidence that men talk more than women we have not found it difficult to continue to believe the myth that women talk too much. This is because we have accepted the deeply entrenched sexist premise that women have few, if any, rights to speak in a patriarchal society. Cora Kaplan (1976) has claimed that there is a taboo against the voice of women in patriarchal society and has some convincing evidence to substantiate her claim. Women do not have the 'authority' to speak and when they do speak, they do so without 'authority'. The stereotype of the female as 'inferior' is subtly woven into sociolinguistic practices and this is clearly illustrated by Joan Roberts:

> The extraordinary idea that women are the talkative sex is a peculiarity of masculist logic . . . If women are in fact more verbally proficient, their continued exclusion from public speech, either spoken or written, seems a flagrant misuse of superior talent. To get out of this illogicality, women's talk is seen as gossip, men's as discourse. When women first publicly broke their angry silence, the shock was not only that they spoke but that they had anything to say. That 'silly chatterboxes' could not only think but also write . . . in a logical manner was a funny joke, an absurdity, barely tolerable and hardly acceptable . . . In historical reality, the female sex is best characterised *not* by talk but by silence born of subjugation (Roberts, 1976; 38).

These are the lessons which students learn before they enter educational establishments. Both sexes bring to the classroom the understanding that it is males who should 'have the floor' and females who should be dutiful and attentive listeners. It would indeed be surprising if these practices were not continued within education, but the ways in which educational institutions actually utilise these understandings, and capitalise on them to reinforce and maximise this double standard, are quite pernicious. Female silence is exploited by educational institutions and contributes to the over-representation of males and the under-representation of females in those who achieve educational success.

Girls do not get the initial message that they shouldn't talk from the school (they get it first at home) but the school certainly reinforces it. Within educational institutions girls are quickly made aware that their talk is evaluated differently from the boys. Girls who take verbal initiative in the classroom, who are verbally 'ostentatious', are likely to find themselves severely reprimanded for being 'loud', 'aggressive' or 'bossy'. Boys who engage in comparable activities are likely to be commended for their verbal facility and praised for demonstrating qualities of leadership. The message delivered in educational institutions is loud and clear; it simply doesn't do for girls to talk like boys. Girls must be more refined, more discreet in their verbal behaviour if they want approval from either the teacher, or the boys, in the classroom.

When Angele Parker (1973) did her research on interaction in the classroom, she not only discovered that the boys talked more but also that both sexes regarded talking in class, particularly in the form of questioning or challenging, as specifically masculine behaviour, and no doubt the same would apply to most teachers as to students. It was perfectly proper that boys should conduct arguments, air their views and query information, but it was not at all proper for girls to do the same thing. The girls, of course, are well aware that there are penalties placed on their talk, particularly if it is serious and marks them as actively intelligent. Not talking in class is a logical form of behaviour. It is also one which is encouraged by the material they are required to talk about.

John Elliot (1974) was disturbed by the lack of female verbal participation in his classroom. He was teaching a topic entitled 'War' and noticed that the girls had very little to say. He tried to remedy this by using his authority as a teacher to provide the girls with the opportunity to talk, but found that there were two (at least) unfortunate effects. If the girls did make a contribution it was quickly ridiculed and put down by the boys. This was 'their' topic, they were the ones who spoke with authority; what could a girl know about war? But Elliot found something else as well. He found that the girls were threatened by being required to talk to boys. Elliot came to the conclusion that he was forcing the girl students to play an 'unfeminine' role when he insisted that they take part in classroom discussion with boys.

> Sometimes I feel like saying that I disagree, that there are other ways of looking at it, but where would that get me? My teacher thinks I'm showing off, and the boys jeer. But if I pretend I don't understand, it's very different. The teacher is sympathetic and the boys are helpful. They really respond if they can show *you* how it is done, but there's nothing but 'aggro' if you give any signs of showing *them* how it is done (Kathy, aged sixteen, Inner London comprehensive).

Matina Horner (1974; 44) has done extensive research on the way in which girls avoid success. Our society, says Horner, has a stereotype of the sexes and a stereotype of intelligence and, in the case of females, the two aren't compatible. We have 'a general inability to reconcile competence, ambition, intellectual accomplishment and success with femininity'. We persist with the image of the female as passive, pliant and polite and we punish any departures from this image. Female students know the way our world works and deliberately set their sights on underachievement because there is less friction that way. According to Horner this is a source of some conflict, particularly at adolescence. Girls are actually faced with the task of deciding whether to opt for reduced achievement, and gain popularity (with, of course, the accompanying reduction in educational attainment, in employment prospects and in financial independence) or whether to opt for maximised achievement and disapproval (and the threat within the prevailing ideology of a lonely and unattractive existence). This is a conflict which is not experienced by male students for whom there is no incompatibility between achievement and popularity. It will not have escaped the attention of either girls or boys that men who do well in the world's terms have little difficulty in finding a partner, whereas women who do well in the same terms are frequently portrayed as partnerless. This single existence is considered uninviting and its origin is frequently attributed to 'female aggression'.

One factor, however, which has never been researched is the possible role that such conflict, in itself, can play in the inhibition of learning. We are all aware that students under pressure, or locked in conflict, cannot function at their best, yet we continue to place these pressures on adolescent girls who are doubly burdened when it comes to educational achievement. Firstly there is the burden which goes with intentionally reducing their performance (and over which they may possess some control) and secondly there is the burden of conflict generated by having to make such a choice (and over which they may have very little control). The girl sitting quietly in class may be nursing valid resentment and frustration and such feelings are hardly advantageous to learning.

Silence can be Golden

However, many girls do perform well in school and there are some teachers who will state that girls are easier to teach because of their docility and diligence. Within the educational system there are often rewards for those who are quiet, conscientious, unquestioning. It has been established that in some educational test situations, girls do better than boys (the outdated eleven-plus, for example). When Katherine Clarricoates (1978; 362) undertook her research in primary schools she found that teacher preference was for 'rigidly conforming girls in order to "facilitate classroom management" ' but she also found that teachers *liked* teaching boys.

> On the whole you can generally say that the boys are far more capable of learning, much nicer to teach.

> Boys are interested in everything and are prepared to take things seriously while girls tend to be more superficial about subjects: they ask the 'right' questions simply because it is expected of them . . .

> Although girls tend to be good at most things in the end you find it's the boy who's going to be your most brilliant pupil.

The teachers just quoted were not using the evidence to hand when they made such judgements for they also readily acknowledged that the girls at this age did better in class than the boys. Although the girls indicated their competence and their superiority, teachers were able to dismiss this and classify it as not genuine ability. When boys ask the right questions, it shows that they are bright; when girls ask them it shows they know what is expected of them. These teachers did not perceive these girls as 'positively intelligent', states Clarricoates, their many virtues—which included better behaviour, better conduct, cleaner and neater work—could all be discounted and seen as of little value. This is nothing short of the 'wholesale theft of true intellectual development in favour of boys', declares Clarricoates (p 358), for even where it is patently obvious that the girls are doing extremely well it can be rationalised as 'not counting'.

When classroom management is the over-riding concern of teachers—and there are many who contend that control is the major educational objective in the classroom (Levy, 1974)—the passivity of girls can be seen as a desirable feature. Again, however, it can work against girls for if they are not interested in the curriculum materials they are presented with, they can choose not to participate and their non-participation can take many forms, few of which are disruptive. They rarely seek to impose their dissatisfaction on the whole class but will elect to withdraw in a variety of unostentatious ways. Girls may not want to talk about war, as John Elliot found out, but at least they are less likely to create chaos if required to endure it. However, when 'girls' topics' are introduced to boys, many teachers are in no position to control the outcome (Clarricoates, 1978). Boys could challenge why they had to do such things, and in the process could bring about the cessation of the lesson. Hence the book lists which are geared primarily to boys, the history texts which are directed towards boys' interests, the English topics which range from motorbikes to violence to football. One of the consequences of girls not talking in class is that their interests do not need to be accommodated. This not only applies in schools but continues into higher education where girls can persist in their passive verbal behaviour which permits the operation of further penalties. Joan Roberts (1976) makes reference to the training in 'selective stupidity' provided for girls which leads not only to a reduction of their horizons but also to pronounced feelings of low self-esteem. Girls may begin by 'choosing' to be stupid but may also come to believe in their own stupidity and to accept that they are not worthy of mention in the curriculum. When girls do not receive the same attention as their male peers, when they are not presented with materials that encompass them, their lack of confidence is confirmed. There is a constant implicit message that they 'do not count'.

This can in turn reinforce a negative self-image, reduce their level of aspiration and lead to even further withdrawal.

Such a cycle needs to be broken. One of the first steps towards that goal is for females to start talking, for there is yet more evidence which suggests that restrictions on female talk can also be restrictions on female learning. Douglas Barnes (1976) points out repeatedly that learning is an active process and requires talk; new information is not absorbed by some osmotic process but must be 'talked into place'. When there are so many pressures on females not to talk, these could well be pressures which work to inhibit learning.

This raises the question of the desirability of mixed versus single-sex schools, a question to which there is no easy answer. In single-sex schools girls do not experience the same constraints upon talk. In an all-girls classroom, those who talk are girls. A range of verbal roles is available, not just the subordinate ones. This can even apply at university level, as Florence Howe found when she talked with female students at Goucher (a single-sex college). One woman stated that she had chosen a single-sex college specifically because she need not 'worry about what boys would think of her' in the daily life in the classroom (Howe, 1974; 72). In a single-sex environment it is possible for girls to pursue their interests without having to hide the results.

This is not true for all women, however. When I talked to women students who had been to single-sex schools they weren't always wholeheartedly enthusiastic about them:

> It really only postpones having to interact with males and I don't think you are automatically better equipped when you are eighteen. My single-sex school sheltered me and when I came here it was an awful shock. I still don't open my mouth in seminars. I'm still scared, easily put down by men. It seems to me that some of the women who went to mixed schools are much better at dealing with this. They have had practice. They have a lot more confidence than I have (Marian, aged twenty-one, university student).

Eileen Byrne has stated that we now need 'a major national debate specifically on co-education or single-sex education' because co-education, which was adopted 'in the hope that the presence of girls would add a slightly civilising element to the boys and that the presence of the boys would act as a spur and incentive to the girls' hasn't fulfilled its expectations (Byrne, 1978; 133). Byrne takes up the argument that in co-educational schools the girls will see that almost all the responsible jobs are held by men; to that we need to add that boys dominate in classroom interaction. While it does not seem that this is conducive to female learning and development it would be wise to be wary before simply advocating the 'return' to single sex education (see: 'The Education of Feminists: The Case for Single Sex-Schools'). It could be that modifications in the mixed classroom would be preferable to segregated education but these modifications would need to be extensive and would need to be accompanied by changes in society.

It is vitally important for women to start to talk but it is not necessary that we emulate the habits of men. Research has indicated that although men talk more, they exert more control over talk, and that they interrupt more (Zimmerman and West, 1975). Women listen more, are more supportive when they do talk (Hirschman, 1973, 1974) and have greater expertise in terms of sustaining conversations (Fishman, 1975). It is precisely these qualities which have been neither valued nor acknowledged. Rather than women learning to talk like men it would seem to be preferable if men were to learn to listen more and to be more supportive of the conversation of others. This could revolutionise our patterns of talk in society, and a vast range of oppressive images, of both men and women, will be undermined.

To be a silent woman is to be an accomplice in female subordination, to reinforce many of the constraints which keep women 'in their place'. The image of female silence as appropriate is maintained by the technique of castigating women and girls for talking and the one way that this image will be broken is for women and girls actually to begin to talk. Talk is a powerful tool. That is precisely why it has been denied to women in patriarchal society. To assert our right to talk is one way of asserting the equal validity of our experience.

RESISTANCE TO CIVIL GOVERNMENT

Henry David Thoreau

[This essay was written in 1859.]

I heartily accept the motto,—"That government is best which governs least;" and I should like to see it acted up to more rapidly and systematically. Carried out, it finally amounts to this, which also I believe,—"That government is best which governs not at all;" and when men are prepared for it, that will be the kind of government which they will have. Government is at best but an expedient; but most governments are usually, and all governments are sometimes, inexpedient. The objections which have been brought against a standing army, and they are many and weighty, and deserve to prevail, may also at last be brought against a standing government. The standing army is only an arm of the standing government. The government itself, which is only the mode which the people have chosen to execute their will, is equally liable to be abused and perverted before the people can act through it. Witness the present Mexican war, the work of comparatively a few individuals using the standing government as their tool; for, in the outset, the people would not have consented to this measure.

This American government,—what is it but a tradition, though a recent one, endeavoring to transmit itself unimpaired to posterity, but each instant losing some of its integrity? It has not the vitality and force of a single living man; for a single man can bend it to his will. It is a sort of wooden gun to the people themselves. But it is not the less necessary for this; for the people must have some complicated machinery or other, and hear its din, to satisfy that idea of government which they have. Governments show thus how successfully men can be imposed on, even impose on themselves, for their own advantage. It is excellent, we must all allow. Yet this government never of itself furthered any enterprise, but by the alacrity with which it got out of its way. *It* does not keep the country free. *It* does not settle the West. *It* does not educate. The character inherent in the American people has done all that has been accomplished; and it would have done somewhat more, if the government had not sometimes got in its way. For government is an expedient by which men would fain succeed in letting one another alone; and, as has been said, when it is most expedient, the governed are most let alone by it. Trade and commerce, if they were not made of India-rubber, would never manage to bounce over the obstacles which legislators are continually putting in their way; and, if one were to judge these men wholly by the effects of their actions and not partly by their intentions, they would deserve to be classed and punished with those mischievous persons who put obstructions on the railroads.

But, to speak practically and as a citizen, unlike those who call themselves no-government men, I ask for, not at once no government, but *at once* a better government. Let every man make known what kind of government would command his respect, and that will be one step toward obtaining it.

After all, the practical reason why, when the power is once in the hands of people, a majority are permitted, and for a long period continue, to rule is not because they are most likely to be in the right, nor because this seems fairest to the minority, but because they are physically the strongest. But a government in which the majority rule in all cases cannot be based on justice, even as far as men understand it. Can there not be a government in which majorities do not virtually decide right and wrong, but conscience?—in which majorities decide only those questions to which the rule of expediency is applicable? Must the citizen ever for a moment, or in the least degree, resign his conscience to the legislator? Why has every man a conscience, then? I think that we should be men first, and subjects afterward. It is not desirable to cultivate a respect for the law, so much as for the right. The only obligation which I have a right to assume is to do at any time what I think right. It is truly enough said, that a corporation has no conscience; but a corporation of conscientious men is a corporation *with* a conscience. Law never made men a whit more just; and, by means of their respect for it, even the well-disposed are daily made the agents of injustice. A common and natural result of an undue respect for law is, that you may see a file of soldiers, colonel, captain, corporal, privates, powder-monkeys, and all, marching in admirable order over hill and dale to the wars, against their wills, ay, against their common sense and consciences, which makes it very steep marching indeed, and produces a palpitation of the heart. They have no doubt that it is a damnable business in which they are concerned; they are all peaceably inclined. Now, what are they? Men at all? or small movable forts and magazines, at the service of some unscrupulous man in power? Visit the Navy-Yard, and behold a marine, such a man as an American government can make, or such as it can make a man with its black arts,—a mere shadow and reminiscence of humanity, a man laid out alive and standing, and already, as one may say, buried under arms with funeral accompaniments, though it may be,—

"Not a drum was heard, not a funeral note,
   As his corse to the rampart we hurried;
Not a soldier discharged his farewell shot
   O'er the grave where our hero we buried."

The mass of men serve the state thus, not as men mainly, but as machines, with their bodies. They are the standing army, and the militia, jailers, constables, posse comitatus, etc. In most cases there is not free exercise whatever of the judgment or of the moral sense; but they put themselves on a level with wood and earth and stones; and wooden men can perhaps be manufactured that will serve the purpose as well. Such command no more respect than men of straw or a lump of dirt. They have the same sort of worth only as horses and dogs. Yet such as these even are commonly esteemed good citizens. Others—as most legislators, politicians, lawyers, ministers, and office-holders—serve the state chiefly with their heads; and, as they rarely make any moral distinctions, they are as likely to serve the Devil, without *intending* it, as God. A very few, as heroes, patriots, martyrs, reformers in the great sense, and *men*,

serve the state with their consciences also, and so necessarily resist it
for the most part; and they are commonly treated as enemies by it. A
wise man will only be useful as a man, and will not submit to be "clay,"
and "stop a hole to keep the wind away," but leave that office to his dust
at least:—

> "I am too high-born to be propertied,
> To be a secondary at control,
> Or useful serving-man and instrument
> To any sovereign state throughout the world."

He who gives himself entirely to his fellow-men appears to them useless and selfish; but he who gives himself partially to them is pronounced
a benefactor and philanthropist.

How does it become a man to behave toward this American government to-day? I answer, that he cannot without disgrace be associated
with it. I cannot for an instant recognize that political organization as *my*
government which is the *slave's* government also.

All men recognize the right of revolution; that is, the right to refuse
allegiance to, and to resist, the government, when its tyranny or its inef-
ficiency are great and unendurable. But almost all say that such is not the
case now. But such was the case, they think, in the Revolution of '75. If
one were to tell me that this was a bad government because it taxed
certain foreign commodities brought to its ports, it is most probable that
I should not make an ado about it, for I can do without them. All machines
have their friction; and possibly this does enough good to counterbalance
the evil. At any rate, it is a great evil to make a stir about it. But when the
friction comes to have its machine, and oppression and robbery are organized, I say, let us not have such a machine any longer. In other words,
when a sixth of the population of a nation which has undertaken to be the
refuge of liberty are slaves, and a whole country is unjustly overrun and
conquered by a foreign army, and subjected to military law, I think that it
is not too soon for honest men to rebel and revolutionize. What makes
this duty the more urgent is the fact that the country so overrun is not
our own, but ours is the invading army.

Paley, a common authority with many on moral questions, in his
chapter on the "Duty of Submission to Civil Government," resolves all
civil obligation into expediency; and he proceeds to say, "that so long as
the interest of the whole society requires it, that is, so long as the established government cannot be resisted or changed without public incon-
veniency, it is the will of God that the established government be obeyed,
and no longer. . . . This principle being admitted, the justice of every particular case of resistance is reduced to a computation of the quantity of
the danger and grievance on the one side, and of the probability and
expense of redressing it on the other." Of this, he says, every man shall
judge for himself. But Paley appears never to have contemplated those
cases to which the rule of expediency does not apply, in which a people,
as well as an individual, must do justice, cost what it may. If I have unjustly wrested a plank from a drowning man, I must restore it to him
though I drown myself. This, according to Paley, would be inconvenient.

But he that would save his life, in such a case, shall lose it. This people must cease to hold slaves, and to make war on Mexico, though it cost them their existence as a people.

In their practice, nations agree with Paley; but does any one think that Massachusetts does exactly what is right at the present crisis?

> "A drab of state, a cloth-o'-silver slut,
> To have her train borne up, and her soul trail in the dirt."

Practically speaking, the opponents to a reform in Massachusetts are not a hundred thousand politicians at the South, but a hundred thousand merchants and farmers here, who are more interested in commerce and agriculture than they are in humanity, and are not prepared to do justice to the slave and to Mexico, *cost what it may.* I quarrel not with far-off foes, but with those who, near at home, coöperate with, and do the bidding of, those far away, and without whom the latter would be harmless. We are accustomed to say, that the mass of men are unprepared; but improvement is slow, because the few are not materially wiser or better than the many. It is not so important that many should be as good as you, as that there be some absolute goodness somewhere; for that will leaven the whole lump. There are thousands who are *in opinion* opposed to slavery and to the war, who yet in effect do nothing to put an end to them; who, esteeming themselves children of Washington and Franklin, sit down with their hands in their pockets, and say that they know not what to do, and do nothing; who even postpone the question of freedom to the question of free-trade, and quietly read the prices-current along with the latest advices from Mexico, after dinner, and, it may be, fall asleep over them both. What is the price-current of an honest man and patriot to-day? They hesitate, and they regret, and sometimes they petition; but they do nothing in earnest and with effect. They will wait, well disposed, for others to remedy the evil, that they may no longer have it to regret. At most, they give only a cheap vote, and a feeble countenance and Godspeed, to the right, as it goes by them. There are nine hundred and ninety-nine patrons of virtue to one virtuous man. But it is easier to deal with the real possessor of a thing than with the temporary guardian of it.

All voting is a sort of gaming, like checkers or backgammon, with a slight moral tinge to it, a playing with right and wrong, with moral questions; and betting naturally accompanies it. The character of the voters is not staked. I cast my vote, perchance, as I think right; but I am not vitally concerned that that right should prevail. I am willing to leave it to the majority. Its obligation, therefore, never exceeds that of expediency. Even voting *for the right* is *doing* nothing for it. It is only expressing to men feebly your desire that it should prevail. A wise man will not leave the right to the mercy of chance, nor wish it to prevail through the power of the majority. There is but little virtue in the action of masses of men. When the majority shall at length vote for the abolition of slavery, it will be because they are indifferent to slavery, or because there is but little slavery left to be abolished by their vote. *They* will then be the only slaves. Only *his* vote can hasten the abolition of slavery who asserts his own freedom by his vote.

I hear of a convention to be held at Baltimore, or elsewhere, for the selection of a candidate for the Presidency, made up chiefly of editors, and men who are politicians by profession; but I think, what is it to any independent, intelligent, and respectable man what decision they may come to? Shall we not have the advantage of his wisdom and honesty, nevertheless? Can we not count upon some independent votes? Are there not many individuals in the country who do not attend conventions? But no: I find that the respectable man, so called, has immediately drifted from his position, and despairs of his country, when his country has more reason to despair of him. He forthwith adopts one of the candidates thus selected as the only *available* one, thus proving that he is himself *available* for any purposes of the demagogue. His vote is of no more worth than that of any unprincipled foreigner or hireling native, who may have been bought. O for a man who is a *man*, and, as my neighbor says, has a bone in his back which you cannot pass your hand through! Our statistics are at fault: the population has been returned too large. How many *men* are there to a square thousand miles in this country? Hardly one. Does not America offer any inducement for men to settle here? The American has dwindled into an Odd Fellow,—one who may be known by the development of his organ of gregariousness, and a manifest lack of intellect and cheerful self-reliance; whose first and chief concern, on coming into the world, is to see that the Almshouses are in good repair; and, before yet he has lawfully donned the virile garb, to collect a fund for the support of the widows and orphans that may be; who, in short, ventures to live only by the aid of the Mutual Insurance company, which has promised to bury him decently.

It is not a man's duty, as a matter of course, to devote himself to the eradication of any, even the most enormous wrong; he may still properly have other concerns to engage him; but it is his duty, at least, to wash his hands of it, and, if he gives it no thought longer, not to give it practically his support. If I devote myself to other pursuits and contemplations, I must first see, at least, that I do not pursue them sitting upon another man's shoulders. I must get off him first, that he may pursue his contemplations too. See what gross inconsistency is tolerated. I have heard some of my townsmen say, "I should like to have them order me out to help put down an insurrection of the slaves, or to march to Mexico;—see if I would go;" and yet these very men have each, directly by their allegiance, and so indirectly, at least, by their money, furnished a substitute. The soldier is applauded who refuses to serve in an unjust war by those who do not refuse to sustain the unjust government which makes the war; is applauded by those whose own act and authority he disregards and sets at naught; as if the state were penitent to that degree that it hired one to scourge it while it sinned, but not to that degree that it left off sinning for a moment. Thus, under the name of Order and Civil Government, we are all made at last to pay homage to and support our own meanness. After the first blush of sin comes its indifference; and from immoral it becomes, as it were, *un*moral and not quite unnecessary to that life which we have made.

The broadest and most prevalent error requires the most disinterested virtue to sustain it. The slight reproach to which the virtue of patriotism is commonly liable, the noble are most likely to incur. Those who, while they disapprove of the character and measures of a government, yield to it their allegiance and support are undoubtedly its most conscientious supporters, and so frequently the most serious obstacles to reform. Some are petitioning the state to dissolve the Union, to disregard the requisitions of the President. Why do they not dissolve it themselves,—the union between themselves and the state,—and refuse to pay their quota into its treasury? Do not they stand in the same relation to the state that the state does to the Union? And have not the same reasons prevented the state from resisting the Union which have prevented them from resisting the state?

How can a man be satisfied to entertain an opinion merely, and enjoy *it*? Is there any enjoyment in it, if his opinion is that he is aggrieved? If you are cheated out of a single dollar by your neighbor, you do not rest satisfied with knowing that you are cheated, or with saying that you are cheated, or even with petitioning him to pay you your due; but you take effectual steps at once to obtain the full amount, and see that you are never cheated again. Action from principle, the perception and the performance of right, changes things and relations; it is essentially revolutionary, and does not consist wholly with anything which was. It not only divides states and churches, it divides families; ay, it divides the *individual*, separating the diabolical in him from the divine.

Unjust laws exist: shall we be content to obey them, or shall we endeavor to amend them, and obey them until we have succeeded, or shall we transgress them at once? Men generally, under such a government as this, think that they ought to wait until they have persuaded the majority to alter them. They think that, if they should resist, the remedy would be worse than the evil. But it is the fault of the government itself that the remedy *is* worse than the evil. *It* makes it worse. Why is it not more apt to anticipate and provide for reform? Why does it not cherish its wise minority? Why does it cry and resist before it is hurt? Why does it not encourage its citizens to be on the alert to point out its faults, and *do* better than it would have them? Why does it always crucify Christ, and excommunicate Copernicus and Luther, and pronounce Washington and Franklin rebels?

One would think, that a deliberate and practical denial of its authority was the only offense never contemplated by government; else, why has it not assigned its definite, its suitable and proportionate penalty? If a man who has no property refuses but once to earn nine shillings for the state, he is put in prison for a period unlimited by any law that I know, and determined only by the discretion of those who placed him there; but if he should steal ninety times nine shillings from the state, he is soon permitted to go at large again.

If the injustice is part of the necessary friction of the machine of government, let it go, let it go: perchance it will wear smooth,—certainly the machine will wear out. If the injustice has a spring, or a pulley, or a rope, or a crank, exclusively for itself, then perhaps you may consider whether the remedy will not be worse than the evil; but if it is of such a nature that it requires you to be the agent of injustice to another, then, I say, break the law. Let your life be a counter friction to stop the machine.

What I have to do is to see, at any rate, that I do not lend myself to the wrong which I condemn.

As for adopting the ways which the state has provided for remedying the evil, I know not of such ways. They take too much time, and a man's life will be gone. I have other affairs to attend to. I came into this world, not chiefly to make this a good place to live in, but to live in it, be it good or bad. A man has not everything to do, but something; and because he cannot do *everything*, it is not necessary that he should do *something* wrong. It is not my business to be petitioning the Governor or the Legislature any more than it is theirs to petition me; and if they should not hear my petition, what should I do then? But in this case the state has provided no way: its very Constitution is the evil. This may seem to be harsh and stubborn and unconciliatory; but it is to treat with the utmost kindness and consideration the only spirit that can appreciate or deserves it. So is all change for the better, like birth and death, which convulse the body.

I do not hesitate to say, that those who call themselves Abolitionists should at once effectually withdraw their support, both in person and property, from the government of Massachusetts, and not wait till they constitute a majority of one, before they suffer the right to prevail through them. I think that it is enough if they have God on their side, without waiting for that other one. Moreover, any man more right than his neighbors constitutes a majority of one already.

I meet this American government, or its representative, the state government, directly, and face to face, once a year—no more—in the person of its tax-gatherer; this is the only mode in which a man situated as I am necessarily meets it; and it then says distinctly, Recognize me; and the simplest, the most effectual, and, in the present posture of affairs, the indispensablest mode of treating with it on this head, of expressing your little satisfaction with and love for it, is to deny it then. My civil neighbor, the tax-gatherer, is the very man I have to deal with,—for it is, after all, with men and not with parchment that I quarrel,—and he has voluntarily chosen to be an agent of the government. How shall he ever know well what he is and does as an officer of the government, or as a man, until he is obliged to consider whether he shall treat me, his neighbor, for whom he has respect, as a neighbor and well-disposed man, or as a maniac and disturber of the peace, and see if he can get over this obstruction to his neighborliness without a ruder and more impetuous thought or speech corresponding with his action. I know this well, that if one thousand, if one hundred, if ten men whom I could name,—if ten *honest* men only,— ay, if *one* HONEST man, in this State of Massachusetts, *ceasing to hold slaves*, were actually to withdraw from this copartnership, and be locked up in the county jail therefor, it would be the abolition of slavery in America. For it matters not how small the beginning may seem to be: what is once well done is done forever. But we love better to talk about it: that we say is our mission. Reform keeps many scores of newspapers in its service, but not one man. If my esteemed neighbor, the State's ambassador, who will devote his days to the settlement of the question of human rights in the Council Chamber, instead of being threatened with the prisons of Carolina, were to sit down the prisoner of Massachusetts, that

State which is so anxious to foist the sin of slavery upon her sister,—though at present she can discover only an act of inhospitality to be the ground of a quarrel with her,—the Legislature would not wholly waive the subject the following winter.

Under a government which imprisons any unjustly, the true place for a just man is also a prison. The proper place to-day, the only place which Massachusetts has provided for her freer and less desponding spirits, is in her prisons, to be put out and locked out of the State by her own act, as they have already put themselves out by their principles. It is there that the fugitive slave, and the Mexican prisoner on parole, and the Indian come to plead the wrongs of his race should find them; on that separate, but more free and honorable ground, where the State places those who are not *with* her, but *against* her,—the only house in a slave State in which a free man can abide with honor. If any think that their influence would be lost there, and their voices no longer afflict the ear of the State, that they would not be as an enemy within its walls, they do not know by how much truth is stronger than error, nor how much more eloquently and effectively he can combat injustice who has experienced a little in his own person. Cast your whole vote, not a strip of paper merely, but your whole influence. A minority is powerless while it conforms to the majority; it is not even a minority then; but it is irresistible when it clogs by its whole weight. If the alternative is to keep all just men in prison, or give up war and slavery, the State will not hesitate which to choose. If a thousand men were not to pay their tax-bills this year, that would not be a violent and bloody measure, as it would be to pay them, and enable the State to commit violence and shed innocent blood. This is, in fact, the definition of a peaceable revolution, if any such is possible. If the tax-gatherer, or any other public officer, asks me, as one has done, "But what shall I do?" my answer is, "If you really wish to do anything, resign your office." When the subject has refused allegiance, and the officer has resigned his office, then the revolution is accomplished. But even suppose blood should flow. Is there not a sort of blood shed when the conscience is wounded? Through this wound a man's real manhood and immortality flow out, and he bleeds to an everlasting death. I see this blood flowing now.

I have contemplated the imprisonment of the offender, rather than the seizure of his goods,—though both will serve the same purpose,—because they who assert the purest right, and consequently are most dangerous to a corrupt State, commonly have not spent much time in accumulating property. To such the State renders comparatively small service, and a slight tax is wont to appear exorbitant, particularly if they are obliged to earn it by special labor with their hands. If there were one who lived wholly without the use of money, the State itself would hesitate to demand it of him. But the rich man—not to make any invidious comparison—is always sold to the institution which makes him rich. Absolutely speaking, the more money, the less virtue; for money comes between a man and his objects, and obtains them for him; and it was certainly no great virtue to obtain it. It puts to rest many questions which he would otherwise be taxed to answer; while the only new question which it puts is the hard but superfluous one, how to spend it. Thus his moral ground is taken from under his feet. The opportunities of living are diminished in proportion as what are called the "means" are increased. The best thing a man can do for his culture when he is rich is to endeavor to carry out those schemes which he entertained when he was poor. Christ answered the Herodians according to their condition. "Show me the tribute-money," said he;—and one took a penny out of his pocket;—if you use money which has the image of Cæsar on it, and which he has made current and valuable, that is, *if you are men of the State,* and gladly enjoy the advantages of Cæsar's government, then pay him back some of his own when he demands it. "Render therefore to Cæsar that which is Cæsar's, and to God those things which are God's,"—leaving them no wiser than before as to which was which; for they did not wish to know.

When I converse with the freest of my neighbors, I perceive that, whatever they may say about the magnitude and seriousness of the question, and their regard for the public tranquillity, the long and the short of the matter is, that they cannot spare the protection of the existing government, and they dread the consequences to their property and families of disobedience to it. For my own part, I should not like to think that I ever rely on the protection of the State. But, if I deny the authority of the State when it presents its tax-bill, it will soon take and waste all my property, and so harass me and my children without end. This is hard. This makes it impossible for a man to live honestly, and at the same time comfortably, in outward respects. It will not be worth the while to accumulate property; that would be sure to go again. You must hire or squat somewhere, and raise but a small crop, and eat that soon. You must live within yourself, and depend upon yourself always tucked up and ready for a start, and not have many affairs. A man may grow rich in Turkey even, if he will be in all respects a good subject of the Turkish government. Confucius said: "If a state is governed by the principles of reason, poverty and misery are subjects of shame; if a state is not governed by the principles of reason, riches and honors are the subjects of shame." No: until I want the protection of Massachusetts to be extended to me in some distant Southern port, where my liberty is endangered, or until I am bent solely on building up an estate at home by peaceful enterprise, I can afford to refuse allegiance to Massachusetts, and her right to my property and life. It costs me less in every sense to incur the penalty of disobedience to the State than it would to obey. I should feel as if I were worth less in that case.

Some years ago, the State met me in behalf of the Church, and commanded me to pay a certain sum toward the support of a clergyman whose preaching my father attended, but never I myself. "Pay," it said, "or be locked up in the jail." I declined to pay. But, unfortunately, another man saw fit to pay it. I did not see why the schoolmaster should be taxed to support the priest, and not the priest the schoolmaster; for I was not the State's schoolmaster, but I supported myself by voluntary subscription. I did not see why the lyceum should not present its tax-bill, and have the State to back its demand, as well as the Church. However, at the request of the selectmen, I condescended to make some such statement as this in writing:—"Know all men by these presents, that I, Henry Thoreau, do not wish to be regarded as a member of any incorporated society which I have not joined." This I gave to the town clerk; and he has it. The State, having thus learned that I did not wish to be regarded as a member of that church, has never made a like demand on me since; though it said that it must adhere to its original presumption that time. If I had known how to name them, I should then have signed off in detail from all the societies which I never signed on to; but I did not know where to find a complete list.

I have paid no poll-tax for six years. I was put into a jail once on this account, for one night; and, as I stood considering the walls of solid stone, two or three feet thick, the door of wood and iron, a foot thick, and the iron grating which strained the light, I could not help being struck with the foolishness of that institution which treated me as if I were mere flesh and blood and bones, to be locked up. I wondered that it should have concluded at length that this was the best use it could put me to, and had never thought to avail itself of my services in some way. I saw that, if there was a wall of stone between me and my townsmen, there was a still more difficult one to climb or break through before they could get to be as free as I was. I did not for a moment feel confined, and the walls seemed a great waste of stone and mortar. I felt as if I alone of all my townsmen had paid my tax. They plainly did not know how to treat me, but behaved like persons who are underbred. In every threat and in every compliment there was a blunder; for they thought that my chief desire was to stand the other side of that stone wall. I could not but smile to see how industriously they locked the door on my meditations, which followed them out again without let or hindrance, and *they* were really all that was dangerous. As they could not reach me, they had resolved to punish my body; just as boys, if they cannot come at some person against whom they have a spite, will abuse his dog. I saw that the State was half-witted, that it was timid as a lone woman with her silver spoons, and that it did not know its friends from its foes, and I lost all my remaining respect for it, and pitied it.

Thus the State never intentionally confronts a man's sense, intellectual or moral, but only his body, his senses. It is not armed with superior wit or honesty, but with superior physical strength. I was not born to be forced. I will breathe after my own fashion. Let us see who is the strongest. What force has a multitude? They only can force me who obey a higher law than I. They force me to become like themselves. I do not hear of *men* being *forced* to live this way or that by masses of men. What sort of life were that to live? When I meet a government which says to me, "Your money or your life," why should I be in haste to give it my money? It may be in a great strait, and not know what to do: I cannot help that. It must help itself; do as I do. It is not worth the while to snivel about it. I am not responsible for the successful working of the machinery of society. I am not the son of the engineer. I perceive that, when an acorn and a chestnut fall side by side, the one does not remain inert to make way for the other, but both obey their own laws, and spring and grow and flourish as best they can, till one, perchance, overshadows and destroys the other. If a plant cannot live according to its nature, it dies; and so a man.

The night in prison was novel and interesting enough. The prisoners in their shirt-sleeves were enjoying a chat and the evening air in the doorway, when I entered. But the jailer said, "Come, boys, it is time to lock up;" and so they dispersed, and I heard the sound of their steps returning into the hollow apartments. My room-mate was introduced to me by the jailer as "a first-rate fellow and a clever man." When the door was locked, he showed me where to hang my hat, and how he managed matters there. The rooms were whitewashed once a month; and this one, at least, was the whitest, most simply furnished, and probably the neatest apartment in the town. He naturally wanted to know where I came from, and what brought me there; and, when I had told him, I asked him in my turn how he came there, presuming him to be an honest man, of course; and, as the world goes, I believe he was. "Why," said he, "they accuse me of burning a barn; but I never did it." As near as I could discover, he had probably gone to bed in a barn when drunk, and smoked his pipe there; and so a barn was burnt. He had the reputation of being a clever man, had been there some three months waiting for his trial to come on, and would have to wait as much longer; but he was quite domesticated and contented, since he got his board for nothing, and thought that he was well treated.

He occupied one window, and I the other; and I saw that if one stayed there long, his principal business would be to look out the window. I had soon read all the tracts that were left there, and examined where former prisoners had broken out, and where a grate had been sawed off, and heard the history of the various occupants of that room; for I found that even here there was a history and a gossip which never circulated beyond the walls of the jail. Probably this is the only house in the town where verses are composed, which are afterward printed in a circular form, but not published. I was shown quite a long list of verses which were composed by some young men who had been detected in an attempt to escape, who avenged themselves by singing them.

I pumped my fellow-prisoner as dry as I could, for fear I should never see him again; but at length he showed me which was my bed, and left me to blow out the lamp.

It was like traveling into a far country, such as I had never expected to behold, to lie there for one night. It seemed to me that I never had heard the town-clock strike before, nor the evening sounds of the village; for we slept with the windows open, which were inside the grating. It was to see my native village in the light of the Middle Ages, and our Concord was turned into a Rhine stream, and visions of knights and castles passed before me. They were the voices of old burghers that I heard in the streets. I was an involuntary spectator and auditor of whatever was done and said in the kitchen of the adjacent village-inn,—a wholly new and rare experience to me. It was a closer view of my native town. I was fairly inside of it. I never had seen its institutions before. This is one of its peculiar institutions; for it is a shire town. I began to comprehend what its inhabitants were about.

In the morning, our breakfasts were put through the hole in the door, in small oblong-square tin pans, made to fit, and holding a pint of chocolate, with brown bread, and an iron spoon. When they called for the vessels again, I was green enough to return what bread I had left; but my comrade seized it, and said that I should lay that up for lunch or dinner. Soon after he was let out to work at haying in a neighboring field, whither he went every day, and would not be back till noon; so he bade me good-day, saying that he doubted if he should see me again.

When I came out of prison,—for some one interfered, and paid that tax,—I did not perceive that great changes had taken place on the common, such as he observed who went in a youth and emerged a tottering and gray-headed man; and yet a change had to my eyes come over the scene,—the town, and State, and country,—greater than any that mere time could effect. I saw yet more distinctly the State in which I lived. I saw to what extent the people among whom I lived could be trusted as good neighbors and friends; that their friendship was for summer weather only; that they did not greatly propose to do right; that they were a distinct race from me by their prejudices and superstitions, as the Chinamen and Malays are; that in their sacrifices to humanity they ran no risks, not even to their property; that after all they were not so noble but they treated the thief as he had treated them, and hoped, by a certain outward observance and a few prayers, and by walking in a particular straight though useless path from time to time, to save their souls. This may be to judge my neighbors harshly; for I believe that many of them are not aware that they have such an institution as the jail in their village.

It was formerly the custom in our village, when a poor debtor came out of jail, for his acquaintances to salute him, looking through their fingers, which were crossed to represent the grating of a jail window, "How do ye do?" My neighbors did not thus salute me, but first looked at me, and then at one another, as if I had returned from a long journey. I was put into jail as I was going to the shoemaker's to get a shoe which was mended. When I was let out the next morning, I proceeded to finish my errand, and, having put on my mended shoe, joined a huckleberry party, who were impatient to put themselves under my conduct; and in half an hour,—for the horse was soon tackled,—was in the midst of a huckleberry field, on one of our highest hills, two miles off, and then the State was nowhere to be seen.

This is the whole history of "My Prisons."

I have never declined paying the highway tax, because I am as desirous of being a good neighbor as I am of being a bad subject; and as for supporting schools, I am doing my part to educate my fellow-countrymen now. It is for no particular item in the tax-bill that I refuse to pay it. I simply wish to refuse allegiance to the State, to withdraw and stand aloof from it effectually. I do not care to trace the course of my dollar, if I could, till it buys a man or a musket to shoot one with,—the dollar is innocent,—but I am concerned to trace the effects of my allegiance. In fact, I quietly declare war with the State, after my fashion, though I will still make what use and get what advantage of her I can, as is usual in such cases.

If others pay the tax which is demanded of me, from a sympathy with the State, they do but what they have already done in their own case, or rather they abet injustice to a greater extent than the State requires. If they pay the tax from a mistaken interest in the individual taxed, to save his property, or prevent his going to jail, it is because they have not considered wisely how far they let their private feelings interfere with the public good.

This, then, is my position at present. But one cannot be too much on his guard in such a case, lest his action be biased by obstinacy or an undue regard for the opinions of men. Let him see that he does only what belongs to himself and to the hour.

I think sometimes, Why, this people mean well, they are only ignorant; they would do better if they knew how; why give your neighbors this pain to treat you as they are not inclined to? But I think again, this is no reason why I should do as they do, or permit others to suffer much greater pain of a different kind. Again, I sometimes say to myself, When many millions of men, without heat, without ill will, without personal feeling of any kind, demand of you a few shillings only, without the possibility, such is their constitution, of retracting or altering their present demand, and without the possibility, on your side, of appeal to any other millions, why expose yourself to this overwhelming brute force? You do not resist cold and hunger, the winds and the waves, thus obstinately; you quietly submit to a thousand similar necessities. You do not put your head into the fire. But just in proportion as I regard this as not wholly a brute force, but partly a human force, and consider that I have relations to those millions as to so many millions of men, and not of mere brute or inanimate things, I see that appeal is possible, first and instantaneously, from them to the Maker of them, and, secondly, from them to themselves. But if I put my head deliberately into the fire, there is no appeal to fire or to the Maker of fire, and I have only myself to blame. If I could convince myself that I have any right to be satisfied with men as they are, and to treat them accordingly, and not according, in some respects, to my requisitions and expectations of what they and I ought to be, then, like a good Mussulman and fatalist, I should endeavor to be satisfied with things as they are, and say it is the will of God. And, above all, there is this difference between resisting this and a purely brute or natural force, that I can resist this with some effect; but I cannot expect, like Orpheus, to change the nature of the rocks and trees and beasts.

I do not wish to quarrel with any man or nation. I do not wish to split hairs, to make fine distinctions, or set myself up as better than my neighbors. I seek rather, I may say, even an excuse for conforming to the laws of the land. I am but too ready to conform to them. Indeed, I have reason to suspect myself on this head; and each year, as the tax-gatherer comes round, I find myself disposed to review the acts and position of the general and State governments, and the spirit of the people, to discover a pretext for conformity.

> "*We must affect our country as our parents,*
> *And if at any time we alienate*
> *Our love or industry from doing it honor,*
> *We must respect effects and teach the soul*
> *Matter of conscience and religion,*
> *And not desire of rule or benefit.*"

I believe that the State will soon be able to take all my work of this sort out of my hands, and then I shall be no better a patriot than my fellow-countrymen. Seen from a lower point of view, the Constitution, with all its faults, is very good; the law and the courts are very respectable; even this State and this American government are, in many respects, very admirable, and rare things, to be thankful for, such as a great many have described them; but seen from a point of view a little higher, they are what I have described them; seen from a higher still, and the highest, who shall say what they are, or that they are worth looking at or thinking of at all?

However, the government does not concern me much, and I shall bestow the fewest possible thoughts on it. It is not many moments that I live under a government, even in this world. If a man is thought-free, fancy-free, imagination-free, that which *is not* never for a long time appearing *to be* to him, unwise rulers or reformers cannot fatally interrupt him.

I know that most men think differently from myself; but those whose lives are by profession devoted to the study of these or kindred subjects content me as little as any. Statesmen and legislators, standing so completely within the institution, never distinctly and nakedly behold it. They speak of moving society, but have no resting-place without it. They may be men of a certain experience and discrimination, and have no doubt invented ingenious and even useful systems, for which we sincerely thank them; but all their wit and usefulness lie within certain not very wide limits. They are wont to forget that the world is not governed by policy and expediency. Webster never goes behind government, and so cannot speak with authority about it. His words are wisdom to those legislators who contemplate no essential reform in the existing government; but for thinkers, and those who legislate for all time, he never once glances at the subject. I know of those whose serene and wise speculations on this theme would soon reveal the limits of his mind's range and hospitality. Yet, compared with the cheap professions of most reformers, and the still cheaper wisdom and eloquence of politicians in general, his are almost the only sensible and valuable words, and we thank Heaven for him. Comparatively, he is always strong, original, and, above all, practical. Still, his quality is not wisdom, but prudence. The lawyer's truth is not Truth, but consistency or a consistent expediency. Truth is always in harmony with herself, and is not concerned chiefly to reveal the justice that may consist with wrong-doing. He well deserves to be called, as he has been called, the Defender of the Constitution. There are really no blows to be given by him but defensive ones. He is not a leader, but a follower. His leaders are the men of '87. "I have never made an effort," he says, "and never propose to make an effort; I have never countenanced an effort, and never mean to countenance an effort, to disturb the arrangement as originally made, by which the various States came into the Union." Still thinking of the sanction which the Constitution gives to slavery, he says, "Because it was a part of the original compact,—let it stand." Notwithstanding his special acuteness and ability, he is unable to take a fact out of its merely political relations, and behold it as it lies absolutely to be disposed of by the intellect,—what, for instance, it behooves a man to do here in America to-day with regard to slavery,—but ventures, or is driven, to make some such desperate answer as the following, while professing to speak absolutely, and as a private man,—from which what new and singular code of social duties might be inferred? "The manner," says he, "in which the governments of those States where slavery exists are to regulate it is for their own consideration, under their responsibility to their constituents, to the general laws of propriety, humanity, and justice, and to God. Associations formed elsewhere, springing from a feeling of humanity, or any other cause, have nothing whatever to do with it. They have never received any encouragement from me, and they never will."

They who know of no purer sources of truth, who have traced up its stream no higher, stand, and wisely stand, by the Bible and the Constitution, and drink at it there with reverence and humility; but they who behold where it comes trickling into this lake or that pool, gird up their loins once more, and continue their pilgrimage toward its fountain-head.

No man with a genius for legislation has appeared in America. They are rare in the history of the world. There are orators, politicians, and eloquent men, by the thousand; but the speaker has not yet opened his mouth to speak who is capable of settling the much-vexed questions of the day. We love eloquence for its own sake, and not for any truth which it may utter, or any heroism it may inspire. Our legislators have not yet learned the comparative value of free-trade and of freedom, of union, and of rectitude, to a nation. They have no genius or talent for comparatively humble questions of taxation and finance, commerce and manufactures and agriculture. If we were left solely to the wordy wit of legislators in Congress for our guidance, uncorrected by the seasonable experience and the effectual complaints of the people, America would not long retain her rank among the nations. For eighteen hundred years, though perchance I have no right to say it, the New Testament has been written; yet where is the legislator who has wisdom and practical talent enough to avail himself of the light which it sheds on the science of legislation?

The authority of government, even such as I am willing to submit to,—for I will cheerfully obey those who know and can do better than I, and in many things even those who neither know nor can do so well,—is still an impure one: to be strictly just, it must have the sanction and consent of the governed. It can have no pure right over my person and property but what I concede to it. The progress from an absolute to a limited monarchy, from a limited monarchy to a democracy, is a progress toward a true respect for the individual. Even the Chinese philosopher was wise enough to regard the individual as the basis of the empire. Is a democracy, such as we know it, the last improvement possible in government? Is it not possible to take a step further towards recognizing and organizing the rights of man? There will never be a really free and enlightened State until the State comes to recognize the individual as a higher and independent power, from which all its own power and authority are derived, and treats him accordingly. I please myself with imagining a State at last which can afford to be just to all men, and to treat the individual with respect as a neighbor; which even would not think it inconsistent with its own repose if a few were to live aloof from it, not meddling with it, nor embraced by it, who fulfilled all the duties of neighbors and fellow-men. A State which bore this kind of fruit, and suffered it to drop off as fast as it ripened, would prepare the way for a still more perfect and glorious State, which also I have imagined, but not yet anywhere seen.

EMPLOYMENT DIVISION, DEPARTMENT OF HUMAN RESOURCES OF OREGON ET AL., PETITIONERS *v.* ALFRED L. SMITH ET AL.

ON WRIT OF CERTIORARI TO THE SUPREME COURT OF OREGON

Syllabus

No. 88–1213. Argued November 6, 1989—Decided April 17, 1990

Respondents Smith and Black were fired by a private drug rehabilitation organization because they ingested peyote, a hallucinogenic drug, for sacramental purposes at a ceremony of their Native American Church. Their applications for unemployment compensation were denied by the State of Oregon under a state law disqualifying employees discharged for work-related "misconduct." Holding that the denials violated respondents' First Amendment free exercise rights, the State Court of Appeals reversed. The State Supreme Court affirmed, but this Court vacated the judgment and remanded for a determination whether sacramental peyote use is proscribed by the State's controlled substance law, which makes it a felony to knowingly or intentionally possess the drug. Pending that determination, the Court refused to decide whether such use is protected by the Constitution. On remand, the State Supreme Court held that sacramental peyote use violated, and was not excepted from, the state-law prohibition, but concluded that that prohibition was invalid under the Free Exercise Clause.

Held: The Free Exercise Clause permits the State to prohibit sacramental peyote use and thus to deny unemployment benefits to persons discharged for such use.

. . .

SCALIA, J., delivered the opinion of the Court, in which REHNQUIST, C. J., and WHITE, STEVENS, and KENNEDY, JJ., joined. O'CONNOR, J., filed an opinion concurring in the judgment, in Parts I and II of which BRENNAN, MARSHALL, and BLACKMUN, JJ., joined without concurring in the judgment. BLACKMUN, J., filed a dissenting opinion, in which BRENNAN and MARSHALL, JJ., joined.

JUSTICE SCALIA delivered the opinion of the Court.
This case requires us to decide whether the Free Exercise Clause of the First Amendment permits the State of Oregon to include religiously inspired peyote use within the reach of its general criminal prohibition on use of that drug, and thus permits the State to deny unemployment benefits to persons dismissed from their jobs because of such religiously inspired use.

I

Oregon law prohibits the knowing or intentional possession of a "controlled substance" unless the substance has been prescribed by a medical practitioner. Ore. Rev. Stat. § 475.992(4) (1987). The law defines "controlled substance" as a drug classified in Schedules I through V of the Federal Controlled Substances Act, 21 U. S. C. §§ 811–812 (1982 ed. and Supp. V), as modified by the State Board of Pharmacy. Ore. Rev. Stat. § 475.005(6) (1987). Persons who violate this provision by possessing a controlled substance listed on Schedule I are "guilty of a Class B felony." § 475.992(4)(a). As compiled by the State Board of Pharmacy under its statutory authority, see Ore. Rev. Stat. § 475.035 (1987), Schedule I contains the drug peyote, a hallucinogen derived from the plant *Lophophorawilliamsii Lemaire.* Ore. Admin. Rule 855–80–021(3)(s) (1988).

Respondents Alfred Smith and Galen Black were fired from their jobs with a private drug rehabilitation organization because they ingested peyote for sacramental purposes at a ceremony of the Native American Church, of which both are members. When respondents applied to petitioner Employment Division for unemployment compensation, they were determined to be ineligible for benefits because they had been discharged for work-related "misconduct". The Oregon Court of Appeals reversed that determination, holding that the denial of benefits violated respondents' free exercise rights under the First Amendment.

On appeal to the Oregon Supreme Court, petitioner argued that the denial of benefits was permissible because respondents' consumption of peyote was a crime under Oregon law. The Oregon Supreme Court reasoned, however, that the criminality of respondents' peyote use was irrelevant to resolution of their constitutional claim—since the purpose of the "misconduct" provision under which respondents had been disqualified was not to enforce the State's criminal laws but to preserve the financial integrity of the compensation fund, and since that purpose was inadequate to justify the burden that disqualification imposed on respondents' religious practice. Citing our decisions in *Sherbert* v. *Verner,* 374 U. S. 398 (1963), and *Thomas* v. *Review Board, Indiana Employment Security Div.,* 450 U. S. 707 (1981), the court concluded that respondents were entitled to payment of unemployment benefits. *Smith* v. *Employment Div., Dept. of Human Resources,* 301 Ore. 209, 217–219, 721 P. 2d 445, 449–450 (1986). We granted certiorari. 480 U. S. 916 (1987).

Before this Court in 1987, petitioner continued to maintain that the illegality of respondents' peyote consumption was relevant to their constitutional claim. We agreed, concluding that "if a State has prohibited through its criminal laws certain kinds of religiously motivated conduct without violating the First Amendment, it certainly follows that it may impose the lesser burden of denying unemployment compensation benefits to persons who engage in that conduct." *Employment Div., Dept. of Human Resources of Oregon* v. *Smith,* 485 U. S. 660, 670 (1988) (*Smith I*). We noted, however, that the Oregon Supreme Court had not decided whether respondents' sacramental use of peyote was in fact proscribed by Oregon's controlled substance law, and that this issue was a matter of dispute between the parties. Being "uncertain about the legality of the religious use of peyote in Oregon," we determined that it would not be "appropriate for us to decide whether the practice is protected by the Federal Constitution." *Id.,* at 673. Accordingly, we vacated the judgment of the Oregon Supreme Court and remanded for further proceedings. *Id.,* at 674.

On remand, the Oregon Supreme Court held that respondents' religiously inspired use of peyote fell within the prohibition of the Oregon statute, which "makes no exception for the sacramental use" of the drug. 307 Ore. 68, 72–73, 763 P. 2d 146, 148 (1988). It then considered whether that prohibition was valid under the Free Exercise Clause, and concluded that it was not. The court therefore reaffirmed its previous ruling that the State could not deny unemployment benefits to respondents for having engaged in that practice.

We again granted certiorari. 489 U. S. ──── (1989).

II

Respondents' claim for relief rests on our decisions in *Sherbert* v. *Verner, supra, Thomas* v. *Review Board, Indiana Employment Security Div., supra,* and *Hobbie* v. *Unemployment Appeals Comm'n of Florida,* 480 U. S. 136 (1987), in which we held that a State could not condition the availability of unemployment insurance on an individual's willingness to forgo conduct required by his religion. As we observed in *Smith I,* however, the conduct at issue in those cases was not prohibited by law. We held that distinction to be critical, for "if Oregon does prohibit the religious use of peyote, and if that prohibition is consistent with the Federal Constitution, there is no federal right to engage in that conduct in Oregon," and "the State is free to withhold unemployment compensation from respondents for engaging in work-related misconduct, despite its religious motivation." 485 U. S., at 672. Now that the Oregon Supreme Court has confirmed that Oregon does prohibit the religious use of peyote, we proceed to consider whether that prohibition is permissible under the Free Exercise Clause.

A

The Free Exercise Clause of the First Amendment, which has been made applicable to the States by incorporation into the Fourteenth Amendment; see *Cantwell* v. *Connecticut,* 310 U. S. 296, 303 (1940), provides that "Congress shall make no law respecting an establishment of religion, or *prohibiting the free exercise thereof....*" U. S. Const. Am. I (emphasis added). The free exercise of religion means, first and foremost, the right to believe and profess whatever religious doctrine one desires. Thus, the First Amendment obviously excludes all "governmental regulation of religious *beliefs* as such." *Sherbert* v. *Verner, supra,* at 402. The government may not compel affirmation of religious belief, see *Torcaso* v. *Watkins,* 367 U. S. 488 (1961), punish the expression of religious doctrines it believes to be false, *United States* v. *Ballard,* 322 U. S. 78, 86–88 (1944), impose special disabilities on the basis of religious views or religious status, see *McDaniel* v. *Paty,* 435 U. S. 618 (1978); *Fowler* v. *Rhode Island,* 345 U. S. 67, 69 (1953); cf. *Larson* v. *Valente,* 456 U. S. 228, 245 (1982), or lend its power to one or the other side in controversies over religious authority or dogma, see *Presbyterian Church* v. *Hull Church,* 393 U. S. 440, 445–452 (1969); *Kedroff* v. *St. Nicholas Cathedral,* 344 U. S. 94, 95–119 (1952); *Serbian Eastern Orthodox Diocese* v. *Milivojevich,* 426 U. S. 696, 708–725 (1976).

But the "exercise of religion" often involves not only belief and profession but the performance of (or abstention from) physical acts: assembling with others for a worship service, participating in sacramental use of bread and wine, proselytizing, abstaining from certain foods or certain modes of transportation. It would be true, we think (though no case of ours has involved the point), that a state would be "prohibiting the free exercise [of religion]" if it sought to ban such acts or abstentions only when they are engaged in for religious reasons, or only because of the religious belief that they display. It would doubtless be unconstitutional, for example, to ban the casting of "statues that are to be used for worship purposes," or to prohibit bowing down before a golden calf.

Respondents in the present case, however, seek to carry the meaning of "prohibiting the free exercise [of religion]" one large step further. They contend that their religious motivation for using peyote places them beyond the reach of a criminal law that is not specifically directed at their religious practice, and that is concededly constitutional as applied to those who use the drug for other reasons. They assert, in other words, that "prohibiting the free exercise [of religion]" includes requiring any individual to observe a generally applicable law that requires (or forbids) the performance of an act that his religious belief forbids (or requires). As a textual matter, we do not think the words must be given that meaning. It is no more necessary to regard the collection of a general tax, for example, as "prohibiting the free exercise [of religion]" by those citizens who believe support of organized government to be sinful, than it is to regard the same tax as "abridging the freedom . . . of the press" of those publishing companies that must pay the tax as a condition of staying in business. It is a permissible reading of the text, in the one case as in the other, to say that if prohibiting the exercise of religion (or burdening the activity of printing) is not the object of the tax but merely the incidental effect of a generally applicable and otherwise valid provision, the First Amendment has not been offended. Compare *Citizen Publishing Co.* v. *United States*, 394 U. S. 131, 139 (1969) (upholding application of antitrust laws to press), with *Grosjean* v. *American Press Co.*, 297 U. S. 233, 250–251 (1936) (striking down license tax applied only to newspapers with weekly circulation above a specified level); see generally *Minneapolis Star & Tribune Co.* v. *Minnesota Commissioner of Revenue*, 460 U. S. 575, 581 (1983).

Our decisions reveal that the latter reading is the correct one. We have never held that an individual's religious beliefs excuse him from compliance with an otherwise valid law prohibiting conduct that the State is free to regulate. On the contrary, the record of more than a century of our free exercise jurisprudence contradicts that proposition. As described succinctly by Justice Frankfurter in *Minersville School Dist. Bd. of Educ.* v. *Gobitis*, 310 U. S. 585, 594–595 (1940): "Conscientious scruples have not, in the course of the long struggle for religious toleration, relieved the individual from obedience to a general law not aimed at the promotion or restriction of religious beliefs. The mere possession of religious convictions which contradict the relevant concerns of a political society does not relieve the citizen from the discharge of political responsibilities (footnote omitted)." We first had occasion to assert that principle in *Reynolds* v. *United States*, 98 U. S. 145 (1879), where we rejected the claim that criminal laws against polygamy could not be constitutionally applied to those whose religion commanded the practice. "Laws," we said, "are made for the government of actions, and while they cannot interfere with mere religious belief and opinions, they may with practices. . . . Can a man excuse his practices to the contrary because of his religious belief? To permit this would be to make the professed doctrines of religious belief superior to the law of the land, and in effect to permit every citizen to become a law unto himself." *Id.*, at 166–167.

Subsequent decisions have consistently held that the right of free exercise does not relieve an individual of the obligation to comply with a "valid and neutral law of general applicability on the ground that the law proscribes (or prescribes) conduct that his religion prescribes (or proscribes)." *United States* v. *Lee*, 455 U. S. 252, 263, n. 3 (1982) (STEVENS, J., concurring in judgment); see *Minersville School Dist. Bd. of Educ.* v. *Gobitis, supra*, at 595 (collecting cases). In *Prince* v. *Massachusetts*, 321 U. S. 158 (1944), we held that a mother could be prosecuted under the child labor laws for using her children to dispense literature in the streets, her religious motivation notwithstanding. We found no constitutional infirmity in "excluding [these children] from doing there what no other children may do." *Id.*, at 171. In *Braunfeld* v. *Brown*, 366 U. S. 599 (1961) (plurality opinion), we upheld Sunday-closing laws against the claim that they burdened the religious practices of persons whose religions compelled them to refrain from work on other days. In *Gillette* v. *United States*, 401 U. S. 437, 461 (1971), we sustained the military selective service system against the claim that it violated free exercise by conscripting persons who opposed a particular war on religious grounds.

Our most recent decision involving a neutral, generally applicable regulatory law that compelled activity forbidden by an individual's religion was *United States* v. *Lee*, 455 U. S. at 258–261. There, an Amish employer, on behalf of himself and his employees, sought exemption from collection and payment of Social Security taxes on the ground that the Amish faith prohibited participation in governmental support programs. We rejected the claim that an exemption was constitutionally required. There would be no way, we observed, to distinguish the Amish believer's objection to Social Security taxes from the religious objections that others might have to the collection or use of other taxes. "If, for example, a religious adherent believes war is a sin, and if a certain percentage of the federal budget can be identified as devoted to war-related activities, such individuals would have a similarly valid claim to be exempt from paying that percentage of the income tax. The tax system could not function if denominations were allowed to challenge the tax system because tax payments were spent in a manner that violates their religious belief." *Id.*, at 260. Cf. *Hernandez* v. *Commissioner*, 490 U. S. —— (1989) (rejecting free exercise challenge to payment of income taxes alleged to make religious activities more difficult).

The only decisions in which we have held that the First Amendment bars application of a neutral, generally applicable law to religiously motivated action have involved not the Free Exercise Clause alone, but the Free Exercise Clause in conjunction with other constitutional protections, such as freedom of speech and of the press, see *Cantwell* v. *Connecticut*, 310 U.S. at 304–307 (invalidating a licensing system for religious and charitable solicitations under which the administrator had discretion to deny a license to any cause he deemed nonreligious); *Murdock* v. *Pennsylvania*, 319 U.S. 105 (1943) (invalidating a flat tax on solicitation as applied to the dissemination of religious ideas); *Follett* v. *McCormick*, 321 U.S. 573 (1944) (same), or the right of parents, acknowledged in *Pierce* v. *Society of Sisters*, 268 U.S. 510 (1925), to direct the education of their children, see *Wisconsin* v. *Yoder*, 406 U.S. 205 (1972) (invalidating compulsory school-attendance laws as applied to Amish parents who refused on religious grounds to send their children to school). Some of our cases prohibiting compelled expression, decided exclusively upon free speech grounds, have also involved freedom of religion, cf. *Wooley* v. *Maynard*, 430 U.S. 705 (1977) (invalidating compelled display of license plate slogan that offended individual religious beliefs); *West Virginia Board of Education* v. *Barnette*, 319 U.S. 624 (1943) (invalidating compulsory flag salute statute challenged by religious objectors). And it is easy to envision a case in which a challenge on freedom of association grounds would likewise be reinforced by Free Exercise Clause concerns. *Cf. Roberts* v. *United States Jaycees*, 468 U.S. 609, 622 (1983) ("An individual's freedom to speak, to worship, and to petition the government for the redress of grievances could not be vigorously protected from interference by the State [if] a correlative freedom to engage in group effort toward those ends were not also guaranteed.").

The present case does not present such a hybrid situation, but a free exercise claim unconnected with any communicative activity or parental right. Respondents urge us to hold, quite simply, that when otherwise prohibitable conduct is accompanied by religious convictions, not only the convictions but the conduct itself must be free from governmental regulation. We have never held that, and decline to do so now. There being no contention that Oregon's drug law represents an attempt to regulate religious beliefs, the communication of religious beliefs, or the raising of one's children in those beliefs, the rule to which we have adhered ever since *Reynolds* plainly controls. "Our cases do not at their farthest reach support the proposition that a stance of conscientious opposition relieves an objector from any colliding duty fixed by a democratic government." *Gillette* v. *United States, supra*, at 461.

B

Respondents argue that even though exemption from generally applicable criminal laws need not automatically be extended to religiously motivated actors, at least the claim for a religious exemption must be evaluated under the balancing test set forth in *Sherbert* v. *Verner*, 374 U.S. 398 (1963). Under the *Sherbert* test, governmental actions that substantially burden a religious practice must be justified by a compelling governmental interest. See *id.*, at 402–403; see also *Hernandez* v. *Commissioner, supra* at ——. Applying that test we have, on three occasions, invalidated state unemployment compensation rules that conditioned the availability of benefits upon an applicant's willingness to work under conditions forbidden by his religion. See *Sherbert* v. *Verner, supra; Thomas* v. *Review Board, Indiana Employment Div.*, 450 U.S. 707 (1981); *Hobbie* v. *Unemployment Appeals Comm'n of Florida*, 480 U.S. 136 (1987). We have never invalidated any governmental action on the basis of the *Sherbert* test except the denial of unemployment compensation. Although we have sometimes purported to apply the *Sherbert* test in contexts other than that, we have always found the test satisfied, see *United States* v. *Lee* 455 U.S. 252 (1982); *Gillette* v. *United States,cf1 401 U.S. 437 (1971). In recent years we have abstained from applying the Sherbert* test (outside the unemployment compensation field) at all. In *Bowen* v. *Roy,* 476 U.S. 693 (1986), we declined to apply *Sherbert* analysis to a federal statutory scheme that required benefit applicants and recipients to provide their Social Security numbers. The plaintiffs in that case asserted that it would violate their religious beliefs to obtain and provide a Social Security number for their daughter. We held the statue's application to the plaintiffs valid regardless of whether it was necessary to effectuate a compelling interest. See *id.*, at 699–701. In *Lyng* v. *Northwest Indian Cemetery Protective Assn.*, 485 U.S. 439 (1988), we declined to apply *Sherbert* analysis to the Government's logging and road construction activities on lands used for religious purposes by several Native American Tribes, even though it was undisputed that the activities "could have devastating effects on traditional Indian religious practices," 485 U.S., at 451. In *Goldman* v. *Weinberger,* 475 U.S. 503 (1986), we rejected application of the *Sherbert* test to military dress regulations that forbade the wearing of yarmulkes. In *O'Lone* v. *Estate of Shabazz,* 482 U.S. 342 (1987), we sustained, without mentioning the *Sherbert* test, a prison's refusal to excuse inmates from work requirements to attend worship services.

Even if we were inclined to breathe into *Sherbert* some life beyond the unemployment compensation field, we would not apply it to require exemptions from a generally applicable criminal law. The *Sherbert* test, it must be recalled, was developed in a context that lent itself to individualized governmental assessment of the reasons for the relevant conduct. As a plurality of the Court noted in *Roy,* a distinctive feature of unemployment compensation programs is that their eligibility criteria invite consideration of the particular circumstances behind an applicant's unemployment: "The statutory conditions [in *Sherbert* and *Thomas*] provided that a person was not eligible for unemployment compensation benefits if, 'without good cause,' he had quit work or refused available work. The 'good cause' standard created a mechanism for individualized exemptions." *Bowen* v. *Roy, supra,* at 708 (opinion of Burger, C. J., joined by Powell and Rᴇʜɴǫᴜɪsᴛ, JJ.). See also *Sherbert, supra,* at 401 n. 4 (reading state unemployment compensation law as allowing benefits for unemployment caused by at least some "personal reasons"). As the plurality pointed out in *Roy,* our decisions in the unemployment cases stand for the proposition that where the State has in place a system of individual exemptions, it may not refuse to extend that system to cases of "religious hardship" without compelling reason. *Bowen* v. *Roy, supra,* at 708.

Whether or not the decisions are that limited, they at least have nothing to do with an across-the-board criminal prohibition on a particular form of conduct. Although, as noted earlier, we have sometimes used the *Sherbert* test to analyze free exercise challenges to such laws, see *United States* v. *Lee, supra,* at 257–260; *Gillette* v. *United States, supra,* at 462, we have never applied the test to invalidate one. We conclude today that the sounder approach, and the approach in accord with the vast majority of our precedents, is to hold the test inapplicable to such challenges. The government's ability to enforce generally applicable prohibitions of socially harmful conduct, like its ability to carry out other aspects of public policy, "cannot depend on measuring the effects of a governmental action on a religious objector's spiritual development." *Lyng, supra,* at 451. To make an individual's obligation to obey such a law contingent upon the law's coincidence with his religious beliefs, except where the State's interest is "compelling"—permitting him, by virtue of his beliefs, "to become a law unto himself," *Reynolds* v. *United States,* 98 U. S., at 167— contradicts both constitutional tradition and common sense.

The "compelling government interest" requirement seems benign, because it is familiar from other fields. But using it as the standard that must be met before the government may accord different treatment on the basis of race, see, *e. g., Palmore* v. *Sidoti,* 466 U. S. 429, 432 (1984), or before the government may regulate the content of speech, see, *e. g., Sable Communications of California* v. *FCC,* 492 U. S. ——, —— (1989), is not remotely comparable to using it for the purpose asserted here. What it produces in those other fields—equality of treatment, and an unrestricted flow of contending speech—are constitutional norms; what it would produce here—a private right to ignore generally applicable laws—is a constitutional anomaly.

Nor is it possible to limit the impact of respondents' proposal by requiring a "compelling state interest" only when the conduct prohibited is "central" to the individual's religion. Cf. *Lyng* v. *Northwest Indian Cemetery Protective Assn., supra,* at —— (BRENNAN, J., dissenting). It is no more appropriate for judges to determine the "centrality" of religious beliefs before applying a "compelling interest" test in the free exercise field, than it would be for them to determine the "importance" of ideas before applying the "compelling interest" test in the free speech field. What principle of law or logic can be brought to bear to contradict a believer's assertion that a particular act is "central" to his personal faith? Judging the centrality of different religious practices is akin to the unacceptable "business of evaluating the relative merits of differing religious claims." *United States* v. *Lee,* 455 U. S., at 263 n. 2 (STEVENS, J., concurring). As we reaffirmed only last Term, "[i]t is not within the judicial ken to question the centrality of particular beliefs or practices to a faith, or the validity of particular litigants' interpretation of those creeds." *Hernandez* v. *Commissioner,* 490 U. S., at ——. Repeatedly and in many different contexts, we have warned that courts must not presume to determine the place of a particular belief in a religion or the plausibility of a religious claim. See, *e. g., Thomas* v. *Review Board, Indiana Employment Security Div.,* 450 U. S., at 716; *Presbyterian Church* v. *Hull Church,*

393 U.S., at 450; *Jones* v. *Wolf*, 443 U. S. 595, 602–606 (1979); *United States* v. *Ballard*, 322 U. S. 78, 85–87 (1944).

If the "compelling interest" test is to be applied at all, then, it must be applied across the board, to all actions thought to be religiously commanded. Moreover, if "compelling interest" really means what it says (and watering it down here would subvert its rigor in the other fields where it is applied), many laws will not meet the test. Any society adopting such a system would be courting anarchy, but that danger increases in direct proportion to the society's diversity of religious beliefs, and its determination to coerce or suppress none of them. Precisely because "we are a cosmopolitan nation made up of people of almost every conceivable religious preference," *Braunfield* v. *Brown*, 366 U. S., at 606, and precisely because we value and protect that religious divergence, we cannot afford the luxury of deeming *presumptively invalid*, as applied to the religious objector, every regulation of conduct that does not protect an interest of the highest order. The rule respondents favor would open the prospect of constitutionally required religious exemptions from civic obligations of almost every conceivable kind—ranging from compulsory military service, see, *e. g., Gillette* v. *United States*, 401 U. S. 437 (1971), to the payment of taxes, see, *e. g., United States* v. *Lee, supra;* to health and safety regulation such as manslaughter and child neglect laws, see, *e. g., Funkhouser* v. *State*, 763 P. 2d. 695 (Okla. Crim. App. 1988), compulsory vaccination laws, see *e. g., Cude* v. *State*, 237 Ark. 927, 377 S. W. 2d 816 (1964), drug laws, see, *e. g., Olsen* v. *Drug Enforcement Administration,* —— U. S. App. D. C. ——, 878 F. 2d 1458 (1989), and traffic laws, see *Cox* v. *New Hampshire*, 312 U. S. 569 (1941); to social welfare legislation such as minimum wage laws, see *Susan and Tony Alamo Foundation* v. *Secretary of Labor*, 471 U. S. 290 (1985), child labor laws, see *Prince* v. *Massachusetts*, 321 U. S. 158 (1944), animal cruelty laws, see, *e. g., Church of the Lukumi Babalu Aye Inc.* v. *City of Hialeah*, 723 F. Supp. 1467 (S. D. Fla. 1989), cf. *State* v. *Massey*, 229 N. C. 734, 51 S. E. 2d 179, appeal dism'd, 336 U. S. 942 (1949), environmental protection laws, see *United States* v. *Little*, 638 F. Supp. 337 (Mont. 1986), and laws providing for equality of opportunity for the races, see, *e. g., Bob Jones University* v. *United States*, 461 U. S. 574, 603–604 (1983). The First Amendment's protection of religious liberty does not require this.

Values that are protected against government interference through enshrinement in the Bill of Rights are not thereby banished from the political process. Just as a society that believes in the negative protection accorded to the press by the First Amendment is likely to enact laws that affirmatively foster the dissemination of the printed word, so also a society that believes in the negative protection accorded to religious belief can be expected to be solicitous of that value in its legislation as well. It is therefore not surprising that a number of States have made an exception to their drug laws for sacramental peyote use. See, *e. g.,* Ariz. Rev. Stat. Ann. § 13–3402(b)(1)–(3) (1989); Colo. Rev. Stat. § 12–22–317(3) (1985); N. M. Stat. Ann. § 30–31–6(D) (Supp. 1989). But to say that a nondiscriminatory religious-practice exemption is permitted, or even that it is desirable, is not to say that it is constitutionally required, and that the appropriate occasions for its creation can be discerned by the courts. It may fairly be said that leaving accommodation to the political process will place at a relative disadvantage those religious practices that are not widely engaged in; but that unavoidable consequence of democratic government must be preferred to a system in which each conscience is a law unto itself or in which judges weigh the social importance of all laws against the centrality of all religious beliefs.

*   *   *   *   *

Because respondents' ingestion of peyote was prohibited under Oregon law, and because that prohibition is constitutional, Oregon may, consistent with the Free Exercise Clause, deny respondents unemployment compensation when their dismissal results from use of the drug. The decision of the Oregon Supreme Court is accordingly reversed.

It is so ordered.

Justice O'Connor, with whom Justice Brennan, Justice Marshall, and Justice Blackmun join as to Parts I and II, concurring in the judgment.

Although I agree with the result the Court reaches in this case, I cannot join its opinion. In my view, today's holding dramatically departs from well-settled First Amendment jurisprudence, appears unnecessary to resolve the question presented, and is incompatible with our Nation's fundamental commitment to individual religious liberty.

I

At the outset, I note that I agree with the Court's implicit determination that the constitutional question upon which we granted review— whether the Free Exercise Clause protects a person's religiously motivated use of peyote from the reach of a State's general criminal law prohibition—is properly presented in this case. As the Court recounts, respondents Alfred Smith and Galen Black were denied unemployment compensation benefits because their sacramental use of peyote constituted work-related "misconduct," not because they violated Oregon's general criminal prohibition against possession of peyote. We held, however, in *Employment Div., Dept. of Human Resources of Oregon*, v. *Smith*, 485 U. S. 660 (1988) (*Smith I*), that whether a State may, consistent with federal law, deny unemployment compensation benefits to persons for their religious use of peyote depends on whether the State, as a matter of state law, has criminalized the underlying conduct. See *id.*, at 670–672. The Oregon Supreme Court, on remand from this Court, concluded that "the Oregon statute against possession of controlled substances, which include peyote, makes no exception for the sacramental use of peyote." 307 Ore. 68, 72–73, 763 P. 2d 146, 148 (1988) (footnote omitted).

Respondents contend that, because the Oregon Supreme Court declined to decide whether the Oregon Constitution prohibits criminal prosecution for the religious use of peyote, see *id.*, at 73, n. 3, 763 P. 2d, at 148, n. 3, any ruling on the federal constitutional question would be premature. Respondents are of course correct that the Oregon Supreme

Court may eventually decide that the Oregon Constitution requires the State to provide an exemption from its general criminal prohibition for the religious use of peyote. Such a decision would then reopen the question whether a State may nevertheless deny unemployment compensation benefits to claimants who are discharged for engaging in such conduct. As the case comes to us today, however, the Oregon Supreme Court has plainly ruled that Oregon's prohibition against possession of controlled substances does not contain an exemption for the religious use of peyote. In light of our decision in *Smith I*, which makes this finding a "necessary predicate to a correct evaluation of respondents' federal claim," 485 U. S., at 672, the question presented and addressed is properly before the Court.

II

The Court today extracts from our long history of free exercise precedents the single categorical rule that "if prohibiting the exercise of religion ... is ... merely the incidental effect of a generally applicable and otherwise valid provision, the First Amendment has not been offended." *Ante*, at 5–6 (citations omitted). Indeed, the Court holds that where the law is a generally applicable criminal prohibition, our usual free exercise jurisprudence does not even apply. *Ante*, at 11. To reach this sweeping result, however, the Court must not only give a strained reading of the First Amendment but must also disregard our consistent application of free exercise doctrine to cases involving generally applicable regulations that burden religious conduct.

A

The Free Exercise Clause of the First Amendment commands that "Congress shall make no law ... prohibiting the free exercise [of religion]." In *Cantwell* v. *Connecticut*, 310 U. S. 296 (1940), we held that this prohibition applies to the States by incorporation into the Fourteenth Amendment and that it categorically forbids government regulation of religious beliefs. *Id.*, at 303. As the Court recognizes, however, the "free *exercise*" of religion often, if not invariably, requires the performance of (or abstention from) certain acts. *Ante*, at 5; cf. 3 A New English Dictionary on Historical Principles 401–402 (J. Murray, ed. 1897) (defining "exercise" to include "[t]he practice and performance of rites and ceremonies, worship, etc.; the right or permission to celebrate the observances (of a religion)" and religious observances such as acts of public and private worship, preaching, and prophesying). "[B]elief and action cannot be neatly confined in logic-tight compartments." *Wisconsin* v. *Yoder*, 406 U. S. 205, 220 (1972). Because the First Amendment does not distinguish between religious belief and religious conduct, conduct motivated by sincere religious belief, like the belief itself, must therefore be at least presumptively protected by the Free Exercise Clause.

The Court today, however, interprets the Clause to permit the government to prohibit, without justification, conduct mandated by an individual's religious beliefs, so long as that prohibition is generally applicable. *Ante*, at 5. But a law that prohibits certain conduct—conduct that happens to be an act of worship for someone—manifestly does prohibit that person's free exercise of his religion. A person who is barred from engaging in religiously motivated conduct is barred from freely exercising his religion. Moreover, that person is barred from freely exercising his religion regardless of whether the law prohibits the conduct only when engaged in for religious reasons, only by members of that religion, or by all persons. It is difficult to deny that a law that prohibits religiously motivated conduct, even if the law is generally applicable, does not at least implicate First Amendment concerns.

The Court responds that generally applicable laws are "one large step" removed from laws aimed at specific religious practices. *Ante*, at 5. The First Amendment, however, does not distinguish between laws that are generally applicable and laws that target particular religious practices. Indeed, few States would be so naive as to enact a law directly prohibiting or burdening a religious practice as such. Our free exercise cases have all concerned generally applicable laws that had the effect of significantly burdening a religious practice. If the First Amendment is to have any vitality, it ought not be construed to cover only the extreme and hypothetical situation in which a State directly targets a religious practice. As we have noted in a slightly different context, " '[s]uch a test has no basis in precedent and relegates a serious First Amendment value to the barest level of minimum scrutiny that the Equal Protection Clause already provides.' " *Hobbie* v. *Unemployment Appeals Comm'n of Florida*, 480 U. S. 136, 141–142 (1987) (quoting *Bowen* v. *Roy*, 476 U. S. 693, 727 (1986) (opinion concurring in part and dissenting in part)).

To say that a person's right to free exercise has been burdened, of course, does not mean that he has an absolute right to engage in the conduct. Under our established First Amendment jurisprudence, we have recognized that the freedom to act, unlike the freedom to believe, cannot be absolute. See, *e. g.*, *Cantwell*, *supra*, at 304; *Reynolds* v. *United States*, 98 U. S. 145, 161–167 (1879). Instead, we have respected both the First Amendment's express textual mandate and the governmental interest in regulation of conduct by requiring the Government to justify any substantial burden on religiously motivated conduct by a compelling state interest and by means narrowly tailored to achieve that interest. See *Hernandez* v. *Commissioner*, 490 U. S. ——, —— (1989); *Hobbie*, *supra*, at 141; *United States* v. *Lee*, 455 U. S. 252, 257–258 (1982); *Thomas* v. *Review Bd.*, *Indiana Employment Security Div.*, 450 U. S. 707, 718 (1981); *McDaniel* v. *Paty*, 435 U. S. 618, 626–629 (1978) (plurality opinion); *Yoder*, *supra*, at 215; *Gillette* v. *United States*, 401 U. S. 437, 462 (1971); *Sherbert* v. *Verner*, 374 U. S. 398, 403 (1963); see also *Bowen* v. *Roy*, *supra*, at 732 (opinion concurring in part and dissenting in part); *West Virginia State Bd. of Educ.* v. *Barnette*, 319 U. S. 624, 639 (1943). The compelling interest test effectuates the First Amendment's command that religious liberty is an independent liberty, that it occupies a preferred position, and that the Court will not permit encroachments upon this liberty, whether direct or indirect, unless required by clear and compelling governmental interests "of the highest order," *Yoder*, *supra*, at 215. "Only an especially important governmental interest pursued by narrowly tailored means can justify exacting a sacrifice of First Amendment freedoms as the price for an equal share of the rights, benefits, and privileges enjoyed by other citizens." *Roy, supra*, at 728 (opinion concurring in part and dissenting in part).

The Court attempts to support its narrow reading of the Clause by claiming that "[w]e have never held that an individual's religious beliefs excuse him from compliance with an otherwise valid law prohibiting conduct that the State is free to regulate." *Ante*, at 6. But as the Court later notes, as it must, in cases such as *Cantwell* and *Yoder* we have in fact interpreted the Free Exercise Clause to forbid application of a generally applicable prohibition to religiously motivated conduct. See *Cantwell, supra*, at 304–307; *Yoder, supra*, at 214–234. Indeed, in *Yoder* we expressly rejected the interpretation the Court now adopts:

> "[O]ur decisions have rejected the idea that religiously grounded conduct is always outside the protection of the Free Exercise Clause. It is true that activities of individuals, even when religiously based, are often subject to regulation by the States in the exercise of their undoubted power to promote the health, safety, and general welfare, or the Federal Government in the exercise of its delegated powers. But to agree that religiously grounded conduct must often be subject to the broad police power of the State is not to deny that there are areas of conduct protected by the Free Exercise Clause of the First Amendment and thus beyond the power of the State to control, *even under regulations of general applicability*. . . .
>
> ". . . A regulation neutral on its face may, in its application, nonetheless offend the constitutional requirement for government neutrality if it unduly burdens the free exercise of religion." 406 U. S., at 219–220 (emphasis added; citations omitted).

The Court endeavors to escape from our decisions in *Cantwell* and *Yoder* by labeling them "hybrid" decisions, *ante*, at 9, but there is no denying that both cases expressly relied on the Free Exercise Clause, see *Cantwell*, 310 U. S., at 303–307; *Yoder*, 406 U. S., at 219–229, and that we have consistently regarded those cases as part of the mainstream of our free exercise jurisprudence. Moreover, in each of the other cases cited by the Court to support its categorical rule, *ante*, at 7–8, we rejected the particular constitutional claims before us only after carefully weighing the competing interests. See *Prince v. Massachusetts*, 321 U. S. 158, 168–170 (1944) (state interest in regulating children's activities justifies denial of religious exemption from child labor laws); *Braunfield v. Brown*, 366 U. S. 599, 608–609 (1961) (plurality opinion) (state interest in uniform day of rest justifies denial of religious exemption from Sunday closing law); *Gillette, supra*, at 462 (state interest in military affairs justifies denial of religious exemption from conscription laws); *Lee, supra*, at 258–259 (state interest in comprehensive social security system justifies denial of religious exemption from mandatory participation requirement). That we rejected the free exercise claims in those cases hardly calls into question the applicability of First Amendment doctrine in the first place. Indeed, it is surely unusual to judge the vitality of a constitutional doctrine by looking to the win-loss record of the plaintiffs who happen to come before us.

B

Respondents, of course, do not contend that their conduct is automatically immune from all governmental regulation simply because it is motivated by their sincere religious beliefs. The Court's rejection of that argument, *ante*, at 9, might therefore be regarded as merely harmless dictum. Rather, respondents invoke our traditional compelling interest test to argue that the Free Exercise Clause requires the State to grant them a limited exemption from its general criminal prohibition against the possession of peyote. The Court today, however, denies them even the opportunity to make that argument, concluding that "the sounder approach, and the approach in accord with the vast majority of our precedents, is to hold the [compelling interest] test inapplicable to" challenges to general criminal prohibitions. *Ante*, at 12.

In my view, however, the essence of a free exercise claim is relief from a burden imposed by government on religious practices or beliefs, whether the burden is imposed directly through laws that prohibit or compel specific religious practices, or indirectly through laws that, in effect, make abandonment of one's own religion or conformity to the religious beliefs of others the price of an equal place in the civil community. As we explained in *Thomas:*

> "Where the state conditions receipt of an important benefit upon conduct proscribed by a religious faith, or where it denies such a benefit because of conduct mandated by religious belief, thereby putting substantial pressure on an adherent to modify his behavior and to violate his beliefs, a burden upon religion exists." 450 U. S., at 717–718.

See also *Frazee* v. *Illinois Dept. of Employment Security*, 489 U. S. ——, —— (1989); *Hobbie*, 480 U. S., at 141. A State that makes criminal an individual's religiously motivated conduct burdens that individual's free exercise of religion in the severest manner possible, for it "results in the choice to the individual of either abandoning his religious principle or facing criminal prosecution." *Braunfield, supra*, at 605. I would have thought it beyond argument that such laws implicate free exercise concerns.

Indeed, we have never distinguished between cases in which a State conditions receipt of a benefit on conduct prohibited by religious beliefs and cases in which a State affirmatively prohibits such conduct. The *Sherbert* compelling interest test applies in both kinds of cases. See, *e. g., Lee*, 455 U. S., at 257–260 (applying *Sherbert* to uphold social security tax liability); *Gillette*, 401 U. S., at 462 (applying *Sherbert* to uphold military conscription requirement); *Yoder, supra*, at 215–234 (applying *Sherbert* to strike down criminal convictions for violation of compulsory school attendance law). As I noted in *Roy* v. *Bowen:*

> "The fact that the underlying dispute involves an award of benefits rather than an exaction of penalties does not grant the Government license to apply a different version of the Constitution. . . .

". . . The fact that appellees seek exemption from a precondition that the Government attaches to an award of benefits does not, therefore, generate a meaningful distinction between this case and one where appellees seek an exemption from the Government's imposition of penalties upon them." 476 U. S., at 731–732 (opinion concurring in part and dissenting in part).

See also *Hobbie, supra*, at 141–142; *Sherbert*, 374 U. S., at 404. I would reaffirm that principle today: a neutral criminal law prohibiting conduct that a State may legitimately regulate is, if anything, *more* burdensome than a neutral civil statute placing legitimate conditions on the award of a state benefit.

Legislatures, of course, have always been "left free to reach actions which were in violation of social duties or subversive of good order." *Reynolds*, 98 U. S., at 164; see also *Yoder*, 406 U. S., at 219–220; *Braunfield*, 366 U. S., at 603–604. Yet because of the close relationship between conduct and religious belief, "[i]n every case the power to regulate must be so exercised as not, in attaining a permissible end, unduly to infringe the protected freedom." *Cantwell*, 310 U. S., at 304. Once it has been shown that a government regulation or criminal prohibition burdens the free exercise of religion, we have consistently asked the Government to demonstrate that unbending application of its regulation to the religious objector "is essential to accomplish an overriding governmental interest," *Lee, supra*, at 257–258, or represents "the least restrictive means of achieving some compelling state interest." *Thomas*, 450 U. S., at 718. See, *e. g., Braunfield, supra*, at 607; *Sherbert, supra*, at 406; *Yoder, supra*, at 214–215; *Roy*, 476 U. S., at 728–732 (opinion concurring in part and dissenting in part). To me, the sounder approach—the approach more consistent with our role as judges to decide each case on its individual merits—is to apply this test in each case to determine whether the burden on the specific plaintiffs before us is constitutionally significant and whether the particular criminal interest asserted by the State before us is compelling. Even if, as an empirical matter, a government's criminal laws might usually serve a compelling interest in health, safety, or public order, the First Amendment at least requires a case-by-case determination of the question, sensitive to the facts of each particular claim. Cf. *McDaniel*, 435 U. S., at 628, n. 8 (plurality opinion) (noting application of *Sherbert* to general criminal prohibitions and the "delicate balancing required by our decisions in" *Sherbert* and *Yoder*). Given the range of conduct that a State might legitimately make criminal, we cannot assume, merely because a law carries criminal sanctions and is generally applicable, that the First Amendment *never* requires the State to grant a limited exemption for religiously motivated conduct.

Moreover, we have not "rejected" or "declined to apply" the compelling interest test in our recent cases. *Ante*, at 10–11. Recent cases have instead affirmed that test as a fundamental part of our First Amendment doctrine. See, *e. g., Hernandez*, 490 U. S., at ——; *Hobbie, supra*, at 141–142 (rejecting Chief Justice Burger's suggestion in *Roy, supra*, at 707–708, that free exercise claims be assessed under a less rigorous "reasonable means" standard). The cases cited by the Court signal no retreat from our consistent adherence to the compelling interest test. In both *Bowen* v. *Roy*, *supra,* and *Lyng* v. *Northwest Indian Cemetary Protective Assn.,* 485 U. S. 439 (1988), for example, we expressly distinguished *Sherbert* on the ground that the First Amendment does not "require the Government *itself* to behave in ways that the individual believes will further his or her spiritual development . . . . The Free Exercise Clause simply cannot be understood to require the Government to conduct its own internal affairs in ways that comport with the religious beliefs of particular citizens." *Roy, supra,* at 699; see *Lyng, supra,* at 449. This distinction makes sense because "the Free Exercise Clause is written in terms of what the government cannot do to the individual, not in terms of what the individual can exact from the government." *Sherbert, supra,* at 412 (Douglas, J., concurring). Because the case *sub judice,* like the other cases in which we have applied *Sherbert,* plainly falls into the former category, I would apply those established precedents to the facts of this case.

Similarly, the other cases cited by the Court for the proposition that we have rejected application of the *Sherbert* test outside the unemployment compensation field, *ante,* at 11, are distinguishable because they arose in the narrow, specialized contexts in which we have not traditionally required the government to justify a burden on religious conduct by articulating a compelling interest. See *Goldman* v. *Weinberger,* 475 U. S. 503, 507 (1986) ("Our review of military regulations challenged on First Amendment grounds is far more deferential than constitutional review of similar laws or regulations designed for civilian society"); *O'Lone* v. *Estate of Shabazz,* 482 U. S. 342, 349 (1987) ("[P]rison regulations alleged to infringe constitutional rights are judged under a 'reasonableness' test less restrictive than that ordinarily applied to alleged infringements of fundamental constitutional rights") (citation omitted). That we did not apply the compelling interest test in these cases says nothing about whether the test should continue to apply in paradigm free exercise cases such as the one presented here.

The Court today gives no convincing reason to depart from settled First Amendment jurisprudence. There is nothing talismanic about neutral laws of general applicability or general criminal prohibitions, for laws neutral toward religion can coerce a person to violate his religious conscience or intrude upon his religious duties just as effectively as laws aimed at religion. Although the Court suggests that the compelling interest test, as applied to generally applicable laws, would result in a "constitutional anomaly," *ante,* at 13, the First Amendment unequivocally makes freedom of religion, like freedom from race discrimination and freedom of speech, a "constitutional nor[m]," not an "anomaly." *Ibid.* Nor would application of our established free exercise doctrine to this case necessarily be incompatible with our equal protection cases. Cf. *Rogers* v. *Lodge,* 458 U. S. 613, 618 (1982) (race-neutral law that " 'bears more heavily on one race than another' " may violate equal protection) (citation omitted); *Castaneda* v. *Partida,* 430 U. S. 482, 492–495 (1977) (grand jury selection). We have in any event recognized that the Free Exercise Clause protects values distinct from those protected by the Equal Protection Clause. See *Hobbie,* 480 U. S., at 141–142. As the language of the Clause itself makes clear, an individual's free exercise of religion is a preferred constitutional activity. See, *e. g.,* McConnell, Accommodation of Religion,

1985 Sup. Ct. Rev. 1, 9 ("[T]he text of the First Amendment itself 'singles out' religion for special protections"); P. Kauper, Religion and the Constitution 17 (1964). A law that makes criminal such an activity therefore triggers constitutional concern—and heightened judicial scrutiny—even if it does not target the particular religious conduct at issue. Our free speech cases similarly recognize that neutral regulations that affect free speech values are subject to a balancing, rather than categorical, approach. See, *e.g., United States* v. *O'Brien,* 391 U. S. 367, 377 (1968); *City of Renton* v. *Playtime Theatres, Inc.,* 475 U. S. 41, 46–47 (1986); cf. *Anderson* v. *Celebrezze,* 460 U. S. 780, 792–794 (1983) (generally applicable laws may impinge on free association concerns). The Court's parade of horribles, *ante,* at 15–16, not only fails as a reason for discarding the compelling interest test, it instead demonstrates just the opposite: that courts have been quite capable of applying our free exercise jurisprudence to strike sensible balances between religious liberty and competing state interests.

Finally, the Court today suggests that the disfavoring of minority religions is an "unavoidable consequence" under our system of government and that accommodation of such religions must be left to the political process. *Ante,* at 17. In my view, however, the First Amendment was enacted precisely to protect the rights of those whose religious practices are not shared by the majority and may be viewed with hostility. The history of our free exercise doctrine amply demonstrates the harsh impact majoritarian rule has had on unpopular or emerging religious groups such as the Jehovah's Witnesses and the Amish. Indeed, the words of Justice Jackson in *West Virginia Board of Education* v. *Barnette* (overruling *Minersville School District* v. *Gobitis,* 310 U. S. 586 (1940)) are apt:

> "The very purpose of a Bill of Rights was to withdraw certain subjects from the vicissitudes of political controversy, to place them beyond the reach of majorities and officials and to establish them as legal principles to be applied by the courts. One's right to life, liberty, and property, to free speech, a free press, freedom of worship and assembly, and other fundamental rights may not be submitted to vote; they depend on the outcome of no elections." 319 U. S., at 638.

See also *United States* v. *Ballard,* 322 U. S. 78, 87 (1944) ("The Fathers of the Constitution were not unaware of the varied and extreme views of religious sects, of the violence of disagreement among them, and of the lack of any one religions creed on which all men would agree. They fashioned a charter of government which envisaged the widest possible toleration of conflicting views"). The compelling interest test reflects the First Amendment's mandate of preserving religious liberty to the fullest extent possible in a pluralistic society. For the Court to deem this command a "luxury," *ante,* at 15, is to denigrate "[t]he very purpose of a Bill of Rights."

III

The Court's holding today not only misreads settled First Amendment precedent; it appears to be unnecessary to this case. I would reach the same result applying our established free exercise jurisprudence.

A

There is no dispute that Oregon's criminal prohibition of peyote places a severe burden on the ability of respondents to freely exercise their religion. Peyote is a sacrament of the Native American Church and is regarded as vital to respondents' ability to practice their religion. See O. Stewart, Peyote Religion: A History 327–336 (1987) (describing modern status of peyotism); E. Anderson, Peyote: The Divine Cactus 41–65 (1980) (describing peyote ceremonies); Teachings from the American Earth: Indian Religion and Philosophy 96–104 (D. Tedlock & B. Tedlock eds. 1975) (same); see also *People* v. *Woody,* 61 Cal. 2d 716, 721–722, 394 P. 2d 813, 817–818 (1964). As we noted in *Smith I,* the Oregon Supreme Court concluded that "the Native American Church is a recognized religion, that peyote is a sacrament of that church, and that respondent's beliefs were sincerely held." 485 U. S., at 667. Under Oregon law, as construed by that State's highest court, members of the Native American Church must choose between carrying out the ritual embodying their religious beliefs and avoidance of criminal prosecution. That choice is, in my view, more than sufficient to trigger First Amendment scrutiny.

There is also no dispute that Oregon has a significant interest in enforcing laws that control the possession and use of controlled substances by its citizens. See, *e. g., Sherbert,* 374 U. S., at 403 (religiously motivated conduct may be regulated where such conduct "pose[s] some substantial threat to public safety, peace or order"); *Yoder,* 406 U. S., at 220 ("activities of individuals, even when religiously based, are often subject to regulation by the States in the exercise of their undoubted power to promote the health, safety and general welfare"). As we recently noted, drug abuse is "one of the greatest problems affecting the health and welfare of our population" and thus "one of the most serious problems confronting our society today." *Treasury Employees* v. *Von Raab,* 489 U. S. ——, —— (1989) (slip op., at 10, 15). Indeed, under federal law (incorporated by Oregon law in relevant part, see Ore. Rev. Stat. § 475.005(6) (1989)), peyote is specifically regulated as a Schedule I controlled substance, which means that Congress has found that it has a high potential for abuse, that there is no currently accepted medical use, and that there is a lack of accepted safety for use of the drug under medical supervision. See 21 U. S. C. § 812(b)(1). See generally R. Julien, A Primer of Drug Action 149 (3d ed. 1981). In light of our recent decisions holding that the governmental interests in the collection of income tax, *Hernandez,* 490 U. S., at ——, a comprehensive social security system, see *Lee,* 455 U. S., at 258–259, and military conscription, see *Gillette,* 401 U. S., at 460, are compelling, respondents do not seriously dispute that Oregon has a compelling interest in prohibiting the possession of peyote by its citizens.

B

Thus, the critical question in this case is whether exempting respondents from the State's general criminal prohibition "will unduly interfere with fulfillment of the governmental interest." *Lee, supra,* at 259; see also *Roy,* 476 U. S., at 727 ("[T]he Government must accommodate a legitimate free exercise claim unless pursuing an especially important interest by narrowly tailored means"); *Yoder*, 406 U. S., at 221; *Braunfield*, 366 U. S., at 605–607. Although the question is close, I would conclude that uniform application of Oregon's criminal prohibition is "essential to accomplish," *Lee, supra*, at 257, its overriding interest in preventing the physical harm caused by the use of a Schedule I controlled substance. Oregon's criminal prohibition represents that State's judgment that the possession and use of controlled substances, even by only one person, is inherently harmful and dangerous. Because the health effects caused by the use of controlled substances exist regardless of the motivation of the user, the use of such substances, even for religious purposes, violates the very purpose of the laws that prohibit them. Cf. *State v. Massey*, 229 N. C. 734, 51 S. E. 2d 179 (denying religious exemption to municipal ordinance prohibiting handling of poisonous reptiles), appeal dism'd *sub nom. Bunn v. North Carolina*, 336 U. S. 942 (1949). Moreover, in view of the societal interest in preventing trafficking in controlled substances, uniform application of the criminal prohibition at issue is essential to the effectiveness of Oregon's stated interest in preventing any possession of peyote. Cf. *Jacobson v. Massachusetts*, 197 U. S. 11 (1905) (denying exemption from small pox vaccination requirement).

For these reasons, I believe that granting a selective exemption in this case would seriously impair Oregon's compelling interest in prohibiting possession of peyote by its citizens. Under such circumstances, the Free Exercise Clause does not require the State to accommodate respondents' religiously motivated conduct. See, *e. g., Thomas*, 450 U. S., at 719. Unlike in *Yoder*, where we noted that "[t]he record strongly indicates that accommodating the religious objections of the Amish by forgoing one, or at most two, additional years of compulsory education will not impair the physical or mental health of the child, or result in an inability to be self-supporting or to discharge the duties and responsibilities of citizenship, or in any other way materially detract from the welfare of society," 406 U. S., at 234; see also *id.*, at 238–240 (WHITE, J., concurring), a religious exemption in this case would be incompatible with the State's interest in controlling use and possession of illegal drugs.

Respondents contend that any incompatibility is belied by the fact that the Federal Government and several States provide exemptions for the religious use of peyote, see 21 CFR § 1307.31 (1989); 307 Ore., at 73, n. 2, 763 P. 2d, at 148, n. 2 (citing 11 state statutes that expressly exempt sacramental peyote use from criminal proscription). But other governments may surely choose to grant an exemption without Oregon, with its specific asserted interest in uniform application of its drug laws, being *required* to do so by the First Amendment. Respondents also note that the sacramental use of peyote is central to the tenets of the Native American Church, but I agree with the Court, *ante*, at 13–14, that because "[i]t is not within the judicial ken to question the centrality of particular beliefs or practices to a faith," *Hernandez, supra*, at —— (slip op., at 17), our determination of the constitutionality of Oregon's general criminal prohibition cannot, and should not, turn on the centrality of the particular religious practice at issue. This does not mean, of course, that courts may not make factual findings as to whether a claimant holds a sincerely held religious belief that conflicts with, and thus is burdened by, the challenged law. The distinction between questions of centrality and questions of sincerity and burden is admittedly fine, but it is one that is an established part of our free exercise doctrine, see *Ballard*, 322 U. S., at 85–88, and one that courts are capable of making. See *Tony and Susan Alamo Foundation* v. *Secretary of Labor*, 471 U. S. 290, 303–305 (1985).

I would therefore adhere to our established free exercise jurisprudence and hold that the State in this case has a compelling interest in regulating peyote use by its citizens and that accommodating respondents' religiously motivated conduct "will unduly interfere with fulfillment of the governmental interest." *Lee*, 455 U. S., at 259. Accordingly, I concur in the judgment of the Court.

JUSTICE BLACKMUN, with whom JUSTICE BRENNAN and JUSTICE MARSHALL join, dissenting.

This Court over the years painstakingly has developed a consistent and exacting standard to test the constitutionality of a state statute that burdens the free exercise of religion. Such a statute may stand only if the law in general, and the State's refusal to allow a religious exemption in particular, are justified by a compelling interest that cannot be served by less restrictive means.

Until today, I thought this was a settled and inviolate principle of this Court's First Amendment jurisprudence. The majority, however, perfunctorily dismisses it as a "constitutional anomaly." *Ante*, at 13. As carefully detailed in JUSTICE O'CONNOR's concurring opinion, *ante*, the majority is able to arrive at this view only by mischaracterizing this Court's precedents. The Court discards leading free exercise cases such as *Cantwell* v. *Connecticut*, 310 U. S. 296 (1940), and *Wisconsin* v. *Yoder*, 406 U. S. 205 (1972), as "hybrid." *Ante*, at 9. The Court views traditional free exercise analysis as somehow inapplicable to criminal prohibitions (as opposed to conditions on the receipt of benefits), and to state laws of general applicability (as opposed, presumably, to laws that expressly single out religious practices). *Ante*, at 11–12. The Court cites cases in which, due to various exceptional circumstances, we found strict scrutiny inapposite, to hint that the Court has repudiated that standard altogether. *Ante*, at 10–11. In short, it effectuates a wholesale overturning of settled law concerning the Religion Clauses of our Constitution. One hopes that the Court is aware of the consequences, and that its result is not a product of overreaction to the serious problems the country's drug crisis has generated.

This distorted view of our precedents leads the majority to conclude that strict scrutiny of a state law burdening the free exercise of religion is a "luxury" that a well-ordered society cannot afford, *ante*, at 15, and that the repression of minority religions is an "unavoidable consequence of democratic government." *Ante*, at 17. I do not believe the Founders thought their dearly bought freedom from religious persecution a "luxury," but an essential element of liberty—and they could not have thought religious intolerance "unavoidable," for they drafted the Religion Clauses precisely in order to avoid that intolerance.

For these reasons, I agree with Justice O'Connor's analysis of the applicable free exercise doctrine, and I join parts I and II of her opinion. As she points out, "the critical question in this case is whether exempting respondents from the State's general criminal prohibition 'will unduly interfere with fulfillment of the governmental interest.' " *Ante*, at 15, quoting *United States* v. *Lee*, 455 U. S. 252, 259 (1982). I do disagree, however, with her specific answer to that question.

I

In weighing respondents' clear interest in the free exercise of their religion against Oregon's asserted interest in enforcing its drug laws, it is important to articulate in precise terms the state interest involved. It is not the State's broad interest in fighting the critical "war on drugs" that must be weighed against respondents' claim, but the State's narrow interest in refusing to make an exception for the religious, ceremonial use of peyote. See *Bowen* v. *Roy*, 476 U. S. 693, 728 (1986) (O'Connor, J., concurring in part and dissenting in part) ("This Court has consistently asked the Government to demonstrate that unbending application of its regulation to the religious objector 'is essential to accomplish an overriding governmental interest,' " quoting *Lee*, 455 U. S., at 257–258); *Thomas* v. *Review Bd. of Indiana Employment Security Div.*, 450 U. S. 707, 719 (1981) ("focus of the inquiry" concerning State's asserted interest must be "properly narrowed"); *Yoder*, 406 U. S., at 221 ("Where fundamental claims of religious freedom are at stake," the Court will not accept a State's "sweeping claim" that its interest in compulsory education is compelling; despite the validity of this interest "in the generality of cases, we must searchingly examine the interests that the State seeks to promote . . . and the impediment to those objectives that would flow from recognizing the claimed Amish exception"). Failure to reduce the competing interests to the same plane of generality tends to distort the weighing process in the State's favor. See Clark, Guidelines for the Free Exercise Clause, 83 Harv. L. Rev. 327, 330–331 (1969) ("The purpose of almost any law can be traced back to one or another of the fundamental concerns of government: public health and safety, public peace and order, defense, revenue. To measure an individual interest directly against one of these rarified values inevitably makes the individual interest appear the less significant"); Pound, A Survey of Social Interests, 57 Harv. L. Rev. 1, 2 (1943) ("When it comes to weighing or valuing claims or demands with respect to other claims or demands, we must be careful to compare them on the same plane . . . [or else] we may decide the question in advance in our very way of putting it").

The State's interest in enforcing its prohibition, in order to be sufficiently compelling to outweigh a free exercise claim, cannot be merely abstract or symbolic. The State cannot plausibly assert that unbending application of a criminal prohibition is essential to fulfill any compelling interest, if it does not, in fact, attempt to enforce that prohibition. In this case, the State actually has not evinced any concrete interest in enforcing its drug laws against religious users of peyote. Oregon has never sought to prosecute respondents, and does not claim that it has made significant enforcement efforts against other religious users of peyote. The State's asserted interest thus amounts only to the symbolic preservation of an unenforced prohibition. But a government interest in "symbolism, even symbolism for so worthy a cause as the abolition of unlawful drugs," *Treasury Employees* v. *Von Raab,* —— U. S. ——, ——(1989) (SCALIA, J., dissenting) (slip op. 8), cannot suffice to abrogate the constitutional rights of individuals.

Similarly, this Court's prior decisions have not allowed a government to rely on mere speculation about potential harms, but have demanded evidentiary support for a refusal to allow a religious exception. See *Thomas,* 450 U. S., at 719 (rejecting State's reasons for refusing religious exemption, for lack of "evidence in the record"); *Yoder,* 406 U. S., at 224–229 (rejecting State's argument concerning the dangers of a religious exemption as speculative, and unsupported by the record); *Sherbert* v. *Verner,* 374 U. S. 398, 407 (1963) ("there is no proof whatever to warrant such fears . . . as those which the [State] now advance[s]"). In this case, the State's justification for refusing to recognize an exception to its criminal laws for religious peyote use is entirely speculative.

The State proclaims an interest in protecting the health and safety of its citizens from the dangers of unlawful drugs. It offers, however, no evidence that the religious use of peyote has ever harmed anyone. The factual findings of other courts cast doubt on the State's assumption that religious use of peyote is harmful. See *State* v. *Whittingham,* 19 Ariz. App. 27, 30, 504 P. 2d 950, 953 (1973) ("the State failed to prove that the quantities of peyote used in the sacraments of the Native American Church are sufficiently harmful to the health and welfare of the participants so as to permit a legitimate intrusion under the State's police power"); *People* v. *Woody,* 61 Cal. 2d 716, 722–723, 394 P. 2d 813, 818 (1964) ("as the Attorney General . . . admits, the opinion of scientists and other experts is 'that peyote . . . works no permanent deleterious injury to the Indian' ").

The fact that peyote is classified as a Schedule I controlled substance does not, by itself, show that any and all uses of peyote, in any circumstance, are inherently harmful and dangerous. The Federal Government, which created the classifications of unlawful drugs from which Oregon's drug laws are derived, apparently does not find peyote so dangerous as to preclude an exemption for religious use. Moreover, other Schedule I drugs have lawful uses. See *Olsen* v. *Drug Enforcement Admin.,* —— U. S. App. D. C. ——, ——, n. 4, 878 F. 2d 1458, 1463, n. 4 (medical and research uses of marijuana).

The carefully circumscribed ritual context in which respondents used peyote is far removed from the irresponsible and unrestricted recreational use of unlawful drugs. The Native American Church's internal restrictions on, and supervision of, its members' use of peyote substantially obviate the State's health and safety concerns. See *Olsen,* —— U. S. App. D. C., at ——, 878 F. 2d, at 1467 ("The Administrator [of DEA] finds that . . . the Native American Church's use of peyote is isolated to specific ceremonial occasions," and so "an accommodation can be made for a religious organization which uses peyote in circumscribed ceremonies" (quoting DEA Final Order)); *id.,* at ——, 878 F. 2d, at 1464 ("for members of the Native American Church, use of peyote outside the ritual is sacrilegious"); *Woody*, 61 Cal. 2d, at 721, 394 P. 2d, at 817 ("to use peyote for nonreligious purposes is sacrilegious"); R. Julien, A Primer of Drug Action 148 (3d ed. 1981) ("peyote is seldom abused by members of the Native American Church"); J. Slotkin, The Peyote Way, in Teachings from the American Faith (D. Tedlock & B. Tedlock, eds., 1975) 96, 104 ("the Native American Church . . . refuses to permit the presence of curiosity seekers at its rites, and vigorously opposes the sale or use of Peyote for non-sacramental purposes"); R. Bergman, Navajo Peyote Use: Its Apparent Safety, 128 Am. J. Psychiatry 695 (1971) (Bergman).

Moreover, just as in *Yoder*, the values and interests of those seeking a religious exemption in this case are congruent, to a great degree, with those the State seeks to promote through its drug laws. See *Yoder*, 406 U. S., at 224, 228–229 (since the Amish accept formal schooling up to 8th grade, and then provide "ideal" vocational education, State's interests in enforcing its law against the Amish is "less substantial than . . . for children generally"); *id.*, at 238 (WHITE, J., concurring opinion). Not only does the Church's doctrine forbid nonreligious use of peyote; it also generally advocates self-reliance, familial responsibility, and abstinence from alcohol. See Brief for Association on American Indian Affairs, et al., as *Amici Curiae* 33–34 (the Church's "ethical code" has four parts: brotherly love, care of family, self-reliance, and avoidance of alcohol (quoting from the Church membership card)); *Olsen*, —— U. S. App. D. C., at ——, 878 F. 2d, at 1464 (the Native American Church, "for all purposes other than the special, stylized ceremony, reinforced the state's prohibition"); *Woody*, 61 Cal. 2d, at 721–722, n. 3, 394 P. 2d, at 818, n. 3 ("most anthropological authorities hold Peyotism to be a positive, rather than negative, force in the lives of its adherents . . . the church forbids the use of alcohol . . . "). There is considerable evidence that the spiritual and social support provided by the Church has been effective in combatting the tragic effects of alcoholism on the Native American population. Two noted experts on peyotism, Dr. Omer C. Stewart and Dr. Robert Bergman, testified by affidavit to this effect on behalf of respondent Smith before the Employment Appeal Board. Smith Tr., Exh. 7; see also E. Anderson, Peyote: The Divine Cactus 165–166 (1980) (research by Dr. Bergman suggests "that the religious use of peyote seemed to be directed in an ego-strengthening direction with an emphasis on interpersonal relationships where each individual is assured of his own significance as well as the support of the group;" many people have " 'come through difficult crises with the help of this religion. . . . It provides real help in seeing themselves not as people whose place and way in the world is gone, but as people whose way can be strong enough to change and meet new challenges' " (quoting Bergman, at 698)); P. Pascarosa and S. Futterman, Ethnopsychedelic Therapy for Alcoholics: Observations in the Peyote Ritual of the Native American Church, 8 (No. 3) J. of Psychedelic Drugs 215 (1976) (religious peyote use has been helpful in overcoming alcoholism); B. Albaugh and P. Anderson, Peyote in the Treatment of Alcoholism among American Indians, 131:11 Am. J. Psychiatry 1247, 1249 (1974) ("the philosophy, teachings, and format of the [Native American Church] can be of great benefit to the Indian alcoholic"); see generally O. Stewart, Peyote Religion 75 *et seq.*

(1987) (noting frequent observations, across many tribes and periods in history, of correlation between peyotist religion and abstinence from alcohol). Far from promoting the lawless and irresponsible use of drugs, Native American Church members' spiritual code exemplifies values that Oregon's drug laws are presumably intended to foster.

The State also seeks to support its refusal to make an exception for religious use of peyote by invoking its interest in abolishing drug trafficking. There is, however, practically no illegal traffic in peyote. See *Olsen*, —— U. S. App. D. C., at ——, ——, 878 F. 2d, at 1463, 1467 (quoting DEA Final Order to the effect that total amount of peyote seized and analyzed by federal authorities between 1980 and 1987 was 19.4 pounds; in contrast, total amount of marijuana seized during that period was over 15 million pounds). Also, the availability of peyote for religious use, even if Oregon were to allow an exemption from its criminal laws, would still be strictly controlled by federal regulations, see 21 U. S. C. §§ 821–823 (registration requirements for distribution of controlled substances); 21 CFR § 1307.31 (1989) (distribution of peyote to Native American Church subject to registration requirements), and by the State of Texas, the only State in which peyote grows in significant quantities. See Texas Health & Safety Code, § 481.111 (1990); Texas Admin. Code, Tit. 37, pt. 1, ch. 13, Controlled Substances Regulations, §§ 13.35–13.41 (1989); *Woody,* 61 Cal. 2d, at 720, 394 P. 2d, at 816 (peyote is "found in the Rio Grande Valley of Texas and northern Mexico"). Peyote simply is not a popular drug: its distribution for use in religious rituals has nothing to do with the vast and violent traffic in illegal narcotics that plagues this country.

Finally, the State argues that granting an exception for religious peyote use would erode its interest in the uniform, fair, and certain enforcement of its drug laws. The State fears that, if it grants an exemption for religious peyote use, a flood of other claims to religious exemptions will follow. It would then be placed in a dilemma, it says, between allowing a patchwork of exemptions that would hinder its law enforcement efforts, and risking a violation of the Establishment Clause by arbitrarily limiting its religious exemptions. This argument, however, could be made in almost any free exercise case. See Lupu, Where Rights Begin: The Problem of Burdens on the Free Exercise of Religion, 102 Harv. L. Rev. 933, 947 (1989) ("Behind every free exercise claim is a spectral march; grant this one, a voice whispers to each judge, and you will be confronted with an endless chain of exemption demands from religious deviants of every stripe"). This Court, however, consistently has rejected similar arguments in past free exercise cases, and it should do so here as well. See *Frazee* v. *Illinois Dept. of Employment Security,* —— U. S. ——, —— (1989) (slip op. 6) (rejecting State's speculation concerning cumulative effect of many similar claims); *Thomas,* 450 U. S., at 719 (same); *Sherbert,* 374 U. S., at 407.

The State's apprehension of a flood of other religious claims is purely speculative. Almost half the States, and the Federal Government, have maintained an exemption for religious peyote use for many years, and apparently have not found themselves overwhelmed by claims to other religious exemptions. Allowing an exemption for religious peyote use would not necessarily oblige the State to grant a similar exemption to other religious groups. The unusual circumstances that make the religious use of peyote compatible with the State's interests in health and safety and in preventing drug trafficking would not apply to other religious claims. Some religions, for example, might not restrict drug use to a limited ceremonial context, as does the Native American Church. See, e. g., *Olsen,* ——— U. S. App. D. C., at ———, 878 F. 2d, at 1464 ("the Ethiopian Zion Coptic Church . . . teaches that marijuana is properly smoked 'continually all day' "). Some religious claims, see n. 8, *supra,* involve drugs such as marijuana and heroin, in which there is significant illegal traffic, with its attendant greed and violence, so that it would be difficult to grant a religious exemption without seriously compromising law enforcement efforts. That the State might grant an exemption for religious peyote use, but deny other religious claims arising in different circumstances, would not violate the Establishment Clause. Though the State must treat all religions equally, and not favor one over another, this obligation is fulfilled by the uniform application of the "compelling interest" *test* to all free exercise claims, not by reaching uniform *results* as to all claims. A showing that religious peyote use does not unduly interfere with the State's interests is "one that probably few other religious groups or sects could make," *Yoder,* 406 U. S., at 236; this does not mean that an exemption limited to peyote use is tantamount to an establishment of religion. See *Hobbie* v. *Unemployment Appeals Comm'n of Fla.,* 480 U. S. 136, 144–145 (1987) ("the government may (and sometimes must) accommodate religious practices and . . . may do so without violating the Establishment Clause"); *Yoder,* 406 U. S., at 220–221 ("Court must not ignore the danger that an exception from a general [law] . . . may run afoul of the Establishment Clause, but that danger cannot be allowed to prevent any exception no matter how vital it may be to the protection of values promoted by the right of free exercise"); *id.,* at 234, n. 22.

III

Finally, although I agree with Justice O'Connor that courts should refrain from delving into questions of whether, as a matter of religious doctrine, a particular practice is "central" to the religion, *ante,* at 16, I do not think this means that the courts must turn a blind eye to the severe impact of a State's restrictions on the adherents of a minority religion. Cf. *Yoder,* 406 U. S., at 219 (since "education is inseparable from and a part of the basic tenets of their religion . . . [just as] baptism, the confessional, or a sabbath may be for others," enforcement of State's compulsory education law would "gravely endanger if not destroy the free exercise of respondents' religious beliefs").

Respondents believe, and their sincerity has *never* been at issue, that the peyote plant embodies their deity, and eating it is an act of worship and communion. Without peyote, they could not enact the essential ritual of their religion. See Brief for Association on American Indian Affairs, et al., as *Amici Curiae* 5–6 ("To the members, peyote is consecrated with powers to heal body, mind and spirit. It is a teacher; it teaches the way to spiritual life through living in harmony and balance with the forces of the

Creation. The rituals are an integral part of the life process. They embody a form of worship in which the sacrament Peyote is the means for communicating with the Great Spirit"). See also Stewart, Peyote Religion, at 327–330 (description of peyote ritual); T. Hillerman, People of Darkness 153 (1980) (description of Navajo peyote ritual).

If Oregon can constitutionally prosecute them for this act of worship, they, like the Amish, may be "forced to migrate to some other and more tolerant region." *Yoder,* 406 U. S., at 218. This potentially devastating impact must be viewed in light of the federal policy—reached in reaction to many years of religious persecution and intolerance—of protecting the religious freedom of Native Americans. See American Indian Religious Freedom Act, 92 Stat. 469, 42 U. S. C. § 1996 ("it shall be the policy of the United States to protect and preserve for American Indians their inherent right of freedom to believe, express, and exercise the traditional religions . . . , including but not limited to access to sites, use and possession of sacred objects, and the freedom to worship through ceremonials and traditional rites"). Congress recognized that certain substances, such as peyote, "have religious significance because they are sacred, they have power, they heal, they are necessary to the exercise of the rites of the religion, they are necessary to the cultural integrity of the tribe, and, therefore, religious survival." H. R. Rep. No. 95–1308, p. 2 (1978).

The American Indian Religious Freedom Act, in itself, may not create rights enforceable against government action restricting religious freedom, but this Court must scrupulously apply its free exercise analysis to the religious claims of Native Americans, however unorthodox they may be. Otherwise, both the First Amendment and the stated policy of Congress will offer to Native Americans merely an unfulfilled and hollow promise.

IV

For these reasons, I conclude that Oregon's interest in enforcing its drug laws against religious use of peyote is not sufficiently compelling to outweigh respondents' right to the free exercise of their religion. Since the State could not constitutionally enforce its criminal prohibition against respondents, the interests underlying the State's drug laws cannot justify its denial of unemployment benefits. Absent such justification, the State's regulatory interest in denying benefits for religiously motivated "misconduct," see *ante,* at 2, is indistinguishable from the state interests this Court has rejected in *Frazee, Hobbie, Thomas,* and *Sherbert.* The State of Oregon cannot, consistently with the Free Exercise Clause, deny respondents unemployment benefits.

I dissent.

ACKNOWLEDGMENTS

Linda Ellerbee, "We Can Kill Off Exit Polling by Lying Our Heads Off." *The Oregonian,* November 8, 1988. © 1988, King Features Syndicate. Reprinted with special permission of King Features Syndicate.

Norman Cousins, "Who Killed Benny Paret?" Published in the *Saturday Review,* May 5, 1962. Reprinted with permission.

Noel Riley, S. M., "Getting a Big Bang Out of Creation Theories." The *Los Angeles Times,* March 10, 1981. Reprinted with permission of the author.

P. J. Wingate, "The Philosophy of H. L. Mencken." Copyright © 1983 by the Enoch Pratt Free Library. All rights reserved. Reprinted from *Meckeniana: A Quarterly Review* 87 (Fall, 1983), 14–16, by permission of the Library and P. J. Wingate.

Tom Welshko, "Mencken and the Great 'Bathtub Hoax.' " Reprinted from *The Baltimore Evening Sun,* September 12, 1984. © 1984, The Baltimore Sun Co.

Geoffrey K. Pullum, "The Great Eskimo Vocabulary Hoax." Reprinted from *The Great Eskimo Vocabulary Hoax and Other Irreverent Essays on the Study of Language,* by Geoffrey K. Pullum, Chicago: University of Chicago Press, 1991. Originally published in *Natural Language and Linguistic Theory* 7(1989), 275–281; © 1989 Kluwer Academic Publishers.

Bamber Gascoigne, "How Masqueraders Think." Reprinted from *Quest for the Golden Hare,* by Bamber Gascoigne, London: Jonathan Cape Ltd., 1983, by permission of the author.

"Interview with Jeremy Rifkin and Bernard Davis." Reprinted from "Pro and Con: Ban Experiments in Genetic Engineering?", in *U.S. News & World Report.* Copyright © October 8, 1984, U.S. News & World Report, Inc.

Mark O. Hatfield, "Peace Through Strength Is a Fallacy." Reprinted with permission of the author.

Margaret Sanger, "The Cause of War." Reprinted from *Women and the New Race,* with permission of Michael Sanger.

Fred L. Smith and Kathy H. Kushner, "Good Fences Make Good Neighborhoods." Reprinted from *The National Review,* April 1, 1990, pp. 31–33, 59. Copyright © by National Review, Inc., 150 East 35th Street, New York, NY 10016. Reprinted with permission.

Donella Meadows, "Our Survival Depends on Saving Other Species." Reprinted from the *Los Angeles Times,* May 20, 1990, with permission of the author.

287

Felice N. Schwartz, "Management Women and the New Facts of Life." Reprinted by permission of *Harvard Business Review* (January/February, 1989). Copyright © 1989 by the President and Fellows of Harvard College; all rights reserved.

Barbara Ehrenreich and Deirdre English, "Blowing the Whistle on the 'Mommy Track.' " Reprinted with permission from *Ms. Magazine,* Matilda Publishing Inc., July/August 1989.

Carol Kleiman, "How to Get 'Em on Track." Reprinted from *Ms. Magazine,* Matilda Publishing Inc., July/August 1989, with permission of the author.

Sinclair Lewis, "Letter to the Pulitzer Prize Committee." Reprinted from *The Man from Main Street,* by Sinclair Lewis, Random House, Inc. Used by permission of the Morgan Guaranty Trust Company of New York.

Henry J. Hyde, "The Culture War." Reprinted from the *National Review,* April 30, 1990, pp. 26–27. Copyright © by National Review, Inc., 150 East 35th Street, New York, NY 10016. Reprinted by permission.

George Orwell, "Politics and the English Language." From *Shooting an Elephant and Other Essays,* copyright 1946 by George Orwell and renewed 1974 by Sonia Orwell. Reprinted by permission of Harcourt Brace Jovanovich, Inc., and the estate of the late Sonia Brownell Orwell and Martin Secker & Warburg Ltd.

Barbara Mellix, "From Outside, In." Originally appeared in *The Georgia Review,* Volume XLI, No. 2 (Summer 1987), © 1987 by Barbara Mellix. Reprinted by permission of Barbara Mellix and *The Georgia Review.*

Alleen Pace Nilsen, "Sexism in English: A 1990s Update." From *The Prose Reader,* 2nd Edition, edited by Kim and Michael Flachmann, Englewood Cliffs, NJ: Prentice-Hall, 1990. Reprinted with permission from the author.

Dale Spender, "Talking in Class." Reprinted from *Learning to Lose: Sexism and Education,* by Dale Spender and Elizabeth Sarah. London: The Women's Press Ltd., 1980.

◆ INDEX ◆